D1153956

The International Yearbook of Environmental and Resource Economics 2003/2004

NEW HORIZONS IN ENVIRONMENTAL ECONOMICS

Series Editors: Wallace E. Oates, *Professor of Economics, University of Maryland, USA* and Henk Folmer, *Professor of General Economics, Wageningen University and Professor of Environmental Economics, Tilburg University, The Netherlands*

This important series is designed to make a significant contribution to the development of the principles and practices of environmental economics. It includes both theoretical and empirical work. International in scope, it addresses issues of current and future concern in both East and West and in developed and developing countries.

The main purpose of the series is to create a forum for the publication of high quality work and to show how economic analysis can make a contribution to understanding and resolving the environmental problems confronting the world in the twenty-first century.

Recent titles in the series include:

The International Yearbook of Environmental and Resource Economics 2003/2004

A Survey of Current Issues

Edited by
Henk Folmer

Professor of General Economics, Wageningen University, The Netherlands and Professor of Environmental Economics, Tilburg University, The Netherlands

Tom Tietenberg

Mitchell Family Professor of Economics, Colby College, USA

NEW HORIZONS IN ENVIRONMENTAL ECONOMICS

Edward Elgar
Cheltenham, UK • Northampton, MA, USA

© Henk Folmer, Tom Tietenberg 2003

All rights reserved. No part of this publication may be reproduced, stored in a retrieval system or transmitted in any form or by any means, electronic, mechanical or photocopying, recording, or otherwise without the prior permission of the publisher.

Published by
Edward Elgar Publishing Limited
Glensanda House
Montpellier Parade
Cheltenham
Glos GL50 1UA
UK

Edward Elgar Publishing, Inc.
136 West Street
Suite 202
Northampton
Massachusetts 01060
USA

A catalogue record for this book
is available from the British Library

ISSN 1460 7352
ISBN 1 84376 212 9 (cased)

Printed and bound in Great Britain by MPG Books Ltd, Bodmin, Cornwall

HC
79
.E5
I616
2003–
2004

Contents

Figures

Tables

Contributors

Trond Bjørndal, Centre for Fisheries Economics (SNF), Bergen, Norway and the Centre for Economics and Management of Aquatic Resources (CEMARE), University of Portsmouth, UK

Thomas D. Crocker, J.E. Warren Professor Emeritus, Department of Economics and Finance, University of Wyoming, Laramie, USA

Michael Finus, Department of Economics, University of Hagen, Germany

Paul K. Freeman, Consultant on natural disaster policy for International Financial Institutions and Member of the Adjunct Faculty, Graduate School of International Studies, University of Denver, USA

Winston Harrington, Senior Fellow, Resources for the Future, Washington, DC, USA

Joseph A. Herriges, Professor of Economics, Iowa State University, Ames, USA

Catherine L. Kling, Professor of Economics and Head, Resource and Environmental Policy Division, Center for Agricultural and Rural Development, Iowa State University, Ames, USA

Bengt Kriström, Department of Forest Economics, The Swedish University of Agricultural Sciences, Sweden

Howard Kunreuther, Cecilia Yen Koo Professor of Decision Sciences and Public Policy, Operations and Information Management Department and Co-Director, Risk Management and Decision Processes Center, Wharton School, University of Pennsylvania, USA

Thomas Laitila, Department of Statistics, Umeå University, Sweden

Virginia McConnell, Senior Fellow, Resources for the Future and Professor of Economics, University of Maryland (UMBC), USA

Gordon Munro, Emeritus Professor of Economics, University of British Columbia, Vancouver, Canada

Clifford S. Russell, Emeritus Professor of Economics, Vanderbilt University, Nashville, TN, and 2003 Sowell Visiting Professor of Economics, Bates College, Lewiston, ME, USA

Jason F. Shogren, Stroock Distinguished Professor of Natural Resource Conservation and Management, Department of Economics and Finance, University of Wyoming, Laramie, USA

William J. Vaughan, Senior Economist (retired), Inter-American Development Bank, USA

Preface

As a discipline Environmental and Resource Economics has undergone a rapid evolution over the past three decades. Originally the literature focused on valuing environmental resources and on the design of policy instruments to correct externalities and to provide for the optimal exploitation of resources. The relatively narrow focus of the field and the limited number of contributors made the task of keeping up with the literature relatively simple.

More recently, Environmental and Resource Economics has broadened its focus by making connections with many other subdisciplines in economics as well as the natural and physical sciences. It has also attracted a much larger group of contributors. Thus the literature is exploding in terms of the number of topics addressed, the number of methodological approaches being applied and the sheer number of articles being written. Coupled with the high degree of specilization that characterizes modern academic life, this proliferation of topics and methodologies makes it impossible for anyone, even those who specialize in Environmental and Resource Economics, to keep up with the developments in the field.

The International Yearbook of Environmental and Resource Economics: A Survey of Current Issues was designed to fill this niche. *The Yearbook* publishes state-of-the-art papers by top specialists in their fields who have made substantial contributions to the area that they are surveying. Authors are invited by the editors, in consultation with members of the editorial board. Each paper is critically reviewed by the editors and by experts in the field.

The editors would like to thank Wallace Oates for his help in getting the project started. We also very much appreciate the assistance of Lee Anderson, Carlo Carraro, Steven Farber, Haynes Goddard, Rognvaldur Hannesson, Lars Hultkrans, Lester Lave, Karl-Gustaf Löfgren, Ståle Navrud, Markku Ollikainen, George Parsons, Kerry Smith and Thomas Sterner in shaping up this collection of papers.

Tom Tietenberg
Henk Folmer

Editorial board

EDITORS

Henk Folmer, Wageningen University and Tilburg University,
   The Netherlands
Tom Tietenberg, Colby College, USA

EDITORIAL BOARD

Kenneth Arrow, Stanford University, USA
Scott Barrett, London Business School, UK
Peter Bohm, Stockholm University, Sweden
Lans Bovenberg, Tilburg University, The Netherlands
Carlo Carraro, University of Venice, Italy
Partha Dasgupta, University of Cambrige, UK
H. Landis Gabel, INSEAD, France
Shelby Gerking, University of Wyoming, USA
Lawrence Goulder, Stanford University, USA
Michael Hoel, University of Oslo, Norway
Per-Olov Johansson, Stockholm School of Economics, Sweden
Bengt Kriström, Swedish Agricultural University, Sweden
Karl-Gustav Löfgren, University of Umeå
Karl-Göran Mäler, The Beijer Institute, Sweden
Mohan Munasinghe, The World Bank, USA
Wallace Oates, University of Maryland, USA
David Pearce, University College London, UK
Charles Perrings, York University, UK
Rudither Pethig, University of Siegen, Germany
Alan Randall, Ohio State University, USA
Michael Rauscher, Kiel University of World Economics, Germany
Kathleen Segerson, University of Connecticut, USA
Mordechai Shechter, University of Haifa, Israel
Horst Siebert, Kiel Institute of World Economics, Germany
V. Kerry Smith, Duke University, USA
Robert Solow, Harvard University, USA

Olli Tahvonen, Finnish Forest Research Institute, Finland
Alistair Ulph, University of Southampton, UK
Aart de Zeeuw, Tilburg University, The Netherlands

1. The management of high seas fisheries resources and the implementation of the UN Fish Stocks Agreement of 1995

Trond Bjørndal and Gordon Munro

1. INTRODUCTION

From 1993 to 1995, the United Nations mounted an international conference, the UN Conference on Straddling Fish Stocks and Highly Migratory Fish Stocks, to address and, it was hoped, to alleviate a worldwide fisheries management crisis, focused on straddling and highly migratory fish stocks. The Conference brought forth an Agreement, popularly referred to as the UN Fish Stocks Agreement,[1] which became available for signing in December 1995. Almost exactly six years later, the Agreement came into force, which is to say that it achieved the status of international treaty law.

In this chapter, we shall attempt to provide an assessment, from an economist's perspective, of the Agreement, and of its prospects. In so doing, we shall:

1. review the history and origins of the Agreement;
2. review the basic economics of management of transboundary fishery resources;
3. assess, with the reviews of the history of the Agreement and the economics of transboundary fishery management in hand, both the problems of implementing the Agreement and the prospects for its success;
4. provide a few illustrative case studies; and
5. present our conclusions.

2. THE HISTORY AND THE ORIGINS OF THE UN FISH STOCKS AGREEMENT OF 1995

The origins of the straddling fish stock/highly migratory fish stock management crisis, and the UN conference to which the crisis gave rise, can be traced back to the UN Third Conference on the Law of the Sea, and the resultant UN Convention on the Law of the Sea (UN, 1982).

Before the UN Third Conference on the Law of the Sea, the extent of jurisdiction of coastal states[2] over fishery resources off their coasts was very limited. Three miles was the norm, while 12 miles was considered exceptional. Under the terms of the UN Convention on the Law of the Sea (Part V), coastal states were to have their jurisdiction over fishery resources extended to 200 nautical miles from shore, through the establishment of exclusive economic zones (UN, 1982, Articles 55 and 57). The key article in Part V of the Convention, and one which is of direct relevance to the UN Fish Stocks Conference of 1992–95, and hence to the UN Fish Stocks Agreement, is Article 56. The article states that:

> In the exclusive economic zone, the coastal State has sovereign rights for the purpose of exploring and exploiting, conserving and managing the natural resources, whether living or non-living . . . (UN, 1982, Article 56)

In time, there was general agreement that the coastal state has property rights to the fishery resources encompassed by the respective exclusive economic zones (EEZs) (McRae and Munro, 1989). The one disputed area concerned highly migratory species found within the EEZ.

The consequence of Part V of the Convention was that vast amounts of renewable resource wealth were transformed from the status of international common property to that of coastal state property. It was estimated, at the close of the UN Third Conference on the Law of the Sea, that 90 per cent of the harvests from marine capture fisheries would be accounted for by fishery resources that are, or would be, encompassed by the EEZs throughout the world (Kaitala and Munro, 1993).

The drafters of the Law of the Sea Convention fully realised that the mobility of fishery resources would result in many fishery resources encompassed by EEZs proving to be transboundary in nature. That is, the resources could be expected to cross the EEZ boundaries. Four, non-mutually exclusive, classes of transboundary resources came to be recognised. While there remains some ambiguity about definitions, a significant number of legal experts agree that the classes can be properly defined and described as follows (Hedley, 2000):

- **'Shared' fishery resources**　These are fishery resources which cross the EEZ boundary into the EEZ (EEZs) of one, or more, neighbouring coastal states.
- **Anadromous species**　These are species (salmon, to all intents and purposes) which are produced in freshwater habitats, live most of their lives in the marine environment, and then return to their fresh-

water habitats to spawn and die. During the course of their lives, the fish migrate between the EEZ and the remaining international waters beyond the EEZs, which are commonly referred to as the 'high seas'. As a result of pressure exerted successfully by Canada and the USA, these resources are effectively covered by a special provision in the Convention – Article 66. As a consequence of the Convention, customary international law now deems directed high seas fishing of salmon to be illegal (Burke, 1991).

- **Highly migratory stocks**   These are fish species designated by the UN as highly migratory (UN, 1982, Annex 1), and are dominated, in economic terms, by the six major tuna species. Being highly migratory, the species naturally move to and from the EEZ and the adjacent high seas. They will also prove, in many instances, to be 'shared' resources.
- **Straddling stocks**   This is a catchall term for all fishery resources, other than anadromous species and highly migratory stocks, which are to be found in both within the EEZ and the adjacent high seas.

The distinction between highly migratory species and straddling stocks is not immediately obvious, and indeed has been the focus of considerable debate. During the UN Third Conference on the Law of the Sea, several distant water fishing nations (DWFNs),[3] the USA in particular, insisted that highly migratory stocks are in fact separate and distinct from straddling stocks. The American position was not unrelated to American distant water fishing interests in tuna. On the other hand, the FAO (Food and Agriculture Organization) maintains that such a distinction cannot be defended on biological grounds (FAO, 1994), while other authorities have stated flatly that the distinction is a false one (for example McRae and Munro, 1989).

In any event, transboundary fishery resources (other than anadromous species) are addressed in Part V of the Convention, through Articles 63 and 64. Paragraphs 1 and 2 of Article 63 deal with 'shared' stocks and straddling stocks respectively, while Article 64, as a whole, addresses the issue of highly migratory stocks. Article 63(2), the straddling stock paragraph, reads as follows:

> Where the same stock or stocks of associated species occur both within the exclusive economic zone and in an area beyond and adjacent to that zone, the coastal State and the States fishing for such stocks in the adjacent area shall seek, either directly or through appropriate subregional or regional organisations, to agree upon the measures necessary for the conservation of these stocks in the adjacent area. (UN, 1982, Article 63(2))

In the reference to 'subregional or regional organisations', one can detect the origins of the concept of regional fisheries management organisations which was to emerge in the UN Fish Stocks Conference. Other than that, the paragraph is no more than a broad admonition to relevant coastal states and distant water fishing nations to cooperate for the purpose of conserving the resources. No guidance is given on the form that such cooperation might take.

Article 64 reads as follows:

> 1. The coastal State and other States whose nationals fish in the region for the highly migratory species listed in Annex 1 shall co-operate directly or through appropriate international organisations with a view to ensuring conservation and promoting the objective of optimum utilisation of such species throughout the region, both within and beyond the exclusive economic zone. In regions for which no appropriate international organisation exists, the coastal State and other States whose nationals harvest these species in the region shall co-operate to establish such an organisation and participate in its work.
> 2. The provisions of paragraph 1 apply in addition to the other provisions of this Part. [V]. (UN, 1982, Article 64)

Paragraph 1 of Article 64 is much stronger than Paragraph 2 of Article 63, calling, as it does, for the establishment of international organisations to manage the resources within, as well as without, the EEZs. This reflected the pressure being exerted by the DWFNs, led by the USA. During the Conference, the USA insisted, as part of its claim that highly migratory stocks were in a class by themselves, that such resources not be deemed to be coastal state property in any sense. The resources should, the USA argued, be managed by true international organisations in which DWFNs (such as the USA) would play a significant role (Munro, 1990a).

Paragraph 2 of Article 64, which implies that Article 56 is relevant to highly migratory stocks within the EEZ, was, it was argued, not entirely compatible with Paragraph 1 of Article 64 (Munro, ibid.). Article 56 grants the coastal state 'sovereign' rights with respect to the exploitation and management of fishery resources within the EEZ. Paragraph 1 of Article 64, on the other hand, implies that relevant DWFNs should share in the management of highly migratory stocks within, as well as without, the EEZ.

The international organisations referred to in Article 64(1) came to be known, in common parlance, as 'Article 64 organisations'. Article 64, and 'Article 64 organisations' in particular, became the source of bitter disputes during the 1980s, worsening US–Latin American fisheries relations and leading to an outright confrontation between the USA and several Pacific Island nations (Munro, ibid.). The USA eventually retreated from its position, and in the revision of the early 1990s of its key piece of legislation governing the American EEZ – the Magnuson Fishery Conservation and

Management Act – acknowledged coastal state jurisdiction over highly migratory stocks within the EEZ (UN, 1992).

This seemed to end the debate on Article 64 organisations. Yet the issue was to emerge again in the UN Fish Stocks Conference. We shall argue that some of the regional fisheries management organisations arising from that conference – and to be discussed at a later point – will take on the attributes of Article 64 organisations. That is, they will be organisations that will enable DWFNs to influence the management policies for relevant fishery resources within, as well as without, the EEZ. One such attempt, it might be observed, takes the form of the Convention on the Conservation and Management of Highly Migratory Fish Stocks in the Western and Central Pacific Ocean.[4] Unlike the original 'Article 64' organisations, the new version applies to straddling stocks, as well as to highly migratory stocks.

Once the USA had acknowledged coastal state jurisdiction over highly migratory stocks within the EEZ, a general consensus on property rights to 'shared' fishery resources appeared to emerge. Consider, for example, two coastal states, A and B, 'sharing' a fishery resource confined to the EEZs of these two states. The emergent view was that the relevant fish, while within the EEZ of A, constitute the property of A, and while within the EEZ of B, constitute the property of B. Thus, one could think of A and B 'owning' the resource on a condominium basis (McRae and Munro, 1989).

By way of contrast, the nature of the property rights to fishery resources to be found both within the EEZ and the adjacent high seas was left unsettled by the Law of the Sea Convention. While the nature of the property rights to the portions of the resources within the EEZ was clear enough, the property rights to the high seas portions of the resources were opaque at best.

Of key relevance to the high seas portions of the aforementioned fishery resources are, not surprisingly, Part VII of the Convention ('High Seas'), along with Articles 63 and 64 of Part V. Within Part VII, Article 87 and Section 2 (Articles 116–20): 'Conservation and Management of the Living Resources of the High Seas', are particularly important.

Article 87 is the 'Freedom of the High Seas' article, which states that 'the high seas are open to all States . . .', and that freedom of the high seas comprises, *inter alia*, freedom of fishing, subject to conditions laid down in Section 2 [Part VII] (UN, 1982, Article 87). Section 2 (Articles 116–20) qualifies a state's right to fish on the high seas by maintaining that such a state (that is, a DWFN) must take into account the interests of relevant coastal states in such resources and must be prepared to cooperate in the conservation of the resource (UN, 1992).

Beyond this general statement, however, Articles 116–20 are models of vagueness and imprecision. The rights and responsibilities of coastal states, as opposed to those of relevant DWFNs, with regard to the portions of straddling/highly migratory stocks in the adjacent high seas, are exceedingly unclear and were left open to conflicting interpretations (Miles and Burke 1989; Kaitala and Munro, 1993).

During the UN Third Conference on the Law of the Sea, the debate over highly migratory stocks focused on Article 64, and the attempt of the USA, in particular, to have these resources subject to management by true international bodies. With respect to straddling stocks, there was a series of proposals, extending up to the last year of the Conference (1982), to acknowledge the 'special interests' of coastal states regarding the high seas portions of straddling stocks, and to grant to coastal states the right to extend their conservation measures to these high seas portions. The proposals were actively resisted by DWFNs, and were never brought to a vote (UN, 1992). If the promoters of the proposals had been successful, then the principle established would presumably have applied with full force to highly migratory stocks, once the Article 64 issue had been resolved.

A probable reason why the issue was not brought to a vote, and why Articles 116–20 were left in such an unsatisfactory state, lies in the fact that, at the close of the Conference in 1982, high seas fishery resources were deemed to be of minor importance. It was, after all, believed that 90 per cent of the harvests from marine capture fisheries would be accounted for by resources encompassed by EEZs throughout the world. Moreover, it can be conjectured that many coastal states were convinced that DWFNs could not harvest the high seas portions of straddling/highly migratory stocks on a commercial basis, unless they were also granted access to the adjacent EEZs. Thus coastal states would have ample bargaining power when having to deal with the DWFNs attempting to exploit such stocks (Kaitala and Munro, 1993).

While the 1982 assessment of the importance of high seas fisheries resources may seem to have been reasonable at the time, the assessment was to prove quite simply wrong. What had appeared in 1982 to be a minor resource management problem became a highly significant problem over the ensuing decade. By the end of the 1980s, there was no longer any doubt that the problem was a major one.

Case after case emerged of straddling/highly migratory stocks that were being subject to severe overexploitation. Two of the more dramatic examples are provided by the Donut Hole in the Bering Sea, and the groundfish fisheries on the Grand Bank of Newfoundland (see Stokke, 2001).

Alaska pollock constitutes one of the larger groundfish resources in the world. Harvests of Alaska pollock throughout the North Pacific had achieved levels of 6.7 million tonnes in the late 1980s and had, at one point, been the largest single species harvested in the North Pacific (FAO, 1994).

A segment of the fishery is to be found in the Donut Hole, a high seas enclave, lying between the American and Russian EEZs. The pollock stocks in the Donut Hole are without question straddling stocks (FAO, 1994).

In 1984, the USA effectively evicted all foreign fleets from its EEZ off Alaska. Before that date, harvests in the Donut Hole had been minor, amounting to no more than 4000 tonnes. Harvests then grew rapidly, and, by 1988, had reached an unsustainable 1.6 million tonnes per annum (Miles and Fluharty, 1991). The fishery had all of the characteristics of an open-access, free-for-all, fishery. The FAO argues that the resources were, to all intents and purposes, plundered (FAO, 1994)

Harvests subsequently declined rapidly, and, by 1992, had fallen to an annual rate of 22000 tonnes. In August of that year, Russia and the USA, along with four DWFNs operating in the area, China, Japan, Republic of Korea and Poland, entered into an agreement to impose a harvest moratorium in the Donut Hole (Kaitala and Munro, 1993). While the moratorium was initially declared for two years, it remains in effect at the time of writing.

The second example concerned the groundfish resources on the Grand Bank of Newfoundland. The 200-mile boundary of Canada's Atlantic EEZ slices off two segments of the Grand Bank, one in the east, the 'Nose of the Bank', and one in the south, the 'Tail of the Bank'. Groundfish resources in the Nose and Tail of the Bank are, virtually by definition, straddling stocks.

Canada attempted to address the problem before the close of the UN Third Conference on the Law of the Sea by establishing the Northwest Atlantic Fisheries Organization (NAFO) in 1979. NAFO had as members Canada and several DWFNs, the most important of which was the EU. NAFO was to oversee the management of the high seas portions of the Grand Bank straddling stocks and to ensure that the management was compatible with the Canadian resource management programme within the EEZ. For a time, NAFO worked reasonably well. In 1985, however, Canada–EU cooperation in NAFO broke down, ostensibly over a dispute concerning management goals (Applebaum, 1990). EU harvests in the NAFO-governed high seas areas exceeded the EU quotas by 400 per cent (Kaitala and Munro, 1993). The situation was aggravated by the fact that NAFO seemed powerless to deal with 'interlopers' – vessels from non-NAFO nations, often flying flags of convenience, which were operating in waters subject to NAFO regulations.

The state of the groundfish stocks off Atlantic Canada in general was deteriorating. Canada argued that DWFN non-cooperation in NAFO was an important contributing factor to the malaise, and complained bitterly about EU overexploitation in particular (Canada Department of External Affairs, 1992).

In late 1992, Canada and the EU signed a Memorandum of Under-standing, which presumably restored Canada–EU fisheries cooperation within NAFO (Canada Department of Fisheries and Oceans, 1993). The Memorandum of Understanding proved to be no more than a temporary truce, however. In early 1995, Canada accused one EU member, Spain, of violating NAFO regulations and overharvesting turbot on the Nose of the Bank. Canada then proceeded to arrest a Spanish trawler on the Nose of the Bank, that is, in waters beyond Canada's EEZ. Canada maintained that it was acting properly to ensure the conservation of fishery resources in which it had a 'special interest'. The EU insisted that Canada had acted improperly, and that its action constituted piracy (Gordon and Munro, 1996; Kaitala and Munro, 1995).

The Donut Hole and the Grand Bank of Newfoundland were but the most dramatic of the straddling/highly migratory stock type of problem, which was becoming pervasive throughout the world. Other examples were provided by pollock resources in the Peanut Hole of the Sea of Okhotsk, and orange roughy on the Challenger Plateau off New Zealand (FAO, 1994).

What then had gone wrong? Why had a minor resource management problem developed into a serious one? What we might refer to as the basis, or foundation, of the problem was provided by two factors. First, the com-fortable coastal state assumption that DWFNs could not operate on a com-mercial basis on the high seas portions of straddling/highly migratory stocks unless they also had access to the adjacent EEZ had proved to be false. Second, DWFN fleets were steadily excluded from many EEZs, often for reasons having little or no economic substance. The excluded DWFN fleets, to the surprise of many, showed little decline (FAO, 1992; 1994). As a consequence, increased pressure on the high seas fishery resources was inevitable.

The non-disappearance of the excluded DWFN fleets is worthy of further comment. A fisheries management issue of growing concern is that of overcapitalisation (excess capacity) (FAO, 1999). It is now recognised that a key aspect of the overcapitalisation problem is the 'non-malleability' of fleet, processing and human capital (Clark et al., 1979; Clark and Munro, 1999). To say that capital is 'non-malleable' is to say that it cannot be quickly and easily withdrawn from a fishery or fisheries without risk of capital loss. If all such capital proved to be perfectly malleable, the over-capitalisation problem would not exist (Clark and Munro, 1999).

One consequence of capital being non-malleable is that, in the short run, the costs relevant to the use of capital are restricted to operating costs (FAO, 1999). With this in mind, consider now the aforementioned DWFN fleets excluded from coastal state EEZs. The capital embodied in the fleets was, more often than not, decidedly non-malleable with respect to world fisheries. The fleet owners were faced with the options of scrapping the vessels, laying them up, or of finding some other form of employment for them, regardless of how unattractive these other forms may have been in the past (Newton, 1999). A set of alternatives, which may well have appeared to be economically unattractive when the DWFN fleets had full access to fisheries now encompassed by EEZs, consisted of the high seas portions of straddling/highly migratory fish stocks. In the new set of circumstances, the high seas resources would have seemed attractive to the DWFN fleet owners if the present value of the expected operating profits to be realised from exploiting the resources exceeded the scrap value of the relevant vessels. The evidence suggests that, in many instances, employing the excluded DWFN fleets in the exploitation of the high seas resources did indeed prove to be more attractive than sending the vessels to the scrapyard, or laying them up.

One aspect of the overcapitalisation problem which is gaining increasing recognition (FAO, 1998) consists of the so-called 'spillover' effect. When non-malleable fleet (and human) capital is removed from a particular fishery, or fisheries, it may, instead of disappearing, 'spill over' into other fisheries (FAO, 1999). The emergence of the high seas fisheries management can be seen, in part, as being the consequence of a massive spillover effect.

While the aforementioned factors provided the foundation for the emergence of the crisis in high seas fisheries management, they are not sufficient, in, of and by themselves, to explain why the crisis did in fact emerge. It is necessary, as well, to look to the review, to follow, of the economics of the management of transboundary fishery resources, where the point will be made that, if joint exploiters of a transboundary fishery resource will not, or cannot, cooperate in the management of the resource, the likely consequence is that the resource will be subject to overexploitation, as exemplified by the Donut Hole and Grand Bank of Newfoundland cases.

The source of the non-cooperation lies in the inadequacies of Part VII, Section 2 (Articles 116–20) of the Convention pertaining to the management of high seas fisheries. We have described the aforementioned Articles 116–20 as constituting a model of imprecision and vagueness. An example of the imprecision is provided by a widely cited article of Miles and Burke (Miles and Burke, 1989). The authors contend that Article 116 of the Convention did, in fact, establish that 'the coastal state has the superior right, duty and interest in the straddling stocks beyond the EEZ' (p. 349). The authors are forced to concede, however, that 'the precise distribution of competences to make these [coastal state right, duty and interest] is not prescribed . . .' (p. 343). The Miles and Burke argument found considerable favour among many coastal states (for example Canada). The same argument was rejected out of hand by the DWFNs (Kaitala and Munro, 1993).

Two mutually incompatible, and hostile, views of the world of straddling/highly migratory stocks emerged after 1982. The first view, the coastal state view, was that uncontrolled harvesting of the high seas portions of straddling/highly migratory stocks by DWFNs could render meaningless the coastal state management regimes for the intra-EEZ portions of these stocks. The powers granted to coastal states by Article 56 of the Convention were thus undermined. The second view, the DWFN view, was that the coastal states had been granted immense transfers of renewable resource wealth under the EEZ regime, at the expense of the DWFNs. Not content with this enormous gain, coastal states were now seeking to extend their jurisdiction yet further to encompass the high seas portions of straddling and highly migratory stocks (UN, 1992). The term 'creeping jurisdictionalism' gained widespread currency among DWFNs.

A key UN preparatory document for the Fish Stocks Conference (UN, 1992) noted that, at the time of writing, the issue remained very much unresolved. As a consequence, the document continued, the admonitions of Articles 63 and 64 for coastal states and DWFNs to cooperate in the management of the aforementioned resources had fallen on deaf ears.

Thus, by the late 1980s, there was deepening concern about the state of straddling and highly migratory stocks throughout the world. This fear led directly to a second fear, namely that, if steps were not taken to correct the situation, coastal states would attempt to extend their jurisdiction unilaterally over the high seas portions of the stocks, and would, as a consequence, undermine the Law of the Sea Convention. Several coastal states did, in fact, threaten to extend their marine jurisdiction unilaterally (Balton, 1996). The Canada–Spain 'fish war' of 1995, which occurred during the Fish Stocks Conference, was, in particular, seen as a portent of things to come, and undoubtedly acted as a spur to the Conference negotiators.

In the year before the Canada–Spain 'fish war', Canada had amended its Coastal Fisheries Protection Act to give itself the authority to seize those non-Canadian vessels in the high seas adjacent to its Atlantic EEZ which Canada deemed to be in violation of NAFO rules and regulations. The amendment was exercised in 1995 when Canada seized the aforementioned Spanish trawler on the Nose of the Bank (Balton, 1996).

The amendment to the Canadian legislation had brought forth protests, not only from the EU, but from the USA as well. The Law of the Sea Convention was the product of compromise. The fear was that attempts by coastal states to extend their jurisdiction unilaterally, as exemplified by the Canadian amendment, would be seen to violate the compromise, and for this reason, would undermine the Convention (Balton, 1996).

The growing sense of alarm brought forth action from the UN. First, the General Assembly in 1989 called for a meeting to discuss sustainability of resources and the environment in general. This led to the UN Conference on Environment and Development (UNCED), which was held in Rio de Janeiro in 1992. The Conference, as well as producing a declaration (Rio Declaration), produced a document, a manifesto if you will; Agenda 21: Programme of Action for Sustainable Development. Chapter 17 of the Agenda deals with oceans and fisheries. The Chapter called for the convening, as soon as possible, of a UN conference on straddling and highly migratory fish stocks. The purpose of such a conference would not be to produce a document that would replace any segment of the Law of the Sea Convention. Rather, the purpose was to produce a document, which would supplement, or buttress, the Convention, with the object of ensuring its effective implementation (Doulman, 1995). In other words, the basic purpose of the conference would be to correct the glaring weaknesses of the Convention as it pertained to high seas fisheries management.

The UN General Assembly responded with dispatch to the UNCED call for a conference. In late 1992, the General Assembly passed a resolution announcing that in 1993 the UN would convene an intergovernmental conference on straddling fish stocks and highly migratory fish stocks. The primary task of the conference would be that of:

(i)   identifying and assessing existing problems related to the conservation and management of straddling fish stocks and highly migratory fish stocks,

(ii)   considering means of improving fisheries cooperation among states, and

(iii) formulating appropriate recommendations. (Doulman, 1995)

Before examining the resultant UN conference of 1993–95, and the agreement that emerged from it, it is necessary to digress and review the basic economics of the management of transboundary fishery resources. It is to this subject that we now turn.

3. THE BASIC ECONOMICS OF THE MANAGEMENT OF TRANSBOUNDARY FISHERY RESOURCES: A REVIEW[5]

Since the straddling/highly migratory stock management issue is a relatively new one, it must be conceded that the economics of the management of these resources is still at an early stage of development (Kaitala and

Munro, 1997; Munro, 2000b). Fortunately, however, the economics of the management of the other class of transboundary fishery resource, 'shared' stocks, is reasonably well developed, to the extent that it now finds its way into official publications (for example OECD, 1997). The economics of 'shared' stock management does, as we shall see, provide a sound basis from which to examine the economics of the management of straddling/highly migratory stocks.

The model most commonly employed by economists in analysing the management of transboundary fishery resources is a blend of the economist's dynamic model of a fishery confined strictly to the waters of a single coastal state, and the theory of games. Since strategic interaction among entities jointly exploiting a transboundary fishery resource is virtually inevitable, the application of game theory becomes all but inescapable.

Let us start with a fishery resource confined to the waters of a single coastal state. For illustrative purposes assume, to begin with at least, that the appropriate underlying biological model is the well-known Schaefer model. The Schaefer model, based upon the logistics population model, rests upon the fundamental assumption that there exists an upper bound to an unharvested fishery resource, determined by the nutrient capacity of the marine environment (see Clark, 1985, for a detailed description of the model).

Assume, as well, that the demand for harvested fish and the supply of labour and capital services, constituting fishing effort, are perfectly elastic. Without going through the details of the well-known dynamic economic model of the fishery (see Clark, 1985; Bjørndal and Munro, 1998), society's objective functional can be expressed as:

$$\max J(x_0, E) = \int_0^\infty e^{-\delta t} \, (px(t) - c)E(t)dt, \tag{1.1}$$

subject to:

$$dx/dt = F(x) - Ex,$$

where x denotes the biomass, x_0 denotes the original biomass, E the rate of fishing effort, c unit fishing effort cost, p the price of harvested fish, and δ the social rate of discount. Finally, $F(x)$ denotes the natural rate of growth of the resource. We have: $F(0) = F(K) = 0$, $F(x) > 0$, for $0 < x < K$, where K denotes the natural upper bound of the resource, also referred to as the carrying capacity of the environment.

In solving equation (1.1), the optimal biomass level x^* is given by the equally well-known decision rule:

$$F'(x^*) + \gamma(x^*) = \delta, \tag{1.2}$$

where $\gamma(x^*)$, the so-called marginal stock effect, is given by:

$$\gamma(x^*) = \frac{-c'(x^*)F(x^*)}{p - c(x^*)}$$

and where $c(x)$ is unit harvesting cost[6] (Clark, 1985). The marginal stock effect reflects the fact that, in this model, unit harvesting costs are inversely related to the size of the biomass (see note 6). Hence the yield, or return, on a marginal investment in the resource (L.H.S., equation (1.2)) has two components. There is, first, the impact upon the sustainable harvest ($F'(x)$), and second, the impact upon harvesting costs ($\gamma(x)$).

If the fishery is a 'common-pool,' 'pure open-access', fishery, we get the H. Scott Gordon result that the resource will be driven down to the bio-economic equilibrium level (Gordon, 1954), given by the following equation:

$$p - c(x_\beta) = 0, \tag{1.3}$$

where x_β denotes the bioeconomic equilibrium level of x. The biomass levels x^* and x_β will be equal, if and only if, $\delta = \infty$ (Clark, 1985).

For future reference, let it be noted that, in the case of species subject to intense schooling, the Schaefer model does not strictly hold. The marginal stock effect becomes small, and, in the limit, approaches zero. The implication is that harvesting costs, in the limit, are effectively independent of x, for all $x > 0$ (Bjørndal, 1988; Bjørndal and Munro, 1998; Clark, 1985). In such circumstances, equation (1.2) reduces to

$$F'(x^*) = \delta. \tag{1.4}$$

There is no solution to equation (1.3), since unit harvesting costs are now independent of x, for all $x > 0$. Extinction of the resource is a decided possibility (Bjørndal, 1988; Bjørndal and Munro, 1998).

Now return to our original example, and suppose that the fishery resource in question is not confined to the waters of a single EEZ, but is rather 'shared' by two neighbouring coastal states. Suppose further that the neighbouring coastal states do not, for whatever reason, cooperate in the management of the resource. To analyse the consequences of non-cooperation, the theory of non-cooperative games is brought to bear.

The consequences of non-cooperation are, with few exceptions, severe. We find ourselves presented with an example of the famous non-cooperative game, 'the prisoner's dilemma'. Even though the two coastal states may be able to exercise iron control over their respective fleets, they will be driven inexorably to overexploitation of the resource, except under unusual circumstances. If the two coastal states are symmetric, that is, alike in all respects, then the theory predicts that the end result will be akin to an open-access wholly domestic fishery, that is, the equivalent of bioeconomic equilibrium (Kaitala and Munro, 1997).

A recent study on Pacific salmon, shared by Canada and the USA, illustrates the point. The two countries attempted to manage the resource cooperatively under a treaty ratified in 1985.[7] The treaty broke down in the early 1990s, and the two sides reverted to competitive behaviour. The consequences for the resource were decidedly harmful. The two countries subsequently signed a Pacific Salmon Agreement in 1999, in an attempt to 'patch up' the treaty. There is no question that the threat of resource destruction provided a powerful incentive to both sets of negotiators to reactivate the treaty (Miller et al., 2001).

The economics of the non-cooperative management of 'shared' stocks can, in fact, be applied, with little or no change, to the non-cooperative management of straddling/highly migratory stocks (Kaitala and Munro, 1997). Thus the overexploitation to be found in many of the straddling and highly migratory stocks in the early 1990s, as exemplified by the Donut Hole and Grand Bank of Newfoundland fisheries, is entirely consistent with the theory. Indeed, the growing crisis in high seas fisheries management of the 1980s and early 1990s stands as a testament to the predictive power of the theory.

Thus cooperation does matter. Return now to our 'shared' resource example. If the joint owners of the resource are able to communicate, and bargain in good faith, it may be possible for them to develop a mutually beneficial cooperative management regime, even though their goals of management differ. In examining the underlying economics of cooperative resource management, the theory of cooperative games is, not surprisingly, brought to bear.

We start out with the simplest case in which there are but two 'players', that is, two coastal states, and suppose that the players, if agreeing on a joint management programme, are prepared to make the agreement a binding one. The example to follow will have Nash's model of a two-person cooperative game as its foundation (Nash, 1953).

Among the many divisions in cooperative games is that between those which allow for so-called 'side-payments' and those which do not. Side-payments are essentially transfers, monetary or non-monetary, between and among players. In the context of a fisheries game, a cooperative game *without* side-payments would be one in which the benefits derived by a player from a fishery would be wholly dependent upon the harvests of that player's fleet within the player's waters.

The chief significance of side-payments is that they can serve both to lead to a solution closer to the global optimum and, perhaps of even greater importance, to broaden the scope for bargaining. The reason for the latter is straightforward enough. What is at issue is the division of the net economic returns, or benefits, from the fishery. If the division is to be determined solely by the harvests of the players' fleets, within their respective waters, then bargaining is subject to a constraint. The Pacific salmon resource, shared by Canada and the USA, provides a case in point. Such a constraint did exist, and did, in the end, prove to be not merely binding, but crippling (Miller et al., 2001).

If there is to be a 'solution' to the two-person cooperative game, two conditions must be met. First, the 'solution' must be Pareto-optimal. Second, the so-called individual rationality constraint must be satisfied. The common-sense meaning of this second condition is that each player must receive from cooperation a 'payoff' at least as great as it would enjoy under non-cooperation. In passing, Nash refers to the set of payoffs rising from non-cooperation as the 'threat point' in the game (Nash, 1953).

In any event, those game outcomes which satisfy both conditions are said to constitute the 'core' of the game. There is no guarantee that the core will be other than empty. If it is empty, attempts to achieve cooperation will not be successful, and the 'players' will revert to competitive behaviour.

We illustrate in Figure 1.1 a possible two-player game (with binding agreements) with and without side-payments. It is assumed that the players are asymmetric, in that they have different management goals. The differences in management could arise, for example, because of differing fishing effort costs, or different social rates of discount, or other reasons (Munro, 1990b). It might be noted, in passing, that in fisheries games asymmetry between, and among, the players is the rule, not the exception.

In any event, a payoff to Player I(II) can be seen as the present value of expected net economic benefits that would accrue to Player I(II) from a particular resource management programme. The curve, concave to the origin, is the Pareto frontier, in the absence of side-payments, and shows the sets of payoffs arising from all cooperative arrangements meeting the criterion of Pareto optimality. The parameter β, $0 \leq \beta \leq 1$, is a bargaining parameter. If $\beta = 1$ (0), then the management preferences of Player I(II) are wholly dominant.

The set of payoffs – θ_0, γ_0 – constitutes the 'threat point' (Nash, 1953). In the absence of side-payments, the segment of the Pareto frontier without side-payments, marked off by the dashed lines emanating from θ_0 and γ_0 constitutes the core of the game. Where the players will end up on the Pareto frontier, what set of payoffs will actually constitute the solution to the game, will be determined by the relative bargaining strength of the two players.

Next, let us turn to the question of side-payments, a question, which, it might be added, has proved to be quite controversial in non-fishery

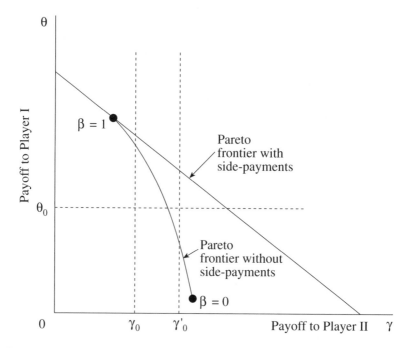

Figure 1.1   Cooperative game with and without side-payments

transboundary issues, particularly those involving the environment (see, for example, Folmer and de Zeeuw, 2000). In the case of fisheries, no one, to our knowledge, has ever considered the possibility of side-payments in cooperative games in which the players are symmetric. Where the players in cooperative fisheries games are asymmetric with regard to management goals, then side-payments have indeed been considered, and have been seen to have merit.

Where management goals differ, it is almost invariably the case that one player will place a higher value on the resource than will the other player, or players. The *optimum optimorum* is achieved by allowing that player to exercise its management preferences unhindered. It will then, in other than exceptional circumstances, be necessary for that player to compensate its fellow player(s) through side-payments (Munro, 1987).

Consider Figure 1.1, where we suppose that Player I places the greater value on the resource. If side-payments are introduced, the two players will seek to maximise the global returns from the fishery, and then bargain over the division of these returns. The Pareto Frontier then becomes a 45° line (see Figure 1.1). Denote the solution payoffs as θ^* and γ^*. If we then denote the cooperative surplus as ϕ^*, where

$$\phi^* = [\theta^* + \gamma^*] - [\theta_0 + \gamma_0],$$

it can be shown (Bjørndal and Munro, 2000) that the solution to the Nash cooperative game with side-payments will be such that:

$$\theta^* = \phi^*/2 + \theta_0$$
$$\gamma^* = \theta_n^*/2 + \gamma_0$$

that is, the two players 'split the difference'.

If the number of players is $n>2$, then sub-coalitions among the players must be considered. The simple 'split the difference' rule in determining a 'fair' distribution of the gains may no longer be considered to be satisfactory. One approach which may be used, the Shapley value, relates the solution payoff to a player to the player's average marginal contribution, or worth, to each coalition in which it might participate (Shubik, 1982).

What, in fact, is really the benefit of side-payments in the example cited? Return to Figure 1.1, and suppose, first, that Player II's threat point payoff is γ_0. It would then certainly be possible to achieve a solution to the co-operative game, without side-payments. Introducing side-payments, and thereby enabling Player I's management preferences to become dominant, however, would be Pareto-improving. In our example, both players could be made better off thereby.

Suppose, on the other hand, that Player II's threat point payoff was not γ_0, but was, rather, γ'_0. In this case, the effect of introducing side-payments would be more substantial. Without side-payments, attempts to achieve a cooperative resource management regime would be futile.

One of the cases to be examined in detail at a later point is that of the Norwegian spring-spawning herring fishery. The resource is currently exploited, on a cooperative basis, by five players: Norway, Iceland, Russia, the Faeroe Islands and the European Union, with Norway being the dominant player, accounting for 60 per cent of the harvest. The nature of the resource is such that the marginal stock effect is small (see equation (1.4)), with the consequence that the resource can be driven to extinction. Arnason et al. (2000) model the fishery as a five-player game. Competition (all against all) can lead to disaster – the extinction of the resource. The economic gains from full cooperation, that is, the five forming a grand coalition, are very substantial. Norway, the leading player, cannot be induced, however, to join and remain in the grand coalition, unless it receives side-payments. Thus, if side-payments are absent, the grand coalition will be inherently unstable. The authors, assuming that each player would receive its Shapley value, are able to calculate the side-payments that each player is to make (all, except Norway), or to receive (Norway).

The model discussed to this point rests upon the implicit assumption that the two players enter into a binding agreement. One lesson, which has been learned over time, is that there is probably no such thing as a 'binding' agreement that will last indefinitely. The Canada–USA treaty governing the joint management of Pacific salmon is as close as one is likely to come to a true binding agreement. Even this agreement, however, was not able to withstand the shock of changing conditions (Miller et al., 2001).

Kaitala and Pohjola (1988) have demonstrated, in a case in which a co-operative agreement was explicitly assumed to be non-binding, the importance of the agreement being 'time-consistent,' that is, recognising that what may appear to be a sound agreement today may not be so tomorrow. In practical terms, this means that the cooperative arrangement must be sufficiently flexible to accommodate unexpected changes in surrounding conditions.

'Time consistency' provides yet another argument for side-payments. The introduction of side-payments can be seen, as we have observed, as having the effect of widening the scope for bargaining. Obviously, the broader the scope for bargaining, the greater the likelihood that the cooperative arrangement will have the requisite flexibility to render it 'time consistent'.

In turning to the cooperative management of straddling/highly migratory stocks, one can state the following. As will be seen, the UN Fish Stocks Agreement calls for the management to be carried out through regional fisheries management organisations (RFMOs), to involve both the coastal states and the DWFNs. If the members of a given RFMO:

(i)   were actively involve in the relevant fishery, or fisheries, at the time of the establishment of the RFMO,
(ii)   are fixed through time, in number and nature,
(iii) can be protected collectively, in the RFMO, from 'interlopers',

then the analysis of cooperative management of 'shared' fishery resources can be applied, without modification. If any one of these conditions cannot be met, then the aforementioned analysis cannot be applied, without significant modification.

There is no guarantee that, under the UN Fish Stocks Agreement, any of the three conditions will be met, for a given RFMO. Let us now turn to the UN Fish Stocks Agreement itself.

4.   THE UN FISH STOCKS AGREEMENT: PROBLEMS OF IMPLEMENTATION

Articles 116–20 of the UN Convention on the Law of the Sea left in doubt the rights and obligations of coastal states versus those of DWFNs, with respect to the high seas portions of the straddling/highly migratory stocks. These doubts helped to ensure, we argued, that the resources would be managed on a non-cooperative basis.

The UN Fish Stocks Agreement (UN, 1995) attempts to deal with the aforementioned inadequacies of the Convention by calling explicitly, in Article 8, for straddling/highly migratory fishery resources to be managed, on a sub-region-by-sub-region basis, by regional fisheries management organisations (RFMOs), or the equivalent thereof. Importantly, the RFMOs are, in effect, to be responsible for the management of the resources within, as well as outside, the EEZ (Munro, 2000b).

Since the RFMO is to oversee the management of the resource within, as well as outside, the EEZ, one issue which arises immediately, and which was a source of considerable controversy at the UN Fish Stocks Conference, is the question of where within the RFMO the locus of power, with regard to resource management, resides. Does it reside with the coastal states alone, or does it reside with both coastal states and relevant DWFNs? Orebech et al. (1998) refer to a 'bottom-up' versus a 'top-down' approach to power over resource management in the RFMO. A 'bottom-up' approach implies that all such power resides with the coastal state(s); a 'top-down' approach that the coastal state(s) share(s) power with the DWFN members. The authors argue that Article 7 of the UN Agreement does, in effect, allow for either approach, with the actual approach being determined on a case-by-case basis.

During the UN Fish Stocks Conference, the coastal states did lobby, not surprisingly, for the mandating within the Agreement of the bottom-up approach. The economic theory of the management of transboundary fishery resources suggests that, had the Agreement in fact mandated a bottom-up approach, the scope for successful negotiation of RFMOs could have been significantly limited. Return to Figure 1.1 and consider now an RFMO consisting of one coastal state and one DWFN, and the resulting cooperative game. Let I (Figure 1.1) denote the coastal state and II the DWFN. A mandated bottom-up approach would be the equivalent of declaring that the only acceptable point on the Pareto frontier would be that at which $\beta = 1$. In the absence of side-payments, the risk would be high that the aforementioned mandate would ensure a cooperative game without a core, with all that that implies (see also Kaitala and Munro, 1993). It is to the credit of the UN Fish Stocks Conference that no such mandate was incorporated in the Agreement.

While the issue of the locus of management power within the RFMO is an important aspect of the UN Fish Stocks Agreement, there are three relevant issues pertaining to the Agreement which, in our view, are central to the question of the long-term economic viability of RFMOs. These are:

(i)   the new member, or participant, issue;
(ii)   the issue of the 'real interest' of the prospective members of an RFMO in the relevant fisheries; and
(iii)   the interloper issue.

All remain essentially unresolved at the time of writing.

In the case of shared fishery resource management, the participants in a cooperative resource management arrangement will not change over time, either in number or nature, except under the most unusual circumstances. The members, or participants, in such a cooperative arrangement can be seen as constituting a closed and stable club. Such is not the case with respect to RFMOs. Some of the members of a given RFMO will be DWFNs, the fleets of which are nothing if not mobile. A DWFN, currently a member of an RFMO, can withdraw. Of even greater importance, a DWFN, not originally a member of the RFMO, may attempt to join as a new member.

Let us refer to the original members of an RFMO as the 'charter' members. The UN Fish Stocks Agreement does not permit such members to bar would-be new members outright. Indeed the Agreement (see, in particular, Articles 8, 10 and 11) permits charter members of an RFMO to exclude would-be new members only on grounds of non-cooperation, that is, if the new members refuse to abide by the terms of the RFMO management regime (Orebech et al., 1998). Moreover, Orebech et al. maintain that Article 8 of the Agreement requires that cooperative would-be new members 'must be offered *just and reasonable* shares of the TAC [total allowable catch] available under an [RFMO] management plan' (*ibid.*, p. 123).

The issue then becomes what constitutes *just and reasonable* shares of the TAC. Kaitala and Munro (1997) demonstrate that if *just and reasonable* implies that upon joining an RFMO, new members should receive, at no further cost, shares of the TAC, or the equivalent on a pro-rata basis, then, when planning is undertaken for the establishment of an RFMO, prospective charter members could well calculate that their expected payoffs from cooperation would fall below their respective threat point payoffs. Hence the RFMO would be stillborn.

This interpretation of *just and reasonable* poses the threat described because it gives rise to a type of 'free-rider' problem. Suppose that a hitherto overexploited straddling, or highly migratory, stock comes under the management of an RFMO consisting of coastal state V, and three DWFNs, W, X and Y. The four charter members undertake the cost and sacrifice of rebuilding the resource over, say, a seven-year period. In the eighth year, the four are in a position to enjoy a return on their resource investment, through harvesting. At the beginning of the eighth year, a prospective new member, DWFN Z, appears. This is a DWFN which had not hitherto participated in the fishery, but which now expresses an interest in it. Recall that DWFN fleets are nothing if not mobile. DWFN fleets have been known to operate around the world (for example, recall that one of the DWFNs operating in the Bering Sea Donut Hole was Poland).

DWFN Z demands access to the RFMO, agrees to abide by the resource management rules, but demands a share of the harvest and, by implication, a share of any resource rent. If DWFN Z's demands were acceded to, Z would effectively be a free-rider. Having incurred none of the costs and sacrifices of investment in the resource, it will enjoy a share of the return on the investment.

Kaitala and Munro (1997) did not discuss the case in which the charter members establish an RFMO, expecting the appearance of no new members, but are then subsequently unpleasantly surprised. None the less, their analysis could readily be extended, and an outcome predicted. The RFMO would be established and might well appear to be successful, initially. When the unpleasant surprise occurs, however, the charter members could be expected to reassess their expected payoffs from cooperation, with the possible consequence that the RFMO would disintegrate.

An example of the problems that could be created by the new member problem is provided by the attempts to manage southern bluefin tuna. The resource had been subject to heavy exploitation. In response, three key countries involved in harvesting the resource, the two coastal states Australia and New Zealand, and the DWFN Japan, came together in 1994 to establish a cooperative resource management regime in the form of the Commission for the Conservation of Southern Bluefin Tuna (Cox et al., 1999; Kennedy, 1999). This regime had, as its express purpose, the rebuilding of the stocks. One might have described the Commission as a pre-UN Fish Stocks Agreement RFMO.

The cooperative management arrangement, in the form of the Commission, initially met with success. It was, however, subsequently threatened with paralysis and breakdown, with the members quarrelling, *inter alia*, over scientific assessments of the stocks. Two recent studies on the Commission, while citing several factors leading to the breakdown, give particular emphasis to the impact of the appearance of major 'new entrants' to the fishery, in the form of Indonesia, the Republic of Korea and Taiwan (Cox et al., 1999; Kennedy, 1999).

Kaitala and Munro (1997) argue that the resolution of the new member problem may call for the creation of *de facto* property rights for the charter members of the RFMO. They raise the question of whether a possible solution might lie in new members being required to 'buy their way in' through the purchase of quota shares. The quotas allocated to charter member states would take on some of the attributes of individual transferable quotas (ITQs).

None of this should come as a surprise. It was, after all, the property rights to straddling/highly migratory fish stocks, so ill defined by the UN Convention on the Law of the Sea, that lay at the heart of the straddling/highly migratory fish stock management crisis in the first place.

At the 1999 Conference on the Management of Straddling Fish Stocks and Highly Migratory Fish Stocks and the UN Agreement,[8] held in Bergen, this issue was raised for discussion. Several of the participants were specialists in international law, some of whom had participated in the UN Fish Stocks Conference. These international law specialists maintained that charter members of RFMO may well have the right to impose charges on new members. Membership does not automatically bring with it free access to a share of the harvests. If that legal opinion should prove to be valid, then we shall indeed have made significant progress towards an effective agreement.

The issue of 'real interest' of prospective RFMO members in the relevant fisheries is somewhat more subtle than the new member issue, but is closely related to it. Article 8, paragraph 3, of the Agreement states that 'States having a real interest in the fisheries concerned may become members of such organisations [that is, RFMOs]' (UN, 1995). The term 'real interest' is not defined in the Agreement. Molenaar (2000) argues that states/entities having a real interest in the relevant fisheries can be taken to include the following:

(a)   coastal states and DWFNs currently engaged in active exploitation of the fisheries;
(b)   DWFNs which are not currently engaged in exploiting the fisheries, but which have done so in the past, and would now like to re-enter the fisheries;
(c)   DWFNs which had never exploited the fisheries, but which would now like to do so.

Article 8, paragraph 5, of the Agreement discusses the establishment of new RFMOs. The paragraph calls upon states falling in category (a), alone to commence the establishment. Article 9, paragraph 2, states that 'States cooperating in the formation of a . . . regional fisheries management organisation [category (a) states] . . . shall inform other States which they are aware have a real interest in the work of the proposed organisation [category (b) and (c) states] . . . of such cooperation' (UN, 1995). Molenaar maintains that one can infer from all of this that, upon so informing such category (b) and (c) states, category (a) states would then invite their (b) and (c) colleagues to enter the RFMO negotiations (that is, become 'charter' members) (Molenaar, 2000). To our untutored eyes, the inference is less than evident.

If the Agreement is interpreted, over time, to mean that category (b) and (c) states must be invited to become charter members, then it is easy to see that the same sort of free-rider problem, threatened by the new member issue, can readily arise. Return to our new member problem example, discussed earlier. Now suppose that states V, W, X and Y are category (a) states. Suppose, further, that Z is now a category (c) state, which demands and receives full and undiluted charter membership. Z incurs no real sacrifice in the rebuilding of the resource, because it had not hitherto been engaged in harvesting the resource. Z will simply bide its time over the seven-year period, and then, when the eighth year arrives, will come to enjoy a share of the return on the resource investment, as the free-rider that it most certainly is. Once again, the possibility of such free-riding could undermine the viability of the RFMO.

The third issue, what we have termed the interloper issue, pertains to the policing of vessels of states which are, by choice, non-members/non-participants of the RFMO. We know from history that the inability to deal effectively with interlopers was a factor undermining pre-UN Agreement organisations designed to manage straddling/highly migratory stocks, such as NAFO (Gordon and Munro, 1996).

The threat posed by an uncontrolled interloper problem is too obvious to be elaborated upon. It is essentially an aggravated and intensified version of the new member problem. The realisation by prospective charter members that they will face a future uncontrollable interloper problem could be sufficient to cause one, or more, prospective charter members to calculate that it (they) would be better off under conditions of non-cooperation.

This issue is addressed in the UN Fish Stocks Agreement through Article 17 (UN, 1995). Article 17(2) admonishes states which are not members/participants in an RFMO, and which decline to cooperate with the RFMO, not to authorise their fishing vessels to operate in the area managed by the RFMO. Article 17(4) then maintains that, when confronted by true interlopers, member/participant states of an RFMO 'shall take measures consistent with this Agreement and international law to deter activities of such vessels which undermine the effectiveness of sub-regional or regional conservation and management measures'. It is not immediately obvious what deterrent powers international law does, in fact, offer RFMO members (Munro, 2000b).

We can take comfort from a recent paper by legal expert and US State Department official David Balton (Balton, 2000), which argues that international law does, in point of fact, grant RFMOs sufficient powers to deal firmly and effectively with interlopers. We can derive even greater comfort from the fact that a major international initiative, spearheaded by the FAO, is now under way to address the interloper problem, referred to as the problem of 'illegal, unreported and unregulated' (IUU) fishing. The FAO has developed an International Plan of Action to combat IUU fishing, which has been formally approved by the FAO's Committee on Fisheries (Doulman, 2000; FAO, 2001). The initiative must be expected to strengthen the hands of RFMO members attempting to repel interlopers through, for example, trade measures and denial of port facilities.

5.   A FEW BRIEF CASE STUDIES

We now turn to a few brief case studies to provide some illustrations of key points made in the earlier sections.

Northwest Atlantic Fisheries Organization (NAFO)

From 1949 until the advent of the UN Third Conference on the Law of the Sea, fishery resources in the Northwest Atlantic beyond the territorial seas were managed by the International Commission for the Northwest Atlantic Fisheries (ICNAF). ICNAF's range extended from Greenland to the Carolinas. Both Canada and the USA implemented 200-mile EEZs unilaterally in 1977. The implementation of the USA–Canada EEZ regimes was incompatible with ICNAF, with the consequence that ICNAF was disbanded.

Faced with the problem of straddling stocks on the Grand Bank of Newfoundland, Canada took the initiative to replace ICNAF with NAFO in 1979, as we noted earlier. Canada's chief partner, it will be recalled, was the EU. There were, however, important non-members, namely the USA, Spain and Portugal. The latter two were not members of the EU at that time. Canada's fisheries relations with the two Iberian DWFNs could have best been described as poisonous.

In its initial phase NAFO was very much a bottom-up organisation, with management powers resting firmly with Canada (Kaitala and Munro, 1993). Canada determined the resource management policy for its Atlantic EEZ. It was then necessary for NAFO to ensure that its management policies for the high seas portions of the straddling stocks were consistent with the Canadian intra-EEZ policies.

NAFO worked reasonably well for the first few years as a cooperative game. Canada's relations with the EU began to fray, however, and then essentially fell apart when Spain and Portugal joined the EU. The deteriorating situation was aggravated, as noted earlier, by NAFO's inability to deal with interlopers, vessels from countries that were not members of NAFO, fishing in waters subject to NAFO regulations. Often the interlopers took the form of DWFN vessels flying flags of convenience (for example Belize).

What had begun as a moderately successful cooperative game did not prove to be time-consistent, which is probably not surprising in light of our previous comments about 'bottom-up' cooperative arrangements. The cooperative game degenerated into a destructive competitive game, as described earlier, culminating in the Canada–Spain fish war. It is probably no exaggeration to say that, by 1995, NAFO was in a state of paralysis.

A revived NAFO has emerged, which uses the UN Fish Stocks Agreement as a framework. NAFO explicitly regards itself as an RFMO (NAFO, 1999), and now has 18 members, including the USA, which joined in November 1995. It is difficult to believe that the American decision to join was not motivated by the concluding of the UN Fish Stocks Conference. Be that as it may, the USA played a key role as intermediary in the Fish Stocks Conference, by virtue of the fact that it had both strong coastal state and DWFN interests. American participation in NAFO should be seen as a decidedly positive development.

The prospective new member problem facing NAFO appears to have been allayed for the foreseeable future by the breadth of the post-1995 NAFO membership, numbering 18. It is difficult to identify a DWFN not already within NAFO which could be taken seriously as a prospective new member. If any of the 18 should, in fact, be regarded as category (b) or (c) states, there is no evidence that they are seen as posing a serious free-rider threat by the others.

The drawback, however, to the all-encompassing membership is that 18 is a very large number of players, which could obviously make effective resource management cooperation difficult to achieve. There is, however, as we have noted, always the possibility of sub-coalitions emerging, which, if cohesive, could reduce the number of effective players. Such sub-coalitions have, in fact, already emerged. Canada and the USA can be thought of as a loose coastal state coalition. Facing this coalition is what might be termed a European coalition, consisting of the EU, the Baltic States, Poland and the Ukraine. Even Iceland and Norway, allies of Canada during the UN Fish Stocks Conference, have shown themselves to be friendly towards the European coalition (Robert Steinbock, Fisheries and Oceans Canada, personal communication).

Interestingly, the new NAFO shows some faint signs of having been transformed from a bottom-up organisation to a top-down, Article 64 type, organisation. In the year 2000 annual meeting of NAFO, there was a heated exchange between the EU and Canada over quotas set by Canada *within* the Canadian EEZ for the severely depleted Northern Cod stock. The EU criticised Canada for setting the quotas at too high a level, on the grounds that the Canadian action would have a negative impact on the resources in the adjacent high seas (NAFO, 1999). The very fact that the EU could raise objections to Canada's intra-EEZ resource management, and be taken seriously, is significant. Objections to Canadian resource management policy within the Canadian EEZ would have been dismissed as impertinent in the pre-1995 NAFO.

NAFO is certainly far from a model of harmony, but the available evidence suggests that it is working far better under the UN Fish Stocks Agreement than it did before. The participants, particularly the DWFNs, have greater security of tenure. Moreover, the new NAFO will have the political, legal and physical power to deal with interlopers, for example through the denial of port facilities and trade sanctions. This provides hope that a successful cooperative fisheries game will emerge.

The Norwegian Spring-Spawning Herring Fishery

In the 1950s and the 1960s, Norwegian spring-spawning herring (*Clupea harengus*) was a major commercial species, harvested by vessels from Norway, Iceland, the Faeroe Islands, the former Soviet Union and several European nations. During this period, the fishable component of the Norwegian spring-spawning herring stock is believed to have measured about 10 million tonnes. However, during this period the stock was subjected to heavy exploitation by several European nations, especially Norway, Iceland and the former Soviet Union, employing new and substantially more effective fishing technology. The annual harvest peaked at two million tonnes in 1966. By this time, however, the stock was in serious decline and a complete stock collapse occurred by the end of the decade. Finally, with catch levels declining to practically nothing in 1970, a fishing moratorium was declared.

Before depletion, the species was a straddling stock migrating through several coastal states and the high seas. In the 1950s and early 1960s, adults would spawn off the south-central coast of western Norway from February through March. The adults would migrate west and south-west through international waters towards Iceland (April and May), spending the summer (June through August) in an area north of Iceland. In September the adults would migrate south to a wintering area east of Iceland before returning to western Norway to spawn. Juveniles, including the recently spawned or 'zero cohort', would migrate north, but remain in Norwegian waters until sexually mature, around age four or five, when they would join the adult migratory pattern.

Because of overfishing and poor recruitment, the spawning biomass fell precipitously in 1968 and 1969, leading to near extinction by 1972. In its depleted state, the adult population ceased migration and both adults and juveniles remained in Norwegian waters year round.

Recruitment remained weak throughout the 1970s and it was not until the strong year class of 1983 joined the adult population in 1986 that the stock began to recover. The main component of the stock has re-established itself on the spawning grounds off western Norway. Now, after spawning, the adult herring begin a westerly migration, passing through the EEZs of the EU, the Faeroe Islands, Iceland and through international waters called the 'Ocean Loop' on their way to the summer feeding area near Jan Mayen Island. In the 1990s, the herring have followed the southern edge of the cold east Iceland stream, north and north-easterly, to winter in the fjords of northern Norway.

The migration pattern of the Norwegian spring-spawning herring takes on importance since, as a straddling stock, the herring are exposed to territorial and possibly distant water fleets with strong incentives to harvest the population before it moves elsewhere. If a cooperative management policy, with an equitable distribution of harvest, cannot be agreed upon, Norway, Iceland, the Faeroe Islands, countries of the EU, Russia and possibly distant water vessels fishing in the Ocean Loop, may resort to 'strategic overfishing' that could jeopardise continued recovery of the stock.

Until recently the situation was quite chaotic. There was no comprehensive regional agreement about the utilisation of the stock. It followed that Norway, Russia, Iceland and the Faeroe Islands were able to harvest the stock at will within their own jurisdictions. Moreover, in international waters the stock could be harvested legally by any interested fishing nation.

In 1995, the Advisory Committee on Fishery Management (ACFM) recommended a total allowable catch (TAC) for the Norwegian spring-spawning herring of 513 000 tonnes. Norway ignored the recommendation and announced an individual TAC of 650 000 tonnes, of which 100 000 tonnes would be allocated to Russian vessels. Iceland and the Faeroe Islands followed suit and announced their own combined TAC of 250 000 tonnes. In total, the collective harvest of Norway, Russia, Iceland, the Faeroe Islands and the EU was approximately 902 000 tonnes of herring, almost twice the quantity recommended by ACFM (Bjørndal et al., 1998). Nevertheless, in spite of these high catch levels, the herring spawning stock continued to increase.

There was, however, progress towards cooperation. In 1996, Norway, Russia, Iceland and the Faeroe Islands reached an agreement for a combined TAC by increasing the quota levels for each country and setting a total TAC of 1 267 000 tonnes. Nevertheless, the EU did not take part in a

TAC commitment and continued fishing at near capacity. In 1997, the EU became a signatory to an agreement limiting the maximum total catch to 1 498 000 tonnes. The significance of this agreement is that the EU, in a commitment to international fisheries cooperation, agreed to reduce their total catch levels from the previous period, whereas the four other member countries again increased individual TACs (Bjørndal et al., 1998). It can be argued that the UN Fish Stocks Agreement provided the necessary framework, albeit with a one-year lag (Munro, 2000a),

The countries involved have agreed to continue cooperation ever since, with management taking place, through the North East Atlantic Fishery Commission (NEAFC). NEAFC is considered a regional fisheries management organisation in the context of the UN Fish Stocks Agreement.

Establishing an RFMO for this fish stock has been important to ensure a sustainable fishery. As Norwegian spring-spawning herring is a schooling stock, it is very vulnerable to overexploitation, as the experience from the 1950s and 1960s clearly shows. Substantial future changes in, for example, the distribution pattern of the herring may conceivably put the agreement under strain. Nevertheless, the countries involved, through NEAFC, have a vehicle that may deal with such problems should they arise. At this stage, the new member problem has yet to occur.

The Atlantic Bluefin Tuna Fishery

The Northern Atlantic and Mediterranean bluefin tuna (*Thunnus Thynnus*) is a large oceanic pelagic fish. It is the largest and one of the most valuable of the tunas, and is, by definition, highly migratory in nature. A dividing line between the East and West Atlantic has been established, separating the stocks in order to facilitate stock assessment. The Bluefin tuna is distributed from the west of Brazil to Labrador, from the east of the Canary Islands to Norway, in the North Sea, in Ireland, in the whole of the Mediterranean and in the south of the Black Sea. Occasionally, it goes to Iceland and Murmansk. The bluefin tuna moves according to food abundance and to water temperature; that is, it moves away from cold waters, seeking warmer areas.

The two existing stocks tend to migrate within their own area. The mixing between stocks is only about 3–4 per cent, that is, the interchange of bluefin tuna is the exception rather than the rule. This allows the two stocks to be managed separately.

The bluefin tuna stock has decreased, especially in the West Atlantic, due to increased catches. The western stock is seriously depleted. In fact, there has been a sharp decrease in this stock, from about 100 000 tonnes in 1970 to below 20 000 tonnes in 1995. The stock is so depleted that strict measures have been enforced to prevent stock extinction, through upper bounds on catches. These measures appear to have had a positive effect, as the bluefin tuna catches decreased and the stock stabilised (Brasão, 2000).

In the East Atlantic, there has also been a substantial decrease in the stock since 1970, but it has remained above 100000 tonnes. In the 1990s, catches have increased, especially in the Mediterranean. If this trend is maintained, a complete depletion of the stock is expected within a few years. Therefore, the East Atlantic is currently the main target of regulations. It is upon this resource that we shall focus in this case study (Brasão et al., 2001: Pintassilgo and Duarte, 2001).

The bluefin tuna fisheries are characterised by a variety of vessel types and fishing gears operating from many countries. The traditional and most important fishing gears are the purse seine, the rod and reel, the longline, the trap and the bait boat. Throughout the years, the importance of each gear has changed. Certain types, such as trap, go back to ancient times. Others, such as the Atlantic longline and the Mediterranean purse seine, reached full development in the mid-1970s.

The spatial distribution of the different gears in the Atlantic and the Mediterranean Sea have changed over the years. The most important change has been the relocation of the longline fishery to latitudes above 40° and longitudes between 20° and 50° west, close to the dividing line between the eastern and western stocks.

Several countries catch bluefin tuna, each country using different gear. In particular the countries in Europe, such as Italy, France or Spain, use bait boat, longline, purse seine and trap. Non-European DWFNs, such as Japan, generally employ longlines. Such a large number of countries harvesting bluefin tuna imposes a severe pressure on the stock. In 1995, 29 countries participated in the fishery, with Japan the most important distant water fishing nation. Historically, however, more than 50 countries have participated. A number of past fishing countries may be new entrants to the fishery should the profitability improve.

The International Commission for the Conservation of Atlantic Tunas (ICCAT) has for decades attempted to manage the bluefin tuna fishery. This has been done through the setting of annual total allowable catch quotas (TACs), which have been allocated by country and gear type. The question is now whether ICCAT can evolve into an effective RFMO (Brasão, 2000).

To date, the outlook has not been encouraging, with ICCAT being unable to ensure that its management policies and recommendations are actually implemented. There are several reasons for this unfortunate state of affairs. Bluefin tuna is a very valuable species. Thus there are strong incentives to harvest tuna, even at low stock levels. The migratory pattern of tuna means that it passes through the EEZs of numerous countries, as well as the Mediterranean and international waters. As a consequence, a large number of countries participate in the fishery. By itself this makes it difficult to reach an agreement, although some countries, for example those of the EU, may form coalitions. Furthermore, should the profitability of the fishery improve, a number of 'new' countries may want to enter the fishery.

In essence, ICCAT, as an RFMO, is plagued by the problem of exceedingly large numbers, and the potential threat of free-riding new members. If ICCAT, or an alternative form of RFMO, does not find ways of overcoming these difficulties, there is good reason to fear that, in time, there will be no East Atlantic–Mediterranean tuna resource left to manage.

6.   CONCLUSIONS

The UN Fish Stocks Agreement of 1995 was concluded in an attempt to address a fisheries resource management crisis involving the class of transboundary fishery resources referred to by the UN as straddling and highly migratory fish stocks. While the foundation for the crisis was provided by DWFN fleet capital 'spilling over' from the newly established EEZs into the high seas, the root cause of the crisis lay in the inadequacies of the UN Convention on the Law of the Sea, as it pertained to the management of high seas fishery resources. The Convention left very much in doubt the rights and duties of coastal states, as opposed to those of DWFNs, with respect to the high seas segments of the straddling and highly migratory fish stocks.

The UN Fish Stocks Agreement of 1995 is an attempt to 'patch up' the Convention on the Law of the Sea. In so doing, the Agreement calls for the aforementioned resources to be managed, on a sub-region-by-sub-region basis, through RFMOs. The Agreement, even before coming into force, had served as a framework for the cooperative management of straddling/ highly migratory fish stocks. The Norwegian spring-spawning herring fishery and NAFO provide striking cases in point.

Attempts to manage the Norwegian spring-spawning herring resource before the advent of the UN Fish Stocks Agreement, proved decidedly unsuccessful. The Agreement provided the necessary framework for the cooperative management of the resource, which has apparently been highly successful to date. Thus, to naysayers who maintained that Agreement was wholly unworkable from the start, one can give the example of Norwegian spring-spawning herring, one of the largest, if not *the* largest, fishery resource in the North Atlantic.

Having said this, however, there are difficulties with the Agreement which could undermine its effectiveness over time. The case of Atlantic bluefin tuna is a sobering counter-example to that of Norwegian spring-spawning herring. We have identified three such difficulties, or problems, which we have termed the new member, the real interest, and the interloper problems.

All three difficulties remain, at the time of writing, very much unresolved. All stand out as areas demanding collaborative research by economists and specialists in international law. If the research is not undertaken and applied, the implementation of the UN Fish Stocks Agreement could prove unsuccessful. Should this be the case, we could then be faced with the threat of coastal states attempting to eliminate the straddling/highly migratory fish stocks problem by extending unilaterally the outward boundaries of their EEZs. That, in turn, could threaten the viability of the UN Convention on the Law of the Sea.

NOTES

1. The full title of the Agreement is the 'Agreement for the Implementation of the Provisions of the United Nations Convention on the Law of the Sea of 10 December 1982 Relating to the Conservation and Management of Straddling Fish Stocks and Highly Migratory Fish Stocks'.
2. Defined by the UN as states with significant marine coastlines, as opposed to landlocked states, and geographically disadvantaged states (for example Singapore).
3. A DWFN can be defined as a fishing nation (entity) some of whose fishing fleets operate well beyond domestic waters.
4. See: http://www.oceanlw.net/texts/westpac.htm.
5. This section draws heavily upon Munro (2000a) and Bjørndal and Munro (2000).
6. That is, $c(x) = c/x$.
7. Treaty between the Government of Canada and the Government of the United States of America Concerning Pacific Salmon, March 1985.
8. See T. Bjørndal et al. (2000b).

REFERENCES

Applebaum, R. (1990), 'The Straddling Stock Problem: The Northwest Atlantic Situation, International Law, and Options for Coastal State Action', in A. H. A. Soons (ed.), *Implications of the Law of the Sea Convention Through International Institutions*, Hawaii: The Law of the Sea Institute, 282–317.

Arnason, R., G. Magnusson and S. Agnarsson (2000), 'The Norwegian Spring-Spawning Herring Fishery: A Stylized Game', *Marine Resource Economics*, **15**, 293–320.

Balton, D.A. (1996), 'Strengthening the Law of the Sea: The New Agreement on Straddling Fish Stocks and Highly Migratory Fish Stocks', *Ocean Development and International Law*, **27**, 125–51.

Balton, D.A. (2000), 'Dealing with the "Bad Actors" of Ocean Fisheries', *Proceedings from the Conference on the Management of Straddling Fish Stocks and*

Highly Migratory Fish Stocks, and the UN Agreement, T. Bjørndal, G. Munro and R. Arnason (eds), Bergen: Centre for Fisheries Economics, Norwegian School of Economics and Business Administration, Papers on Fisheries Economics 38.

Bjørndal, T. (1988), 'The Optimal Management of North Sea Herring', *Journal of Environmental Economics and Management*, **15**, 9–29.

Bjørndal, T. and G. Munro (1998), 'The Economics of Fisheries Management: A Survey', in T. Tietenberg and H. Folmer (eds), *The International Yearbook of Environmental and Resource Economics 1998/1999*, Cheltenham, UK and Northampton, USA: Edward Elgar.

Bjørndal, T. and G. Munro (2000), 'The Management of High Seas Fishery Resources and the Implementation of the UN Fish Agreement of 1995: Problems and Prospects', prepared for the 10th Biennial Conference of the International Institute of Fisheries Economics and Trade, Corvallis, July.

Bjørndal, T., G. Munro and R. Arnason (eds) (2000a), 'Introduction', *Proceedings from the Conference on the Management of Straddling Fish Stocks and Highly Migratory Fish Stocks, and the U.N. Agreement*, Bergen: Centre for Fisheries Economics, Norwegian School of Economics and Business Administration, Papers on Fisheries Economics 38.

Bjørndal, T., V. Kaitala, M. Lindroos and G. Munro (2000b), 'The Management of High Seas Fisheries', *Annals of Operations Research*, **94**, 183–96.

Bjørndal, T., A.D. Hole, W.M. Slinde and F. Asche (1998), 'Norwegian Spring Spawning Herring – Some Biological and Economic Issues', Norwegian School of Economics and Business Administration, Centre for Fisheries Economics Working Paper No. 3/1998.

Brasão, A. (2000), 'Ensaios em Economia dos Recursos Naturais', Faculdade de Economia, Universidade Nova de Lisboa.

Brasão, A., C. Costa Duarte and M.A. Cunha-e-Sá (2000), 'Managing the Northern Atlantic Bluefin Tuna Fisheries: The Stability of the UN Fish Stock Agreement Solution', *Marine Resource Economics*, **15**(4), 341–60.

Burke, W. (1991), 'Anadromous Species and the New International Law of the Sea', *Ocean Development and International Law*, **22**, 95–131.

Clark, C.W. (1980), 'Restricted Access to Common-Property Fishery Resources', in P. Liu (ed.), *Dynamic Optimization and Mathematical Economics*, New York: Plenum, 117–32.

Clark, C.W. (1985), *Bioeconomic Modelling and Fisheries Management*, New York: John Wiley and Sons.

Clark, C.W. and G. Munro (1999), 'Fishing Capacity and Resource Management Objectives', Food and Agriculture Organization of the UN. Technical Consultation on the Measurement of Fishing Capacity, Mexico City, Mexico, 29 November–3 December 1999-11-02. Document Number 12.

Clark, C.W., F.H. Clark and G.R. Munro (1979), 'The optimal exploitation of renewable resource stocks: problems of irreversible investment', *Econometrica* **47**, 25–47.

Cox, A., M. Stubbs and L. Davies (1999), *Southern Bluefin and CITES: An Economic Perspective*, Report for Fisheries Research Fund and Environment Australia, ABARE Research Report 99–2. Canberra: Australian Bureau of Agricultural and Resource Economics.

Department of External Affairs and International Trade Canada (1992), News Release, 24 December.

Department of Fisheries and Oceans Canada (1993), Memorandum of

Understanding Between the European Community and the Government of Canada on Fisheries Relations.

Doulman, D.J. (1995), *Structure and Process of the 1993–1995 United Nations Conference on Straddling Fish Stocks and Highly Migratory Fish Stocks*, FAO Fisheries Circular No. 898, Rome: Food and Agriculture Organization of the United Nations.

Doulman, D.J. (2000), 'Events Leading to the Elaboration of an International Plan of Action to Combat Illegal, Unreported and Unregulated Fishing', prepared for the International Conference on Fisheries Monitoring, Control and Surveillance, Brussels, Belgium, 24–27 October 2000.

Folmer, H. and A. de Zeeuw (2000), 'International Problems and Policy', in H. Folmer and H.L. Gabel (eds), *Principles of Environmental and Resource Economics*, Cheltenham, UK and Northampton, USA: Edward Elgar, 447–78.

Food and Agriculture Organization of the United Nations (FAO) (1992), 'International Fisheries Bodies: Considerations for High Seas Management', Technical Consultation on High Seas Fishing, Rome FI/HSF/TC/92/6.

Food and Agriculture Organization of the United Nations (FAO) (1999), 'Managing Fishing Capacity: Selected Papers on Underlying Concepts and Issues', Rome: FAO Fisheries Technical Paper 386.

Food and Agriculture Organization of the United Nations (FAO) (1994), *World Review of Highly Migratory Species and Straddling Stocks*, Rome: FAO Fisheries Technical Paper 337.

Food and Agriculture Organization of the United Nations (FAO) (2001), *International Plan of Action to Prevent, Deter and Eliminate Illegal, Unreported and Unregulated Fishing*, www.fao.org/docrep/003/x6729e00.htm.

Gordon, D.V. and G.R. Munro (eds) (1996), *Fisheries and Uncertainty: A Precautionary Approach to Resource Management*, Calgary: University of Calgary Press.

Gordon, H.S. (1954), 'The Economic Theory of a Common Property Resource: The Fishery', *Journal of Political Economy*, **62**, 124–42.

Hedley, C. (2000), 'International Relations and the CFP: the Legal Framework', in A. Hatcher and D. Tingley (eds), *International Relations and the Common Fisheries Policy*, Portsmouth: Centre for the Economics and Management of Aquatic Resources, University of Portsmouth, 38–61.

Kaitala, V. and G.R. Munro (1993), 'The Management of High Seas Fisheries', *Marine Resource Economics*, **8**, 313–29.

Kaitala, V. and G.R. Munro (1997), 'The Conservation and Management of High Seas Fishery Resources Under the New Law of the Sea', *Natural Resource Modeling*, **10**, 87–108.

Kaitala, V. and M. Pohjola (1988), 'Optimal Recovery of a Shared Resource Stock', *Natural Resource Modeling*, **3**, 91–119.

Kennedy, J. (1999), 'A Dynamic Model of Cooperative and Non-cooperative Harvesting of Southern Bluefin Tuna With an Open Access Fringe', presented to the 1999 World Conference on Natural Resource Modeling, Halifax.

McRae, D. and G. Munro (1989), 'Coastal State "Rights" within the 200 Mile Exclusive Economic Zone', in P. Neher, R. Arnason and N. Mollet (eds), *Rights Based Fishing*, Dordrecht: Kluwer, 97–112.

Miles, E. and W. Burke (1989), 'Pressures on the United Nations Convention on the Law of the Sea of 1982 Arising from New Fisheries Conflicts: The Problem of Straddling Stocks', *Ocean Development and International Law*, **20**, 343–57.

Miles, E. and D.L. Fluharty (1991), 'U.S. Interests in the North Pacific', *Ocean Development and International Law*, **22**, 315–42.

Miller, K., G. Munro, T. McDorman, R. McKelvey and P. Tyedemers (2001), *The 1999 Pacific Salmon Agreement: A Sustainable Solution?*, Canadian American Public Policy Occasional Paper No. 47, Orono: The Canadian–American Center, University of Maine.

Molenaar, E. (2000), 'The Concept of "Real Interest" and Other Aspects of Co-operation through Regional Fisheries Management Mechanisms', *The International Journal of Marine and Coastal Law*, **15**, 475–631.

Munro, G.R. (1987), 'The Management of Shared Fishery Resources Under Extended Jurisdiction', *Marine Resource Economics*, **3**, 271–296.

Munro, G.R. (1990a), 'Extended Jurisdiction and the Management of Pacific Highly Migratory Species', *Ocean Development and International Law*, **21**, 289–307.

Munro, G.R. (1990b), 'The Optimal Management of Transboundary Fisheries: Game Theoretic Considerations', *Natural Resource Modeling*, **4**, 403–26.

Munro, G.R. (2000a), 'An Economic Review of the United Nations Agreement for the Implementation of the United Nations Convention on the Law of the Sea of 10 December 1982 Relating to the Conservation and Management of Straddling and Highly Migratory Fish Stocks. December 1995', *Proceedings from the Conference on the Management of Straddling Fish Stocks and Highly Migratory Fish Stocks, and the U.N. Agreement*, T. Bjørndal, G. Munro and R. Arnason (eds), Bergen: Centre for Fisheries Economics, Norwegian School of Economics and Business Administration, Papers on Fisheries Economics 38.

Munro, G.R. (2000b), 'The United Nations Fish Stocks Agreement of 1995: History and Problems of Implementation', *Marine Resource Economics*, **15**, 265–80.

Nash, J. (1953), 'Two-Person Cooperative Games', *Econometrica*, **21**, 128–40.

Newton, C. (1999), 'Review of Issues for the Control and Reduction of Fishing Capacity on the High Seas', FAO of the UN, *Managing Fishing Capacity: Selected papers on Underlying Concepts and Issues*, Rome: FAO Fisheries Technical Paper no. 386, 49–74.

Northwest Atlantic Fisheries Organization (NAFO) (1999), 21st Annual Meeting of NAFO 7–17 September 1999, press release.

Orebech, P., K. Sigurjonsson and T.L. McDorman (1998), 'The 1995 United Nations Straddling and Highly Migratory Fish Stocks Agreement: Management, Enforcement and Dispute Settlement', *The International Journal of Marine and Coastal Law*, **13**, 119–41.

Organisation for Economic Co-operation and Development (1997), *Towards Sustainable Fisheries: Economic Aspects of the Management of Living Marine Resources*, Paris: OECD.

Pintassilgo, P. and C. Costa Duarte (2001), The New-Member Problem in the Cooperative Management of High Seas Fisheries', *Marine Resource Economics*, **15**, 361–78.

Shubik, M. (1982), *Game Theory in the Social Sciences*, Cambridge, MA: The MIT Press.

Stokke, O. (2001), *Governing High Seas Fisheries: The Interplay of Global and Regional Regimes*, Oxford: Oxford University Press.

United Nations (UN) (1982), United Nations Convention on the Law of the Sea, UN Doc. A/Conf. 62/122.

United Nations (UN) (1992), *The Law of the Sea: The Regime for High Seas Fisheries: Status and Prospects.* New York: Division for Ocean Affairs and the Law of the Sea, Office of Legal Affairs.

United Nations (UN) (1995), United Nations Conference on Straddling Fish Stocks and Highly Migratory Fish Stocks. Agreement for the Implementation of the Provisions of the United Nations Convention on the Law of the Sea of 10 December 1982 Relating to the Conservation and Management of Straddling Fish Stocks and Highly Migratory Fish Stocks, UN Doc. A/Conf./164/37.

2. Choosing environmental risks

Thomas D. Crocker and Jason F. Shogren*

1. INTRODUCTION

Over the past decade, we have argued that environmental risk is endogenous. By endogenous risk, we mean that people have some control over
the probability and severity of the environmental risks they confront. They
defend themselves; they invest scarce resources to increase the odds that
good things happen and bad things do not. While we appreciate that both
nature and the government affect the level of personal risk, we have maintained the classical liberal viewpoint that neither biology nor collective
action is destiny. Individual choices affect nature and collective action just
as nature and governments affect our private choices. We go so far as to
argue that endogenous risk arises whenever economic systems and environmental systems are jointly determined, which seems to apply to nearly all
environmental questions.

Examples of endogenous risk in which a person can choose to alter environmental outcomes abound. Common sense and everyday evidence
demonstrate that human actions and reactions make environmental risks
non-synonymous with environmental hazards. Most people take care of
themselves. When confronting risks from pathogens, people self-protect by
washing their hands, storing food, and cooking food well. They buy bottled
water if they suspect their drinking water is polluted. They apply sunscreen
to protect their skins from UV radiation. The success of collective mandates to promote safety depends on individual choices. Use of auto seat
belts reduces both the probability and the severity of any injury but their
mandatory installation cannot guarantee that passengers will choose to
wear them. People substitute self-care for the care supplied by collective
safety programs. They also supplement these programs with self-care.

*We thank our reviewers and editors for their numerous helpful comments. Senior authorship
is shared. Although the US Environmental Protection Agency provided financial support
through grant #R82871601, this research has not been subjected to the Agency's required peer
and policy review, and therefore does not necessarily reflect the views of the Agency. Thanks
to the Economic Research Service of the US Department of Agriculture for their funding
support as well.

Examples include more thorough weeding and crop storage in response to the prospect of drought and improved nutrition and exercise regimens to cope with health hazards. Each person's value for any collectively supplied risk reduction program is then conditional on his private preparation and forearming efforts (Ehrlich and Becker, 1972; Courbage, 2001).

If one views this as stating the obvious, remember that many educated people presume the insertion of economics into natural science, or vice versa, will not change the core concepts of either discipline. The dominant view in environmental risk assessment/risk management studies is still that risk is exogenous, beyond the control of everyday people who might suffer from undesirable outcomes. This belief continues to guide the risk assessment–risk management bifurcations sanctified by the National Academy of Sciences (1983) in the early 1980s and approvingly discussed by former USEPA Administrator William Ruckelshaus (1984). The presumption has also encouraged the expert natural scientist to view the lay person's risk judgment as frequently irrational or misinformed, allowing the specialist to label the nonspecialist as unqualified to apprehend the consequences of environmental hazards (Freudenberg, 1988). This has arguably led economists to focus attention more on the properties of risk preference than on the technologies of risk control when explaining behavior under risk (Shogren, 1991). Exogenous risk presumes that lay people cannot privately prepare and forearm themselves when confronting risks – that they must resign to a future no more than a whim of the gods or of the state and that the person can do little beyond adapting *ex post* to the idiosyncrasies of his surroundings (Sahlins, 1974).

Environmental risk has two features that affect a person's private choices to protect himself – his perception of the likelihood an event unfavorable to him will take place and the severity of the consequences if the event is realized. If the person cannot prepare and forearm for the threat an environmental hazard poses him, this likelihood and severity is directly delivered by the hazard. Risk would be exogenous to this person and the only way to reduce his risks is some form of collective action to reduce the hazard. The great bulk of the literature, economic and noneconomic, on environmental risk views risk reduction as a pure public good which exists independent of any person's actions and which the relevant collective agency finances by sure payments from all affected by the hazard.[1] And even though thoughtful discussions have been held over the last two decades looking for ways to integrate more behavior into risk assessment, the fundamental bifurcation sanctioned by the NRC holds to this day, and spills over into discussions on how to use risk analysis to help guide all governmental policies (see for example Charnley et al., 2000).

But people protect themselves privately every day. They protect against environmental risk by making investments to reduce the likelihood that bad states of nature occur; they adapt to risk by changing production and consumption decisions to reduce the severity of a bad state if it does occur. Risk is endogenous. Both collective action and private investments jointly determine the risks people choose and the costs to reduce them. And since private citizens have the freedom to self-protect on their own accord, a policy-maker should consider these private responses when choosing the appropriate degree of public action. Otherwise, a policy is more expensive than need be with no additional reduction in environmental risk.

Intuitively, policy-makers and researchers would agree with this logic – private risk reduction efforts affect the costs and benefits of collective action. And yet this obvious point is neglected in actual policy-making whenever decisions are fragmented into the assessment–management paradigm.[2] An illustrative example is endangered species. The conservation biologist maintains that identifying the threshold of extinction endangerment for a species is strictly a biological question as determined by the present sizes, trends, and spatial distributions of populations and their interactions with the stochastic forces of nature (for example Beissinger and Perrine, 2001). But species survival also depends on key economic parameters such as relative prices of sites with and without their habitat, and on the preferences, resources, and productivities of the site users who generate these relative prices. Assessing the risks to the survival of a species is an economic as well as a biological problem. Risks to species are endogenous too. This view implies the use of either natural science or of economic analysis in isolation to assess the consequences of environmental risks leads to biased and inconsistent estimates.[3]

Climate change policy is another instructive example. Based on the Rio agreement and the Framework Convention on Climate Change (UNFCCC, 1992), the international climate change community has maintained a separation between mitigation and adaptation that has pervaded most thinking at top levels of decision-making, and is reflected in research budgets and agendas (USOSTP, 1999). Mitigation means efforts to curtail carbon emissions to reduce the risk of climate change; adaptation means investments to reduce the severity if a bad climate state is realized. A good example is the most recent assessment of the scientific, technical and socio-economic dimensions of climate change by the International Panel on Climate Change (IPCC, 2001a,b). IPCC Working Group II reported on adaptation, while the separate Working Group III reported on mitigation; neither report debated the specifics of how the economic circumstances that affect adaptation drive mitigation or visa versa. Rather they sketch out emission scenarios that suggest mitigation might be less likely if all people take a more 'global' perspective. But since both mitigation and adaptation jointly determine climate risks and the costs to reduce them, and since private citizens can adapt on their own accord, a policy-maker must consider these adaptive responses when choosing the optimal degree of public mitigation. Otherwise, policy actions increase costs without reducing climate risk (Kane and Shogren, 2000).[4]

Endogenous risk implies that observed risks are functions of natural-science parameters and of a person's preparation and forearming decisions against a perceived hazard. The basis on which people make decisions about risk vary across people and across situations with the relative marginal productivities of their efforts to protect themselves and family, even though the properties of the natural hazards triggering these efforts may apply equally to everyone. It follows that attempts to assess risk levels solely in terms of natural science or in terms of economics may be highly misleading – costly self-care is endogenous and may vary systematically in the observed risk data. The sources of the systematic variation are relative prices, incomes, and other economic and social parameters that influence any person's self-care decisions. Endogenous risk implies that risk assessors must explicitly address the simultaneous nature of how a person's behaviors affect observed risk *and* how the natural-science features of hazards affect these behaviors.

Incomplete markets imply endogenous risk (Marshall, 1976). Settings in which arbitrage among different beliefs or values about states-of-the-world is costly create opportunities for private risk reduction. With their open access, consumption indivisibility, nonconvex response, and asymmetrically distributed informational properties, among others, environmental goods are the touchstone case of goods for which economically efficient markets in which arbitrage exhausts all gains from trade are difficult, frequently even impossible, to form and to maintain. With complete markets, the economic analysis of environmental issues would serve only as a scholarly curio rather than being driven in at least equal parts by potential policy applications and intellectual curiosity. If environmental hazards are to be analyzed in terms of exogenous risk, then one presumes that an insurance (Arrow–Debreu contingent claim) contract can be written and enforced for every conceivable risk in every conceivable state. But because moral hazard, adverse selection, and jointness of risks make the writing and enforcement of contracts costly, complete contracts rarely if ever exist, especially for environmental risk. The person must choose *ex ante* between contractually defining states of nature or of making an effort to alter the likelihood and the prospective severity of states of nature. Environmental risk is usually endogenous.

Hirshleifer (1966) and Quiggin (1992) endeavor to preserve the scope of applicability for the exogenous risk framework by arguing it is always possible to redefine a problem such that the state of nature is independent of human action (also see Chambers and Quiggin, 2000). One need only assume the marginal productivity of risk reduction in terms of ambient risk reduction to be independent of the realized state of nature. Consider, however, a household which suspects bacterial groundwater contamination threatens its drinking water. The household can alter its probability of illness by boiling the water. An analyst might define the situation as additively separable from the household's actions by focusing solely on the groundwater contamination, over which the household likely has no control. But this treatment is irrelevant if the question is the household's response to and damages from the threat groundwater contamination poses to its drinking water. Household members are concerned with the probability of being made ill and the severity of any realized illness, and they are able to exercise some control over these events (see Crocker et al., 1991; Poe and Bishop, 1999). A plausible circumstance in which additive separability of consequence from ambient hazard might be a constant occurs when collective protection is a perfect substitute for the private version (Shogren and Crocker, 1999).[5]

But this case has to be the exception, not the rule. Suppose two states of nature exist – contamination or non-contamination of groundwater. It is hard to imagine a case in which the realized state will not affect the marginal productivity of protection. The marginal productivity of boiling the household's drinking water would be positively affected by contamination, negatively affected by non-contamination. Alternatively, if the sign of the effect of the hazard upon the marginal productivity of protection is always the same, such that one utility prospect always dominates, the household is wasting its time and effort by trying to prepare for the hazard. Separability essentially makes risk irrelevant to this household's decisions since it removes the risk from the risk–cost of protection tradeoff.

The concept of endogenous risk is by no means foreign to the general economics literature. Beginning with Arrow (1963), the concept is familiar under the label 'moral hazard', in which private actions are private information. Ehrlich and Becker (1972) defined the two basic technologies of endogenous risk – self-protection and self-insurance.[6] Self-protection reduces the probability of an undesired state; self-insurance reduces the severity of consequences if the state is realized. Numerous researchers have since explored analytically the behavioral implications of self-protection and self-insurance, mainly while investigating the properties of insurance markets. Examples include Cook and Graham (1977), Laffont (1980), Boyer and Dionne (1983), Arnott and Stiglitz (1988), Lewis and Nickerson (1989), Stewart (1994), and Heyes (2001). A major conclusion of this literature is that the endogenous risk concept describes a broader range of behavior than does the standard exogenous risk framework. This less constrained range of behavior comes into play because the endogenous risk concept encompasses preferences over both outcomes and the lotteries that define these outcomes.

This chapter reviews applications of the endogenous risk concept to environmental valuation problems, and suggests a few plausible extensions. We consider the contributions this literature has made to a better understanding of environmental issues and to the evaluation of environmental policy. We adapt the concepts of self-protection and self-insurance to individuals' decisions about manipulating or tempering their potential consequences of exposures to environmental hazards. The chapter focuses on using endogenous risk as an aid in understanding the choices people actually make as opposed to suggesting the choices they should make. We explore the core analytical developments of the endogenous risk concept to valuation issues, review a sampling of empirical applications, and draw conclusions about the current status of the concept and its future use prospects. We do not present an exhaustive listing of particularized models shaped to specific environmental decision problems. We instead try to identify different modeling strategies by using specific models as illustrations. The next section reviews the basic exogenous and endogenous risk concepts for the person in the context of the expected utility theory. We also speak to analytical extensions of the basic endogenous risk concept. Implications of endogenous risk for risk valuation exercises are considered in a third section, and existing empirical applications are briefly reviewed. We conclude with brief remarks on productive research agendas and environmental applications of the endogenous risk concept that this review does not cover.

2. CHOICES

We now consider in more detail the formal differences between the exogenous and endogenous risk perspectives. We also explore how choice under endogenous risk is affected by uncertain productivity and protection premia, alternative risk reduction technologies, non-convex preferences created by self-protection opportunities, and risks of irrational behavior.

2.1 Exogenous Risk

Expected utility (EU) theory is the economic theory of individual decision making under risk. As presented in the seminal works of von Neumann and Morgenstern (1947), Savage (1954), de Finetti (1974), and Dreze (1987), among others, it defines economically rational behavior for the person who makes risky decisions – choices made before the consequences are revealed. It says a person's expected utility from a lottery is a weighted average of his utility in each realized state of nature or consequence, with his subjective probabilities of the states being the weights. EU theory gives an answer to the question of how people combine probabilities and consequences when confronted with probabilistic alternative choices. The model simultaneously captures their mindsets about probabilities and about consequences, and presumes that people think about these two elements simultaneously and not in sequence. For the widely examined exogenous risk case in which a person cannot manipulate the state probabilities or the states themselves, his expected utility function for the two-state case of no loss and a loss is:

$$EU = pU_1(M - L) + (1 - p)U_2(M), \qquad (2.1)$$

where the states are mutually exclusive and jointly exhaustive, implying that the probabilities are additive. EU is the von Neumann–Morgenstern (1947) expected utility index, p is the probability of the undesirable state, M is predetermined wealth, and L is the money equivalent of damages if the undesirable state 1 is realized.

Risk aversion is commonly assumed such that $U_i'(\cdot) > 0, U_i''(\cdot) < i = 1,2$, where primes denote the relevant order of the derivative. The utility function for money is positive and concave and is independent of state. Given the person cannot manipulate either M or L, analysis of expression (2.1) reduces to asking for that outside payment which would make the person indifferent in utility terms between the two states. This payment would be L if the person were risk-neutral, that is, indifferent between the gamble and a sure thing, which is the probability weighted average of the state utilities. The payment would be more than L if he were averse to the gamble and less than L if he preferred it. His price of insurance is 'actuarially fair' when it equals his expected loss. A person's only problem in a world of complete contingent claims markets is how much insurance to buy taking account of his risk preference.

Machina (1987) provides an especially clear presentation of the axioms sufficient to make the exogenous case of EU a theory of rational individual choice.[7] Empirical evidence is plentiful, however, that people routinely violate one or more of these axioms. The exogenous EU paradigm frequently fails to bridge the gap between economists' conjectures and everyday observations of human behavior. Three vivid examples of the gap include the Allais (1953) paradox, the Ellsberg (1961) paradox, and the preference reversal phenomenon. Allais (1953) showed that people do not preserve their initial rank orderings between two lotteries when a third lottery is introduced, a violation of the independence axiom central to the exogenous case *EU* paradigm. Intuitively, the Allais paradox says the rank ordering of a pair of lotteries depends on the context in which they are offered rather than only upon their consequences. In environmental policy terms, the Allais paradox implies that policy-makers can manipulate public perceptions of the net benefits of alternative programs by judiciously framing them.

In the Ellsberg (1961) paradox, many people have an irrational aversion to ambiguous risk – they may choose a gamble with known probabilities over a gamble with ambiguous or uncertain probabilities, even though the ambiguous or uncertain gamble has higher expected utility. This implies that the public irrationally fears environmental problems whose associated risks are unclear, putting excessive pressure on policy-makers to do something – anything – now.

Preference reversals also imply that people do not think about environmental risk in the manner *EU* theory requires. *EU* theory supposes that people think about the odds of an event and of its consequences jointly. But a great deal of empirical work in a broad range of settings says that they separate the two, first deciding one and then the other (for example Grether and Plott, 1979; Shogren, 1998). For example, a person might rank an alternative as better than another because it has good odds, but be willing to pay more to realize the lower-ranked alternative because, if realized, it has a bigger payoff. Upon which of these choices is a policy-maker to focus? The exogenous case *EU* paradigm provides him no guidance.

Some economists have adopted two modes of argument to contest the empirical evidence that individuals' behaviors in risky environments frequently do not conform to the exogenous case *EU* paradigm. One mode challenges the experimental procedures used by those who report violations of exogenous case *EU* rationality. The procedures are said to be poorly suited to problems involving risk because they are one-shot, in which inexperienced subjects do not have the opportunity to learn and to acquire feedback (Grether and Plott, 1979), that normal decision aids such as prices are withheld (Edwards and von Winterfeldt, 1986), and that the incentives used are weak, at best, at matching rewards to performances (Grether, 1994).

The second mode seeks out restrictions on utility functions that reconcile the theoretical implications with the empirical evidence of how people actually behave when confronted with risky choices. The economics literature of the last few decades has abundant papers submitting elegant 'non-expected-utility theories' to the profession, submissions of different theories which now add up well into double figures. Starmer (2000) provides a thorough review of the static versions of these theories. Kreps and Porteus (1978) and Selden (1978), for example, create a temporal lottery approach, in which both the payoff vector and the timing of resolution of uncertainty matter. Their model allows a person to have a preference for delayed revelation of information by dropping the reduction of compound lotteries axiom. Such dynamic non-expected-utility theories with recursive preferences have occasionally found applications in the economics of renewable resources (see Peltola and Knapp, 2001).

Some of these theories retain the *EU* prior that people try to maximize utility – people try to maximize the extent to which their preferences are satisfied and they do so by optimizing their behavior in a thoroughly holistic fashion. The trick is then to suggest how the preference structure changes as the level or the type of risk changes, for example Machina (1982). These theories typically relax the independence axiom requiring linearity in probabilities, allowing more complex notions of tastes to be introduced. Other theories discard the optimizing rule altogether, to replace it with alternative decision rules which people purportedly use to simplify their choices (for example Kahneman and Tversky, 1979).

Nevertheless, without exception, the non-expected-utility theory alternatives to the conventional *EU* specification in expression (2.1) make conjectures about the structure of people's preferences. They do so by selectively distinguishing among potential consequences in terms of the anxiety, regret, anticipation, suspicion, disappointments, and other emotions which gambles might elicit (for example Sugden, 1985; Elster, 1998). But never in this wide body of non-expected-utility theories and taxonomies of the emotions is there allowed any interplay among these emotions. Moreover, with the singular exception of Machina (1989), no concern is expressed as to where one might draw the line about the extent to which the analyst is permitted to distinguish among outcomes by appealing to his perceptions of the person's anticipated feelings. In fact, Harless and Camerer (1994) show that many non-expected-utility theories are too 'fat' in that they predict too many behavioral patterns never actually observed in practice.

Non-expected-utility theorists must focus on the structures of preferences because starting from specifications like expression (2.1) leaves them no choice. Expression (2.1) requires people to adapt their preferences to circumstances; it does not allow them to adapt circumstances to their preferences. We suggest that the endogenous risk case of *EU* theory preserves the theory's capacity to organize behavior while expanding its descriptive and explanatory powers. It makes *EU* theory appear less stressed to the outside observer. We submit that it is worthwhile to see what can be achieved by refining our understanding of how people's beliefs of what they can do to the world around them operates on their choices. Much might be gained by acquiring insights into the relation between how a risk is reduced and tastes for outcomes and the lotteries that define these outcomes.[8] Though we focus on the potential contributions an endogenous risk perspective can make to more robust *EU* theory, we grant the underexplored possibility it could do the same for some non-expected-utility theories as well.

2.2 Endogenous Risk

Think, for example, of a risk-averse person who must decide *ex ante* on self-protection, z, and self-insurance, x, as he confronts the prospect of having some valuable personal asset such as his house or his health harmed by an environmental hazard. Because of moral hazard, adverse selection, and non-independence of risks, this person cannot acquire enough market insurance to assure his *ex ante* utility level is maintained whether or not the harm occurs. The person *ex ante* selects z and x to maximize his von Neumann–Morgenstern (1947) utility index, *EU*,

$$EU = \int_a^b U(M - L(\gamma;x) - c(x, z))dF(\gamma;z,r), \qquad (2.2)$$

where $W = M - L(\gamma;x) - c(x, z)$ is net wealth, M is endowed income, $L(\gamma;x)$ is the money equivalent of realized damage severity from hazard exposure, γ is a random variable such as health or hazard exposure conditional on self-protection and self-insurance choices defined by the distribution $F(\gamma;z,r)$ bounded over the support $[a,b]$, $c(x,z)$ is the cost function for self-care and r is an index of exogenous background riskiness such as the level of ambient air pollution. Assume $U_W > 0$, $L_x < 0$, $L_\gamma < 0$ and $c_i(x, z) > 0$, $i = x,z$. Also let $F_z < 0$, and $F_r > 0$, in the sense of first-order stochastic dominance.[9] No restrictions need be placed on the signs of F_{zz}, F_{rr}, and F_{zr} in the immediate neighborhood of the expected utility-maximizing level of self-protection, z^*. Shogren and Crocker (1999) show that the parameterized formulation set forth in (2.2) is formally equivalent to a state-space formulation (exogenous state of nature) of the same problem, suggesting the choice between them rests on the relative restrictiveness of the assumptions necessary to make each tractable for a specific application.[10] In either case, the person is making self-care choices, *ex ante*, of lotteries over potential outcomes of the random variable rather than choosing self-care at each and every potential *ex post* outcome.

The necessary conditions from (2.2) for this person's optimal levels of self-protection and self-insurance are

$$z: -\int_a^b U_W(M - L(\gamma;x)) - c(x, z))c_z(x, z)dF(\gamma;z,r)$$

$$+ \int_a^b U(M - L(\gamma;x) - c(x, z))L_\gamma F_z(\gamma;z,r)d\gamma = 0 \qquad (2.3)$$

$$x: -\int_a^b U_W(M - L(\gamma;x) - c(x, z))[L_x(\gamma;x) + c_x(x, z)]dF(\gamma;z,r) = 0 \quad (2.4)$$

Expressions (2.3) and (2.4) state the standard result that a person maximizes expected utility by equating the marginal cost of influencing probability or severity to the marginal wealth gained. The second or marginal benefit term in (2.3) registers the distinctive feature of the endogenous risk concept. Integration by parts of the term shows that the marginal benefits of self-care are realized directly in the utility function and indirectly in this function through a first-order stochastically dominating change in outcomes induced by the person's risk reduction technology.[11]

We devote the rest of this section to brief demonstrations of the analytical suppleness of the endogenous risk concept – its ability to capture at the level of the individual behavioral features otherwise previously unrecognized or thought too complex or amorphous for analytical treatments. We start with the idea of protection premia, move on to a discussion of access to and effectiveness of risk reduction technologies, describe how nonconvex preferences can arise, and, finally, review how a form of seeming irrationality can be made rational. For simplicity, we assume throughout that all marginal rates of substitution are wealth-independent.[12]

2.3 Protection Premia

The endogenous risk specification in expression (2.2) assigns risk to the consequences of a known exposure to an environmental hazard. But risk can also join the exposure itself because of a person's incomplete knowledge about the effectiveness of a particular risk reduction technology. A farmer may be unsure about whether a pesticide he applies will rid him of a pest; a parent may doubt the cleanliness of a childcare facility. Yet for any pest incidence, the farmer may be clear about the consequences for his crop output. Similarly, for any level of cleanliness, the parent may be certain about the consequences for her child's health. Shogren (1991) uses the concept of a protection premium to examine the interaction between a person's use of a risk reduction technology and his risk preferences. The protection premium accounts for a person's aversion to riskiness about the productivity of a risk reduction technology rather than his aversion to the risky consequences of a hazard.

Shogren (1991) defines a protection premium as the utility equivalent of the burden imposed on a person by the chance that a particular risk reduction technology will be ineffective. Pratt's (1964) traditional premium for preference risk aversion in the exogenous case of *EU* theory burdens wealth; Shogren's protection premium burdens efforts to use a risk reduction technology successfully. The protection premium reflects the value a person attaches to the resolution of the risk that a technology directed at reducing the risk of undesirable consequences from a hazard will not work. A person may be willing to pay a premium to obtain a known value of a stochastic variable instead of having to deal with a mixed lottery involving the possibility the selected risk reduction technology is ineffective.

Consider the self-protection, z, and the self-insurance, x, decision problems of a person who is unsure about the efficacy of a risk reduction technology in a binary lottery setting consisting of a loss, L, and of a no-loss state. The curvature of $U_i, i = 1,2$, does not differ between the two states. This self-protection problem is

$$\underset{z}{Max}\left[\int_{a}^{b} [p(z+\eta)U_1(M-L)+(1-p(z+\eta))U_2(M-L-z)]dG(\eta;r)\right], \quad (2.5)$$

and his self-insurance problem is

$$\underset{x}{Max}\left[\int_{a}^{b} [pU_1(M-x)+(1-p)U_2(M-L(x+\eta))-x]dG(\eta;r)\right]. \quad (2.6)$$

In (2.5) and (2.6), η is the risk attached to the effectiveness of the risk reduction technology, $p(z+\eta)$ is the probability of no loss from the hazard, $L(x+\eta)$ is the loss from the hazard, $p' > 0$, $p'' < 0$, and $L' < 0$, $L'' \geq 0$, by assumption. $G(\cdot)$ is the cumulative distribution function defined over the support $[a, b]$.

The first-order necessary conditions for interior maxima of (2.5) and (2.6) are

$$z: \quad p'(\cdot)Q - p(\cdot)U'_1 - (1-p(\cdot))U'_2 = 0 \quad (2.7)$$

$$x: \quad -pU'_1 - (1-p)U'_2(L'+1) = 0, \quad (2.8)$$

where $Q = U_1 - U_2$, and $-Q''/Q' = \hat{R}(z) = -(U'_1 - U'_2)/(U_1 - U_2) \geq 0$ is a first-order approximation of the Arrow–Pratt measure of absolute risk aversion. Both risk reducing technologies in the form of p' and L', and taste effects in the form of $\hat{R}(z)$ and $U_i, i = 1,2$ affect these first-order optimality conditions.

The protection premium model suggests that risk reduction technologies play a key role in how people approach risks from environmental hazards. It follows then that the utility function needs fewer restrictions to explain individuals' behaviors under risk. The model suggests the economic analysis of individuals' behaviors under risk can gain by devoting more attention to details of the sources of risk, the technologies describing combinations of risk reduction inputs, and the interactions of these sources and technologies with tastes. More significantly, the results highlight the question of causality raised by Stigler and Becker (1977). They call risk aversion in preferences one of the primary *ad hoc* assumptions in economics. Their question is, do people pay a risk premium because they are presumed to be risk-averse, or are they risk-averse because they pay a risk premium? In exogenous risk models, the only way a premium arises is by the presumption of risk aversion in preferences. People with identical tastes must value a risk reduction identically. With endogenous risk and the protection premium, a person might pay a premium for a less chancy risk reduction technology irrespective of presumed preferences about risk. In fact, the person could be assumed risk-neutral in preferences, and he could still pay a protection premium to reduce the uncertainty about the effectiveness of the risk reduction technology. This protection premium is based on the curvature of the probability function, not the utility function (also see Lee, 1998). According to the effectiveness of the risk reduction each person employs, this curvature may differ across people, whether their tastes be similar or dissimilar.

2.4   Choosing among Risk Reduction Technologies

Our treatment of exogenous risk has assumed the person who wishes to self-protect or self-insure has only a single risk reduction technology available. But people confronted with an environmental hazard can draw upon a wide range of such technologies, differing in accessibility and in effectiveness for any given level of risk about potential consequences the hazard poses. The critical point here is that self-protection and self-insurance involve considerably more than merely selecting an effort level and waiting for nature to make a random draw. Consider, for example, the exposures to lead of a young child from a poor, single-mother household living in a rundown old neighborhood in a traffic-congested urban area. To reduce the child's exposures and its associated body lead burden the parent might remove leaded paint from the family home, have the child drink bottled rather than tap water, not allow the child to play in the outside dirt, or even have the child chelated. But lead paint removal and chelation are costly and access to them may be beyond the mother's physical capabilities or her financial reach. Or with the same result as no access, she may not even know lead exposure harms her child. Even if she knows about this harm, having the child drink bottled rather than tap water offers the child less than fully effective protection if the major source of the child's exposures is leaded paint in the residence. Finally, even if the mother has access to a means of removing the leaded paint, she may remove only a portion of it. Or she may monitor where her child plays when outside some but not all of the time.

As in Archer et al. (2002), consider the example of a risk-neutral parent who can use various combinations of own health, own time, home environment, and child-specific inputs to protect and to insure her child's health from a particular environmental hazard. Assume the parent knows both the likelihood her child suffers from the hazard and what childcare techniques – various combinations of her child protection and child insurance efforts – do to reduce this likelihood successfully. Any given child protection technique can come to naught for two reasons – access failure and effectiveness failure. Access failure occurs when the parent cannot gain access to a childcare technique; effectiveness failure occurs when exogenous conditions render a technique completely ineffective. The rational parent cares for her child by investing time and money resources to reduce the probabilities of access and effectiveness failures, thereby increasing her expected wealth.

Let z be the parent's child protection efforts directed at the specific environmental hazard and x be her child insurance efforts. Assume the mother perceives two mutually exclusive and jointly exhaustive states: a better state implying less severe losses in her child's health and a bad state implying a worse loss. The probability, $p(z)$, of the better state is a function of child protection, z, where $p'(z) > 0$. The bad state occurs with probability $1 - p(z)$.

Child protection represents the quality of childcare as defined by flexibility and technical efficiency. Flexibility measures the relative absence of access failure. It refers to the weighted percentage of the number of sources of the hazard against which the parent's childcare efforts offer protection. The weights are the frequency of occurrence of a particular source of the hazard during a given time interval. A parent who can remove leaded paint in the home and provide the child bottled water rather than tap water has greater flexibility than does the parent who can provided bottled water but cannot remove the leaded paint.

Technical efficiency, which measures effectiveness, deals with the productivity of a technique in terms of the extent to which a particular level of its use completely removes the threat of exposure to the hazard. The complete removal of lead paint would be 50 percent efficient if it reduced the child's lead exposure from the collection of *all sources* by 50 percent. Greater flexibility or efficiency implies a technique has greater quality as reflected in the parent's enhanced ability to respond to and to cope with the threat the hazard poses the child. The unit cost of a childcare technique is $c(z)$, where $c'(z) > 0$. This cost comes from the setup costs (time, transportation, durable goods outlays) when resources are devoted to adding a new technique to an existing set.

Child insurance, x, refers to the quantity or level of use of a childcare technique. Insurance applies, for example, to the extent to which the parent removes lead paint. Low use of an accessible technique can fade into child neglect. Note a difference between the notion of child self-insurance we employ here and that standard for self-insurance in endogenous risk discussions where only the level of use of a single technique is at issue. For the single-technique case, self-insurance reduces the loss from a failure, reducing wealth variability across states. But when multiple techniques exist which differ in their accessibility or effectiveness, wealth losses can occur in both the better and the worse states. For example, to reduce losses in child health, a childcare technique must be accessible and effective. Greater accessibility and effectiveness drive the wealth positions of the two states farther apart by increasing returns in the better state.

To continue with the child health example, the damage, $L(\gamma)$, to the parent's wealth equivalent of the child's health is a positive function of hazard exposure, γ. Let r again be an index of riskiness to parent wealth as when only collectively supplied risk reduction processes are available. If a childcare technique is accessible, the child's exposures to the health hazard are determined by the level of use, $\gamma(x)$, of the technique such that $L'(\gamma)\gamma'(x) < 0$, where $\gamma'(x) < 0$. The childcare technique indirectly affects damages. Through the hazard exposure function, $\gamma(x)$, the intensity with which the childcare technique is used reduces the hazard exposure, γ. The hazard, working through the damage function, $L(\gamma)$, influences childcare. The marginal product of x depends on the structure of both the hazard exposure and the damage functions.

Total parent wealth consists of her predetermined money wealth, M_0, and the money equivalent for her of the child's current health and her discounted value of its future prospects. The parent's utility is a state-dependent positive function of her residual wealth – the wealth remaining to her after child health losses have been deducted. This residual wealth is not invested in the child.

The parent maximizes her expected wealth $E(W)$, by selecting z and x:

$$\max_{z,x} E(W) = p(z)\{M_0[1 - L(\gamma(x))] - c(z)x\}$$

$$+ (1 - p(z))\{M_0[1 - L(r)] - \beta c(z)x\}. \qquad (2.9)$$

For simplicity, we treat access probabilities and effectiveness probabilities as separate cases. In reality the parent may decide them jointly. Assume β is a binary (0–1) variable. Let $\beta = 1$ for an effectiveness failure in which a child protection technique proves to be utterly useless. In spite of this uselessness, the cost, $c(z)x$, of gaining access to and of using the technique is nevertheless borne in both states. Let $\beta = 0$ for an access failure since the parent incurs no cost of the child protection technique in the bad state. She cannot use a technique if she has no access to it. The first term in expression (2.9) represents the parent's expected wealth if there is no failure of technique access or effectiveness; the second term represents such failure.

The first-order conditions for expression (2.9) to have a maximum are:

$$\frac{\partial E(W)}{\partial z} = p'(z)\{M_0[L(r) - L(\gamma)] - (1 - \beta)c(z)x\}$$
$$- c'(z)x\{\beta + (1 - \beta)p(z)\} = 0 \qquad (2.10)$$

and

$$\frac{\partial E(W)}{\partial \chi} = -p(z)M_0L'(\gamma)\gamma'(x) - \{(1 - \beta)p(z)c(z) + \beta c(z)\} = 0. \quad (2.11)$$

The first term on the right-hand side of expression (2.10) is the parent's marginal benefit of child protection, z, in increasing the probability of successful childcare. For the access case, the benefits of reduced wealth damages with the successful child protection of the better state are partially offset by the added cost of gaining access to and of using the childcare technique. For the effectiveness case, this offset does not occur since the technique is used in both states – there is effectiveness failure but no access failure in the worse state. The second term in (2.10) represents the realized marginal cost of z for the access case.

In expression (2.11), the first term represents the expected marginal benefit of child insurance, x, in reducing wealth losses from child health damages. The second term is the realized unit price of the childcare technique for the effectiveness case and the expected unit price of this technique for the access case. Given that the parent instantaneously decides upon how much insurance to use, she chooses x for the access case so that the marginal benefit of x in the better state is equal to its marginal cost in this same case.

2.5 Nonconvex Preferences

Crocker and Shogren (2001) build upon a moral hazard model originally set forth by Arnott and Stiglitz (1988) to show that risk reduction technologies may make nonconvex a landowner's preferences for alternative ecosystem states on his land. Because landowners cannot easily respond to new information that arrives subsequent to committing to a land use, these commitments are risky. By committing, the owner forgoes his options to make other commitments (Dixit and Pindyck, 1994), and the use decisions of adjacent owners, exogenous natural events, and public environmental policies make unclear how a particular commitment ultimately translates into his fortunes. Also, many land-use commitments, whether on the extensive or the intensive margins, are discrete: whether or not to build a dam across a stream, to introduce an exotic species, to use more or less environmentally benign pesticide types. Different land-use commitments foster different ecosystem states, the relations between which can be portrayed as owner risk reduction technologies. Viewed as lotteries, these technologies have varying degrees of effectiveness in lessening the owner's likelihood (self-protection) or severity (self-insurance) for untoward events that originate off the owner's land. The owner has preferences over both the outcomes of ecosystem states and over the ecosystem state lotteries themselves.

For example, wetlands can buffer the owner's fortunes from natural and man-made shocks by tempering precipitation runoff and by providing water purification and habitat services. People purchase open space adjacent to their existing properties to add to and to protect the ecological services their property provides them. An owner realizes the benefits of these natural risk reduction technologies by refraining from the practice of extractive, natural ecosystem-altering activities such as intensive logging, damming, plowing, and residential development. But this voluntary hobbling of his property rights to extract from and to develop his land has opportunity costs as well as benefits for him. Development generates a flow of income which the owner forgoes when he practices self-restraint on his land.

Crocker and Shogren (2001) depict the owner as confronting two mutually exclusive and jointly exhaustive ecosystem states. $U_0 = U_0(M)$, $U_0' > 0$, $U_0'' < 0$ is the utility the owner receives under the good ecosystem state in which he allows the ecosystem to buffer him. The buffer does not fail, which implies the utility he receives is safe. But in the bad state the buffer might fail. Again let L be the money equivalent of the owner's loss and M his wealth. Assuming $L < M$, let $EU_1 = \int_a^b U_1(M - L)dF(L;r)$ reflect his expected utility under the bad state where the ecosystem might fail to serve its protection function. Increases in the index of damage riskiness, r, to the owner's fortunes are due to a loss of ecosystem resilience, an ecological measure of the change a natural asset can endure before being shifted into another state (Hollings, 1986). Assume EU_1 is concave in wealth and declines for a first-order stochastic dominant shift, $F_r < 0$, in the distribution of damages.

Let p^i and $1 - p^i$ be the probabilities of realizing the good or the bad ecosystem states. Allow the owner to influence these odds by prudence in how he uses his land. Let c^i be the opportunity costs in utility terms of this self-restraint, where $i = H, D$ represents high (H) and low (D) levels of self-restraint such that $c^H > c^D$, and $p^H > p^D$. The owner's choice between the two self-restraint alternatives affects the utility loss he suffers from a given level of riskiness. Given the level of riskiness, his expected utility when he practices high self-restraint by treading gently on his land is

$$EV^H \equiv p^H U_0(M) + (1 - p^H)EU_1(M - L) - c^H. \qquad (2.12)$$

When he practices low self-restraint by clearing, developing, or by digging up his land, his expected utility is

$$EV^D \equiv p^D U_0(M) + (1 - p^D)EU_1(M - L) - c^D. \qquad (2.13)$$

While presuming that the utility opportunity costs and benefits of self-restraint are separable and independent of wealth, define separate sets of indifference curves in wealth–risk space for the high and for the low self-restraint cases. The owner's willingness to trade off risk for wealth is higher in the high self-restraint case than in the low self-restraint case because a low self-restraint owner needs more wealth than does a high self-restraint owner to accept more risk if he is to maintain constant utility. This implies the two sets of indifference curves intersect when in the same wealth–risk space. Since the slope of one set of curves is steeper than the other set, any two curves, one for each case, representing a given utility level must intersect. The envelope of these curves depicts nonconvex expected utility in wealth and the risk of damages to the owner's fortunes. The degree of nonconvexity is greater the larger the difference in the slopes of the sets of the high and the low self-restraint indifference curves. At the intersection of any two curves of equal utility, the owner is indifferent between high and low self-restraint but in the immediate neighborhood of the intersection he switches from one level of self-restraint to the other.

Risks of Irrationality

Expected utility theory in the exogenous case provides the benchmark for rational individual behavior under risk. But rationality can disappoint – controlled experimental evidence is abundant that people frequently do not behave rationally in risky situations. They do not always exploit potential gains from trade and they sometimes even engage in behaviors that allow or encourage others to exploit these gains. A person's potential gain from trade need not persist if he does not take advantage of it because he risks having someone else exploit the opportunity. He risks losing his opportunity to gain.

People have cognitive and computational limitations which can make the recognition and the exploitation of potential gains from trade costly to them (Simon, 1973). Consider, for instance, a valuable real-estate property to be sold at public auction for non-payment of property taxes. For two people with equal money resources and obligations, the busy working man or woman may not even be aware of the auction, whereas the courthouse lawyer is first in line to bid. These limitations confront the person with yet another form of a risk – wealth tradeoff. He can reduce the risk of losing the wealth that rationality brings by making a costly effort to temper his cognitive and computational failings. He can learn to identify and to exploit gains from trade. The working man can try to find out about the environmental hazards at a site he is considering for his home. He must decide how to decide whether to purchase the site. This is a tough task for the socially isolated person, who does not even know where to look for or whom to seek out for information about potential hazards.

The burden of deciding how to decide is considerably reduced if he can gain access to effective exchange institutions. These institutions make trading opportunities visible to him and perform many of the computations he needs to exploit them fully (Becker, 1962). The working man can hire advice from an expert in site-specific environmental hazards. To plead rationality, one need not view this person as embodying in his person an anonymous, competitive market that never fails to hear and to respond to the beat of the exchange opportunity drummer. It is exchange institutions that pressure the person to behave in accordance with the *EU* maximization paradigm (see Gode and Sunder, 1993, and Hayes et al., 1995, among others, for strong evidence of induced rationality emerging within controlled lab experiments). Exchange institutions can be regarded as risk-reducing technologies in the sense that by gaining access to one or more of them (the market, the club, the family, the firm), a person reduces the risk he misses out on lucrative trading opportunities, and engages in unprofitable opportunities.

But the effectiveness with which exchange institutions spur a person to submit his beliefs and preferences to them may differ across people and across exchange institutions, and a person may well have preferences over the manner of submission (Crocker, 1973). For example, someone may prefer the anonymity of the nonstrategic, competitive market over a public-good club which compels him to divulge more about himself than he would like in interminable meetings for which he does not care. Given that pressures to be rational and costs of participation differ across exchange institutions, the person's rationality is endogenous because his irrational risk–wealth tradeoff differs across exchange institutions. He chooses allocations of his learning efforts across the irrationality risk-reducing technologies which constitute alternative exchange institutions.

Crocker et al. (1998) define irrationality in terms of de Finetti's (1974) logic, where there exists a positive difference between one's greatest buying price and lowest selling price, where the greatest buying price corresponds to the greatest credible odds one attaches to a state and the lowest selling price corresponds to the lowest credible odds. This difference can be interpreted as an incomplete belief, that is, as an index of the risk, r, the person is irrational because another person could win a positive sum by either buying a lottery ticket from him or by selling him a lottery ticket. The rational price is then the no-arbitrage price at which belief is complete, implying that no other person could win a positive sum by buying low from and selling high to the same person. The decision problem of a person who wants to reduce his irrationality can then be stated as

$$\max_{\theta_{ij}} E(W) \equiv E(V) + E(M)$$

$$\equiv \sum_i \sum_j \{K_i - (1 - \theta_{ij})[r_{ij}(\theta_{ij}) - E(r_{ij}(\theta_{ij}))] - c_{ij}(\theta_{ij})\}. \qquad (2.14)$$

$E(V)$ is the person's expected wealth when he only self-provisions; $E(M)$ is his expected wealth when he bothers to engage exchange institutions. Let θ_{ij} represent the productivity of the agent's efforts to gain access to and to use the jth exchange institution, $j = 1, \ldots, m$, in the ith state, $i = 1, \ldots, n$, to generate the wealth, K_i, that would be generated for him in a world of non-strategic, anonymous, complete, competitive markets. Assume θ_{ij} is continuous, lying within the interval $[0,1]$, where the upper bound implies the person is fully effective in capturing all potential wealth and the lower bound says he is totally ineffective. Let $r'_{ij}(\theta_{ij})$ represent the distribution of the risk-neutral person's incomplete beliefs defined in terms of the difference between his greatest and lowest credible odds for a state being realized. Let $E[r'_{ij}(\theta_{ij})]$ be his expected utility consequence of engaging the ith institution in the jth state. Let $c_{ij}(\theta_{ij})$ be the person's cost of gaining access to and using an exchange institution. Further assume $r'_{ij}(\theta_{ij}) > 0$, $c'_{ij} > 0$, $r''_{ij} < 0$, and $c''_{ij} > 0$.

The Kuhn–Tucker first-order necessary condition, ℓ, for expression (2.14) is

$$\ell = \sum_i \sum_j [r_{ij}(\theta_{ij}) - (1 - \theta_{ij})r'_{ij}(\theta_{ij}) - c'_{ij}(\theta_{ij}) + (1 - \theta_{ij})E(r'_{ij}(\theta_{ij}))$$

$$- E(r_{ij})] \le 0, \qquad (2.15)$$

where $\theta_{ij} \ge 0$, and $\theta_{ij}\ell = 0$.

The first two terms in expression (2.15) are the indirect and the direct benefits of trading in the exchange institution. The third term is the cost of doing so.

These three terms imply that a person's marginal cost of gaining access to and operating in an exchange institution must be less than the marginal benefits. The inequality implies that gaining access is not worthwhile in all states because the cost of putting forth any effort to do so exceeds the benefits.

The last two terms in expression (2.15) represent the indirect and the direct marginal impacts of θ_{ij} upon the person's rationality. To become less irrational by making beliefs less incomplete and thereby to increase the wealth he can gain from trade, the person has to distribute his exchange activities across institutions such that he maximizes the wealth he acquires from what he learns. Assuming an interior solution such that the first two (benefit) terms in expression (2.15) equal the last three (cost) terms, it follows that this person distributes his social activities across exchange institutions such that the net marginal benefits of greater rationality are equal across institutions.

3.   IMPLICATIONS FOR VALUING RISK REDUCTIONS

We now illustrate how an endogenous risk perspective affects the basic theory of environmental economics by considering the problem of valuing environmental risk reductions. We present several provocative propositions which emerge from the basic framework and the extensions about the value people place on risk reductions. Without exception, these propositions motivate detailed attention to the physical and the biological realities underlying environmental hazards if the impact on valuation of *how* people prefer to reduce risk is to be explained. These same propositions also imply that the physical and the biological manifestations of environmental change depend as much upon producer and consumer decision processes as upon the biological and physical phenomena that start up the economic reactions. The endogenous risk concept requires that the simultaneous nature of how economic decisions affect observed risk and how the natural science features affect economic decisions be addressed.[13]

Under the endogenous risk framework defined in Section 2.2, simultaneous solution of the first-order conditions in expressions (2.3) and (2.4) yields demand functions for self-protection, z^*, and self-insurance, x^*, which solve the implicit function

$$\int_a^b U(M - L(\gamma;x^*) - c(x^*,z^*))dF(\gamma;z^*,r) - \int_a^b U^* = 0 \qquad (2.16)$$

where U^* denotes maximum expected utility given predetermined wealth, M, the random variable, γ, an index of background riskiness, r, and for notational ease, the support [a,b] is suppressed. Application of the implicit function rule to (2.16) and differentiation with respect to r yields the compensating variation version of willingness to pay for a risk reduction in terms of the tradeoff between the person's wealth and the marginal reduction in risk (Silberberg, 1978, ch. 8). We now review a selection of the propositions that arise from within this framework about the value of risk reduction.

3.1 Selected Propositions

Proposition A Self-protection expenditures need not be a lower bound on a person's willingness to pay for a risk reduction (Shogren and Crocker, 1991, 1999).

Actual self-protection expenditures seem like a natural lower bound on willingness to pay for risk reduction. The connection, however, is complicated by both preferences and risk reduction technology choices (also see USEPA, 2000). To see this, let a parsimonious version of expression (2.2) be translated, as in Quiggin (1992), into state-space independent of the person's actions such that $\theta = F(\gamma;s,r)$ or $\gamma = F^{-1}(\theta;s,r)$, where $\theta \in [0,1]$, and $s = s(z, x)$ for self-care. The person's EU maximization problem is then

$$\max_{s} \left[\int_0^1 U(M - F^{-1}(\theta;s,r) - s)d\theta \right], \quad (2.17)$$

with the first-order condition

$$-E[U_M F_s^{-1}] - EU_M = 0. \quad (2.18)$$

The first term in (2.18) is the expected marginal utility of self-care given $F_s^{-1} < 0$, and the second term is the expected marginal disutility.

The comparative static for a change in risk is

$$\frac{\partial s}{\partial r} = -\frac{1}{D}[E(U_{MM}F_s^{-1}F_r^{-1} - U_M F_{sr}^{-1}) + E(U_{MM}F_r^{-1})], \quad (2.19)$$

where $D < 0$ by the second-order sufficiency condition. For self-care to be an unambiguous lower bound, the sign of (2.19) must be positive. The second term in (2.19), the change in the expected marginal disutility of self-care, is negative by convention. The sign of the first term, the change in the expected marginal utility, is ambiguous. The term depends on how changes in risk affect self-care marginal productivity, F_{sr}^{-1}. The sign of the marginal productivity of a risk reduction technology is problem-specific. Marginal productivity increases if $F_{sr}^{-1}<0$ such that self-care and risk are technological complements as Berger et al. (1987) and Quiggin (1992) each suppose, but this marginal productivity may decrease when they are substitutes, $F_{sr}^{-1}>0$. The effectiveness of a fence in keeping children from sneaking into a toxic waste site does not become greater as the toxicity of the site increases. An increase in the risk of harm to the children raises both the marginal benefits and the marginal costs of childcare for the parents. When parental costs dominate, investment in childcare declines as the risk of harm to the child increases. When benefits dominate, parental investment in childcare increases. *A priori*, the sign of net benefits is an empirical question influenced by the properties of the risk reduction technology. Accurate valuation requires detailed specification of both the person's preferences and his risk reduction technology.

Proposition B   Marginal willingness to pay for the randomly selected individual includes unobservable utility terms unless his marginal rate of substitution between self-care and risk is additively separable from the random variable (Shogren and Crocker, 1991, 1999). Direct valuation methods that focus on a single risk reduction mechanism and do not address the range of alternative reduction technologies could underestimate the actual demand for risk reduction.

We can see this proposition by rewriting (2.18) as

$$- EU_M EF_s^{-1} - \text{cov}(U_M, EF_s^{-1}) - EU_M = 0. \qquad (2.20)$$

For the utility terms to disappear from expression (2.20), it must be that $\text{cov}(U_M, EF_s^{-1})=0$, which would mean that the sign of the expression would depend only on the technical relation between the marginal productivity of self-care and risk. If the additive separability condition is unrealistic, it seems that assessments of aggregate willingnesses to pay by multiple individuals for reductions in the risk of untoward consequences from environmental hazards must admit interpersonal comparisons of utility.

Quiggin (1992) obtains sharp results (for example, marginal willingness to pay increasing with the background risk level) when the additive separability condition is combined with the state-space approach. The sharpness results because, as expression (2.20) demonstrates, preferences vanish. The human actions and reactions which these preferences induce, and which help determine the likelihood and the severity of events, can then play no role. Risk assessment then belongs solely to the natural scientist and only 'objective' risk matters in value determination and policy formation. In effect, given the absence of the protection premia involved in expressions (2.7) and (2.8), the additive separability condition makes risk exogenous. People may engage in self-care behaviors, but these behaviors are viewed as matters of habit rather than of choice. Natural scientists have no incentive to account for the interactions between human behavioral responses and natural phenomena if economists, by opting for the sharp results obtained via the additive separability condition, allow the scientist to infer that the abstract condition translates into the practical conclusion that risk must be exogenous.

This additive separability condition must be invoked to make the numerous estimates of a VSL, the value of statistical life or limb (Viscusi, 1993), logically coherent. A VSL is the cost of a randomly selected person's death or personal illness or injury weighted by a probability that is uniform across people. But even if people have identical preferences, substantial differences exist in their opportunities for or costs of altering probabilities. The VSL idea fails to address the differences in individual probabilities caused by the differences in self-care alternatives that people choose.

Unless private and collective risk reduction technologies are perfect substitutes, undiscriminating invocation of the additive separability condition between random events and self-care using direct valuation methods like contingent valuation exercises can lead to undervaluations of environmental improvements that reduce risk. Any person who has ready access to private risk reduction technologies values collective provision less than otherwise. The undervaluation caused by a singular focus on collective provision could increase with the success of the provision. As the marginal effectiveness of collective provision declines, the relative effectiveness and the value of the person's private provision increase. A complete assessment of this person's value for a given risk reduction requires taking account of changes in his self-provisioning as well as recognizing what the collective provision does for him (see also Chapman and Hariharan, 1996; and Laffont, 1995). The exclusive VSL focus on collective provision which logically follows from the exogenous risk perspective engendered by the additive separability condition undervalues risk reductions for this average person and endorses economically excessive levels of environmental degradation for him.

The undervaluation of risk reductions caused by inattention to the determinants of the randomly selected person's choices over risk reduction technologies extends as well to his time-distributed risks. Blackorby et al. (1984) and Keen (1990) show that unless one incorporates the person's preferences toward the temporal availabilities of goods with incomplete markets into analysis, program evaluations for these goods based on an independently derived discount rate are biased. This bias occurs even when utility is intertemporally separable. The bias is caused by the custom of first estimating a time stream of instantaneous net benefits and then applying a discount rate to obtain an estimate of the present value of the stream. Applying the discount factor only after having estimated the stream changes the relative values of the instantaneous surpluses. A person who could do so would then intertemporally redistribute his consumption and investment activities so as to make equal his marginal utility of income across periods. The person's marginal rate of time preference obviously depends on this intertemporal redistribution. Le Chatelier effects imply the analyst who shuts his eyes to opportunities people have for these redistributions underestimates the present value of a time stream of risk reductions and overestimates the present value of risk increases. Given that contingent claims markets are incomplete and that access to these markets differs among people, marginal rates of time preference are endogenous. It is then inappropriate to apply a discount rate uniform across people to a time-distributed risk reduction (Crocker et al., 1991).

Proposition C   The value of statistical life (VSL) based on real-world wage-fatality risks trade offs tends to be biased upward if it does not account for the diversity of workers' unobservable skill to cope privately with job risk (Shogren and Stamland, 2002a).

Many VSL estimates are based on the results of compensating wage differential (hedonic wage) studies (see Freeman, 1993, ch. 12, for a review) in which discriminating between the average and the marginal person becomes relevant to calculating the value of risk reductions. Risks in the wage–risk literature are treated as exogenous either through self-selection or through the private market. Pearce (2000) expresses this perspective as follows:

> [the analysis] suggests that wage–risk studies may be measuring endogenous risk, whereas the risks of relevance to public policy will tend to be exogenous. Indeed, it is unclear if endogenous risks should be the subject of policy at all since they can be argued to be internalized in the relevant market, in this case the labour market.

Shogren and Stamland (2002a), however, show that VSL estimates based on these studies of labor markets are likely to be systematically upward biased. Again, the reason is that workers differ in their risk preferences and in their skills at protecting themselves from on-the-job hazards to life and health. One would expect workers in a more risky occupation to be more skilled, or more tolerant to risk, or both. This implies the marginal worker in a particular occupation is not randomly selected. Rather he is the person among those who have selected the occupation who demands the highest compensation for *his* risk on the job. This compensation is for some combination of his risk tolerance and his lack of self-protection skills relative to other workers who have been sorted into the same occupation. Relative to other workers, he has either lower risk tolerance or lower protection skills or both. When this marginal worker's wage differential used in hedonic wage studies is divided by the statistical risk (that is, the risk for the average person in the occupation), the resulting VSL estimate is upward biased. The VSL estimate is upward biased because the highest required wage differential among the workers is divided by their average risk. The result holds even if one allows workers to self-select among occupations with differing statistical risks.

Consider the essences of the skill–VSL model. Workers differ in two *unobservable* respects: they are unequally skilled, which implies they face different probabilities of a fatal accident in the same job; and they disagree on the value of life, which means they have different tradeoffs between wages and risk. The safe job pays w_s, and all workers face the same probability of a fatal accident, $p \geq 0$. The dangerous job pays w_d, and the likelihood of an accident decreases with the worker's skill. The wage differential, $w_d - w_s$, is set to compensate the worker in the dangerous job who requires the highest compensation for the additional risk.

Assume T workers are in the dangerous job, each with his own value of life, $VOL_t > 0$, and his own risk, $q_t \geq p$. Denote the workers' utility function by $u(t,P,W) = W - P \cdot VOL_t$, where t denotes the worker's type, $P \in \{p,q_t\}$ is the worker's fatality risk in a job, and $W \in \{w_s,w_d\}$ is the worker's wage. The wage differential is determined by $w_d = w_s + \max_{t \in \{1,2,\dots,T\}} \{(q_t - p)VOL_t\}$. The probability a randomly selected worker dies in the safe job is $P_s \equiv p$, and in the dangerous job is $P_d = (1/T)\Sigma_{t=1}^{T} \equiv \bar{q}$. Using the wages and the probabilities, we infer the VSL by taking the ratio of the wage differential to the risk differential, $VSL = (w_d - w_s)/(P_d - P_s)$,

$$VSL = \frac{\max_{t \in \{1,2,\dots,T\}} \{(q_t - p)VOL_t\}}{\bar{q} - p} = \frac{(q_\tau - p)VOL_\tau}{\bar{q} - p},$$

where τ denotes the marginal worker in the dangerous job. Define $\overline{VOL} \equiv (1/T)\Sigma_{t=1}^{T} VOL_t$. We now have the key expression,

$$\frac{\overline{VOL}}{VSL} = \frac{(\bar{q} - p)\overline{VOL}}{(q_\tau - p)VOL_\tau}.$$

By the definition of τ, this means that *VSL* overestimates the average value of life unless the condition $(q_t - p)VOL_t \leq (\bar{q} - p)\overline{VOL}$ $\forall t$ holds, which is unlikely since there must be a strong inverse relationship between $(q_t - p)$ and VOL_t.

This VSL bias can be corrected if one can account for the highly multi-dimensional heterogeneity that existing single-equation methods cannot handle. Shogren and Stamland (2002b) propose a general method of moments (GMM) approach to identify all the parameters affecting a person's willingness to pay for mortality risk reduction. This allows one to obtain a consistent estimator of the value of statistical life. They use simulations to show that the GMM estimator of the value of statistical life performs well even when combining data from different sources that are sampled at different, low frequencies.

Proposition D   Marginal valuations of risk reductions can increase (Shogren and Crocker, 1991).

Even when it allows people some choice about how to deal with risk, the literature on risk valuation typically takes declining marginal valuation of risk reductions as a maintained hypothesis (for example, Berger et al. 1987; Kahneman and Tversky, 1979; Smith and Desvousges, 1986). Differentiation of the willingness-to-pay expression associated with the parameterized distribution problem in expression (2.2) yields an equation involving an assortment of direct and indirect effects – entangled utility curvature terms, cross-product terms between the risk index and the random variable that affect severity and costs, and cross-product terms between the risk index and self-care which affect the cumulative distribution function. The equation demonstrates that strong convexity defined as all of increasing marginal costs of self-care, increasing marginal severity of consequences, convexity of the distribution function, and declining marginal productivity of self-care are not sufficient to sign the equation. Similarly, strong nonconvexity with all of decreasing marginal costs, decreasing marginal severity, nonconvexity of the distribution function, and increasing marginal productivity are insufficient. The equation simply contains too many terms, including utility curvature terms, whose relative magnitudes must be known to obtain an unambiguous signing. Intuitively, this confusion results because both marginal self-protection probability effects and marginal self-insurance severity effects are present in the equation. Shogren and Crocker (1991, p. 11) suggest that the assumption of zero marginal severity effects is sufficient to yield strong convexity. Except for risks which result in death, the assumption that severity is unchanging with respect to changes in the risk index seems an insubstantial basis on which to ground an entire theory of environmental hazard valuation dealing with prospective injuries to human bodies and spirits.

A maintained hypothesis of strong convexity or an assumption of zero marginal severity, which as in Weinstein et al. (1980) slips strong convexity in through the back door, can mislead policy makers about the distributional consequences of a collective risk reduction. Strong convexity implies that those who have greater wealth are willing to pay more for a given collectively provided risk reduction. But if strong convexity is not admitted, then one challenges the distributional conclusion following from the standard strong convexity view. Concerns about 'environmental justice' for the poor are given analytical legitimacy. The endogenous risk framework can capture the possibility that the poor may have fewer and more costly opportunities for self-protection and self-insurance and may value a given collective risk reduction more highly than do the wealthy. Moreover, because of a lack of education and lesser access to information about self-care technologies, the poor may view the efficacy of these technologies as more risky than do their better-educated and wealthier compatriots.[14]

Proposition E Self-protection expenditures need not be a lower bound on the person's willingness to pay for a risk reduction from an environmental hazard when the effectiveness of the reduction technology is itself risky (Shogren, 1991).

Totally differentiating expressions (2.5) and (2.6) and substituting in the appropriate first-order condition, the comparative statics of an increased risk of harm from an environmental hazard clearly illustrate the relationships between taste and technology for a risky risk reduction technology. For self-protection we have

$$\frac{\partial z}{\partial r} = -\frac{1}{D_z}\left[\int_a^b Q'_p[R(\hat{z})\Gamma(z)G_r d\eta]\right] \tag{2.21}$$

and for self-insurance

$$\frac{\partial x}{\partial r} = \frac{1}{D_x}\left[\int_a^b (1-p)L'U'_2[\Gamma_0(x) - \hat{R}(z)L']G_r d\eta\right], \tag{2.22}$$

where the second-order conditions, D_z and D_x, are negative by assumption. Denote $\Gamma(z) = p''/p'$ as the measure of absolute aversion to risk about self-protection effectiveness, and $\Gamma_0(x) = L''/L'$ as the measure of absolute aversion to risk about self-insurance effectiveness.

Note in expressions (2.21) and (2.22) that traditional preference risk neutrality can exist, $\hat{R}(z) = 0$ as defined in expression (2.7), in the presence of positive aversion to risk about the effectiveness of self-protection or self-insurance technologies. But the sign of (2.21) is ambiguous when both preference risk aversion and aversion to risk about protection effectiveness are present. In (2.21), a person with preference risk aversion engages in less of the activity that encourages the undesirable consequences of the hazard than a risk-neutral person. The protection premium for a risky technology causes the opposite reaction – increased risk from the hazard increases self-protection because the person wants to increase his likelihood of being in the no-loss state. The ambiguous sign attached to (2.21) implies that expenditures on risky self-protection cannot, just as with non-risky self-protection, be interpreted as a lower bound on the marginal willingness to pay for a reduction in the index of riskiness from the hazard unless preference risk neutrality is present. In (2.22), however, increased risk from the hazard unambiguously increases the demand for self-insurance whether or not preference risk aversion is present.

Proposition F   Different sources of risk have different implications for successful risk reduction and for the valuation of this reduction (Archer and Shogren, 1996; Archer et al. 2002).

We see this proposition by defining $p(z)$ in expression (2.9) as in Hiebert (1983):

$$p(z) = p_o + vh(z), \tag{2.23}$$

with $h'(z) > 0$, with p_o and v as positive constants, and with an increase in the probability of damages being a decline in either p_o or in v. A decline in p_o represents an increase in the probability of damages that is independent of flexibility or efficiency. The probability cannot be tempered with self-protection. In contrast, a decrease in v represents an increase in the probability of damages that increases proportional to z. Think of it as a decrease in the efficacy of self-protection.

Substituting expression (2.23) into expression (2.9) and then performing comparative statics demonstrates a tradeoff between the quality (self-protection) and the quantity or intensity of use (self-insurance) of risk reduction technologies. Demonstrating the tradeoff acknowledges that there are many ways to accomplish something. Changed circumstances can cause one to consider the accessibility and the effectiveness of these alternative ways rather simply changing the magnitude of one's usual strategy. The quality (self-protection in terms of access and effectiveness) and the quantity (self-insurance in terms of intensity of use) are stochastic substitutes. Whether p_o or v changes affects this tradeoff. For example, it can be shown that a decline in p_o increases self-insurance and increases self-protection. In contrast, a decrease in the efficacy of self-protection reduces self-protection and may increase self-insurance. Different sources of change in risk for a child have different implications for the quality and the quantity of childcare. Since self-protection can only be changed by varying care quality, which involves using alternative care technologies, it follows that public policies aimed at encouraging private use of a particular risk reduction technology may, if successful, reduce the use of alternative care technologies. The net impact of the policy could increase the risk the person suffers and increase the value of a collective risk reduction to him. To ascertain whether the net effect is positive or negative, the structure of the tradeoffs people make among access to, effectiveness of, and intensity of use of alternative risk reduction technologies must be understood.

Proposition G   In the presence of discrete, risky alternative states, preference risk aversion can be endogenous (Ng, 1965; Crocker and Shogren, 2001).

A person's degree of preference risk aversion need not be a preordained, immutable feature of his character. Again consider the landowner who enhances the likelihood of a good ecosystem state for his land if he practices high self-restraint with his land use but who increases the chance of a bad ecosystem state if he practices low self-restraint. If the bad state is realized, his fortunes are adversely affected. Let his willingness to pay, M^H, for a collectively supplied guarantee that the good state is realized when he practices high self-restraint be

$$U(M - M^H) = V^H \qquad (2.24)$$

and for low self-restraint

$$U(M - M^D) = V^D. \qquad (2.25)$$

The guarantee might, for example, be a public flood control project or insect-spraying program. From expressions (2.12) and (2.13), we see that the comparative levels of expected utility depend on the relative magnitudes of the benefits $(U_0 - EU_1)$ and the costs $[(c^H - c^D)/(p^H - p^D)]$ of self-restraint:

$$V^H \underset{<}{\overset{>}{=}} V^D \, as \, (p^H - p^D)(U_0 - EU_1) \underset{<}{\overset{>}{=}} (c^H - c^D). \qquad (2.26)$$

From expressions (2.12), (2.13), and (2.24)–(2.26), the two levels of the owner's willingness-to-pay to secure the collectively supplied guarantee can be compared as

$$M^D \underset{<}{\overset{>}{=}} M^H \text{ as } (p^H - p^D)(U_0 - EU_1) \underset{<}{\overset{>}{=}} c^H - c^D. \tag{2.27}$$

Even though convexity of preferences is assumed for each level of self-restraint, Figure 2.1 illustrates that the *ex ante* willingness-to-pay function to remove various degrees of risk, r, of realizing the bad ecosystem state is nonconvex given these relative benefits and costs of high and low self-restraint. The owner's value function is represented by the dashed lower envelope of the willingness-to-pay curves, M^H and M^D. He switches from being a low self-restraint landowner to a high self-restraint owner at a level of risk, a. But with fair insurance, the owner is better off with any combination of damage risks connecting d on M^D and h on M^H than he is by practicing a level of self-restraint entailing any damage risk in the neighborhood of a. The chord connecting d and h shows that a lottery involving these two risk levels permits a lower outlay to achieve any expected level of risk lying between d and h. The owner prefers the lottery to a more certain world – he is a risk lover rather than a risk averter over the $[d, h]$ interval. Of course, he has to invent ways to produce the convexification that the chord embodies, perhaps by choosing to participate in political lotteries about the spatial and temporal placement of public infrastructure and property rules that can be capitalized into the value of his ownership. If it is possible for him to achieve any convexification, his risk preferences become endogenous.

Crocker and Shogren (2001, pp. 258–64) show that convexification or the lack of opportunity to induce it has at least three important policy

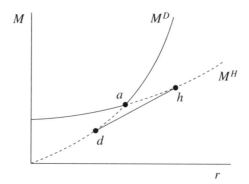

Figure 2.1   Nonconvex willingness to pay

implications. First, policy-maker neglect of nonconvex owner preferences implies the policy maker exaggerates the benefits of collectively mandated provision of natural areas on private lands. He does so because he disregards the risk-reducing actions of the people who own and live on the land. This exaggeration can be shown to occur whether the policy maker views the private owner as always practicing low self-restraint or as always practicing high self-restraint. Second, policies which prohibit risk levels greater than some threshold for some set of sites increase the likelihood that no lotteries can be constructed which allow smoothing to occur. The possibilities for construction of lotteries are truncated. Finally, even though owners may initially have identical nonconvex preferences, any opportunities to smooth produce heterogeneous joint distributions over space of ecosystem configurations and self-restraint practices. Smoothing can accentuate already existing differences in ecosystem configurations at various locations; it also concentrates degradation at selected locations rather than distributing it evenly over space (Helfand and Rubin, 1994). Public policies that repress smoothing discourage land-use heterogeneity and specialization.

Proposition H   The rationality a person applies to a particular commodity and his valuation of that commodity can depend on the rationality other people apply to that commodity and on the rationality he applies to other commodities (Crocker et al., 1998; Cherry et al., 2003).

Rationality spillovers can exist, which means that the rationality learned in active exchange markets that punish inconsistent behavior can be transferred to choices in non-market settings free from market pressure. Consider a simple model consistent with expression (2.14) where, with two people, A and B, we allow individual B's efforts to organize and to participate in exchange institutions to affect those of A parametrically. Alternatively, for a single person, A could be a commodity the person pursues in an isolated, nonsocial setting, and B could be another commodity he pursues in a complete market setting. Following the multiple-person interpretation, let B first select his mix of exchange institutions in which to participate and then let A select his. Person A's surplus extraction problem is:

$$\max E(M^A) = \sum_i \sum_j [K_i - (1 - \theta_{ij}^A) r_{ij}^A(\theta_{ij}^A, \theta_{ij}^B) - c_{ij}(\theta_{ij}^A, \theta_{ij}^B)]. \quad (2.28)$$

Person B's organizing and participation efforts in the institution influence both A's risk of irrationality and his costs of operating and participating.

After differentiating the first-order conditions for expression (2.28) with respect to a parametric shift in B's mix of exchange institutions, one obtains an expression the sign of which, apart from maintained hypotheses about the signs of first and second derivatives of various risk reduction and cost terms, depends upon the signs and the relative magnitudes of two cross-partials, $\partial r^A/\partial\theta^A\partial\theta^B$, and $\partial c^A/\partial\theta^A\partial\theta^B$. If their net effects are negative, B's organizing and participation efforts reduce those A must exercise to reduce his irrationality. B's efforts complement those of A. Examples of this complementarity in environmental settings are easily identified. For example, the existence of people who are knowledgeable about the attributes of a recreation site allows unknowledgeable people to observe the choices of the knowledgeable and thereby enhance the surplus the unknowledgeable can extract from the area. If the net effects of the cross-partials are negative, B's activities make A less rational. More effort by B results in lower surplus extraction by A.

The key point is that rationality, or the risk of irrationality, is endogenous. By selecting the exchange institutions in which they participate and their degree of participation, people choose how rational they will be. These institutions act as technologies that reduce the person's risk of irrational behaviors.

When viewed as a package, Propositions A though H renew an earlier refrain of this chapter. The endogenous risk concept demands the economist step outside his professional boundaries to draw on information from the disciplines that study technologies, broadly interpreted to include any process that contributes to the attainment of human objectives. We confess we find it odd that the economics discipline, which explicitly recognized the policy relevance of incomplete markets, is reluctant to use information from other disciplines to simulate or to stimulate the results of a complete market. As Alfred Marshall (1920, p. 636) noted, 'specialists who never look beyond their own domain are apt to see things out of true proportion.' We now review the empirical evidence for supporting detailed attention by economists to the institutional, physical, and biological realities which, in addition to preferences, hold up the endogenous risk concept.

3.2   Evidence from Controlled Experiments

Controlled laboratory experiments involving the buying and the selling of real goods to real people in a context of replication and repetition can isolate and control how different auctions and exchange institution settings affect values. Experiments with repeated market experience provide a well-defined incentive structure that encourages a person to learn that accurate and precise revelation of preferences in his best strategy. Subjects in these experiments learn the actual monetary or surplus consequences of their behaviors (see for example Smith, 1982; Shogren, 2002).

Several of the selected endogenous risk propositions we have reviewed have been subjected to controlled experiments. For example, Shogren and Crocker (1994) allow for the choice of exchange institution in risk valuation by having people choose between private or collective self-protection and self-insurance. The values revealed in their lab experiments suggested that private reduction was preferred to collective reduction and that an exclusive focus on collective action would undervalue risk reduction. Shogren (1990) had earlier shown that even when self-protection and collective protection are perfect substitutes in risk reduction, the upper bounds on the values participants in controlled experiments attached to these reductions were consistently associated with self-protection. Collective protection always represented the lower bound. These results suggest the risk reduction mechanism matters to valuation. When private reduction was available prior to collective action, people placed a greater value on the private action. But if private action was accessed after collective action, values were independent of the action. Note, however, Di Mauro and Maffioletti's (1996) laboratory experiments on valuing risk reduction generated no evidence that the mechanisms constituted a 'frame' – values seemed independent of method to reduce the risk. In another experiment examining risk reduction mechanisms, McClelland et al. (1993) observe a persistent bimodal distribution of bidding behavior for private self-insurance. Some people always bid zero, others bid much more than the expected value of the potential loss. Their results do not contradict evidence that people either dismiss the low-probability risks completely or have an alarmist reaction to them.[15]

Cherry et al. (2003) designed an experiment to ascertain whether people learn their preferences or their valuations when they participate in an exchange institution. In non-arbitrage treatments, irrational behaviors were observed in about one-third of the subjects and this rate persisted over 15 trials. Once arbitrage was introduced, the proportion of irrational behaviors declined with the number of trials, whether the focus was money or environmental goods. Rationality spillovers from the arbitraged to the non-arbitraged setting were also observed, again whether the focus was money or environmental goods. Finally, the experimental subjects adjusted valuations rather than preferences. The results of the experiment are consistent with the idea that, though isolated people fail to behave rationally according to the exogenous expected utility paradigm, this irrationality can be overcome if these same people receive information and discipline from an exchange institution. Exchange institutions produce rationality (Becker, 1962).

Other reported experiments are, however, consistent with the preference learning hypothesis (Crocker and Shogren, 1991), which suggests that the risk of irrationality framework set forth in Crocker et al. (1998) and in Cherry et al. (2003) may be too thin to explain some portion of irrational behaviors under risk. With the exception of endogenous risk preferences (Ng, 1965; Crocker and Shogren, 2001), the endogenous risk concept treats preference orderings as immutable. Yet Hayes et al. (1995) and Shogren et al. (2000) explain their results in terms of preference learning rather than value learning. They do not suggest that risk preference is what is being learned. These results warn that though the endogenous risk concept appears to broaden the domain to which expected utility theory is applicable, one should be cautious about presuming it sufficiently robust to explain all human behaviors observed in risky settings.

Other experimental evidence for the endogenous risk concept is equally unsettled. Hayes et al. (1995) report that the values experiment subjects attached to reducing risks from five foodborne pathogens changed little with substantial differences in the probabilities and the severities of the illnesses caused by the pathogens. Yet marginal willingness to pay in the form of option prices declined as risk increased. List and Shogren (1999) find that posted pieces affect bidding behaviors for products unfamiliar to the subjects of their experiment but that this effect dissipates when bidders receive non-price information about the products or if they are familiar with the products prior to participating in the experiment.

2.3   Evidence from the Field

Field studies employing econometric or survey techniques to test endogenous risk propositions about the value of risk reductions in environmental settings are few. Those inquiries available counsel that the endogenous risk concept be taken seriously – that the burden of proof be placed upon those who would dismiss it rather than upon those who advocate it. Consider the following results from field studies. Babcock and Shogren (1995) and Lence and Babcock (1995) conclude in their studies of agricultural production risks from weed infestations that a producer's willingness to pay to resolve this risk may be driven more by the uncertain technical efficacy of herbicides than by traditional risk preferences. Babcock and Shogren (1995) find that the risk reduction technology makes up 60–80 percent of the producer's risk premium. Lence and Babcock (1995) conclude that it makes up no less than 20 percent of this premium.

Most field studies of endogenous risk have dealt with human health. They show that mediating behavioral interactions originating in individuals' attempts to protect personal and family human capital stocks can make substantial differences in predicted outcomes and in valuations. For example, Kremer (1996) takes the person's chosen frequency of sexual activity and number of partners to be a function of the prevalence of AIDS within a predetermined pool of candidate partners. He specifies and simulates conditions under which these choices accentuate and attenuate AIDS incidence and associated welfare effects.

Agee and Crocker (1996) find that an endogenous risk approach to parents' willingness to pay to reduce their children's body burdens of lead yields estimates at least twice those of an exogenous risk treatment. But in an earlier paper, Agee and Crocker (1994) also find that from a societal perspective, these same parents underinvest in more precise information about the future consequences of these body burdens for their children. These underinvestments occurred even though the new information caused some parents to alter their risk perceptions and to engage in risk-reducing behaviors. Agee and Crocker (2003) show that an endogenous risk framework allows one to assess the tradeoffs parents make between own consumption, own health, and child health. They estimate that parents who smoke value the health of their young children a bit more than they value their own health. Other explicit estimates of this tradeoff are unavailable.

But one can compare the Agee and Crocker (2003) relative magnitude to that formed by dividing VSL estimates of the value adults attach to own health independent of child health (Viscusi, 1993) by estimates of the value parents attach to child health independent of own health (for example, Carlin and Sandy, 1991; Viscusi et al., 1987). These independent VSL and child health estimates suggest that parents value own health somewhat more than the health of their child. There is then at least one bit of evidence that taking account of the endogeneity inherent in the tradeoffs between parental consumption and health and child health produces a different estimate of the relative magnitude of parental and child health valuations than when this endogeneity is not considered.

Finally, in a survey study on the value of reducing the risks of death and illness from dioxin exposure, Kask et al. (2002) find people had clear preferences for four reduction mechanisms: private insurance, private protection, collective insurance, and collective protection. Considering all risks, most people preferred collective protection to collective insurance. Looking strictly at the risk of death, people preferred the private to the collective mechanisms. People with less education who considered the health risk to be less serious preferred the private action. These results support the notion that people can make rational choices about the risk reduction mechanism – most respondents choose the mechanism they considered to be more effective, more easily implemented, and less costly.

4. CONCLUDING REMARKS

No doubt, circumstances exist in which people either have total control over risk through complete markets or they have no control due to overwhelming natural or collective maltreatment. But these conditions surely have to be the exception for most people facing most environmental risks – markets are notoriously incomplete, nature is not always so cruel, government edicts can be dodged. Private citizens choose to create and to control environmental risk. Risk and its private avoidance are internal to the system. Granted reducing risk privately requires both the will and the means to do so, but that is exactly the point. Risks are endogenous because they depend on the economic circumstances a person confronts. Poverty reduces options to reduce risk, but it does not eliminate the choice to reduce them. Relative prices that favor collective action over private control promote more government regulations to reduce risk, but this action still does not eliminate the choice to adopt or adapt privately with one's own resources. Understanding just how these personal economic circumstances work with ecological systems to help create and control environmental hazards should be a research priority.

Many, if not most, natural scientists would agree with the logic that people choose both to create and reduce risk. They might even agree that economic circumstances affect these choices. But not all of them would agree with the next step in our logical chain that the economic circumstances which make risk endogenous can matter to the core of the natural sciences, and that accounting for relative prices and relative wealth is essential for a well-specified human health or ecological system and well-reasoned set of risk assessment and policy recommendations. Convincing these scientists that economics could perhaps play a role in their own core disciplines requires considerably more effort from economists to show why endogenous risk affects environmental policy through how we frame choice, structure analysis, evaluate policy, and compare policies (Crocker, 2001; Settle et al., 2002). Even better, scientists and economists should take up the task of providing criteria to determine when serious error of omission and commission might take place in policy applications when the possibility of endogenous risk is arbitrarily dismissed.

Others now share our view. Lutter et al. (2002, p. 6) recognize the importance of endogenous risk in the case of evaluating the benefits of mercury emission regulations. They point out that 'people protect themselves from risks and that changes in such self-protection can alter the effectiveness of regulatory efforts to control risks.' And if fishermen eat more fish after a program of emissions reductions is in place, they note 'their total exposure may not be reduced as much as estimated here and could even be unaffected by the emissions cuts.' Likewise Smith et al. (2002) recognize that endogenous risk matters in valuation. In explaining why their results on the behavior of the 'near-elderly' using a wage hedonic model should be taken seriously, Smith et al. suggest that more researchers should take on the endogenous risk perspective for valuation work. They find that

> risk/money tradeoffs change with voluntary behavior and with new health conditions. They imply people are altering behavior in response to their subjective risk perceptions. Such responses require that the definitions used for relevant baseline risk and marginal valuations we infer from observed behavior for risk changes take account of the available mitigation opportunities available to the people being studied. (Smith et al., 2002, p. 12)

We have discussed one key facet of endogenous risk in this chapter – how private choices to protect one's self and one's family affect the economic value of environmental risk reduction policies. Endogenous risk captures the technology of risk reduction by simultaneously examining actions and reactions to the environmental system. We highlighted how not addressing private actions can underestimate the value of risk reduction elicited through stated preferences, and can overestimate preferences estimated through revealed preferences. We examined why a person might pay a risk premium even if his preferences were risk-neutral – the curvature of his risk reduction technology matters too. We also considered how the institution one operates within could endogenously determine a person's preferences for risk.

We have not discussed how one can also use the endogenous risk framework to help frame the institutional underpinnings of environmental policy. We did not explore insights about how the control of risk affects conflict and cooperation in managing environmental hazards, private insurance markets and liability rules, or the design of collectively mandated mechanisms to reduce environmental hazards. Elsewhere discussions can be found on how endogenous risk aids the examination of new policies sought to correct for weaknesses in existing policy leading to conflict (for example, Hurley and Shogren, 1997); helps structure the interaction of private choices and cooperative public policy (for example, Rhoads and Shogren, 2001); affects thinking about environmental liability rules and regulations (for example, Yoder, 2002); guides the implementation of current policy (for example, Agee and Crocker, 1998; Crocker and Shogren, 1997; Freeman and Kunreuther, 2002; Immordino, 2000); shows how to account for the joint determination of economic and human health or ecological systems (for example, Chen et al., 2002; Crocker and Tschirhart, 1992); and creates a self-enforcing process for economic growth (see Antoci and Borghesi, 2001). We save that review for another day.

NOTES

1. The dose-response functions natural scientists estimate make no allowance for human choice even though the results of these estimates are used to recommend modes of human behaviors. Witness the following statement from a prestigious medical journal: 'Research on exogenous causes of hypertension has focused on diet, physical activity and psychological factors' (Lefant, 1996, p. 1605). For economic examples of inattention to the human propensity to prepare and forearm for contingencies, consider the abundant literature on option values appearing from the 1970s into the 1990s.
2. Wilhite (2001) argues the desire for protection of one's self might have been the catalyst for early community formation. Using a simple agent-based model, his results suggest the gains from social protection might have been one contributing factor in the growth of social order.
3. Also see Shogren et al. (1999), who discuss other reasons why economics matters more to endangered species policy than many natural scientists think. Also see Perrings (2001), who considers how private choices of trade make the risks of invasive species endogenous to individual firms and people.
4. Economists have initiated the few studies that have explored policy options using both mitigation and adaptation (see for example Nordhaus, 1994; Weyant and Hill, 1999).
5. Plenty of empirical evidence exists to suggest people do not regard collective and private protection as perfect substitutes. See, for example, Crocker and Shogren (1998), Johannesson et al. (1996), Shogren (1990), and Shogren and Crocker (1994).
6. Self-protection and self-insurance have also been called averting behavior, defensive actions, and protective investments. Self-protection is also referred to as *loss prevention* or *mitigation*; self-insurance as *loss reduction* or *adaptation*. And Ehrlich and Becker (1972) point out that the line between self-protection and self-insurance can sometimes be blurry. Some actions influence both the probability and the severity of an event.
7. The minimal set of axioms that yields a von Neumann–Morgenstern index of rational preferences for risky choices is completeness, transitivity, continuity, and independence. Formal explanations of the axioms and the properties of the associated preference function are widely available. See for example Mas-Colell et al. (1995, ch. 6).
8. Stigler and Becker (1977) take a similar position in the context of a riskless setting. See also Viscusi (1989).
9. The distribution $F(\gamma)$ first-order stochastically dominates the distribution $G(\gamma)$ when $F(\gamma) \leq G(\gamma)$ for all $\gamma \in [a,b]$, which is equivalent to obtaining $F(\gamma)$ from $G(\gamma)$ by shifting the probability mass to the right.
10. The model easily accommodates second-order stochastic dominance or mean-preserving spreads by integrating twice by parts. Bresnahan and Dickie (1995) model self-protection as a complete vector of contingent actions, one for each state the individual might confront.
11. The relation between the parameterized distribution and the state-space characterizations of the decision problem is analogous to that between reduced forms and structural models in econometrics (Mirrlees, 1974). The state-space representation is supposed to depict the entire structure of the relations among possible states, input choices, and random variables; the parameterized distribution compresses this structure into a single relation based on observed events among outcomes, input, and random variables. Shogren and Crocker (1999, pp. 48–9) argue that the parameterized distribution formulation will generally be easier to apply to environmental problems. These problems frequently involve a complex array of multiple causes acting in concert; complexity causes errors in scientific tests and protocols and definitions of states are paradigm-specific but natural scientists, especially biologists, frequently do not agree on the paradigm appropriate to an environmental problem.
12. Evans and Viscusi (1991) present empirical evidence that consumers treat minor impacts upon personal non-pecuniary assets such as health as a drop in income. But Viscusi and Evans (1990) find that on-the-job injuries reduce the marginal utility of income.

13. It is instructive to review the USEPA guidelines on risk assessments for environmental hazards (USEPA, 1993). First general information about the molecular, chemical, and physical properties of the hazard is amassed. Second, where the hazard enters the environment along its chain of production, distribution, use, and disposal is examined. Third, the exposure pathways are determined. Fourth, ambient concentrations are measured for environmental media. Fifth, exposure assessments ascertain the exposed population by size, characteristics, location, and habits. Sixth, a risk characterization combines concentration estimates with the exposed population to construct an exposure profile. Finally, the characterization describes the statistical robustness of the procedure. Only the assessors themselves, the technical experts, make choices – their human subjects are, at best, viewed as creatures of habit.

14. Eom (1995) examines how information affects the valuation for safer food in a two-period endogenous risk model. She argues that people with more information about health threats are less likely to overreact to low-probability risks.

15 In an experiment considering self-protection, Kunreuther et al. (1998) examine the behavior of people asked to choose between and to value protection with an immediate cost and extended benefits that accrue over time. Their results suggest that most people either discounted or ignored the long-term benefits. Most people were willing to buy protection, but they behaved inconsistently with a discounted utility model.

REFERENCES

Agee, M.D. and T.D. Crocker (1994), 'Parental and Social Valuations of Child Health Information,' *Journal of Public Economics*, **55**, 89–105.

Agee, M.D. and T.D. Crocker (1996), 'Parental Altruism and Child Lead Exposure,' *The Journal of Human Resources*, **31**, 677–91.

Agee, M.D. and T.D. Crocker (1998), 'Economics, Human Capital, and Natural Assets: Forming Empirical Linkages,' *Environmental and Resource Economics*, **11**, 261–71.

Agee, M.D. and T.D. Crocker (2003), 'Smoking Parents' Valuations of Own and Child Health,' Working paper, Department of Economics and Finance, University of Wyoming, Laramie.

Allais, M. (1953), 'Le Comportement de l'Homme Rationnel devant le Risque, Critique des Postulats et Axiomes de l'Ecole Américaine,' *Econometrica*, **21**, 503–46.

Antoci, A. and S. Borghesi (2001), 'Working Too Much in a Polluted World: A North–South Evolutionary Model,' working paper No. 334, Dipartimento Di Economia Politica, Università degli Studi di Siena, on-line at www.econpol.unisi.it/quaderni/334.pdf.

Archer, D.W. and J.F. Shogren (1996), 'Endogenous Risk in Weed Control Management,' *Agricultural Economics*, **14**, 103–22.

Archer, D.W., T.D. Crocker and J.F. Shogren (2002), *Choosing Children's Environmental Risk*, Working paper, Department of Economics and Finance, University of Wyoming, Laramie.

Arnott, R. and J. Stiglitz (1988), 'The Basic Analytics of Moral Hazard,' *Scandinavian Journal of Economics*, **90**, 383–413.

Arrow, K.J. (1963). 'Uncertainty and the Welfare Economics of Medical Care,' *American Economic Review*, **53**, 941–73.

Babcock, B. and J.F. Shogren (1995), 'The Cost of Agricultural Production Risk,' *Agricultural Economics*, **12**, 141–50.

Becker, G.S. (1962), 'Irrational Behavior and Economic Theory,' *Journal of Political Economy*, **70**, 1–13.

Beissinger, S.R. and J.D. Perrine (2001), 'Extinction, Recovery and the Endangered Species Act,' in J.F. Shogren and J. Tschirhart (eds), *Protecting Endangered Species in the United States*, New York, NY: Cambridge University Press, 51–71.

Berger, M., G. Blomquist, D. Kenkel and G. Tolley (1987), 'Valuing Changes in Health Risk: A Comparison of Alternative Measures,' *Southern Economic Journal*, **53**, 967–83.

Blackorby, C., D. Donaldson and D. Maloney (1984), 'Consumer's Surplus and Welfare Change in a Simple Dynamic Economy,' *Review of Economic Studies*, **51**, 171–6.

Boyer, M. and G. Dionne (1983), 'Variations in the Probability and the Magnitude of Loss: Their Impacts on Risk,' *Canadian Journal of Economics*, **16**, 406–19.

Bresnahan, B.W. and M. Dickie (1995), 'Averting Behavior and Policy Evaluation,' *Journal of Environmental Economics and Management*, **29**, 378–92.

Carlin, P.S. and R. Sandy (1991), 'Estimating the Implicit Value of a Young Child's Life,' *Southern Economic Journal*, **58**, 186–202.

Chambers, R. and J. Quiggin (2000), *Production, Uncertainty, Choice, and Agency: The State-contingent Approach*, New York: Cambridge University Press.

Chapman, K. and G. Hariharan (1996), 'Do Poor People Have a Stronger Relationship between Income and Mortality than Do the Rich? Implications of Panel Data for Wealth–Health Analysis,' *Journal of Risk and Uncertainty*, **12**, 51–64.

Charnley G., J.D. Graham, R.F. Kennedy Jr, and J.F. Shogren (2000), 'Assessing and Managing Risks in a Democratic Society,' *Risk Analysis* (annual meeting plenary session), **20**, 301–16.

Chen, S.-N., J.F. Shogren, P. Orazem and T. Crocker (2002), 'Prices and Health: Identifying the Effects of Nutrition, Exercise, and Medication Choices on Blood Pressure,' *American Journal of Agricultural Economics*, 84, 990–1002.

Cherry, T., T.D. Crocker and J.F. Shogren (2003), 'Rationality Spillovers,' *Journal of Environmental Economics and Management*.

Cook, P.J. and D.A. Graham (1977), 'The Demand for Insurance and Protection: The Case of Irreplaceable Commodities,' *Quarterly Journal of Economics*, **91**, 143–56.

Courbage, C. (2001), 'Self-Insurance, Self-Protection and Market Insurance within the Dual Theory of Choice,' *Geneva Papers on Risk and Insurance Theory*, **26**, 43–56.

Crocker, T.D. (1973), 'Contractual Choice,' *Natural Resources Journal*, **13**, 561–77.

Crocker, T.D. (2001), 'Some Economics Questions about the Biology of Biodiversity Protection: Comments on Gibbons, Brown and Layton, and Beissinger and Perrine,' in J. Shogren and J. Tschirhart (eds), *Protecting Endangered Species in the United States: Biological Needs, Political Realities, Economic Choices*, New York: Cambridge University Press, 72–88.

Crocker, T.D. and J.F. Shogren (1991), 'Preference Learning and Contingent Valuation Methods,' in F.J. Dietz, F. van der Ploeg, and J. van der Straaten (eds), *Environmental Policy and the Economy*, Amsterdam: North-Holland, 77–94.

Crocker, T.D. and J.F. Shogren (1997), 'Endogenous Risk and Environmental Program Evaluation,' in G. Knaap and T.J. Kim (eds), *Environmental Program Evaluation: A Primer*, Urbana, IL: University of Illinois Press, 255–69.

Crocker, T.D. and J.F. Shogren (1998), 'On the Bounds of the Economic Lore of "Nicely Calculated Less or More" for Natural Environments,' in S. Mahendrarajah, D. Jakeman, and M. McAleer (eds), *Modeling Changes in Integrated Economic Systems*, Chichester, UK: John Wiley & Sons, 61–86.

Crocker, T.D. and J.F. Shogren (2001), 'Ecosystems as Lotteries,' in H. Folmer, H.L. Gabel, S. Gerking, and A. Rose (eds), *Frontiers of Environmental Economics*, Cheltenham, UK and Northampton, USA: Edward Elgar, 250–71.

Crocker, T.D. and J. Tschirhart (1992), 'Ecosystems, Externalities, and Economies,' *Environmental and Resource Economics*, **2**, 551–67.

Crocker, T.D., B.A. Forster and J.F. Shogren (1991), 'Valuing Potential Groundwater Benefits,' *Water Resource Research*, **27**, 1–6.

Crocker, T.D., J.F. Shogren and P.R. Turner (1998), 'Incomplete Beliefs and Nonmarket Valuation,' *Resource and Energy Economics*, **20**, 139–62.

de Finetti, B. (1974), *Theory of Probability*, Vol. I, New York, NY: John Wiley & Sons.

Di Mauro, C. and A. Maffioletti (1996), 'An Experimental Investigation of the Impact of Ambiguity on the Valuation of Self-insurance and Self-protection,' *Journal of Risk and Uncertainty*, **13**, 53–71.

Dixit, A. and R. Pindyck (1994), *Investment under Uncertainty*, Princeton, NJ: Princeton University Press.

Dreze, J. (1987), *Essays on Economic Decisions under Uncertainty*, Cambridge, UK: Cambridge University Press.

Edwards, W. and D. von Winterfeldt (1986), 'On Cognitive Illusions and Their Implications,' in H.R. Arkes and K.R. Hammond (eds), *Judgment and Decision Making*, New York, NY: Cambridge University Press, 124–51.

Ehrlich, I. and G. Becker (1972), 'Market Insurance, Self-Insurance, and Self-Protection,' *Journal of Political Economy*, **80**, 623–48.

Ellsberg, D. (1961), 'Risk Ambiguity and the Savage Axioms,' *Quarterly Journal of Economics*, **75**, 643–9.

Elster, J. (1998), 'Emotions and Economic Theory,' *Journal of Economic Literature*, **36**, 47–74.

Eom, Y. S. (1995), 'Self-Protection, Risk Information, and Ex Ante Values of Food Safety and Nutrition,' in J. Caswell (ed.), *Valuing Food Safety and Nutrition*, Boulder, CO, and Oxford: Westview Press, 27–49

Evans, W.N. and W.K. Viscusi (1991), 'Estimation of State-Dependent Utility Functions Using Survey Data,' *The Review of Economics and Statistics*, **73**, 94–104.

Freeman, A.M. III (1993), *The Measurement of Environmental and Resource Values*, Washington, DC: Resources for the Future.

Freeman, A.M. III and H. Kunreuther (2002), 'Environmental Risk Management for Developing Countries,' *Geneva Papers on Risk and Insurance*, **27**, 196–214.

Freudenburg, W.R. (1988), 'Perceived Risk, Real Risk: Social Science and the Art of Probabilitistic Risk Assessment,' *Science*, **242**, 44–9.

Gode, D. and S. Sunder (1993), 'Allocative Efficiency of Markets with Zero Intelligence Traders: Markets as a Partial Substitute for Individual Rationality,' *Journal of Political Economy*, **101**, 119–38.

Grether, D. and C. Plott (1979), 'Economic Theory of Choice and the Preference Reversal Phenomenon,' *The American Economic Review*, **69**, 623–38.

Grether, D.M. (1994), 'Individual Behavior and Market Performance,' *American Journal of Agricultural Economics*, **76**, 1079–83.

Harless, D. and C. Camerer (1994), 'The Predictive Utility of Generalized Expected Utility Theories,' *Econometrica*, **62**, 1251–89.

Hayes, D., J. Shogren, S. Shin and J. Kliebenstein (1995), 'Valuing Food Safety in Experimental Auction Markets,' *American Journal of Agricultural Economics*, **77**, 40–53.

Helfand, G. and J. Rubin (1994), 'Spreading versus Concentrating Damages: Environmental Policy in the Presence of Nonconvexities,' *Journal of Environmental Economics and Management*, **27**, 84–91.

Heyes, A. (2001), 'A Note on Defensive Expenditures: Harmonised Law, Diverse Results,' *Environmental and Resource Economics*, **19**, 257–66.

Hiebert, L.D. (1983), 'Self-Insurance, Self-Protection, and the Theory of the Competitive Firm,' *Southern Economic Journal*, **50**, 160–8.

Hirshleifer, J. (1966), 'Investment Decisions under Uncertainty: Applications of the State-Theoretic Approach,' *Quarterly Journal of Economics*, **80**, 252–77.

Holling, C. (1986), 'Resilience of Ecosystems: Local Surprise and Global Change,' in W. Clark and R. Munn (eds), *Sustainable Development of the Biosphere*, New York, NY: Cambridge University Press.

Hurley, T. and J.F. Shogren (1997), 'Environmental Conflicts and the SLAPP,' *Journal of Environmental Economics and Management*, **33**, 253–73.

Immordino, G. (2000), 'Self-Protection, Information and the Precautionary Principle,' *Geneva Papers on Risk and Insurance Theory*, **25**, 179–87.

Intergovernmental Panel on Climate Change (IPCC) Working Group II (2001a), *Climate Change 2001: Impacts, Adaptation, and Vulnerability*, J. McCarthy, O. Canziani, N. Leary, D. Dokken, K. White (eds), Cambridge: Cambridge University Press.

Intergovernmental Panel on Climate Change (IPCC) Working Group III (2001b), *Climate Change 2001: Mitigation*, B. Metz, O. Davidson, R. Swart and J. Pan (eds), Cambridge: Cambridge University Press.

Johannesson, M., P.-O. Johansson and R. O'Conor (1996), 'The Value of Private Safety Versus the Value of Public Safety,' *Journal of Risk and Uncertainty*, **13**, 262–76.

Kahneman, D. and A. Tversky (1979), 'Prospect Theory: An Analysis of Decision Under Risk,' *Econometrica*, **47**, 263–91.

Kane, S. and J.F. Shogren (2000), 'Linking Adaptation and Mitigation in Climate Change Policy,' *Climatic Change*, **45**, 75–102.

Kask, S., T. Cherry, J. Shogren and P. Frykblom (2002), 'Using Flexible Scenarios in Benefits Estimation: An Application to the Cluster Rule and the Pulp and Paper Industry,' in J. List and A. de Zeeuw (eds), *Recent Advances in Environmental Economics* Cheltenham, UK and Northampton, USA: Edward Elgar, 232–56.

Keen, M. (1990), 'Welfare Analysis and Intertemporal Substitution,' *Journal of Public Economics*, **42**, 47–66.

Kremer, M. (1996), 'Integrating Behavioral Choice into Epidemiological Models of AIDS,' *Quarterly Journal of Economics*, **111**, 549–74.

Kreps, D.M. and E. Porteus (1978), 'Temporal Resolution of Uncertainty and Dynamic Choice Theory,' *Econometrica*, **46**, 185–200.

Kunreuther, H., A. Onculer and P. Slovic (1998), 'Time Insensitivity for Protective Investments,' *Journal of Risk and Uncertainty*, **16**, 279–99.

Laffont, J. (1995), 'Regulation, Moral Hazard and Insurance of Environmental Risks,' *Journal of Public Economics*, **58**, 319–36.

Laffont, J.-J. (1980), *Essays in the Economics of Uncertainty*, Cambridge, MA: Harvard University Press.

Lee, K. (1998), 'Risk Aversion and Self-Insurance-cum-Protection,' *Journal of Risk and Uncertainty*, **17**, 139–50.

Lefant, C. (1996), 'High Blood Pressure: Some Answers, New Questions, Continuing Challenges,' *Journal of the American Medical Association*, **275**, 1604–6.

Lence, S. and B. Babcock (1995), 'Endogenous Risk, Flexibility, and the Protection Premium,' *Theory and Decision*, **38**, 29–50.

Lewis, T. and P. Nickerson (1989), 'Self-Insurance against Natural Disasters,' *Journal of Environmental Economics and Management*, **16**, 209–23.

List, J. and J. Shogren (1999), 'Price Information and Bidding Behavior in Repeated Second-price Auctions,' *American Journal of Agricultural Economics*, **81**, 942–9.

Lutter, R., E. Mader and N. Knuffman (2001), 'Regulating Mercury Emissions: What Do We Know About Costs and Benefits?', AEI-Brookings Joint Center for Regulatory Studies, Regulatory Analysis 01–03.

Machina, M. (1982), '"Expected Utility" Theory Without the Independence Axiom,' *Econometrica*, **50**, 277–323.

Machina, M. (1987), 'Choice Under Uncertainty: Problems Solved and Unsolved,' *Journal of Economic Perspectives*, **1**, 121–54.

Machina, M. (1989), 'Dynamic Consistency and Non-Expected Utility Models of Choice Under Uncertainty,' *Journal of Economic Literature*, **27**, 1622–88.

Marshall, A. (1920), *Principles of Economics*, 8th edn, London: Macmillan.

Marshall, J. (1976), 'Moral Hazard,' *American Economic Review*, **66**, 880–90.

Mas-Colell, A., M.D. Whinston and J.R. Green (1995), *Microeconomic Theory*, New York, NY: Oxford University Press.

McClelland, G., W.D. Schulze and D. Coursey (1993), 'Insurance for Low-Probability Hazards: A Bimodal Response to Unlikely Events,' *Journal of Risk and Uncertainty*, **7**, 95–116.

Mirrlees, J. (1974), 'Notes on Welfare Economics, Information, and Uncertainty,' in M. Balch, D. McFadden, and S. Wu (eds), *Essays on Economic Behavior under Uncertainty*, Amsterdam, The Netherlands: North-Holland, 163–74.

National Academy of Sciences (1983), 'Risk Assessment in the Federal Government: Managing the Process,' Washington, DC: National Academy Press.

Ng, Y.-K. (1965), 'Why Do People Buy Lottery Tickets? Choices Involving Risk and the Indivisibility of Expenditure,' *Journal of Political Economy*, **73**, 530–35.

Nordhaus, W. (1994), *Managing the Global Commons*, Cambridge, MA: MIT Press.

Pearce, D. (2000), 'Valuing Risks to Life and Health: Towards Consistent Transfer Estimates in the European Union and Accession States,' paper prepared for the European Commission (DGXI) Workshop on Valuing Mortality and Valuing Morbidity, 13 November, Brussels.

Peltola J. and K. Knapp (2001), 'Recursive Preferences in Forest Management,' *Forest Science*, **47**, 455–65.

Perrings, C. (2001), 'Trade, the Harmonisation of Environmental Policy and the Subsidiarity Principle,' Workshop on Trade and the Environment in the Prospect of European Union Enlargement, Milan, www.york.ac.uk/depts/eeem/resource/perrings/tradehar.pdf.

Poe, G. and R. Bishop (1999), 'Valuing the Incremental Benefits of Groundwater Protection When Exposure Levels are Known,' *Environmental and Resource Economics*, **13**, 341–67.

Pratt, J.W. (1964), 'Risk Aversion in the Small and in the Large,' *Econometrica*, **32**, 122–36.

Quiggin, J. (1992), 'Risk, Self-Protection, and Ex Ante Economic Value: Some Positive Results,' *Journal of Environmental Economics and Management*, **23**, 40–53.

Rhoads, T. and J.F. Shogren (2001), 'Coasean Bargaining and Collaborative Environmental Policy,' in A. Heyes (ed.), *The Law and Economics of the Environment*, Cheltenham, UK and Northampton, USA: Edward Elgar, 18–43.

Ruckelshaus, W. (1984), 'Risk Assessment and Risk Management,' *Risk Analysis*, **4**, 157–62.

Sahlins, M. (1974), *Stone Age Economics*, London: Tavistock Press.

Savage, L. (1954), *The Foundation of Statistics*, New York, NY: John Wiley & Sons.

Selden, L. (1978), 'A New Representation of Preferences over "Certain x Uncertain" Consumption Pairs: The Ordinal "Certainty Equivalent" Hypothesis,' *Econometrica*, **46**, 1045–60.

Settle, C., T.D. Crocker and J.F. Shogren (2002), 'On the Joint Determination of Economic and Biological Systems,' *Ecological Economics*, **42**, 301–11.

Shogren, J.F. (1990), 'The Impact of Self-Protection and Self-Insurance on Individual Response to Risk,' *Journal of Risk and Uncertainty*, **3**, 191–204.

Shogren, J.F. (1991), 'Endogenous Risk and Protection Premiums,' *Theory and Decision*, **31**, 241–56.

Shogren, J.F. (1998), 'Coasean Bargaining with Symmetric Delay Costs,' *Resources and Energy Economics*, **20**, 309–26.

Shogren, J.F. (forthcoming), 'Experimental Methods and Valuation,' in K.-G. Mäler and J. Vincent (eds), *Handbook of Environmental Economics*, Amsterdam: Elsevier.

Shogren, J.F. and T.D. Crocker (1991), 'Risk, Self-Protection, and Ex Ante Economic Value,' *Journal of Environmental Economics and Management*, **20**, 1–15.

Shogren, J.F. and T.D. Crocker (1994), 'Rational Risk Reduction Given Sequential Reduction Opportunities,' *Economics Letters*, **44**, 241–8.

Shogren, J.F and T.D. Crocker (1999), 'Risk and Its Consequences,' *Journal of Environmental Economics and Management*, **37**, 44–52.

Shogren, J.F. and T. Stamland (2002a), 'Skill and the Value of Life,' *Journal of Political Economy*, **110**, 1168–72.

Shogren, J.F. and T. Stamland (2002b) 'Consistent Estimation of the Value of Statistical Life,' working paper, Department of Economics and Finance, University of Wyoming.

Shogren, J.F., J. List and D. Hayes (2000), 'Preference Learning in Consecutive Experimental Auctions,' *American Journal of Agricultural Economics*, **82**, 1016–21.

Shogren, J.F., J. Tschirhart, T. Anderson, A. Ando, S. Beissinger, D. Brookshire, G. Brown, Jr, D. Coursey, R. Innes, S. Meyer and S. Polasky (1999), 'Why Economics Matters for Endangered Species Protection,' *Conservation Biology*, **13**, 1257–67.

Silberberg, E. (1978), *The Structure of Economics: A Mathematical Analysis*, New York, NY: McGraw-Hill.

Simon, H.A. (1973), 'The Structure of Ill-Structured Problems,' *Artificial Intelligence*, **4**, 181–201.

Smith, V.K. and W. Desvousges (1986), 'An Empirical Analysis of the Economic Value of Risk Change,' *Journal of Political Economy*, **95**, 89–115.

Smith, V.K., H. Kim and D. H. Taylor, Jr. (2002). 'Do the "Near" Elderly Value Mortality Risks Differently?', working paper, North Carolina State University.

Smith, V.L. (1982), 'Microeconomic Systems as an Experimental Science,' *American Economic Review*, **72**, 589–97.

Starmer, C. (2000), 'Developments in Non-Expected Utility Theory: The Hunt for a Descriptive Theory of Choice Under Risk,' *Journal of Economic Literature*, **38**, 332–82.

Stewart, J. (1994), 'The Welfare Implications of Moral Hazard and Adverse Selection in Competitive Insurance Markets,' *Economic Inquiry*, **32**, 193–208.

Stigler, G.J. and G.S. Becker (1977), 'De Gustibus Non Est Desputandum,' *American Economic Review*, **67**, 76–90.

Sugden, R. (1985), 'Regret, Recrimination, and Rationality,' *Theory and Decision*, **19**, 77–99.

United Nations Framework Convention on Climate Change, 29 May 1992, 31 I.L.M. 849.

United States Environmental Protection Agency (1993), *A Guidebook to Comparing Risks and Setting Environmental Priorities*, Washington, DC.

United States Environmental Protection Agency (2000), *Guidelines for Preparing Economic Analysis*, EPA 240-R-00-003, Washington, DC. On-line at yosemite.epa.gov/EE/Epa/eed.nsf/pages/guidelines.

United States Office of Science and Technology Policy (1999), *Our Changing Planet: The FY 2000 US Global Change Research Program*, Washington, DC.

Viscusi, W.K. (1989), 'Prospective Reference Theory: Toward an Explanation of the Paradoxes,' *Journal of Risk and Uncertainty*, **2**, 235–64.

Viscusi, W.K. (1993), 'The Value of Risks to Life and Health,' *Journal of Economic Literature*, **31**, 1912–46.

Viscusi, W.K. and W.N. Evans (1990), 'Utility Functions that Depend on Health Status: Estimates and Economic Implications,' *American Economic Review*, **80**, 353–74.

Viscusi, W.K., W. Magat and J. Huber (1987), 'An Investigation of the Rationality of Consumer Valuations of Multiple Health Risks,' *Rand Journal of Economics*, **18**, 465–79.

von Neumann, J. and O. Morgenstern (1947), *Theory of Games and Economic Behavior*, Princeton, NJ: Princeton University Press.

Weinstein, M.C., D.S. Shephard and J.S. Pliskin (1980), 'The Economic Value of Changing Mortality Probabilities: A Decision-Theoretic Approach,' *Quarterly Journal of Economics*, **94**, 373–96.

Weyant, J. and J. Hill (1999), 'Introduction and Overview: The Costs of the Kyoto Protocol – A Multi-model Evaluation,' *Energy Journal*, Special Issue: vii–xliv.

Wilhite, A. (2001), 'Protection and Social Order,' manuscript, 7th International Conference of the Society of Computational Economics, Yale University, cas.uah.edu/wilhitea/papers/bandits/CEFpaper.pdf.

Yoder, J. (2002), 'Prescribed Fire: Liability, Regulation, and Endogenous Risk,' working paper, Department of Agricultural and Resource Economics, Washington State University.

3. Stability and design of international environmental agreements: the case of transboundary pollution

Michael Finus

1. INTRODUCTION

Concern about international environmental problems[1] has grown immensely over the last four decades. This led to the signature of several international environmental agreements (IEAs), as for instance the Helsinki and Oslo Protocols on the reduction of sulphur signed in 1985 and 1994, respectively, the Montreal Protocol on the reduction of chlorofluorocarbons (CFCs) that deplete the ozone layer signed in 1987 and the Kyoto Protocol on the reduction of greenhouse gases causing global warming signed in 1997.[2,3] This concern is also reflected in numerous papers on the economics of international environmental problems. In this chapter I survey the game-theoretical literature on coalitions analysing the formation and stability of IEAs. The fundamental result motivating all analyses is that as long as environmental problems are not of purely local nature, global welfare can be raised through cooperation. The fundamental assumption of all models is that there is no international agency that can establish binding agreements.[4] Consequently, cooperation faces three fundamental constraints (see section 2.1 for details): (1) IEAs have to be profitable for all potential participants; (2) the parties must agree on the particular design of an IEA by consensus; and (3) the treaty must be enforced by the parties themselves. The main feature according to which models can be structured is the type of free-riding they capture. Two types of free-riding can be distinguished. The first type implies that a country is either not a member of an IEA or is a member of an agreement

* I have benefited from grant No. 213800/059748 (WIMEK), University of Wageningen, The Netherlands, from discussions with Carlo Carraro, Alfred Endres, Michaela Hodyas, Pierre van Mouche, Carsten Müssig, Bianca Rundshagen and Ekko van Ierland and would like to acknowledge research assistance by Frank Brockmeier and Eva Schreiner. I also would like to thank the editors of this volume and two anonymous referees for many constructive comments. I am particularly indebted to Henk Folmer, who provided me with many suggestions that substantially improved the exposition of the material.

that contributes less to the improvement of environmental quality than members of other agreements. This type of free-riding is captured by models that I call 'membership models', where the first aspect is modelled in 'traditional' single-coalition games and the second aspect in 'new' multiple-coalition games. The second type of free-riding implies that a country is a member of an IEA but does not comply with the terms of the agreement. This type of free-riding is analysed in models that I call 'compliance models'. Since the bulk of the theoretical literature that I review is related to pollution problems, I restrict myself, by and large, to this variety, though most of the qualitative results also apply to other problems, as for instance the depletion of fish stocks and the deforestation of tropical rain forests.

In what follows, I present empirical evidence on the problems of co-operation (section 2.1) and on important issues of treaty design (section 2.2). I introduce a basic framework for the analysis of international pollution problems (section 2.3) and give an overview of the features of possible extensions (section 2.4). Subsequently, I provide a summary of important results obtained with membership models (section 3) and with compliance models (section 4), critically review the models with respect to their theoretical consistency, their ability to contribute to the understanding of real-world phenomena and the extent to which they capture the three fundamental constraints of cooperation. Finally, I point out topics for future research in section 5.

2. BACKGROUND INFORMATION AND FUNDAMENTALS

2.1 Problems of Cooperation

Profitable agreements
Profitability implies that countries must find it beneficial to participate in an IEA. For instance, in spring 2001 President Bush announced that the USA would withdraw from the Kyoto Protocol since abatement costs from the 7 per cent emission reduction, as agreed in 1997, were expected to exceed the benefits from reduced global warming. Also many developing countries did not sign this protocol, given their priority for economic development over environmental issues. Generally, although cooperation raises global welfare, individual countries may be worse off. This may happen for ambitious and/or efficient abatement policies if countries have heterogeneous welfare functions, and has been confirmed by many empirical studies, for instance on global warming (IPCC, 2001) or acid rain (Mäler, 1994). In these cases some countries' abatement obligations are too high compared

to perceived benefits from abatement, rendering an IEA unprofitable for them. For instance, an efficient allocation of abatement burdens requires that developing countries with low marginal abatement cost contribute more than industrialized countries to the reduction of greenhouse gases, although developing countries value associated benefits on average less than industrialized countries. Thus, if differences are pronounced enough, developing countries may be worse off from joining an IEA as long as they receive no compensation.

Consensus agreements

Since there are several options in designing a treaty that is profitable for all participants, countries usually find it hard to agree on a particular design. Critical issues are the level of abatement, the allocation of abatement burdens, and the level, kind, as well as the net donors and recipients, of compensation payments. The struggle for consensus is evident from considering how long it takes from the recognition of an environmental problem to the start of negotiations, the signature of an IEA, and its ratification and enforcement. Generally, it seems relatively easy for countries agreeing on 'framework conventions', which are mainly declarations of intention, but far more difficult agreeing on 'protocols' with explicit and serious emission reductions.[5] For instance, the problem of protecting the ozone layer was first discussed at a meeting of the United Nations Environmental Program in 1976. Preparation for a treaty started no earlier than 1981, and concluded with the adoption of the Framework Convention in Vienna in 1985. First reduction targets for ozone-depleting substances were agreed upon in the Montreal Protocol in 1987, which entered into force in 1989. For greenhouse gases the negotiation time was even longer: the Framework Convention on Climate Change (FCCC) was signed in Rio de Janeiro in 1992, but preliminary emission ceilings were agreed no earlier than 1997 under the Kyoto Protocol, modified and relaxed ceilings (without participation of the USA) were only accepted in 2001 at the meeting in Marrakesh. As of August 2002 this treaty had not yet come into force. In addition, acidification of water and soil was first noticed in 1972 at the UN conference in Sweden, and the Framework Convention on Long-Range Transboundary Air Pollution (LRTAP) was signed in 1979 in Geneva, but serious action was taken only in 1985 when the Helsinki Protocol on sulphur reduction was signed. However, not only the agreements on protocols but also on their amendments frequently reflect only the lowest common denominator. For instance, according to Article 20 of the Kyoto Protocol, amendments can only be passed by unanimity. If no consensus can be reached, the changes are only binding for those participants that accepted the amendments. Similar articles are part of almost all protocols.

Therefore, it is not surprising that amendment protocols, which successively tighten emission standards, are signed by substantially fewer countries than the original protocols (see evidence below).

Self-enforcing agreements

Even if countries can agree on the design of a treaty that is profitable for all participants, free-riding jeopardizes the success of IEAs. A country is usually better off either by remaining a non-participant (first type of free-riding) or by acceding to an IEA but violating its terms (second type of free-riding). The first type of free-riding is obvious when it is seen that in most IEAs the number of signatories falls short of the total number of countries involved in the externality problem. This is true at least for those IEAs with explicit and ambitious abatement targets. For instance, the pollutants CFCs and greenhouse gases affect all countries, a total of roughly 200, but only 38 industrialized countries have accepted emission ceilings under the Kyoto Protocol. Also only 26 countries signed the Montreal Protocol in 1987, though participation has risen substantially over recent years to 180 parties at present. However, the more ambitious amendment protocols number fewer participants (London 1990: 153, Copenhagen 1992: 128, Montreal 1997: 63, Beijing 1999: 11; for details see Appendix 3.1). Moreover, though sulphur is a major air pollutant, the 1985 Helsinki Protocol counts currently only 22 parties, of which 16 are EU countries. In contrast, participation in the framework conventions without specific abatement obligations preceding these protocols is very high (FCCC: 186 parties, Vienna Convention: 180 parties and LRTAP: 48 parties).

There is also ample evidence that the second type of free-riding jeopardizes the success of IEAs. Keohane (1995, p. 217) writes: 'compliance is not very adequate. I believe that every study that has looked hard to compliance [of all major IEAs] has concluded . . . that compliance is spotty.' Also Brown Weiss and Jacobson (1997, p. 87ff.) found instances of violations of all IEAs covered by their extensive study. For instance, no less than over 300 infractions of CITES[6] have been counted per year (Sand, 1997, p. 25). Moreover, all important parties breached the International Convention for the Regulation of Whaling (Heister, 1997, p. 68).[7]

Effective agreements

In the light of the three fundamental constraints it is evident that as a general conclusion it would be wrong to claim that small IEAs are inferior to large IEAs.[8] Among a small group of countries it might be easier to agree on ambitious abatement targets and compliance might be easier to enforce. Also an inefficient may be superior to an efficient allocation of abatement burdens if it leads to a more symmetrical distribution of the gains from cooperation.

This may ensure a higher rate of participation and compliance and may put less strain on critical countries so that they agree on higher abatement targets. From the discussion it is also evident that success of a treaty cannot be inferred from a high participation rate and degree of compliance. This is not only obvious when considering framework conventions but may also be true for other protocols. If an IEA sets only low abatement targets and/or targets that are close to non-cooperative levels, participation and compliance will be no problem. Thus, success can only be measured if abatement targets under an IEA are compared with estimated abatement levels in the absence of a treaty and, ideally, are evaluated in terms of costs and benefits. For instance, two econometric studies by Murdoch and Sandler (1997a, b) suggest that agreed sulphur reduction under the Helsinki Protocol signed in 1985, and agreed CFC reductions under the Montreal Protocol signed in 1987, though they may seem large, are more in line with non-cooperative than with cooperative behaviour of governments. For the Helsinki Protocol their conclusion can be supported by noting that some members and even some non-members had already achieved the reduction target in 1985 when the treaty was signed, and that not only all members but also most non-members met and even overfulfilled the 30 per cent sulphur reduction target in 1993. This conclusion is also supported by the game-theoretical analysis of Finus and Tjøtta (forthcoming), which evaluates sulphur targets under the successor agreement, the Oslo Protocol, signed in 1994 (see section 4).

2.2   Treaty Design

Abatement targets
The level and allocation of abatement targets affect welfare of countries and thus also participation and compliance with treaty obligations. Under many 'old' IEAs uniform emission reduction quotas have been negotiated, which implies that countries have to reduce their emissions by the same percentage for some base year. The list of examples is long and includes several protocols under the umbrella of the framework convention LRTAP. For instance, the Helsinki Protocol suggested a 30 per cent reduction of sulphur emissions from 1980 levels by 1993. Moreover, the Protocol Concerning the Control of Emissions of Nitrogen Oxides or Their Transboundary Fluxes, signed in Sofia in 1988, called on countries uniformly to freeze their emissions at 1987 levels by 1995 and the Protocol Concerning the Control of Emissions of Volatile Organic Compounds or Their Fluxes, signed in Geneva in 1991, required parties to reduce 1988 emissions by 30 per cent by 1999. Only 'modern' IEAs apply the 'principle of different responsibilities', including the Oslo, Kyoto and Montreal Protocols. However, even though the Montreal Protocol allows developing countries to be exempted

from certain regulations, to claim a transition period until full compliance is required and to draw on support from various financial mechanisms to meet their targets (see evidence below), it calls on uniform reductions of various CFC pollutants in the different amendments.[9] Also in the original draft of the Kyoto Protocol greenhouse gas emission reductions of the major global players are very similar (USA: 7 per cent, Japan and Canada: 6 per cent and EU: 8 per cent).[10]

Barrett (1992a, b) and Hoel (1992) suggest that uniform abatement obligations constitute some kind of focal point on which bargaining partners can agree relatively easily. However, their models provide little evidence that helps to explain the prominence of uniform quotas. Endres (1996, 1997), Endres and Finus (1998, 1999, 2002), Eyckmans (1999) and Finus and Rundshagen (1998b) compare the outcome and stability of negotiations under different policy regimes, assuming that countries agree on the lowest common denominator. Their main finding is that although uniform quotas are inefficient, the negotiation outcome may be superior in terms of global emission and welfare as well as stability compared to efficient policy regimes since the interests of the blocking country (the country that makes the smallest proposal) are better accounted for in the negotiations. This is also confirmed in the coalition model of Finus and Rundshagen (1998a), where the choice of the policy regime is endogenized (see section 4).

Compensation measures
Transfers are an obvious instrument to compensate the losers from co-operation, to increase participation in an IEA and to encourage compliance. Possible compensation measures are monetary and in-kind transfers, which comprise for instance technical assistance to developing countries from industrialized countries. Whereas monetary transfers directly target compensation, in-kind transfers do so only indirectly and hence the aim of compensation is often blurred and overlapped by other aims. Therefore, theoretically, the efficiency of in-kind transfers is lower than that of monetary transfers. However, the order of frequency of the application of these instruments is reversed in practice. Almost all IEAs have no provisions for monetary transfers. One prominent exception is the Montreal Protocol, under which a multilateral fund has been established to which industrialized countries are supposed to contribute and from which developing countries and countries in transition can receive support. However, recipients can only claim compensation for their incremental costs of abatement (Jordan and Werksman 1996, pp. 247ff. and Kummer, 1994, p. 260).[11] Moreover, payment started only in 1991, but has risen constantly ever since. Outstanding contributions amount to roughly 12 to 16 per cent per year, transfers are often delayed, some donors only issued promissory notes and

some have fulfilled their obligations only in the form of in-kind transfers.[12] A second prominent exception is the Convention of Biological Diversity signed in 1992 in Rio de Janeiro, where developing countries can receive support from the 'Global Environmental Facility'. However, this fund also covers only incremental costs, and the backlog of transfers is very large.[13] Another exception, though different, is the Kyoto Protocol. Among Annex 1 countries transfers are paid indirectly under joint implementation (Articles 3 and 4), where countries can jointly meet their targets in the form of a bubble and paid directly under the emission trading system (Article 17). Under the clean development mechanism (CDM; Article 12) Annex 1 countries can reduce their abatement burdens by financing 'project activities resulting in certified emission reductions' in countries not included in Annex 1 of the protocol.[14] In contrast to monetary transfers, the number of IEAs including provisions for technical exchange and assistance between industrialized and developing countries is larger, though a closer reading reveals that obligations are usually very vague.

Until now, the literature on IEAs has presented little evidence that helps to explain the resistance of governments to pay monetary transfers. Two intuitive arguments are due to Mäler (1990): first, transfers provide an incentive for governments to strategically misrepresent their preferences in order to extract larger compensation payments or to pay low transfers. For instance, under CDM, developing countries may certify emission reductions that they would have undertaken anyway. Also, under the Montreal Protocol, if a developing country indicates non-compliance despite 'best intentions' to the Implementation Council, it may receive additional financial assistance. Second, governments may fear that if they pay transfers they are judged as weak bargainers, which may weaken their position in future negotiations. Further arguments have been developed in three models. First, paying transfers to non-participants for additional abatement efforts may provide a disincentive to join an IEA (Hoel and Schneider, 1997; see section 3.3.4). Second, there is a compliance problem between donor and recipient (Finus, 2002a; see section 4.2). Either the recipient may take the money but does not fulfil its promised abatement obligation or the recipient fulfils its part of the deal but the donor does not pay the promised transfers. Third, there is a compliance problem within the group of donor countries (Barrett, 1994a; see section 4.2). Individual donors are better off if they free-ride, though the group of donors as a whole benefits from transfers through higher participation and compliance.

Issue linkage
An alternative compensation measure is issue linkage, where concessions in one agreement are exchanged for concessions in another agreement. Since

package deals are sometimes secretly negotiated, it is not that easy to gather empirical evidence. Most reported examples include bilateral links (Ragland, 1995 and Bennett et al., 1998). For instance, Krutilla (1975) suggests that the Columbia River Treaty of 1961 between the USA and Canada which – viewed as a single issue was to the disadvantage of the USA – was built on concessions by Canada involving North American defence. In the context of multilateral agreements only a wider interpretation allows us to detect issue linkage. One example is the Montreal Protocol, where the import and export of controlled substances with non-parties is banned (Article 4) or the efforts to include environmental issues in the World Trade Organization (WTO), which may be interpreted as a link between an IEA and a trade agreement. Also the provision of technical assistance and exchange under many protocols may be interpreted as a link between an IEA and an agreement to share the cost of R&D. Moreover, considering that the various transboundary pollutants have initially been regulated in separate agreements (sulphur: Helsinki and Oslo Protocols, nitrogen oxides: Sofia, and volatile organic compounds: Geneva) but are now treated together in the Gothenburg Protocol signed in 1999, and that the Kyoto Protocol deals with several global pollutants in one agreement, suggests some kind of issue linkage under the last two mentioned protocols. In the literature, it has been suggested that issue linkage can raise participation (section 3.3.5) and compliance (section 4.5) in an IEA.

Sanctions
Obvious measures to control free-riding are sanctions. However, empirical evidence tells us that either most IEAs have no provision for sanctions or they have hardly been used in the past. Probably, the only exception of sanctioning non-participation is the above-mentioned Article 4 under the Montreal Protocol. For sanctioning non-compliance most IEAs have only a provision for the establishment of an arbitration and dispute settlement committee if one party accuses another of violating the spirit of an agreement (Marauhn, 1996, pp. 696ff.; Széll, 1995, pp. 97ff.; and Werksman, 1997, pp. 85ff.). Due to the voluntary character of the arbitration scheme and since the provision contains no threat of punishment, it is not surprising that there are no reported instances of application (Sand, 1996, p. 777). Again, the ozone regime is an exception, where the parties first agreed on an indicative list of measures (Annex V) at their fourth meeting in Copenhagen in 1992 and then defined non-compliance at their sixth meeting in Nairobi in 1994.[15] The measures include (a) assistance in the collection and the reporting of data, technical assistance, technology transfers and financial assistance, (b) issuing cautions and (c) suspension of specific rights and privileges, including transfers of technology, financial mechanism and institutional arrangements. It is

evident that only item (c) can be regarded as sanctions. Moreover, these sanctions can only be used against developing countries since only these can claim assistance and enjoy specific rights and privileges (for example, they are allowed a longer transition period until they have to meet the targets of the various protocols) under Article 5 of the ozone regime.[16] However, any formal statement of non-compliance by the Implementation Committee has to be passed by unanimity.[17] Another exemption is the Kyoto Protocol, where the parties agreed at the meeting in Marrakesh in 2001 on 'Consequences Applied by the Enforcement Branch' (Annex XV).[18] Similar to the Montreal Protocol, most measures include assistance to meet the targets rather than tough sanctions, and complicated voting procedures precede any formal statement of non-compliance. However, two tough punishment options have been decided: a party (a) may be excluded from the emission trading system and (b) must reduce 30 per cent more of its assigned emissions in the second commitment period (2013–17). It remains to be seen whether these sanctions will be used in the future.

In contrast to Chayes and Chayes (1993, 1995), I interpret the empirical evidence on sanctions not to imply that free-riding is not a problem, but to suggest that the design of effective sanctions faces credibility, institutional and technical problems in reality (Finus, 2002a):[19]

1. Sanctioning countries for not acceding to an IEA is at odds with the notion of voluntary participation.
2. Sanctions often also have a negative effect on those countries carrying out the punishment. Thus harsh sanctions are not always credible and constitute themselves as a public good that is subject to free-riding.
3. Sanctioning non-compliance is flawed by the fact that under most treaties signatories can withdraw from the agreement after giving notice three (Kyoto Protocol, Article 27) or four years (Montreal Protocol, Article 19) in advance.
4. Sanctions may be in conflict with the regulations of other treaties (for example, trade sanctions and WTO).
5. Coordination of sanctions among signatories is often time-consuming and costly.

2.3   Basic Framework[20]

Let there be N countries, $i \in I = \{1, ..., N\}$, and the welfare of country i, π_i, be given by

$$\pi_i = \beta_i(e_i) - \phi_i \left(\sum_{j=1}^{N} a_{ij} e_j \right) \qquad (3.1)$$

Country i benefits from its own emissions, e_i, where it is usually assumed that benefits increase $(\beta_i' > 0)$ at a decreasing rate $(\beta_i'' \le 0)$. Thus emissions can be viewed as an input in the production and consumption of goods where the law of diminishing returns applies. Country i also suffers damages from its own (e_i) and foreign $(e_j, j \ne i)$ emissions. The transportation coefficient $a_{ij}, 0 \le a_{ij} \le 1$, indicates the portion of emissions of country j, which is deposited in country i. Whereas for local pollutants, $a_{ii} = 1$ and $a_{ij} = a_{ij} = 0$, the transportation coefficients will be between zero and one for transboundary pollutants, as for instance the acid rain pollutant sulphur. For an upwind country, like the UK, a_{ii} and a_{ij} will be small and for a downwind country, like Norway, these coefficients will be large. For global pollutants, like CFCs and greenhouse gases, all coefficients are one since emissions disperse uniformly in the atmosphere.[21] The standard assumption is that damages increase in depositions $(\phi_i' > 0)$ at an increasing rate $(\phi_i'' \ge 0)$. Hence, due the limited absorption and regeneration capacity of most environmental systems, environmental damages increase more than proportionally with increasing depositions.

Since benefits from abatement correspond to reduced damages from depositions and cost of abatement correspond to a loss of benefits from reduced emissions (opportunity cost of abatement), a country's welfare function (also called payoff function in the game-theoretical terminology) has also been modelled in terms of abatement in the literature. Since qualitative results are not affected by such a change, I will relate all subsequent models to (3.1) in order to use a uniform terminology.

If each of the N countries pursues its own interest, that is, all countries behave non-cooperatively, each country maximizes (3.1) with respect to its own emissions ($\max_{e_i} \pi_i$), taking emissions from other countries as given. The simultaneous solution of the N first-order conditions $\beta_i' = a_{ii}\phi_i'$ [22] delivers the non-cooperative Nash equilibrium emission vector $e^N = (e_1^N, ..., e_N^N)$. Since this equilibrium *de facto* implies that countries form singleton coalitions, it seems plausible to assume that it represents the *status quo* before an IEA is signed. In contrast, if governments were to pursue the common interest, that is, they behaved *fully cooperatively*, they would maximize the aggregate payoff over all countries ($\max_{e_1,...,e_N} \Sigma_{i=1}^N \pi_i$). Again, the simultaneous solution of the N first-order conditions $\beta_i' = \Sigma_{j=1}^N a_{ji}\phi_j'$ delivers the fully cooperative (also called globally or socially optimal) emission vector $e^S = (e_1^S, ..., e_N^S)$. This may be interpreted as if all countries form a grand coalition and jointly maximize the aggregate welfare of their coalition. Since $e^S \ne e^N$ as long as there is some transboundary pollution ($a_{ji} \ne 0$ for some $j \ne i$), global welfare could be raised through cooperation, that is, $\Sigma_{i=1}^N \pi_i(e^N) < \Sigma_{i=1}^N \pi_i(e^S)$. This is also true for more pragmatic solutions (which most IEAs are), where either the grand coalition chooses more moderate abatement targets than in the social optimum or only a subgroup of countries forms a coalition (coalitions), implying a partially cooperative emission vector $e^* = (e_1^*, ..., e_N^*)$. However, in the basic framework, no form of cooperation can be enforced. In a static game, any strategy of conditional cooperation ('I will cooperate provided you also cooperate') would be irrational since it cannot be rewarded at later stages. Thus any other emission vector different from the (static) Nash equilibrium would imply that at least one country has an incentive to revise its decision. Thus, to explain any form of cooperation requires extending the basic framework (see section 2.4).

In order to study the free-riding behaviour of countries in the context of coalition formation, it is helpful to note that the first-order conditions derived from the maximization behaviour of single countries or coalitions for any coalition structure[23] different from the grand coalition can be interpreted as best-reply functions. A best-reply function describes the optimal choice of emissions of a country (coalition) for a given level of emissions of outsiders (and given transportation coefficients). Total differentiation of the first-order conditions delivers the slopes of the reaction functions that approximate the direction and the extent of change of emissions of countries (coalitions) to an external change of emissions. Usually, these functions are negatively sloped since an increase (decrease) of external emissions increases (reduces) marginal damages and a best reply calls on a country (coalition) to reduce (increase) emissions, which increases (reduces) marginal benefits in order to equalize marginal benefits and damages. Only under special conditions ((a) $a_{ii} = 0$, (b) $a_{ij} = 0$ and (c) linear damage cost functions) is the optimal choice of a country (coalition) independent of external emissions (dominant strategy) and the slope of a country's (coalition's) reaction function zero. The literature refers to the standard case as non-orthogonal and to the special case as orthogonal best-reply functions.[24]

2.4 Extended Framework

Table 3.1 provides an overview of important features (column 1), sub-features (column 2) and characteristics (columns 3 and 4) according to which various coalition models can be structured. Those characteristics that can be related to the basic model are indicated in italic. All other entries are related to extended frameworks, which suggests that the number of possible extensions is large. Therefore, in order not to lose track at this stage of the discussion, I will only briefly sketch some important issues of Table 3.1 and encourage the reader to return to this subsection after reading

Table 3.1 Structure of coalition models

Main features	Sub-features	Characteristics	
Time	Framework	Implicit dynamic	Explicit dynamic
	Horizon		Finite or infinite
	Interval		Discrete or continuous
Payoff	Structural relation	*Independent* (flow pollution)	Dependent (stock pollution)
	Arguments	*Only material payoffs*	Also non-material payoffs
	Transfers	*No*	Yes
Equilibrium concepts	Strategic relation	*Independent*	Dependent
	Sanctions	Different degrees of harshness and credibility of sanctions	
	Deviations	*Single*	Multiple
Number of issues		*Single*	Multiple
Rules of coalition formation	Sequence of coalition formation	Simultaneous	Sequential
	Number of coalitions	Single	Multiple
	Membership	Open	Exclusive
	Consensus	Different degrees of consensus with respect to membership	

sections 3 and 4 to gain a full understanding of the driving forces of coalition models and their classification.

The first main feature and an important prerequisite for cooperation is '*Time*'. Whereas non-cooperative behaviour is the only equilibrium strategy in the static basic model (conditional cooperation is not possible), cooperative behaviour is possible in a dynamic extended model since countries can condition their strategies on previous behaviour and/or can react to deviations from agreed strategies through some form of punishment.[25] However, in some models the dynamic aspect is not immediately obvious. I call this an 'implicit dynamic framework', which means that time is not explicitly modelled and the dynamic story is exogenous to the model. In contrast, an 'explicit dynamic framework' implies that 'real' time is captured and modelled. In the case of an explicit dynamic time framework, the time horizon can be either finite or infinite and the time intervals can be either discrete or continuous. An infinite time horizon does not necessarily imply an infinite life of agents but only that the end of the game is not known with certainty. Discrete time implies that strategies can only be revised at certain points in time whereas strategies can immediately be revised if time is continuous.

The second main feature is '*Payoff*'. The first sub-feature, 'Structural relation', is closely related to the dynamics of a model (main feature 'Time'). 'Structural independence' means that payoffs at time t depend only on strategies (that is, emissions) at time t whereas structural dependence implies that they also depend on previous strategies. Since in the context of IEAs most coalition models capture only structural dependence with respect to damages from emissions, the line of distinction can also be drawn between the assumption of flow and stock pollutants. This sub-feature can also be related to three important games. Repeated games assume the same payoff function at each point in time and usually discrete time intervals, though we will encounter a version with continuous time in section 3.2. In contrast, difference and differential games capture structural dependence of payoffs where the former assume discrete and the latter continuous time (Dockner et al., 2000 and de Zeeuw and van der Ploeg, 1991). Of course, trivially, since the basic model is static, its payoff structure can be classified as independent. The second sub-feature concerns the arguments in countries' payoff functions. Whereas 'material payoffs' refer to benefits and costs from emissions as captured in the basic model in equation (3.1), all other dimensions such as reputation and fairness that usually favour more co-operation are captured by the term 'non-material payoffs'. The same positive effect usually applies to the third sub-feature, 'Transfers', which may be seen as an additional strategy to emissions to achieve cooperation.

The third main feature is captured by the term 'Equilibrium concepts', where the first two sub-features, 'Strategic relation' and 'Sanctions' also have a close connection to the dynamics of a model. Strategic independence implies that strategies are chosen once and for all and cannot be revised, whereas strategic dependence implies that strategies at time t are conditioned on previous actions and can be revised if new information becomes available.[26] Consequently and trivially, there is no strategic dependence in the basic model due to its static nature. The second sub-feature, 'Different degrees of harshness and credibility of sanctions', is related to two facts. First, in a dynamic setting the free-rider incentives (of type 1 and 2) do not vanish but may be controlled through either implicit or explicit threats of sanctions. Second, threats of punishment have to be credible to be deterrent, which corresponds to different notions of equilibrium concepts discussed in subsequent sections. Those notions are also related to the third sub-feature, 'Deviations'. Whereas we defined stability in the basic model as a state that is immune to single deviations (Nash equilibrium), some coalition models define stability in terms of multiple deviations. Of course, in the basic model, this simple definition was sufficient since cooperative agreements were not stable anyway, but is less obvious in extended models where full or partial cooperation is possible.

The fourth main feature is the '*Number of issues*'. Whereas the basic model restricted attention to one issue, that is, one pollutant, some coalition models also consider multiple issues, as for instance additional pollutants, trade flows, investment in R&D and so on. Multiple issues can improve upon the possibilities of establishing cooperation between countries if issues are cleverly and strategically linked. The success of issue linkage depends on a number of factors, which are discussed in subsequent sections, but the main reason is that issue linkage, like transfers, increases the number of policy options (strategies) to achieve cooperation.

The fifth main feature is the 'Rules of coalition formation'. The rules may be interpreted as the institutional setting in which countries strike informal or formal cooperative agreements with other countries. At this stage it suffices to point out that the rules of coalition formation have a crucial impact on the outcome, but its role has only recently been analysed in a strand of literature that I call 'new coalition theory', discussed in subsection 3.3.6.

In summarizing the preliminary discussion, five conclusions seem important. First, a dynamic time framework is the most important ingredient and extension compared to the basic model in order to capture the phenomenon of cooperation. Second, it will become apparent from sections 3 and 4 that the extensions non-material payoffs, transfers and issue linkage will usually have a positive effect on the possibility of cooperation. In terms of the rules of coalition formation it will be evident that the possibility of forming multiple coalitions instead of only one coalition, restricting membership to an IEA (exclusive membership) instead of allowing any country to join and requiring a high instead of a low degree of consensus with respect to membership in an IEA will lead to superior outcomes in terms of global welfare and emissions. Third, no clear-cut conclusions about the effect of characteristics of other sub-features that constitute an extension to the basic model can be drawn. This will depend on the specifics of models. Fourth, roughly speaking, the right-hand-side characteristics (fourth column) in Table 3.1 imply a higher degree of sophistication than the left-hand-side characteristics (third column). However, sophistication comes at the cost of complexity. Therefore, it will become apparent that all models make some exogenous assumptions and solve for the remaining endogenous variable in order to keep the analysis tractable. For instance, all coalition models assume certain rules of coalition formation when determining equilibrium coalition structures but do not derive these rules from the negotiation process between the potential participants to an IEA. Moreover, all models focus either on the first or the second type of free-riding and capture the other type of free-riding only deficiently. I take this phenomenon as the fundamental feature to structure the following discussion. I call models that focus on the first type of free-riding 'membership models' (M-models; section 3) and those that focus on the second type of free-riding 'compliance models' (C-models; section 4). M-models are concerned with the coalition formation process and stability of membership. They analyse whether a country remains a non-participant or participates in a coalition and, if it participates, with which countries it will form a coalition. However, M-models are not concerned with whether and how agreed emission ceilings within a coalition are enforced. This is the focus of C-models, which emphasize the role of sanctions in enforcing compliance. However, C-models usually start their analysis from a given membership and give less attention to the process of coalition formation and issue of membership.[27] Fifth, it will be apparent that if structural dependence is modelled (which is only the case in some M-models, applying the stability concept of the core; subsection 3.2), this is only done in terms of emissions. The reason is simple: in all models payoffs are a function of emissions and transfers, which are only indirectly a function of membership. Moreover, whereas for emissions a strategic dependence is interesting because of stock pollutants, it is less interesting for transfers as long as it is assumed that transfers at time t are paid out of the gains from cooperation at time t. Also, if strategic dependence is assumed, it is usually only modelled in terms of emissions and transfers (which is the case in some M-models applying the stability concept of the core; subsection 3.2, and in all C-models; section 4), though it would generally be possible (and very useful) to capture strategic dependence in terms of membership.

3   MEMBERSHIP MODELS

3.1   Introduction

Membership has been analysed within cooperative and non-cooperative game theory. The classical distinction is that cooperative game theory assumes the possibility of binding agreements whereas non-cooperative game theory neglects this possibility. However, it will become apparent that this distinction is not very helpful since all M-models share some fundamental features.[28] First, not only cooperative but also non-cooperative game-theoretical M-models assume some form of commitment within coalitions. That is, all M-models assume that countries comply with their emission reduction and transfer obligations if they form a coalition and therefore free-rider problems of real IEAs are underestimated. Second, not only M-models belonging to non-cooperative game theory but also those belonging to cooperative game theory assume some form of punishment if countries leave an agreement. Third, all M-models check stability of membership in an implicit dynamic framework. That is, they analyse whether a country or group of countries have an incentive to move from a particular coalition structure (state 1) to another coalition structure (states 2, 3, ...), where the time path to switch from one to another state is not modelled. Therefore, I propose to distinguish both theories in terms of their tools and foci.

The first attempts to study coalition formation are rooted in cooperative game theory.[29] The analytical tool is the characteristic function (see Definition 1, below) that assigns to each coalition a worth, which is the aggregate payoff a coalition can get irrespective of the behaviour of outsiders. What irrespective means depends on the specific assumptions associated with this function and will be discussed in subsection 3.2.1. The focus of the analysis is on the allocation of the gains from cooperation, but not that players may choose inefficient strategies. Therefore, in games with externalities, stability of the grand coalition implementing the socially optimal strategy vector is analysed. The central question of the analysis is: which transfer scheme or bargaining rule enables the grand coalition to be sustained?

Proponents of non-cooperative game theory criticize three features of cooperative coalition theory: (1) for rational actors it seems natural to assume that they base their decision about membership on individual rather than on aggregate payoffs; (2) some assumptions of cooperative game theory about the behaviour of countries outside a coalition are difficult to justify since they require irrational behaviour of countries (see section 3.2.1 for details); (3) cooperative game theory cannot explain why most IEAs are inefficient in terms of participation and emission reductions. Therefore, scholars of non-cooperative game theory propose analysing coalition formation based on a valuation function (see Definition 1) that assigns an individual payoff to each player for any possible coalition structure, assuming that each coalition pursues its own interests, and not restricting coalition formation to the grand coalition. Hence the behaviour of insiders and outsiders is guided by self-interest and is based on the same assumption of rationality. That is, countries cooperate within their coalition but behave non-cooperatively against outsiders. Therefore, higher than globally optimal emissions and inefficient coalition structures (different from the grand coalition) typically emerge in equilibrium. The central question of the analysis is: which coalition structure can be sustained as an equilibrium for a given transfer scheme or bargaining rule?

Definition 1: Characteristic and Valuation Function   Let I^J denote a subset of countries forming a coalition and let I^{NJ} denote the set of all other countries, then the worth (characteristic function) of coalition I^J is given by $w(I^J) = \Sigma_{i \in I^J} \pi_i(e^J, e^{NJ})$, where emission vector e^{NJ} follows from some assumption about the behaviour of countries outside coalition I^J, I^{NJ}, and emission vector e^J from the maximization of the aggregate payoff of the countries belonging to coalition I^J, $\max_{e^J} \Sigma_{i \in I^J} \pi_i(e^J, e^{NJ})$.

Let $c = (c^1, ..., c^k, ..., c^M)$ be a coalition structure with M coalitions, then the valuation (function) of country i belonging to coalition c^k is given by $v_i(c^k, c) = \pi_i(e) + t_i$, where the emission vector $e = (e^1, ..., e^k, ..., e^M)$ follows from the maximization of each coalition $c^k \subset c$ where the members of c^k maximize the aggregate payoff of the countries belonging to their coalition, $\max_{e^k} \Sigma_{i \in c_k} \pi_i(e^k, e^{-k})$, where the emission vector e^{-k} follows from the maximization of other coalitions, and t_i is a transfer paid ($t_i < 0$) or received ($t_i > 0$) by country i that follows from some transfer scheme.

The main differences between the analytical tools of cooperative and non-cooperative game theory – are discussed above – are also evident from Definition 1. First, whereas $w(I^J)$ gives the aggregate payoff of a coalition, $v_i(c^k, c)$ is based on individual payoffs. Second, whereas in $w(I^c)$ the choice of emissions of insiders and outsiders may follow from different assumptions, in $v_i(c^k, c)$ choices are based on the same assumption. The main difference between the foci and the results of the two approaches will become apparent from the following subsections. In particular, it will be evident that each theory has its merits and shortcomings and a selection should be motivated by the focus of research. Therefore, it is not surprising that in the context of IEAs roughly half of the M-models belong to co-operative and half to non-cooperative game theory. More surprising is that only one equilibrium concept has been applied within each theory. Scholars of cooperative game theory applied the concept of the core (section 3.2) and those of non-cooperative game theory the concept of internal and external stability (section 3.3) to study coalition formation. Only recent contributions of non-cooperative theory consider other concepts (section 3.3.6).

3.2   Cooperative Game Theory

3.2.1   The concept of the core
In the context of IEAs cooperative game theory analysed stability of the grand coalition implementing the socially optimal emission vector. The payoff of each country depends – as in the basic model – on benefits and damages from emissions, but also on possible transfer payments among

countries. The set of payoffs resulting from the socially optimal emission vector and possible transfer payments is called an 'imputation'. According to the concept of the core an imputation is called stable, that is, it lies in the core, if each country receives a high enough share from the gains from co-operation, so that no group of countries (including single countries), I^J, finds it profitable to form another coalition different from the grand coalition.

Definition 2: Core　Let π_i^S be the payoff in the social optimum, t_i a transfer, $\Sigma_{i=1}^N t_i = 0$ and $\pi_i^* = \pi_i^S + t_i$, then an imputation $\pi^* = (\pi_1^*, ..., \pi_N^*)$ lies in the core if $\Sigma_{i \in I^J} \pi_i^* \geq w(I^J) \ \forall \ I^J \subset I$.

From Definition 2 it is evident that profitable deviations are defined in terms of the characteristic function $w(I^J)$. Recalling Definition 1, this has four implications. First, counter-intuitively, the term 'coalition' is *not* used for the group of cooperating countries (as this is common in non-cooperative game theory), but for the group of deviating countries. Thus the members of the coalition I^J are the 'bad guys' and all remaining countries, I^{NJ}, are the 'good guys'.[30] Second, a deviation is not only considered as profitable if each country of this deviating coalition receives more than in the imputation but also if the aggregate payoff of the coalition increases through the deviation. Third, whether deviations of coalition I^J are profitable depends on the assumption how the set of remaining countries, I^{NJ}, will react. This in turn depends on the definition of the characteristic function where in the context of IEAs two functions are important. The α-characteristic function, $w^\alpha(I^J)$, assumes that each country in I^{NJ} chooses its highest emission level, e_j^{max}, in order to minimize the aggregate payoff of the deviators I^J.[31] The coalition members will adjust to this punishment by choosing their best reply, which follows from maximizing aggregate payoffs of the coalition for the punishment vector e^{max}.[32] In contrast, the γ-characteristic function, $w^\gamma(I^J)$, assumes that after a deviation the remaining countries break up into singletons, where each singleton maximizes its individual payoff as this has been described for the basic model in the Nash equilibrium. The deviators also choose their optimal strategy in a Nash equilibrium fashion, except that they act as one single player and maximize the aggregate payoff to their coalition. Hence the emission vector after a deviation follows from the simultaneous maximization of payoffs of deviators and punishers and has therefore been called 'a partial-agreement Nash equilibrium between the coalition and other countries' (Chander and Tulkens, 1995 and 1997). Fourth, the worth tells a dynamic story, which is not explicitly modelled, which explains my statement that membership is checked in an implicit dynamic framework.

　　When comparing the assumptions of the α- and γ-characteristic function, it is evident that the punishment in the former case is stronger than in the latter. The reason is that damages increase in own but also foreign emissions. Consequently, the higher are foreign emissions, the lower will be aggregate payoffs of the deviators for any given level of domestic emissions. Since the α-characteristic function assumes that the punishers choose their highest possible emission level, the γ-characteristic function must imply a weaker punishment. Hence $w^\gamma(I^J) \geq w^\alpha(I^J)$ holds for any deviation of a subgroup of countries I^J (Chander and Tulkens, 1995). Consequently, it is easier to satisfy the inequalities characterizing a stable coalition in Definition 2 and therefore the set of imputations that lie in the γ-core, C^γ, is a subset of those lying in the α-core, C^α. That is, $C^\gamma \subset C^\alpha$.

When evaluating the core concept, three issues seem import. First, the notion of profitable agreements is captured in the γ-core since Definition 2 implies that an imputation is only stable if each country receives at least its payoff in the *status quo* where all countries are singletons. To see this, assume that only one country deviates. Then the coalition comprises only one single country, $I^J = \{i\}$, and all $N-1$ other countries would react by breaking up into singletons. Thus all countries are singletons and maximize their individual payoffs. Hence, in this case the partial-agreement Nash equilibrium is the same as the Nash equilibrium (known from the basic game in section 2.3) and hence, according to Definition 2, stability requires that $\pi_i^* \geq w^\gamma(\{i\}) = \pi_i(e^N) \,\forall\, i$ holds, where we may recall that e^N denotes the Nash equilibrium emission vector. In the case of the α-core, profitability is only ensured if we assume that in the *status quo* all countries would emit their maximum emissions because then $\pi_i^* \geq w^\alpha(\{i\}) = \pi_i(e^{max})$.[33] Since the Nash equilibrium is a plausible assumption for the *status quo* but not the only possible assumption, it could therefore be argued that the α-core also captures the notion of profitable agreements. Second, the core concept captures the notion of consensus agreements since all coalition members must unanimously prefer the grand coalition (and the allocation of the gains from cooperation) to alternative coalition structures. Thus the coalition formation game may be viewed as a bargaining game where countries bargain on the allocation of transfers, where alternative coalition structures function as threat points. Unfortunately, however, there is usually not only one imputation that lies in the core and therefore the solution of the bargaining game may not be unique. Third, the notion of self-enforcing IEAs rests on strong and probably non-credible punishments and therefore the possibilities of controlling free-riding in reality are most likely overestimated. This is obvious in the case of the α-core, where the punishers behave as sadists but also as masochists in the case of a deviation since they not only inflict the maximum punishment on the free-riders but also substantially harm themselves. In fact, some punishments (depending on how many countries deviate) will imply that the punishers receive lower payoffs than without the agreement (Nash equilibrium payoffs). However, even the assumption of the weaker punishment in the case of the γ-core is not innocuous for at least two reasons.[34] First, the complete break-up of the remaining countries after a deviation is not related to the rules of coalition formation and therefore does not logically follow from the rational behaviour of countries. For instance, it might well be the case that it is in the interest of at least some of the remaining countries to continue cooperation. Second, compared to the cooperative state, punishment will also hurt the punishers. Hence deviators will find it easy to persuade punishers to forget about punishment and to resume cooperation, which questions the credibility of the threat of punishment in the first place. Thus, in a strong sense, this weaker punishment may also be regarded as not credible.[35] Another disadvantage of the core concept is that only stability of the grand coalition is tested and that the profitability of deviations is checked in terms of aggregate and not individual payoffs. However, this concept also has its merits since not only single but also multiple deviations are considered.

3.2.2 Results

Usually, it is not possible to determine the set of imputations that lie in the core. Therefore, most papers prove the opposite. For instance, Scarf (1971) showed that the α-core is not empty in static externality games. Recent contributions extend this result, demonstrating that a particular imputation possesses the core properties. Though the various papers assume different transfer schemes, they are all very similar to that proposed in Chander and Tulkens (1995 and 1997) in the context of a global pollutant,[36] a static game and the γ-core:

$$t_i = [\beta_i(e_i^N) - \beta_i(e_i^S)] - \frac{\phi_i'(e^S)}{\Sigma_{k=1}^N \phi_k'(e^S)} \cdot \left[\sum_{k=1}^N \beta_k(e_k^N) - \sum_{k=1}^N \beta_k(e_k^S) \right], \quad (3.2)$$

where I use the notation introduced in section 2.3 (the superscripts S and N stand for social optimum and Nash equilibrium, respectively, β_i and ϕ_i denote benefits and damages from emissions, respectively, and primes denote derivatives), $t_i > 0$ ($t_i < 0$) implies that a transfer is received (paid) by a country and transfers are balanced since $\Sigma_{i=1}^N t_i = 0$ (see Definition 2). The first term (first square bracket) is a payment *to* each country, compensating for the individual loss of benefits when moving from the Nash equilibrium to the social optimum. The second term is a payment *by* each country in proportion to the fraction of marginal damages in each country to aggregate marginal damages in all countries (term in front of the second square bracket) covering the total decrease of benefits (second square bracket). That is, those countries which benefit more from emission reduction in the form of reduced marginal damages have to carry a larger portion of the total opportunity costs of cooperation (total loss of benefits). In other words, countries have to contribute to the provision of the public-good 'clean environment' according to their preferences for this good and therefore (3.2) may be interpreted as a (opportunity) cost-sharing rule. Whether a country is a net donor or receiver of transfers depends on whether the first term is larger or smaller than the second. In any case, however, it can be shown that (3.2) ensures that each country is at least as well off when co-operating as in the Nash equilibrium.[37]

In the case of non-uniform spillovers (see note 1), (3.2) will be slightly modified to account for different transportation coefficients, and in the case of dynamic models similar transfer schemes to (3.2) are implemented at each point in time. In the following, I review results of selected publications, proceeding according to the historical development in the field. A summary of the main features of various models is provided in Appendix 3.3.

Tulkens (1979), Chander and Tulkens (1991 and 1992) and Kaitala et al. (1995)   The first group of papers extends the analysis to a dynamic payoff structure with a continuous time horizon, sticking to the assumption of a flow pollutant. Thus the payoff structure is that of a repeated game except that time is continuous.[38] The central idea is that countries do not immediately jump to the social optimum but gradually adjust their emissions towards this 'steady state'. The motivation is that emission reduction takes time and that countries may know their benefits and damages only in the neighbourhood of their current emissions (local information). In Tulkens (1979) it is shown that the time-iterative process converges to the steady state and in Chander and Tulkens (1991 and 1992) it is demonstrated that an imputation with a transfer scheme similar to (3.2) lies in the α-core at each point in time, when countries are sharing a common resource. The transfer scheme is illustrated for the acid rain problem between Finland, Russia and Estonia in Kaitala et al. (1995).[39]

Chander and Tulkens (1995 and 1997)   The second group of papers extends the analysis to the γ-core but is more restrictive in that it assumes a static payoff structure and global pollution. These papers establish the γ-core properties for the transfer scheme in (3.2) under the following conditions: (a) damage functions are linear, (b) $\forall = I^c \subset I$, $|I^J| \geq 2$, $\Sigma_{k \in I^J} \phi'_k(e^S) \geq \phi_i'(e^N) \; \forall \; i \in I^{J}$[40] and (c) countries are symmetric. Whereas Chander and Tulkens (1995) establish the γ-core property only for condition (a), they (1997) prove this property for all three conditions in a more sophisticated though also more complicated model. However, in Finus (2001, ch. 13) it is shown that all results of the 1997 paper also hold in the

basic model of section 2.3, and Helm (2001) established the γ-core properties under even more general conditions.

Germain et al. (1996a and b)   The third group of papers analyses, similar
to the first set of papers, the general case of transboundary pollution,
assumes a dynamic, though independent payoff structure (flow pollutant),
but considers discrete time intervals and uses the definition of the γ-core of
the second set of papers. Hence the payoff structure is that of a repeated
game. The motivation is that governments revise their emission strategies
only occasionally. However, discrete time introduces a great many compli-
cations so that the γ-core properties can only be shown to hold for linear
damage cost functions (though concave benefit functions). Both papers
illustrate the transfer scheme for the acid rain problem as in Kaitala et al.
(1995).

Germain et al. (1998a), Germain et al. (1998b) and Germain et al. (2000)
The fourth group of papers considers a global stock pollutant, assuming
continuous time, implying a differential game in terms of emissions. In
Germain et al. (1998a) the γ-core properties are established for linear
damage cost functions and only for the overall game. Thus the stability
check is similar to that in Chander and Tulkens (1995 and 1997), except that
countries base their one-shot decision whether to free-ride on the discounted and not on the static payoff. Germain et al. (1998b) extend the
analysis by checking stability along the entire time path and in Germain et
al. (2000) stability is also established for strictly convex damage cost functions where payoff functions satisfy some concavity properties in the local
games.[41] These assumptions imply non-orthogonal best-reply functions
and therefore the distinction between strategic independent (open-loop)
and strategic dependent (closed-loop) Nash equilibrium emissions strategies becomes important.[42] The authors show that the γ-core properties
hold for both types of strategy.[43]

Eyckmans and Tulkens (1999) and Germain and van Ypersele (1999)   The
papers belonging to the fifth group are the only ones that establish the
γ-core properties empirically in the context of the greenhouse effect since
for their example the assumptions of the theoretical papers (for example,
linear damages and concavity of the local games) do not hold. Both papers
use the data and the climate model of Nordhaus and Yang (1996). Whereas
Eyckmans and Tulkens (1999) check the γ-core properties only for the
overall game, assuming open-loop Nash equilibrium strategies, Germain
and van Ypersele (1999) check stability for all local games, assuming closed-
loop Nash equilibrium strategies (note 43 applies).

3.2.3 Evaluation

1. The theoretical results are derived for relatively general properties of the payoff function, though the assumptions of punishment and the focus on the grand coalition are very restrictive. The empirical papers nicely illustrate the implications of the transfer scheme.
2. Not only in models with a static but also with a dynamic payoff structure, deviations from the grand coalition trigger immediate reactions by fellow countries, and thus in all models stability of membership is checked in an implicit dynamic framework.
3. Testing stability along the entire time path is a remarkable theoretical achievement but also captures an important condition for successful cooperation in reality.[44]
4. In the context of flow pollutants, the time-iterative process is a major step in capturing the evolution of many IEAs where abatement obligations are successively increased over time, starting with framework conventions and continuing with various amendments of protocols. Of course, due to the focus on the grand coalition, the increasing participation in many IEAs over time cannot be explained.
5. Considering stock pollutants is an important step in order to capture the structural dependence of most pollutants.
6. The transfer scheme is interesting in that it shows a way to guarantee profitability in a world with heterogeneous countries. However, transfer formula (3.2) provides an incentive for biased reporting. Since payments depend on the fraction $\phi_i'(e^S)/\Sigma\phi_k'(e^S)$, a country has an incentive to bias its estimation of marginal damages downward. By the same token, countries will bias their opportunity costs of abatement (loss of benefits; $\beta_i(e_i^N) - \beta_i(e_i^S)$) upward so as to receive higher transfers (see also Chander and Tulkens, 1992, pp. 396ff.).
7. The core is mainly a normative concept since it exclusively focuses on first best solutions. Consequently, it cannot explain suboptimal treaties, which, of course, most IEAs are.

3.3 Non-cooperative Game Theory

3.3.1 The concept of internal and external stability

The concept of internal and external stability (I&E-S) goes back to d'Aspremont et al. (1983), who used it to study cartel formation in an oligopoly. In the context of IEAs it has been applied to study coalition formation in global pollution control, though it seems that most qualitative results could also be reproduced for other transboundary pollutants. Moreover, all models assume a static payoff structure though preliminary results in Rubio and Ulph (2001) indicate that an extension to a dynamic payoff structure is possible. I&E-S assumes that there is one group of participants forming a coalition (good guys) and that non-participants (bad guys) play as singletons. A coalition is called stable, that is, it is internally and externally stable, if no participant finds it profitable to leave the coalition to become a non-participant and no non-participant finds it profitable to become a member of the coalition.

Definition 3: Internal and external stability Denote the set of participants forming a coalition by c^{k*}, a particular participant by i, $i \in c^{k*}$, non-participants by $j \notin c^{k*}$ and let the equilibrium coalition structure be given by $c^* = (c^{k*}, 1, ..., 1)$, where c^{k*} is the coalition and 1 indicates single countries, then a coalition structure is called stable if it satisfies the following two conditions:

1. Internal stability: $v_i(c^{k*}; c^{k*}, 1, ..., 1) - v_i(i; c^{k*} - i, 1, ..., 1) \geq 0 \ \forall \ i \in c^{k*}$. That is, there is no incentive for a participant to leave the coalition.
2. External stability: $v_j(j; c^{k*}, 1, ..., 1) - v_j(c^{k*} + j; c^{k*} + j, 1, ..., 1) > 0 \ \forall \ j \notin c^{k*}$. That is, there is no incentive for a non- participant to join the coalition.

From Definition 3 it is evident that profitable deviations are defined in terms of the valuation function. Recalling Definition 1, this has four implications. First, deviations are considered as profitable if individual countries gain. Second, the valuation function assumes that coalition members maximize the aggregate payoff to their coalition.[45] Consequently, a change of membership implies that all countries reoptimize their emission strategies under the new conditions. Thus, if a participant leaves a coalition, punishment only implies that the remaining participants reduce their abatement efforts and hence global emissions increase. Thus, leaving a coalition is (not) profitable if increased damages fall short of (exceed) additional benefits from increased emissions. By the same token, if a non-participant joins a coalition, total abatement efforts of the enlarged coalition increase and hence total emissions decrease. Thus, joining a coalition is (not) profitable if reduced damages exceed (fall short of) lower benefits from reduced emissions. Third, the previous remarks reveal that there is some (not modelled) underlying dynamic story, which explains why I claimed that non-cooperative M-models also check stability in an implicitly dynamic framework. Fourth, the valuation and hence the equilibrium will depend on the specifics of the maximization procedure of countries. The standard assumption of non-cooperative coalition theory is that all countries choose their emissions simultaneously. Hence, as in the γ-core, in a given coalition structure, the emission vector constitutes a partial-agreement Nash equilibrium, except that now the role of the good and bad guys is reversed. However, since internal and external stability implies a simple game structure (there can be only one non-trivial coalition), some papers (for example, Barrett, 1994b and 1997b) have departed from the standard assumption and assume a sequential choice of emissions where participants are the Stackelberg leader and non-participants the Stackelberg followers. Since there is a close similarity between the emission game and an output cartel in oligopoly theory, the simultaneous choice of emissions has been called the Nash–Cournot assumption and the sequential choice the Stackelberg assumption.[46] This similarity also carries over to the interpretation and evaluation of the Stackelberg assumption. (a) An immediate interpretation of the Stackelberg assumption is that participants have a strategic advantage over non-participants. (b) Wider interpretations are that participants have an informational or second-mover advantage since they choose their optimal emissions based on the information about the best reply of non-participants. (c) The Stackelberg assumption is an interesting extension for studying how assumptions drive results. (d) In the context of IEAs, it turns out that this assumption allows us to capture a broad spectrum of different agreements that can be related to the fundamental parameters of the model (see subsection 3.2.2). (e) Introducing asymmetry between players is difficult to justify if this assumption does not follow from the analysed problem itself. This is particularly evident in those models in section 3.2.2 that assume symmetric countries. One, though not elegant way around this problem is to tell some plausible story that is exogenous to the model. For instance, in the context of IEAs the case could be made that participants are better informed than non-participants about emission-relevant data since they coordinate their environmental policies. Another story could be that the proportion of industrialized coutries is larger than that of developing countries participating in IEAs and for non-participants this relation is reversed (see the empirical evidence in subsection 2.2). Thus, the strategic advantage of participants could be related to the often-claimed greater power of industrialized compared to developing countries. Moreover, participants cooperate by forming a 'political bloc' against outsiders and therefore assume a stronger position in international politics than non-participants who 'only' pursue their self-interests as singletons. (f) The Stackelberg assumption implies that a participant loses its strategic advantage once it leaves the coalition to become a non-participant, which is difficult to defend rationally by any means.

When evaluating the concept of internal and external stability, three items seem important. First, the concept captures the notion of profitable agreements since it can be shown that if a coalition is internally stable it is also profitable; that is, all participants receive more than in the *status quo*.[47] Second, whether the notion of consensus agreements is captured depends on the specific assumptions of the various models. In the case of symmetric countries or heterogeneous countries and transfers, the assumption of joint welfare maximization of the coalition seems uncontroversial, though in most models transfers are allocated according to stylized bargaining rules of cooperative game theory. In the case of heterogeneous countries and no transfers this assumption seems less obvious and probably overestimates the rationale for cooperation of governments. Third, the notion of self-enforcing IEAs rests on a weak punishment since after a participant leaves the coalition the remaining participants stick together and only reoptimize their strategies. In this sense punishment is credible and reflects the limited punishment options countries face in reality. However, in another and strong sense, punishment may regarded as not credible as in the case of the core.[48] (a) The assumption that the remaining participants do not revise their decisions about membership after a deviation does not follow from the rules of coalition formation and can therefore not be related to rational behaviour of countries. (b) Compared to the cooperative state, the reoptimization strategy may very well imply a loss to the punishers. Finally, note two difference to the core: (a) I&E-S analyses not only stability of the grand coalition but of any coalition structure, though only those with one non-trivial coalition. (b) Stability is defined in terms of only single but not multiple deviations.

3.3.2 Symmetric countries
The simplest method of studying the I&E-S of IEAs is to assume symmetric countries and no transfers (Nash–Cournot assumption: Carraro and Siniscalco, 1991, 1993 and Stackelberg assumption: Barrett, 1991, 1992c, 1994b). The analysis is based on specific payoff functions, though it seems that the results are far more general if viewed together (Barrett, 1997a; Carraro, 2000; and Finus, 2001; ch. 13). It appears that qualitative results depend on the sequence of the choice of emissions and the slopes of the best-reply functions.[49] In the present context the slopes of the best-reply functions indicate by how much emission reductions of participants are offset by an expansion of emissions by non-participants (leakage effect, Hoel, 1991).[50] I group payoff functions in three categories (types 1, 2 and 3) according to the associated slopes of best-reply functions, and illustrate results for each category with an example in Table 3.2. The main conclusions that can be derived from Table 3.2 are summarized in Result 1.[51]

Table 3.2 *Equilibrium coalition size*

Payoff functions	Slopes of the best-reply functions	Choice of emissions	
		Nash–Cournot	Stackelberg
Type 1 $\pi_i = b\left(de_i - \dfrac{1}{2}e_i^2\right) - \dfrac{c}{N}\left(\displaystyle\sum_{k=1}^{N}e_k\right)$	0	$N^* = 3$	$N^* = 3$
Type 2 $\pi_i = b\left(de_i - \dfrac{1}{2}e_i^2\right) - \dfrac{c}{2N}\left(\displaystyle\sum_{k=1}^{N}e_k\right)^2$	Between 0 and -1	$N^* \in \{1, 2\}^\dagger$	$N^* \in [2, N]^\dagger$, $\partial N^*/\partial\gamma < 0$
Type 3 $\pi_i = be_i - \dfrac{c}{2N}\left(\displaystyle\sum_{k=1}^{N}e_k\right)^2$	-1	$N^* = 1$	$N^* = N$

Notes: b, d, c and N are parameters, where N denotes the total number of countries and $\gamma = b/c$; N^* denotes the equilibrium number of participants; † means that the coalition size depends on parameter values. The results in the column 'Choice of emissions' apply to the examples.

Result 1

(a) The number of participants usually falls short of the grand coalition.
(b) The number of participants and global welfare is at least as high under the Stackelberg than under the Nash–Cournot assumption.
(c) The steeper the best-reply function (that is, the higher the absolute value of the slope of the best-reply functions), the lower (higher) is the number of participants under the Nash–Cournot (Stackelberg) assumption.

Part (a) of Result 1 is due to the fact that that the more countries accede to an IEA, the more attractive it is for a participant to leave and the less attractive it is for a non-participant to join the coalition. Since the free-rider incentive increases sharply with the number of participants, N^* is usually small compared to N. Part (b) of Result 1 can be explained by noting that for any coalition size a strategic asymmetry (Stackelberg assumption) secures participants a higher payoff and implies for non-participants a lower payoff than in the standard case (Nash–Cournot assumption). Hence, it is more attractive to join a coalition and less attractive to leave a coalition which leads to larger stable coalitions, involving also a higher global welfare. A less technical interpretation of this result is that an informational advantage puts participants of an IEA in the position to better control leakage effects. Only in the case of payoff functions of type 1 does this advantage not materialize since all countries have dominant strategies (the slope of the best-reply function is zero). In other words, in the case of payoff functions of type 1 (orthogonal best-reply functions), the sequence of the choice of emissions is irrelevant (no distinction between the Nash–Cournot and Stackelberg assumptions is necessary) since both assumptions lead to the same outcome. Also part (c) of Result 1 is related to the slopes of countries' reaction functions. First note that the absolute value of the slope of the best-reply function increases from payoff function of type 1 to type 3. The absolute value of the slope of the best-reply function implied by payoff function of type 2 is somewhere between the two benchmarks 0 and 1 and decreases in the benefit–cost ratio from emissions, $\gamma = b/c$. The reason is that the higher b and the lower c, the more beneficial and the less costly it is for countries to expand emissions if other countries reduce emissions. That is, countries are less sensitive to a change of external emissions. Second, under the Nash–Cournot assumption the larger the absolute value of the slope of the best-reply functions, the larger are leakage effects, undermining the abatement efforts of participants. For instance, in the case of payoff function of type 3 with a slope of -1, no nontrivial coalition is stable since any emission reduction would be completely offset by non-participants. Under the Stackelberg assumption this relation is exactly reversed, though this result should be interpreted with a grain of salt. This is evident by considering again payoff function of type 3. For any coalition smaller than the equilibrium number of participants, coalition members choose higher emissions than non-participants, recognizing that an expansion of emissions is offset by a decrease of emissions of non-participants. Thus, any coalition comprising not all countries is not externally stable (though internally stable) since no country wants to be a Stackelberg follower. Consequently, only the grand coalition is internally and externally stable.[52] In the case of payoff function of type 2 it is evident from Table 3.2 that the number of participants decreases in the benefit–cost ratio γ. The reason is that – as pointed out above – the absolute value of the slope of the reaction function decreases in γ and hence also the strategic advantage of participants over non-participants. Finally, in the case of payoff function of type 1, the equilibrium number of participants is small since orthogonal best-reply functions imply that participants can make no use of their strategic advantage.

As suggested in section 2.2, success of an IEA cannot be inferred from the number of signatories. This requires benchmarking an IEA with the no-treaty situation.[53]

Result 2 Let the degree of externality without an IEA be measured by $I_1 := (\Sigma e_k^N - \Sigma e_k^S)/\Sigma e_k^S$ and $I_2 := (\Sigma \pi_k^S - \Sigma \pi_k^N)/\Sigma \pi_k^S$ and with an IEA by $I_3 := (\Sigma e_k^* - \Sigma e_k^S)/\Sigma e_k^S$ and $I_4 := (\Sigma \pi_k^S - \Sigma \pi_k^*)/\Sigma \pi_k^S$ where the superscripts N, S and $*$ stand for Nash equilibrium, social optimum and coalition equilibrium, respectively. Then the degree of externality measured by the four indices (weakly) increases in the number of countries N and (weakly) decreases in the benefit–cost ratio $\gamma = b/c$ for the three examples in Table 3.2.

First note that since coalition formation can improve upon the non-cooperative status, indices I_1 and I_2 can be interpreted as the gap between the first-best solution (social optimum; full cooperation) and third-best solution (Nash equilibrium; no cooperation) and indices I_3 and I_4 as the gap between first-best solution (social optimum) and second-best solution (coalition equilibrium; partial cooperation). Second, the results related to indices I_1 and I_2 provide conditions under which cooperation would be particularly useful from a global point of view. The results reflect typical features of public-good problems. The more countries are involved in an externality problem and the higher environmental damages are compared to the benefits from emissions, the larger is the degree of externality.[54] A large N implies that the influence of single countries on environmental quality is only marginal and hence individual contributions to global abatement in the non-cooperative equilibrium fall substantially short of those required from a global point of view. Moreover, a large benefit–cost ratio implies that damages are small compared to benefits from emissions and hence even from a global point of view it is sensible to reduce emissions only marginally compared to the *status quo*. Hence the degree of externality is small. The opposite applies to a small benefit–cost ratio. For reference reasons, I call large values of N and low values of γ, implying a high degree of externality in the *status quo*, 'critical parameter values'. Third, the results related to indices I_3 and I_4 provide information about the conditions under which coalition formation is successful. The results indicate that whenever the gap between first- and third-best is large this is also true for the gap between first- and second-best and vice versa (Barrett, 1994a). In other words, whenever cooperation is most needed from a global point of view, IEAs achieve only little. This may seem paradoxical but simply suggests that even if countries coordinate their strategies within an agreement, their abatement efforts are jeopardized by free-riding where the free-rider incentive is particularly strong for large N and small γ.

Although the results are derived from a stylized model, they may be related to the Montreal Protocol signed in 1987 and the Kyoto Protocol (Barrett, 1994b, 1999a). For the interpretation I assume payoff function of type 2 and Stackelberg leadership of signatories since this allows us to relate differences in the two agreements to the benefit–cost ratio from emissions.[55] Both agreements regulate a global pollutant from which severe damages to the environment are expected (high value of c). Currently, most studies also estimate high abatement cost for greenhouse gases (high value of b) but low abatement cost for CFCs (low value of b). In particular, there is evidence that substitution of CFCs has become increasingly cheap over the last decade (Heister, 1998). This implies a lower benefit–cost ratio $\gamma = b/c$ for CFCs than for greenhouse gases where the absolute value of γ is small for CFCs. Thus Result 1 suggests that participation in the Montreal Protocol should be high but Result 2 questions the efficacy of this agreement.[56] In contrast, Result 1 predicts a low participation for the Kyoto Protocol but Result 2 is more optimistic with respect to its efficacy. Obviously, the current status of participation under both protocols confirms the theoretical conclusions based on Result 1. Moreover, the conclusions of Result 2 are in line with the empirical evidence on the (low) efficacy of the Montreal Protocol reported in section 2.2 and in the case of the Kyoto Protocol they are confirmed by those empirical studies that find that the Kyoto targets are very ambitious (Nordhaus and Yang, 1996).

Thus, taken together, the models in this section contribute a great deal to explaining real-world phenomena, although they are simple. In particular, the models help to explain why and under which conditions it is difficult to establish successful cooperation in international pollution control. Of course, all results have to be interpreted in qualitative terms since quantitative results are sensitive to specific assumptions (symmetric countries and specific payoff functions; see also note 51).

3.3.3   Heterogeneous countries and no transfers

Bauer (1992) and Hoel (1992) assume payoff functions of type 1 so that the sequence of emission choices is irrelevant (see Table 3.2). Both authors index countries from 1 to N. In Hoel's model countries differ in the perception of damages where damages increase with the index. Since benefits from emissions are the same for all countries, those countries with a higher index gain more from joint abatement than those with a lower index. In Bauer's model damages also increase in the index. Moreover, countries also differ in benefits from emissions where benefits decrease in the index. Following Bauer, who suggests interpreting the index as the size of a country, this implies that global emissions cause more damages in large countries but the same amount of emission reduction is associated with lower opportunity costs of abatement than in small countries. Consequently, large countries gain more from joint abatement than small countries. Hoel departs from the valuation approach and considers several maximization procedures and abatement allocation rules for the grand coalition and tests for profitability and stability. Although some larger coalitions are profitable, the largest stable coalition comprises only two signatories. Bauer sticks to the standard valuation function approach, assuming joint welfare maximization of coalitions, but extends the I&E-S concept to allow for multiple coalitions. She finds that only coalitions of two countries of similar size (for example, countries 2 and 3, 4 and 5) are stable but not those comprising countries with rank difference larger than 1 (for example, countries 2 and 4).

Thus both papers confirm the intuition that cooperation should be more difficult in the absence of transfers if countries are heterogeneous: an IEA comprises three symmetric countries (see Table 3.2) but only two heterogeneous countries in the case of payoff functions of type 1. Bauer's result that only countries with similar interests will form a coalition is in line with the empirical finding that participants and non-participants can be sorted according to their stage of economic development (for example, Montreal and Kyoto Protocols) or regional patterns (for example, Helsinki Protocol; see section 2.1). The finding that several agreements will emerge in equilibrium suggests that if the strategy to get as many countries as possible into one boat fails due to strong free-rider incentives, the alternative strategy of forming separate agreements may be more successful. This is confirmed by the multiple-coalition models discussed in section 3.3.6.

3.3.4 Transfers, commitment and non-material payoffs

The central question of this section is whether transfers, commitment and non-material payoffs have a positive effect on cooperation and how different transfer schemes affect coalition formation. All papers assume that transfers have to be paid out of the gains from cooperation (self-financed transfers).

Ex-ante transfers Botteon and Carraro (1997) and Barrett (1997b) assume, in the tradition of the valuation function, joint welfare maximization of coalition members and that transfers within coalitions are *ex ante* specified for each possible coalition structure. Based on this assumption, they compute I&E-S coalition structures. This may be interpreted as if participants are committed to transfers *ex ante*. Botteon and Carraro use estimates from Musgrave (1994) to calibrate payoff functions of type 1 for five world regions. They point out that their data set does not necessarily reflect the 'true' incentive structure of the greenhouse gas problem but rather serves as an example to study the effect of transfers. They consider two bargaining rules of cooperative game theory. The Shapley value allocates the gains from joint welfare maximization according to the average marginal contribution of each member to the success of the coalition. It assumes tranferable utility which implies an unconstrained maximization where the gains from cooperation are subsequently allocated via a transfer scheme, similar to that in the context of the core (subsection 3.2.2). The Nash bargaining solution allocates the gains in proportion to the payoffs in the no-treaty situation. The authors assume non-transferable utility, which is a constrained maximization of the weighted payoffs of the coalition members where weights reflect the payoffs in the Nash equilibrium (singleton coalition structure).[57] Thus, under Nash bargaining coalition members only choose a Pareto-optimal emission vector, whereas under the Shapley value they choose the 'socially' optimal emission vector for their coalition. Botteon and Carraro find that for the Nash bargaining solution three coalition structures are internally and externally stable, and for the Shapley value three coalitions structures are internally stable, of which only one is externally stable. The set of participants differs under the two bargaining rules, though in all equilibria coalitions comprise three countries. The three equilibria under the Nash bargaining solution differ in terms of global emissions and welfare but are all inferior compared to the unique equilibrium under the Shapley value.

Botteon and Carraro (1997) illustrate four important issues of treaty design. First, a clever allocation rule of the gains from cooperation can raise participation in an IEA. Under both bargaining rules the equilibrium number of signatories is three, as in the case of symmetric countries and payoff function of type 1, but was only two in Bauer's and Hoel's model of heterogeneous countries and no transfers. Second, though the superiority of the Shapley value over the Nash bargaining solution is not surprising, the exercise stresses that the nature and design of allocation rules have a crucial impact on the success of cooperation. Third, it is shown that membership has an effect on the success of an IEA. Under the Nash bargaining rule there are three equilibria with different membership, implying different global emissions and welfare. This suggests that international organizations could play a role as a coordination device. Even though they have no enforcement power, and hence only stable coalition structures are feasible, they may influence negotiations leading to IEA to achieve 'optimal membership'. Fourth, although the authors do not mention this, the rules of coalition formation have an effect on the stability of coalitions. Since two coalition structures are externally unstable (stability is upset by non-participants joining the coalition) under the Shapley value, they could be stabilized if coalition members can refuse to allow outsiders to join their club. This implies altering the rules of coalition formation from open to exclusive membership – an issue that will be discussed in more detail in subsection 3.3.6.

In a theoretical model, Barrett (1997b) considers payoff functions of type 1 and 2, a Shapley value transfer scheme and Stackelberg leadership of participants.[58] Barrett investigates various forms of heterogeneity and conducts several simulation exercises. He finds that if the heterogeneity is large enough in the absence of transfers, participation will be lower than in the case of symmetric countries, confirming the results of subsection 3.3.3. In these cases, transfers can lead to larger coalitions, implying higher global welfare and lower global emissions, confirming Botteon and Carraro's result above. Moreover, Barrett confirms a central conclusion obtained for symmetric countries in subsection 3.3.2, namely, whenever cooperation is needed most, a coalition achieves only little (see Result 2).

Ex post transfers to increase participation   Carraro and Siniscalco (1993) and Botteon and Carraro (1997) investigate the possibility of enlarging a stable coalition via transfers if members compensate non-participants for joining their club. I call these *ex post* transfers since, starting from stable coalition structures, the role of transfers for the expansion of coalitions is analysed. An expansion is regarded as successful if it implies a Pareto improvement for all coalition members and if the larger coalition is internally stable despite old signatories allocating some of the additional gains from cooperation to new members. This may be interpreted as if transfers were paid conditional on the success of the expansion. That is, expansion is not always successful is demonstrated by Carraro and Siniscalco for the benchmark case of symmetric countries with a simple argument. Rewriting the condition of an externally stable coalition of size c_k^* without transfers, $\pi_j(1; c^{k*}, 1, ..., 1) - \pi_j(c^{k*} + 1; c^{k*} + 1, 1, ..., 1) > 0$, reveals that a coalition of size $c_k^* + 1$ is internally unstable: $\pi_i(c^{k*} + 1, c^{k*} + 1, ..., 1) - \pi_i(1; c^{k*}, 1, ..., 1) < 0$. Since coalition members i have to pay a transfer t_i in order to induce non-participants j to accede to the coalition, they will receive only $\pi_i(c^{k*} + 1; c^{k*} + 1; 1, ..., 1) - t_i$ in the enlarged coalition and thus internal stability cannot hold. Thus, Carraro and Siniscalco conclude that self-financed transfers can only enlarge a coalition in the case of heterogeneous countries. This is investigated in Botteon and Carraro (1997), where they show for their example that from any of the three stable coalition structures under the Nash bargaining solution enlargement is not possible, whereas from the equilibrium coalition structures under the Shapley value an expansion to four and even five countries (grand coalition) is possible. Once more, the result stresses that the nature and design of transfers have an impact on the success of IEAs.

Ex post transfers and commitment to increase participation   Commitment refers to the assumption that countries cooperate irrespective of their free-rider incentive and pay transfers to non-participants in order to raise participation in an IEA. Internal commitment implies that some, all, or also 'new' participants are committed to cooperation when expanding a coalition. External commitment means that non-participants pay other non-participants to join the coalition. Any form of commitment requires only that expansion be beneficial for the payee and, in the case of internal commitment, also to the entire coalition. The original idea goes back to Carraro and Siniscalco (1993), who study various forms of internal and external commitment assuming symmetric countries. The main conclusion is that the more countries are committed, the larger the gains are from expanding the coalition, and the lower the free-rider incentives, the easier it is to expand a coalition, though full participation may not always be possible. For internal commitment this result is illustrated with an example in Jeppesen and Andersen (1998) and confirmed by Petrakis and Xepapadeas (1996) for the case of heterogeneous countries.[59] For the example considered in Botteon and Carraro (1997) it is shown that it is now possible to expand any of the three coalition structures under the Nash bargaining solution to the grand coalition if only one out of three signatories is committed.

From a theoretical point of view, the results are not surprising and commitment is not compatible with the notion of self-enforcing IEAs. In fact, assuming enough commitment, any problem of cooperation can trivially be solved. From a practical point of view, the results may be more interesting if it were possible to find out under which conditions governments pursue a commitment strategy, but I am not aware of any empirical evidence.

Non-material payoffs Jeppesen and Andersen (1998) and Hoel and Schneider (1997) add a term to the 'classical payoff function', which the former call a 'non-material payoff', representing the idea of fairness, and the latter 'non-environmental cost of breaking the agreement'. These terms may also be interpreted as reputation or political correctness. Both papers assume that all countries' payoffs are benefit minus damage costs (material payoff) but that non-participants also receive disutility from being outsiders (non-material payoff), where disutility increases with the number of countries participating in an IEA. Though the papers differ with respect to their particular assumptions,[60] they both find that the higher the disutility of being an outsider, the larger will be the equilibrium coalition. Indeed, this result seems so obvious that it should be expected that it could be established at a far more general level. From a practical point of view the result is more interesting since intuition and casual evidence suggest that reputation effects may play some role in international politics. However, the withdrawal of the USA from the Kyoto Protocol suggests that reputation effects may not always be strong enough to neutralize free-rider incentives.

A theoretically more interesting finding in Hoel and Schneider's model is that side-payments lead to smaller coalitions, which may imply lower global welfare and higher global emissions than in the absence of transfers. Since this result contrasts with all the previous findings, I examine more closely the driving forces of this model. Hoel and Schneider assume that all countries have the same benefits and damages from emissions but different non-environmental costs provided they remain non-participants. Hence those countries that face the highest non-environmental costs have the largest incentive to join the coalition. The authors assume that participants offer non-participants side-payments for additional emission reductions but that the recipient countries remain non-participants. Non-participants are compensated for lower benefits from emissions minus the additional benefits from reduced damage costs. Hence non-participants break even compared to the situation without transfers, and in order to generate Hoel and Schneider's result participants' payoffs must be lower, so that it is more attractive to leave an IEA and less attractive join an IEA. This leads me to the conjecture that Hoel and Schneider's negative result is due to two inefficiency and two strategic effects. The first inefficiency effect is evident from noting that if non-participants joined the coalition if they receive compensation, they would receive an additional benefit from cooperation since they would no longer have to carry non-environmental costs. Hence, if transfers were conditioned on participation in the coalition, either lower compensation payments would be needed to achieve the same abatement target or more abatement could be achieved with the same amount of transfers. The second inefficiency effect is only apparent from a closer study of the technical details of Hoel and Schneider's model, from which it appears that the first-order conditions of participants when bribing non-participants imply that non-participants should choose lower emissions than participants. Hence marginal benefits from emissions of non-participants are higher than those of non-participants, which is a source of inefficiency in a model with identical benefit functions. Thus participants could increase their payoffs at the margin by increasing their abatement efforts, requiring less abatement from non-participants and paying lower transfers. The first strategic effect is related to the allocation of transfers. It is evident from recalling the driving forces responsible for the positive effect of transfers in the 'classical' case of *ex ante* transfers. A clever transfer scheme applied within a coalition raised payoffs of critical countries and made it more attractive to join and stay in a coalition. Hoel and Schneider's transfer scheme also implies *ex ante* transfers; however, transfers are paid from coalition members to outsiders. Hence, compared to the classical case, it is now more attractive to remain a non-participant and to leave a coalition. The second strategic effect is related to the commitment to transfers. This is evident from recalling that the positive effect of *ex post* transfers rests on the assumption that transfers are only paid if expansion is successful. Therefore, no expansion of the coalition was possible through conditional *ex post* transfers in the case of symmetric countries. Now suppose that participants are committed to transfers. Then not only the coalition of $c_k^* + 1$ but also the coalition of c_k^* (or even smaller coalitions) would be internally unstable if internal stability of the c_k^* coalition holds at the margin. Hence, in this case, a commitment to transfers reduces the coalition size, implying higher global emissions and lower global welfare. The same forces are at work in Hoel and Schneider's model, though their model assumes heterogeneity with respect to non-environmental costs.

From a theoretical point of view it seems that the basic flaw of the model is the construction of inefficient transfer payments (second inefficiency effect), so that the negative result almost follows by assumption. The role of 'cooperating' non-participants in this model also indicates that here, in particular, participation cannot be a measure of the success of an IEA but only global emissions and welfare. Of course, this first inefficiency effect could be defended by interpreting it as just a different institutional setting compared to previous models. This is definitely true for the two strategic effects, which leads me to the following general policy conclusions. First, participants of an IEA should first pay attention to the stability of their coalition before using transfers to raise the global abatement level (avoiding the first strategic effect). Second, governments should not commit to transfers *ex ante* if they intend to ensure high participation in an IEA. Instead, a group of core countries should first form an IEA and then try to increase participation via transfers (avoiding the second strategic effect). Third, non-participants should only receive transfers if they join an IEA (avoiding the first inefficiency effect). Fourth, the way transfers are paid should be selected carefully in order to ensure efficiency (avoiding the second inefficiency effect). Hence these conclusions support the transfer scheme under the Montreal Protocol, where the multilateral fund has been established after the initial protocol was signed and where developing countries only receive financial support after becoming members. However, the conclusions question the construction of the clean development mechanism (CDM) under the Kyoto Protocol. First, developing countries may receive transfers for 'certified emission reductions' without joining the protocol. Second, including development countries in the trading system would be a more efficient way of paying transfers than CDM.

3.3.5   Issue linkage

The central motivation to analyse issue linkage in M-models is due to the following conjecture (Carraro, 1997): IEAs are public-good agreements that suffer from free-riding since the gains from cooperation are non-exclusive to signatories, whereas club-good agreements enjoy a higher participation since the gains from cooperation are exclusive to signatories. Consequently, linking a public- to a club-good agreement may increase participation and the success of IEAs.

Examples of club-good agreements that have been studied in the literature include agreements on R&D (Botteon and Carraro, 1998; Carraro and Siniscalco, 1997 and Katsoulacos, 1997) and trade agreements (Barrett, 1997c and Finus and Rundshagen, 2000).[61] Though the specifics of the models differ, they assume simultaneous membership in both agreements, firms competing in a Cournot oligopoly. Under an R&D agreement firms in member countries share the costs of R&D, implying that those firms reduce their marginal and average production costs compared to firms in non-member countries. The lower the spillovers of R&D to outsiders, the higher the degree of excludability and the larger the competitive advantage of firms in member countries over firms in non-member countries. Also, in a trade agreement firms in member countries have a competitive advantage over outsiders. Barrett assumes that trade with non-participants is completely banned whereas in Finus and Rundshagen participants can only impose an external tariff on non-participants and plant location of firms is endogenous. Thus cooperation is easier in Barrett's model since the degree of excludability is higher and since firms cannot leave their country if they face high environmental standards in their home country. The central findings of all models may be summarized as follows.

Result 3

1. Increasing the participation in an IEA via the linkage to a club-good agreement may be a successful policy (for example, Barrett, 1997c and Katsoulacos, 1997).
2. Issue linkage may not achieve full participation (for example, Carraro and Siniscalco, 1997 and 1998).
3. In some cases issue linkage reduces the participation in an IEA and global welfare (Carraro and Siniscalco, 1997 and Finus and Rundshagen, 2000).

Though there are many forces at work in the various models, the intuition of the results is the following (Carraro, 1997; Carraro and Marchiori, 2001; Finus, 2002a). Issue linkage implies that the two conditions for internal and external stability in each of the isolated games reduce to two conditions in the linked game, and stability depends exclusively on the aggregate payoff countries receive in the two isolated games. Consequently, participation in the linked agreement cannot be lower but also not higher than in any of the isolated games. Thus, parts 1 and 2 of Result 3 represent the 'classical' case where participation in the linked agreement is at least as high as in the IEA since participation in the club-good agreement is higher than in the IEA. Full participation in the club-good agreement may not be obtained (and therefore also not in the linked agreement) due to diminishing returns of holding a club membership, which decrease with the number of participants. For instance, consider an R&D agreement. Though cooperation initially increases profits of firms in countries belonging to the agreement, the more countries participate in the R&D agreement, the more competition will increase and profits eventually shrink at some participation rate. If the returns of holding a membership in the club-good agreement decrease sufficiently fast, participation in the club-good agreement and therefore also in the linked agreement may be lower than in the IEA, which is part 3 of Result 3.

From an applied point of view, it seems that the models capture the empirical evidence presented in section 2.2 quite well. However, in reality, membership will be mixed and it will be more difficult to exclude countries from a trade agreement or defence pact if they do not join an IEA. Moreover, the positive effects may be overestimated, since in the context of many countries issue linkage may involve time-consuming negotiations. From a theoretical point of view, four issues for future research come to mind. First, previous results in subsection 3.3.2 and the discussion of Hoel and Schneider's model in section 3.3.4 suggest that high participation does not necessarily imply high global welfare and vice versa. Moreover, even if issue linkage raises participation from the perspective of the IEA, it may lower participation from the perspective of the club-good agreement. Hence, more attention should be devoted to measuring carefully the success of issue linkage. Second, all papers (except Finus and Rundshagen, 2000) derive their results from simulations and therefore results should be generalized. Some guidance in this direction is provided in Carraro (1997) and Carraro and Marchiori (2001), who classify valuation functions of isolated and linked games according to their functional forms. Some hints may also be found in the following. Third, the intuitive explanation that the success of issue linkage is due to the exclusivity of the club-good agreement may be misleading since it suggests that there are no externalities between participants and non-participants under the club-good agreement. One obvious negative externality imposed by participants on non-participants is that in all models production of firms in non-member countries is substituted for production of firms in member countries. However, there is also a positive externality, since cooperation in an oligopoly implies that firms in member countries can raise their profits by reducing production from which firms in non-member countries also benefit through higher prices. Therefore, I suggest classifying games as positive or negative externality games for which some general properties and results have been established in the 'new coalition theory' literature (see subsection 3.3.6, in particular note 62). Although an IEA is unambiguously a positive externality game, for club-good agreements the evidence may be mixed. Nevertheless, it may be possible to show that for those parameter values where the club-good agreement is a negative externality game, issue linkage will unambiguously be a success. Fourth, the very definition of club-good agreements and the construction of the linked game suggest that membership should be exclusive though the definition of internal and external stability implies open membership. Results in Finus and Rundshagen (2000) suggest that when removing this inconsistency the effect of issue linkage may be less positive. However, more research is needed on the effect of the rules of membership on the success of issue linkage. The next subsection and the literature cited in note 62 may provide some inspiration for this task.

3.3.6   New coalition theory

I include in the term 'new coalition theory' recently developed coalition games and equilibrium concepts but also new interpretations of old concepts in the context of the valuation function. One general conclusion of this literature is that economic problems can be categorized as positive and negative externality games and that most results of the first category are reversed for the second category of games. In positive externality games (formation of IEAs or cartels in a Cournot oligopoly) outsiders benefit if

other players form coalitions or if coalitions merge, and in negative externality games (formation of customs unions and joint ventures) this is
reversed.[62] For each category general properties can be derived, applying to
a large group of payoff functions, which allow us to determine equilibrium
coalition structures under more general conditions than in previous sections. Another general conclusion is that the rules of coalition formation
and the equilibrium concept, applied to determine the outcome of a game,
should be clearly distinguished for analytical reasons but also in order to
derive sound policy recommendations (Finus, forthcoming). In the following I report on some selective findings in the context of IEAs and refer the
reader for details of assumptions and proofs to Carraro (2000), Carraro
and Marchiori (2002) and Finus and Rundshagen (2001a, b, c, 2002).

As a starting point, assume the following rules of coalition formation:
all countries simultaneously announce their decision for membership;
countries can only form one coalition but membership is open to all countries. Suppose that a coalition structure is stable if decisions are mutually
best responses and no country has an incentive unilaterally to change its
decision. In new coalition theory, this is called a Nash equilibrium in a
simultaneous open membership single coalition game and, obviously, corresponds to the 'old' definition of an I&E-S coalition structure. Note that
under the 'new' terminology the rules of coalition formation and the equilibrium concept are clearly distinguished from each other whereas they are
included in one definition under the 'old' terminology.

The role of multiple coalitions   If coalition formation is not restricted to one
coalition, multiple coalitions emerge in equilibrium. This is for instance true
in Yi and Shin's (1995) open membership game, which is identical to the
simultaneous open membership single coalition game mentioned above,
except that it does not restrict coalition formation to one coalition, but also
operates for other multiple-coalition games. A multiple-coalition structure
does not necessarily imply that coalitions are larger (because of internal
instability) but that some singletons form their own coalition – a result
confirmed by Bauer's model (section 3.3.3). This leads to lower global
emissions, larger global welfare and larger individual welfare of countries.
Comparing the theoretical results with the empirical finding that all IEAs
constitute single agreements, two controversial conjectures come to mind.
First, if existing IEAs are the result of an unrestricted coalition formation
process, then the predictions of the models are wrong. One reason may be that
some assumptions of the models (for example, joint welfare maximization)
do not reflect important aspects of real treaty making, although it should be
pointed out that the results are very robust to different specifications of the
rules of coalition formation. Second, if coalition formation has been

restricted for institutional and/or political reasons in the past, this suggests that the rules should be altered in the future. For instance, under the Kyoto Protocol the USA insisted that it would only ratify the treaty if developing countries also acceded to this agreement. Thus it may be the case that more could have been achieved if separate agreements had been designed for industrialized countries, developing countries and countries in transition. This last remark points to the possibility of reconciling both conjectures. Taking a broader perspective, some modern IEAs, as for instance the Montreal Protocol, may be interpreted as separate agreements under the umbrella of one treaty since they impose differentiated abatement obligations on participants. Nevertheless, more research is needed to construct models that make a close link between the assumptions of theory and real institutional arrangements under existing IEAs.

The role of exclusive membership   Any coalition structure which is stable under open membership is also stable under exclusive membership rules but not vice versa. This is not only true for single- but also for multiple-coalition games and also if multiple instead of only single deviations are considered. The reason is simple. Any coalition structure is subject to the same amount of possible deviations, except that in exclusive membership games a country or group of countries cannot join another coalition if the members reject their application.[63] Usually, at least some of those additional equilibria under exclusive membership lead to a large degree of cooperation, implying lower global emissions and higher global welfare. The theoretical superiority of the exclusive over the open membership rule contrasts with the empirical evidence on the protocols of all major past IEAs, which have no provision that restricts membership. This suggests that it may also be worthwhile to adopt an exclusive membership rule, which is typical of club agreements, for the public-good IEA in future treaties.

The role of consensus   There is a set of simultaneous exclusive membership games that differ in the degree of consensus needed to form a coalition (Δ- and Γ-game of Hart and Kurz, 1983 and H-game of Finus and Rundshagen, 2002). However, here consensus does not mean agreement on abatement levels but agreement on the selection of coalition members. It appears that any coalition structure that is stable under a lower degree of consensus is also stable under a higher degree of consensus but not vice versa. Roughly speaking, the higher the degree of consensus, the harsher the implicit punishment if agreement fails. Typically, those additional equilibria are coalition structures with a higher degree of cooperation, implying lower global emissions and higher global as well as individual welfare. Thus, although it is usually argued that the need for consensus within international organizations and governments implies that only unambitious policies can be implemented, in the present context consensus is conducive to cooperation.

Internal and external stability versus core: a new interpretation As pointed out above, the rules of coalition formation of I&E-S imply simultaneous choice of membership, a single coalition, open membership, and hence no consensus with respect to membership is needed to form coalitions. The rules are represented by the simultaneous open membership single coalition game. The equilibrium concept is that of a Nash equilibrium considering only single deviations. In Finus and Rundshagen (2002) it is shown that the γ-core can also be classified according to the new terminology. The rules imply simultaneous choice of membership, multiple coalitions, exclusive membership and high degree of consensus. A representation in the context of the valuation function approach is called a simultaneous exclusive membership H-coalition game. The equilibrium concept is that of a strong Nash equilibrium, considering multiple deviations, if the stability check is extended to all coalition structures and not restricted to the grand coalition. Hence, I&E-S and γ-core differ in the equilibrium concept and in three rules of coalition formation. Consequently, in order to isolate effects, it is important to construct a sequence of coalition games where each game in this sequence differs only in one rule with respect to the previous game, covering the entire spectrum between I&E-S and γ-core and to determine equilibrium coalition structures by applying the same equilibrium concept (either Nash equilibrium or strong Nash equilibrium, but it could also be another equilibrium concept). This allows us to attribute different results to different rules of coalition formation. Hence, based on the discussion above, we are not surprised that the higher degree of cooperation under the γ-core (see subsection 3.2.2) than under I&E-S (see subsections 3.3.2 to 3.3.4) is due to the possibility of forming multiple coalitions, exclusive membership and a high degree of consensus necessary to form coalitions. The exercise also stresses my previous claim that the difference between cooperative and non-cooperative game theory is not the difference between the assumption of making binding agreements and non-binding agreements. The difference is the tool, which has been levelled out by using the valuation function also for the core, and the foci, which has been levelled out by extending the stability analysis of the core to all coalition structures (Finus, forthcoming).

The role of equilibrium concepts Two extensions to capture the possibility of not only single but also multiple deviations are the concepts of a strong Nash equilibrium and a coalition-proof Nash equilibrium (Aumann, 1959; Bernheim et al., 1987), where the latter concept is more sophisticated since it allows only deviations which are self-enforcing. Apart from the fact that these extensions are theoretically more convincing than the concept of a Nash equilibrium, they have the advantage that they reduce the amount of equilibria in multi-coalition games considerably. Another mode of extension is Chwe's (1994) concept of a farsighted equilibrium.[64] A coalition structure is 'farsighted stable' if countries have no incentive to form any other coalition structure, taking all possible counter-reactions of other countries into account. Since this concept does not specify the sequence and direction of deviations, it turned out to be too difficult in practice, and more pragmatic concepts have been developed. One is Ray and Vohra's (1997) equilibrium binding agreement. Roughly speaking, this considers a given coalition structure and checks whether countries have an incentive to break apart, taking into account that this may trigger further deviations. Though their concept assumes multiple coalitions, exclusive membership of the Δ-type, it can be applied to almost any other type of coalition game (Carraro and Machiori, 2002; Ecchia and Mariotti, 1997; Eyckmans, 2000 and 2001; Rundshagen, 2002). The implications are best explained in the context of I&E-S (Carraro and Moriconi, 1998). Assume payoff function of type 1 in Table 3.2 for which it is known that any coalition larger than three members is not internally stable. However, suppose that five countries form a coalition. Then each member knows that if it leaves the coalition a second country will follow suit. Thus, if a member's payoff is higher than the payoff it would receive as a non-member if three countries form a coalition, a coalition of five countries will be farsighted stable. By repeating this procedure it can be shown that a coalition of eight countries is stable since a deviation would trigger an additional two deviations until only five members are left. Thus, if governments took a farsighted instead of a myopic view of international pollution control, cooperation would be more successful. On the one hand, this is not a very surprising result and it seems that the concept overestimates the visionary character of governments. On the other hand, this concept models reactions after a deviation in a consistent and best-reply fashion, different from I&E-S and the γ-core where membership is not revised or the entire coalition breaks apart.[65]

The role of sequential coalition formation   Bloch's (1995, 1996) sequential move unanimity game assumes that an initiator proposes a coalition. If all prospective members accept, the remaining countries may form coalitions on their own. If a government rejects a proposal, it can make a new one. A stable coalition structure follows from a sequence of accepted proposals. The advantage of this game is that it captures an important feature of actual coalition formation, which rarely happens in a one-shot fashion (see section 2.1). It also captures farsightedness since any government making a proposal must anticipate the reaction of prospective members but also of outsiders. Moreover, it captures an interesting strategic and commitment problem: any country would like to remain a singleton while all other countries form a coalition but has to take into account that if other governments follow a similar strategy this may lead to an inferior outcome. The only disadvantage of this game is that, due to its complexity, theoretical results can only be established for special assumptions (Bloch, 1997 and Finus and Rundshagen, 2001c).

4 COMPLIANCE MODELS

4.1 Introduction

Studying the conditions of compliance with treaty obligations is only interesting in a non-cooperative game theoretical setting where there is a time lag between violation (second type of free-riding) and discovery through other participants. This requires a payoff structure with discrete time intervals and hence only difference and repeated games are potential candidates for C-models.[66] Theoretically, difference games are superior to repeated games since they not only capture strategic but also structural dependence. In practice, this relation is reversed since difference games are very complex and few general results are available.[67] Therefore, the literature on IEAs has exclusively focused on repeated games where the applied literature restricted attention to supergames (infinite time horizon).[68] In these games only three phases are strategically relevant (Abreu, 1986, 1988): cooperative, free-rider and punishment phase. An IEA is called stable if the incentive to free-ride can be controlled by threats to punish deviations. The exact notion of stability depends on the equilibrium concept; the most important are displayed in Table 3.3. The entries in a particular row imply additional aims, features and conditions to those listed in the rows above. In the remainder of this section, I first discuss important variables for stability and then illustrate and evaluate different equilibrium concepts. I abstract from transfers and discuss their implications in section 4.2.

Important variables for stability are discount factors, cooperative and punishment emission levels (Finus, 2002a). The discount factor, $0 \leq \delta_i \leq 1$, by which payoffs are discounted is defined as $\delta_i = p_i/(1 + r_i)$, with $0 \leq p_i \leq 1$ the (subjective) probability that the game is continuous and r_i the discount rate or time preference rate (Gibbons, 1992, p. 90 and Osborne and Rubinstein, 1994, p. 135). The probability p_i justifies analysing compliance of IEAs in supergames since those treaties typically do not specify the termination of a treaty, and therefore the end of the game is not known with certainty ($p_i > 0$). The larger the discount factor δ_i, that is, the larger the

Table 3.3   Equilibrium refinements in supergames

Equilibrium	Aim	Main feature	Condition
NE	Deterrence to free-riding during cooperation	Compliance during cooperative phase is a best reply	Discounted payoff from cooperation is larger than taking a free-ride and subsequently being punished
SPE	Deterrence to free-riding during punishment	Compliance during punishment phase is a best reply	Discounted payoff from punishment is larger than taking a free-ride and subsequently being punished
WRPE	Deterrence to renegotiating conditions of punishment	Compliance during the repentance phase is a best reply	Free-rider: discounted payoff from repentance is larger than punishment Punishers: discounted payoff from repentance is larger than cooperation
SRPE	Deterrence to renegotiating conditions of cooperation	Selection of efficient WRPE agreements	Discounted payoff from cooperation is not Pareto-dominated by any other WRPE agreement
SSPE	Avoidance of inefficient components of a contract	Selection of efficient SRPE with efficient punishment	Discounted payoff in each phase is not Pareto-dominated by any other possible agreement

Notes: NE = Nash equilibrium; SPE = subgame-perfect equilibrium; WRPE and SRPE = weakly and strongly renegotiation-proof equilibrium; SSPE = strong subgame perfect equilibrium.

probability p_i and the lower the discount rate r_i, the easier it is to enforce compliance since future payoffs from cooperation receive more weight compared to short-term gains from free-riding and subsequent punishment. The lower are own emissions and those of other signatories during cooperation, the larger will be the free-rider incentive. The harsher the punishment, that is, the longer punishment lasts and the lower the payoff during the punishment phase, the easier it is to sustain compliance. However, punishment must be credible to be deterrent. Hence a necessary condition for compliance is that each participant receive an average discounted payoff from cooperation exceeding that during punishment.

A typical subgame-perfect equilibrium (SPE) punishment is the suspension of an IEA. This is credible as long as all participants receive more than in the no-treaty situation: non-cooperative emissions are by definition mutually best replies in any stage t (see section 2.3) and therefore also if chosen continuously. Therefore not only does the punished country go along with the punishment but also the punishers, since otherwise they are subject to punishment. A weakly renegotiation-proof equilibrium (WRPE) captures the notion that threats of punishment implying a lower payoff to punishers than during cooperation are subject to renegotiations and therefore lose their credibility. If defection occurred, it would be in the interest of all countries to treat bygones as bygones and punishment not be carried out. Consequently, the suspension of an IEA is no longer a feasible threat and more sophisticated punishment strategies are needed. This requires in particular that the punished country reduce emissions below cooperative emissions, which raises payoffs to punishers above cooperative levels. The trick is that the free-rider prefers repentance to retaliation so that all countries can return to normal terms after some time. Thus punishment cannot be too harsh and cannot last too long but should also not be too weak since otherwise free-riding would pay in the first place. A strong renegotiation-proof equilibrium (SRPE) also requires that countries agree on an efficient IEA, so that there is no incentive to switch to another agreement. That is, an IEA is not only internally but also externally stable. Finally, a strong subgame-perfect Nash equilibrium (SSPE) requires that in each phase efficient strategies are played, which implies that countries agree not only on efficient emission ceilings but also that punishment is conducted efficiently.[69]

In C-models the notion of profitable agreements is not directly captured since it is assumed that if punishment can deter free-riding, countries join an IEA. However, imposing an appropriate upper bound on punishment emission levels (for example, *status quo* emissions), this notion can be captured indirectly because then compliance only holds if each country receives a higher payoff from cooperation than in the *status quo*. Whether and how the notion of consensus treaties is captured depends on the specifics of the models and will be apparent from the subsequent discussion. The way in which the notion of self-enforcing treaties is captured improves along the sequence of equilibrium refinements, though the requirement for efficient punishments in an SSPE seems unduly restrictive for practical purposes. The notion of renegotiation-proof equilibrium nicely captures the difficulties in reality of imposing sanctions. It explains why most IEAs have either no provisions for sanctions or that sanctions have hardly been imposed in the past. Moreover, it allows us to evaluate the punishment strategies agreed upon in Marrakesh under the Kyoto Protocol (see section 2.2).

The requirement of an additional 30 per cent emission reduction in the second commitment period 2013–17 might be a successful threat to enforce compliance. This punishment would compensate punishers and – given that parties can leave the protocol after informing the secretariat three years in advance – seems short enough so that the free-rider goes along with the punishment instead of leaving the IEA. However, the exclusion from the permit trading system may be a less successful punishment strategy. For instance, if the free-rider is Russia (Japan) – a potential seller (buyer) of permits – this measure may imply a loss to the punisher, the permit buyers (sellers), violating a fundamental condition of renegotiation-proof punishment. Finally, note that all concepts consider only single deviations. However, this seems less problematic since all papers assume that coalition formation is restricted to a single coalition. Hence free-riding is most attractive for a single country and if other countries do not follow suit.[70]

4.2   TRANSFERS

Introducing transfers in a C-model implies that there is a free-rider incentive between donor and recipients (Finus, 2002a) and within the group of donors (Barrett, 1994a). The first incentive is captured by assuming that transfers are only used to balance asymmetric payoffs between donors and recipients. Compared to the case of no transfers, this assumption has the following implications: a donor country receives a lower payoff during cooperation and it will not only expand emissions but will also suspend transfer payments if it free-rides. However, the only punishment against a donor remains emissions. Consequently, compliance will be more difficult to enforce. In contrast, a recipient country receives a higher payoff during cooperation and the suspension of transfer provides an additional punishment tool. Hence, compliance will be easier to enforce. Thus, if there is an abundance of enforcement power on the side of donors and a lack on the side of recipients, transfers can increase the chances for cooperation. They are an ideal instrument to sanction developing countries as regards renegotiation-proofness, as developed under the Montreal Protocol (see section 2.2): suspension of transfers provides donors with an additional gain during punishment. Does this result also hold for in-kind transfers? Yes, but only partially. On the one hand, in-kind transfers, like the installation of clean technology in developing countries, reduce the free-rider incentive between donors and recipients. Recipients cannot abuse in-kind transfers for other purposes and donors will only enjoy the benefits from transfers when they have completed the project. On the other hand, in-kind transfers are a less flexible tool for sanctioning developing countries since they usually cannot be retrieved. Thus, given that in-kind transfers have been more frequently used than monetary transfers (see section 2.2), this suggests that in reality either the net advantage of in-kind transfers is higher than of monetary transfers or the possibility of using monetary transfers to enforce compliance of developing countries has only recently been discovered. However, given that theory draws a generally positive picture of the role of transfers, there remains the question of why both types of transfers have rarely been used in the past. The answer is simple: though transfers are globally rational, individually, each donor is better off not paying transfers – a phenomenon captured in Barrett (1994a).

In his 'biodiversity supergame' Barrett assumes symmetric industrialized countries, which contribute to an environmental fund, buying biological conservation from developing countries. Hence payments represent the input in the production of the public good 'biodiversity'. Industrialized countries receive benefits from total payments, where benefits increase at a decreasing rate. Costs from individual payments increase at an increasing rate. Thus the structure of this game is identical to a global emission game with payoff function of type 2, except that strategies are not emissions but monetary contributions (see Barrett, 1994b below). Barrett checks the SSPE stability of the grand coalition, assuming discount factors close to one and socially optimal contributions. From his simulations he concludes that only if the number of contributors is sufficiently small can free-riding be deterred. For those parameter values where the difference in welfare between social optimum and Nash equilibrium is large, the grand coalition will not be stable and vice versa. Thus his model illustrates the public-good nature of transfers by capturing the free-rider incentive within the group of donor countries. Moreover, interestingly, his result is similar to that obtained in the context of M-models in section 3.3.2. It is evident that some of his assumptions over- and some underestimate stability problems. For instance, if compliance within a large group of contributors and of socially optimal levels cannot be enforced, it may nevertheless be possible to establish a fund involving more moderate contributions among a smaller group of contributors. Also the assumption of efficient punishment may be unduly restrictive. In contrast, the free-rider incentive between industrialized and developing countries is not captured and the assumption of discount factors close to one provides the most favourable conditions for stability. The deficiencies of the models of Barrett and Finus suggest constructing a model that simultaneously captures the free-rider incentive between donors and recipients and within the group of donor countries.

4.3   Grand Coalition

Barrett (1994b) and Finus and Rundshagen (1998b) analyse stability of the grand coalition in a theoretical and Finus and Tjøtta (forthcoming) and Mäler (1994) in an empirical model. Since not only the assumptions and structure but also the results in Barrett's (1994a) global emission and Barrett's (1994b) biodiversity supergame are similar, I refer the reader to the discussion above. In their global emission game Finus and Rundshagen (1998b) extend Barrett's analysis in two directions. First, they assume heterogeneous countries as in Hoel (1992), where countries are indexed from 1 to N. Damages increase in this index and the decisive parameters are the number of countries N and the benefit–cost ratio $\gamma = b/c$ from emissions as in the context of M-models (see in particular subsection 3.3.2). Second, they consider two policy regimes: a uniform tax and a uniform emission reduction quota. For each regime they consider three agreement procedures. Countries agree on (a) the globally optimal contract, (b) the median country proposal and (c) country 1's proposal. Country 1's proposal is the smallest of all proposals and thus reflects an agreement on the lowest common denominator. Since a uniform tax is efficient in the context of global pollutants, a globally optimal contract is identical to the social optimum, and the median and lowest country proposal are at least cost-efficient. In contrast, a uniform quota is inefficient and thus even a globally optimal contract is only a constrained optimum. Since Finus and Rundshagen test not only stability of efficient contracts, they apply the WRPE concept. They conduct a large set of simulations for different values of N and $\gamma = b/c$, of which I report only those results for the assumption of discount factor close to one. First, irrespective of the treaty design, the grand coalition is not stable for the critical parameter values (large N and small $\gamma = b/c$; see subsection 3.3.2). Thus, they confirm Barrett's (1994b) result under more general conditions. Second, even for non-critical parameter values (except for very small values of N), neither the agreement on globally optimal policy levels nor on the median country proposal are stable, though the smallest tax and quota proposals may be stable. This emphasizes that a large participation in an IEA is only possible if participants agree on very moderate abatement targets. Third, whenever the smallest tax proposal is stable this is also true for the quota proposal but not vice versa, and, except for small N, the quota proposal leads to higher global welfare and lower global emissions than the tax proposal. This indicates that there may be some rationale behind the frequent application of emission reduction quotas in past IEAs. Though the quota regime is inefficient, it leads to a more symmetric distribution of the gains from cooperation and provides more favourable conditions to critical countries than the tax regime. Consequently, not only can critical countries agree on a higher abatement target, which makes up for the inherent inefficiency of the quota regime, but also stability is less of a problem.

Mäler (1994) and Finus and Tjøtta (forthcoming) analyse the acid rain game – a term coined by Mäler (1989) – based on benefit and damage cost functions of sulphur emissions for all major European countries, including all states of the former Soviet Union. Mäler's data cover the time before the first sulphur protocol (Helsinki 1985), whereas Finus and Tjøtta's data are related to the second protocol (Oslo 1994). Both papers compute socially optimal emissions and find that they imply large welfare gains compared to non-cooperative emissions but that they are not self-enforcing without transfers. For instance, the UK receives only a low payoff since, as a down-wind and low-abatement-cost country, it has to contribute a great deal to a socially optimal contract but benefits only little from emission reductions. However, both papers draw different conclusions from this result. Mäler assumes in a second step that the gains in the social optimum are shared equally among all participants through transfers and that the probability that the game continues is one ($p_i = 1$). He finds that if the former Soviet Union discounts payoffs by not more than 19 per cent it will comply and for most other countries this critical discount rate is much higher. Mäler concludes that it should not be a problem to implement a socially optimal contract and therefore he argues that the supergame approach cannot contribute much to a positive analysis of actual IEAs. However, it seems that he makes four assumptions that lead to an underestimation of stability problems. First, in reality p_i will be lower than one. Second, neither the Helsinki nor the Oslo Protocol makes provision for transfers. Third, Mäler tests stability with a simple SPE-trigger strategy, which does not satisfy the requirement of renegotiation-proof punishment. Fourth, he calibrates linear damage cost functions, implying orthogonal reaction functions, and hence low free-rider incentives. Moreover, concluding that a model lacks explanatory power seems premature without benchmarking the social optimum against the actual agreement.

This is the motivation for Finus and Tjøtta to test WRPE stability, assuming quadratic damage cost functions as well as no transfers, and benchmarking the Oslo Protocol against the socially optimal contract and the non-cooperative equilibrium. This implies computing annual emissions and welfare under three scenarios for the target year 2000 of this protocol, where the non-cooperative equilibrium may be interpreted as the business-as-usual scenario (BAU). Finus and Tjøtta find that agreed emission ceilings under the Oslo Protocol, though they are stable, are close to or even higher than BAU emissions, and substantially higher than socially optimal emissions. Since the Oslo ceilings would imply a welfare loss for some participants compared to BAU, the authors conclude that the Oslo Protocol is not, as commonly claimed, the great leap forward and that there is an incentive for participants to overfulfil the terms of this IEA in their self-interest, as has been observed under the Helsinki Protocol (see section 2.1). Due to this negative result, Finus and Tjøtta investigate whether more ambitious abatement targets could have been realized in a self-enforcing IEA. They show that, even for discount factors close to one, the maximal self-enforcing abatement level only marginally exceeds the BAU scenario. They suggest that free-rider problems are the main obstacle to implementing more ambitious abatement targets. However, they do not analyse the formation of subcoalitions and multiple agreements, which, given previous and subsequent results, might lead to more optimistic findings.

4.4   Subcoalitions

The central question of this section is whether subcoalitions can achieve more than the grand coalition. Barrett (2000) analyses this question assuming symmetric countries, global pollution, no discounting and WRPE strategies. He considers two types of treaties. In the consensus treaty all countries participate and choose the maximal emission reduction that is self-enforcing. In the focal treaty only a subgroup of countries form a coalition. They choose emission reductions that maximize the payoff to their coalition. The equilibrium number of participants is the maximum number of countries for which the focal treaty is stable. Countries will implement the consensus treaty if the expected welfare is higher than under the focal treaty and vice versa. Barrett considers two specific payoff functions. For the first function he finds that countries always prefer a consensus treaty over a focal treaty. For the second function this is only true for two conditions: (a) cost and benefit parameters implying that only few countries participate in the focal treaty and (b) large number of countries affected by global pollution. The specific assumptions and the mixed evidence suggest that more research is needed to derive more general conclusions. Moreover, result (b) indicates that the assumption of symmetric countries overestimates the superiority of the consensus treaty. Intuition suggests that if countries have heterogeneous interests, it will be particularly difficult to enforce and to agree on ambitious abatement targets among a large number of countries and therefore the formation of subcoalitions should be more attractive than the grand coalition. This intuition is confirmed in the paper by Finus and Rundshagen (1998b) discussed in the previous section.

Finus and Rundshagen assume a sequential coalition formation process where participants have to agree simultaneously on the level and kind of policy instrument and the members of an IEA. Within a coalition each country makes a tax or quota proposal, participants agree on the smallest proposal, decide by majority voting which of the two proposals is adopted and decide either by majority or unanimity whether new members are asked for participation. Those countries with the highest environmental preference kick off coalition formation, which are countries N and $N-1$. Based on their preliminary agreement, they decide whether to expand their coalition. Three factors determine the equilibrium agreement. First, expanding the coalition implies fewer free-riders and that more countries can shoulder abatement. Second, additional participants imply that it is more difficult to agree on ambitious abatement targets. As long as the first dominates the second effect, the coalition is expanded, and the break-even point determines the equilibrium size of the coalition. Third, although the high index initiator countries prefer a tax over a quota regime, they may nevertheless vote for the quota proposal if this implies that more countries join the coalition and that higher abatement targets can be agreed and implemented self-enforcingly. Finus and Rundshagen find that in particular for the critical parameter values (large N and small $\gamma = b/c$; see subsection 3.3.1) a subcoalition achieves more than the grand coalition in terms of global emission reduction and welfare, even assuming that the grand coalition implements not the smallest proposal but the maximal stable emission reduction. As long as N is not very small, participants will agree on a uniform emission quota. Thus the results confirm a finding in the context of M-models, namely that success of an IEA cannot be inferred from the number of participants and small coalitions may achieve more than large coalitions. They are also in line with the empirical evidence that agreements with serious abatement targets always enjoy a lower participation than framework conventions. Therefore, the results support the European strategy under the Kyoto Protocol to achieve an agreement that does not include all countries but does include the most important industrialized countries. Finally, they also provide a rationale for the application of uniform emission reduction quotas in many IEAs despite their inefficiency (see section 2.2).

4.5   ISSUE LINKAGE

In the context of C-models issue linkage has been studied by Bennett et al. (1998), Cesar and de Zeeuw (1996), Folmer et al. (1993), Folmer and van Mouche (1994) and Ragland (1995); an overview is provided in Finus (2001, ch. 8; 2002) and Folmer and van Mouche (2000). The main finding is that issue linkage either improves upon the chances for cooperation or leaves them unchanged.[71] This unambiguously positive conclusion differs from that obtained in M-models. Recall that Result 3, part 3, in subsection 3.3.5 states that issue linkage may also have a negative impact. Of course, this difference could be due to the fact that in M-models the focus is on the strategy membership and stability has been tested with internal and external stability, whereas in C-models the focus is on the strategy emissions and on the second issue and stability is tested with some of the equilibrium concepts listed in Table 3.3. However, I do not believe this is the reason. Despite the danger of oversimplifying, I argue that different conclusions are only due to one trivially different assumption since the driving forces of issue linkage in both frameworks are almost identical. For illustrative purposes, I restrict the discussion to two issues.

Linking two games implies adding the payoffs of the two isolated games and requiring that stability conditions hold for the linked game – an interpretation I have already provided in the context of M-models in subsection 3.3.5. Thus if one or some stability conditions fail in the isolated games, they may be satisfied in the linked game and thus cooperation may become easier. Thus issue linkage implies that countries have more strategies available to achieve cooperation. These additional strategies allow us to balance slack and lack of enforcement power – an interpretation similar to the one I provided for transfers in the context of C-models in subsection 4.2. However, in the context of issue linkage, it is the strategic link between issue 1 and issue 2 which increases the strategic options, whereas in the context of transfers it is the strategic link between issue 1 and transfers. That is, issue linkage balances slack and lack of enforcement power between countries indirectly, whereas transfers do so directly. In any case, in M- and C-models the effect of additional policy options on the overall game can be classified as positive, neutral or negative. Consequently, only in the last case do additional policy options have a negative impact, which is part (c) of Result 3 in the context of M-models and which would also apply to C-models. However, all C-models assume that issue linkage is not used if it has a negative impact.[72]

In the following I provide a list of future research issues. First, most papers motivate the analysis of issue linkage by pointing out that transfers played a minor role in past IEAs. Though this observation is certainly true, it seems that theory does not provide an explanation why countries should prefer issue linkage to transfers. As argued above, there is a close similarity of the incentive structure and the balancing effect of both instruments, but the crucial problem of transfers, namely that there is a free-rider incentive within the group of donor countries (section 4.2), is not captured by the issue linkage models above. In an N-country context, each country is a net donor with respect to some issues and therefore countries have an individual incentive not to offer their preferred issue for compensation. Second, most papers have studied issue linkage assuming SPE strategies and considering prisoner's dilemma type of games. However, considering the simple structure of issue linkage, it should also be possible to establish the main result for more sophisticated equilibrium concepts and for a larger group of games. Some guidance in this direction is provided in Cesar and de Zeeuw (1996) and Finus (2001), who study issue linkage assuming WRPE and SRPE strategies, and in Finus (2002a), who considers general social dilemma types of games. Third, a more difficult and still open question is under which conditions issue linkage strictly improves the chances of cooperation and by how much. That is, what kind of mirror asymmetry in the isolated games is needed for the success of issue linkage (Folmer and van Mouche, 2000)? Fourth, the assumption that payoffs of the isolated games are simply added is very restrictive. One modification is considered in van Mouche (2000), who shows that the main results also apply to additive payoffs with different weights and to any linear transformation of payoffs through issue linkage. A second modification is considered in Spagnolo (1996), who assumes non-separable utility functions in the two issues and shows that only if issues are substitutes in governments' welfare function does issue linkage have a positive effect.[73] Fifth, all papers analyse stability assuming that all countries participate in the linked agreement but do not consider the formation of subcoalitions.

4.6   Evaluation, Extensions and Practical Issues

C-models are an important tool for a positive analysis of IEAs: they nicely illustrate the benefits and problems of transfers, the problems of enforcing ambitious and efficient abatement targets and help to clarify the role of emission quotas and subcoalitions as well as the conditions of effective IEAs. However, all models restrict attention to a single coalition and the issue of membership is captured insufficiently. Due to the nature of C-models, it is assumed that either countries accede to an IEA if it is stable (Barrett, 1994a, b) or some exogenous coalition formation process is constructed, though the one assumed in Finus and Rundshagen (1998a) seems very close to what is going on in actual treaty making. Moreover, all models assume that free-riding is immediately discovered and sanctioned, and that punishments will be optimal in the sense that they are as harsh as possible, given the restrictions on credible punishments. In reality, however, monitoring relies mainly on self-reporting and establishing the link between an increase in global emissions and the depletion of fish stocks, and non-compliance is not always straightforward due to incomplete information and natural fluctuations. Since any violation has to be proved unambiguously by international law before punishment starts, compliance will be more difficult to enforce. Also, punishment faces practical problems. First, coordination of punishment takes time and thus punishment will be delayed. Second, punishment will be simple in reality in order to ensure a high transparency of the rules of sanctions and to keep transaction costs low. Third, once abatement measures have been taken, it will not be that easy for punishers to increase emissions. Assuming that emissions can only be increased marginally above cooperative levels suggests that the more ambitious abatement targets have been implemented in an IEA, the less deterrent punishment becomes. Fourth, it will also be difficult for the punished country to lower emissions below cooperative levels in order to show repentance. Again, the lower emissions are already in the cooperative phase, the more difficult it will be to show repentance. Fifth, considering that the evolvement of an IEA typically implies that emissions standards are sequentially tightened suggests that enforcement of an IEA becomes increasingly difficult over time. Sixth, international law suggests that any misconduct should only be punished in relation to the severity of non-compliance. Although international law is non-binding, it may nevertheless be expected that it provides some guidance to 'good conduct' to countries and therefore restricts punishment in reality.[74]

5.   FINAL REMARKS

M- and C-models capture a different type of free-rider incentive but derive similar results. This is at least true for M-models belonging to non-cooperative game theory. Although I have emphasized the difference between the groups of models, there is also close similarity. If a country leaves a coalition, this may also be interpreted to mean that it does not comply with treaty obligations. Similarly, if a country does not comply with treaty obligations it *de facto* leaves a coalition. Thus it remains for the future to study the relation between both types of models more intensively, as in Barrett (1999b). It also became apparent that there is much work ahead to generalize some results. One important issue is the relation between the design of a treaty and its success. I suggest five routes for future research. First, the conditions under which small coalitions are more successful than large coalitions and when issue linkage is a successful strategy need to be clarified. Second, in the absence of transfers, an optimal abatement allocation rule must be developed, since although joint welfare maximization implies a coalitionally efficient allocation, it does not necessarily guarantee the highest success of a treaty. Third, in the presence of transfers, an optimal scheme must be constructed. This implies establishing whether there are other transfer schemes than the Shapley value or that developed by Chander and Tulkens which lead to more effective IEAs, taking into account the free-rider incentives between donor and recipients but also those within the group of donors. In this context, the question arises whether transfers should be viewed as just an additional strategy or whether the allocation of transfers should be seen as a game in its own right (Folmer and de Zeeuw, 2000). Fourth, the agreement procedure on the design of a treaty should be modelled as an endogenous decision of signatories, taking into account the struggle for consensus. Though this will be a difficult task, some guidance on optimal consensus treaties is provided in Ray and Vohra (1999). However, it would also be important to explain why treaty obligations are often inefficient. Fifth, the preliminary results of new coalition theory (subsection 3.3.6) suggest that research should be intensified to analyse how the rules of coalition formation affect the outcome. It would be interesting to endogenize the choice of rules in order to explain why particular rules have emerged in the past (Carraro et al., 2001) and to analyse which role international institutions can play in shaping these rules (Ecchia and Mariotti, 1998).

It also became evident that some aspects of actual treaty formation are not yet sufficiently captured. I name only four. One aspect is the development of a treaty (Barrett, 1998). Only some papers in the context of the core model the change of emission ceilings over time but not the evolvement of participation since they only consider the grand coalition. A simple extension could be to stick to the assumption of a constant payoff structure over time either as in Chander and Tulkens (1992) or in Germain et al. (1996a, b) but to apply one of the non-cooperative equilibrium concepts used in M-models. A more involved extension could be based on a differential or difference game (structural dependence of payoffs in terms of emissions) with a strategic dependence in terms of emissions and membership. The second extension has been pursued by Rubio and Ulph (2001) and Courtois et al. (2001), where preliminary results indicate that this is a promising route for future research. A second aspect is incomplete information and uncertainty. Although this topic is not new in the economic literature, there is not much work in the context of the formation of IEAs. Since incomplete information and uncertainty may persist in reality with respect to many issues associated with international environmental problems, it should be easy to find new research topics. For incomplete information about emissions possible extensions could for instance be based on work by Avenhaus (1992), Güth and Pethig (1992) and Russell (1992) on incomplete monitoring of emissions, work by Abreu et al. (1986) and Green and Porter (1984) on cartel stability when prices or quantities cannot be observed and work by Fudenberg and Levine (1992) and Fudenberg et al. (1994) on equilibrium concepts capturing incomplete information. For uncertainty, some inspiration may be found by consulting the work of Chichilnisky (2000), Chichilnisky and Heal (1998), Endres and Ohl (2001), Kolstad (2000) and Ulph (1998). A third aspect is to include public choice. All models assume governments' decisions as a black box and abstract from interest groups (Carraro and Siniscalco, 1992 and 1998). The main problem of extension is that in the international context the number of interest groups is N times larger than in the national context and that there may be interaction between groups across borders. Nevertheless, a pragmatic approach could be developed along the lines in Congleton (1996), Endres and Ohl (2002), and Hillman and Ursprung (1994). Moreover, casual empirical evidence tells us that prestige and power are influential factors in negotiations leading to a treaty but also when enforcing a treaty. For instance, it is hardly conceivable that countries sanction the USA for their withdrawal from the Kyoto Protocol, but it is easily conceivable that developing countries could be sanctioned under the Montreal Protocol if they do not join this treaty or do not comply with its terms, either by all participants or unilaterally by the USA if there is no consensus on conducting the punishment. Also, an industrialized country like the Netherlands may be more affected by a loss of prestige if non-compliance is detected than a developing country. The main problem of integrating those aspects in a model is that either the link between assumptions and results is too obvious, as I suggested for the models considering reputation effects in subsection 3.3.4, or that almost any result can be generated. Hence those non-material payoff components should be selected carefully and only introduced into a model if they can be supported empirically. Fourth, almost all models abstract from institutional issues. On the one hand, this applies to local and international organizations that are involved in negotiations but also in the implementation of treaties. On the other hand, this applies to the legal aspects associated with international treaties, as shown in note 3. Of course, international law and game theory take very different perspectives. Nevertheless, it would be fruitful to establish a closer link between both perspectives, which may be an interesting research agenda, in particular for those scholars who are more interested in applications than in hard theory.

Finally, it is also evident that more research is needed to combine game theory and empirical modelling. Particularly fruitful seems an approach that is based on cost–benefit data of general equilibrium models, like some papers in the context of the core, applying concepts and approaches of new coalition theory. This will be a great intellectual challenge since the concepts of game theory will have to be operationalized for empirical analysis, but in my view, will also be one of the most rewarding routes for future research.

NOTES

1. I use this term for environmental problems which are not confined to the boundaries of nations. In the context of pollution, this is referred to as 'transboundary pollution', including (a) spillovers from one nation to another (unilateral spillovers), (b) spillovers from one nation to another and vice versa (bilateral spillovers) and (c) spillovers among several nations and in different directions (multilateral spillovers). 'Global pollution' is a special case of transboundary pollution and refers to 'multilateral uniform spillovers', that is, pollutants (for example, CFCs and greenhouse gases) which mix uniformly in the atmosphere and which affect all nations. For a detailed classification of environmental problems see for instance Mäler (1990) and Siebert (1985).

2. A list of all IEAs mentioned in this chapter, including their objectives and status of membership, is provided in Appendix 1.

3. In international law 'signature' means merely that countries declare their intention to become members of an agreement. Only if countries 'ratify' an agreement (which requires in most democracies the approval of signature by parliament) do they become official members of an agreement. Hence, signatories are only those countries that signed an agreement at the initial stage. Countries that become members at a later stage do not 'sign' but 'accede' to an agreement, where 'accession' implies *de facto* declaration of intention to become a member and ratification at the same time. Signatories which have ratified an agreement and countries which have acceded to an agreement are called 'parties'. Most agreements require a certain number of parties (minimum participation clause) before they come into force (become legally binding for parties but not for signatories, which have not ratified the agreement). For details see http://untreaty.un.org/English/guide.asp. In contrast to the legal jargon, the game-theoretical terminology is less differentiated since most models abstract from the development and the legal status of IEAs (see also note 4). In the game-theoretical literature, a 'signatory' is a country that coordinates its abatement (emission) strategy with other countries within a coalition and 'to accede to a coalition' means to become a signatory. In order to avoid misunderstandings, I will use the legal terms when I provide empirical background information, and the terms 'members' and 'participants' and the phrases 'to join' or 'to become a member of a coalition' in the context of game-theoretical models.

4. In this literature international law is regarded as non-binding since the International Court of Justice can only open a trial if the accused party agrees.

5. Framework conventions (sometimes just called conventions) are IEAs, which only state the general concern of nations about an environmental problem and their intention to deal with it in the future. A framework convention typically precedes an IEA (usually called a protocol) that suggests concrete steps to tackle an environmental problem (for example, emission reductions to be achieved at some future date). Most protocols require that a country first becomes a party to the framework convention before it can become a party to a protocol. However, being a party to a framework convention does not necessarily also imply being a party to a protocol. Amendments comprise changes of or additional provisions to an original protocol and become legally binding only for those countries that ratify the amendments.

6. The Convention on International Trade in Endangered Species of Wild Fauna and Flora (CITES).

7. Moreover, many IEAs have a very poor compliance record with respect to reporting (Bothe, 1996, pp. 22ff.; GAO, 1992, p. 3; and Sand, 1996, p. 55). Since official monitoring of most IEAs relies exclusively on self-reporting of states, some suspicion with respect to the good official compliance records of some IEAs seems to be justified (Ausubel and Victor, 1992, pp. 23ff.).

8. I use the terms 'small' and 'large' for the number of participants in relation to the total number of countries affected by an international environmental problem. Nevertheless, these terms are and probably must remain vague since there is no exact definition.

However, as a benchmark, if more (less) than 50 per cent of the affected countries are members of an IEA, this may be called large (small).

9. Details can be found at http://www.ea.gov.au/about/annual-report/99-00/ozone.html. Note that as long as I do not refer to a specific date of signature, I use the term 'Montreal Protocol' or 'ozone regime' for the Montreal Protocol signed in 1987 and all its amendments.

10. http://www.umwelt-schweiz.ch/imperia/md/content/oekonomie/klima/kyoto/33.pdf.

11. Incremental costs are those that occur in excess of abatement activities compared to the *status quo*. This implies for most developing countries that they just break even compared to the *status quo*.

12. http://www.unmfs.org/documents/3458_E.pdf.

13. See http://www.biodiv.org.

14. Annex 1 (non-Annex 1) countries are signatories that (have not) accepted emission ceilings under the Kyoto Protocol and which comprise mainly industrialized countries (developing countries).

15. See www.unep.ch/ozone/4mop_chp.shtml and www.unep.ch/ozone/6mop_nbo.shtml.

16. For instance, if a developing country does not report baseline data within one year, it is no longer given Article 5 status (Greene, 1998).

17. This happened for the first time in 1995 in the case of Russia, though non-compliance was later 'accused' (Victor, 1998, p. 155).

18. http://www.unfccc.int/cop 7/documents/accords_draft.pdf.

19. Barrett (1997a) was originally a proponent of Chayes and Chayes, but is now more or less in line with my interpretation above (Barrett, 1999a, b).

20. A mathematically rigorous exposition including proofs may be found in Finus (2001), Folmer and van Mouche (2002), van Mouche (2001) and Welsch (1993). The second and third references cover the general case of transboundary pollution, whereas the other references deal only with global pollutants.

21. Equation (3.1) neglects background emissions from natural sources for simplicity.

22. I make the standard assumption of interior solutions throughout the chapter. Corner solutions are discussed for instance in Finus (2001), ch. 9.

23. For instance, in the case of three countries there are five possible coalition structures: $(\{1\},\{2\},\{3\})$; $(\{1,2\},\{3\})$; $(\{1,3\},\{2\})$; $(\{1\},\{2,3\})$ and $(\{1,2,3\})$. The first coalition structure is the singleton coalition structure, the second, third and fourth coalition structures comprise coalitions of two countries and the last coalition structure is the grand coalition.

24. A formal and detailed discussion of best-reply functions and their properties is provided in Appendix 3.2.

25. Note that unconditional cooperative behaviour is not compatible with the notion of rationality.

26. Note that there is a crucial difference between strategic and structural dependence. See also Friedman (1986, p. 72) on this point.

27. I use the terms 'membership models' and 'compliance models' to emphasize the focus of the analysis and to allow for a very general classification of current but also future models. Alternative terms found in the literature in the case of membership models are coalitional games or reduced-stage games and in the case of compliance models repeated games. This terminology stresses more the technical aspect of these models, seems more specific and more closely related to the current state of the art.

28. This is why I did not relate the discussion of the structure of coalition models to co-operative versus non-cooperative game theory.

29. See Bloch (1997) for an excellent survey of the historical development of coalition theory.

30. These terms are due to Tulkens (1998).

31. Whether the non-deviating countries conduct the punishment jointly or individually is not important. This is different for the γ-characteristic function discussed below.

32. The β-characteristic function, $w^{\beta}(P)$, makes a similar assumption, except that coalition members choose first their optimal response strategy and then the remaining countries choose their punishment strategy. Since in the current context (emission game) the

sequence of emission choices has no effect on the worth (that is, $w^\alpha(I^J) = w^\beta(I^J)$, I restrict attention to the α-characteristic function in the following discussion. For details see Chander and Tulkens (1997) and Finus (2001), ch. 13.

33. $w^\alpha(\{i\}) \geq \pi_i(e^{max})$ simply follows from the fact that in $\pi_i(e^{max})$ all countries choose their maximum emissions, whereas in $w^\alpha(\{i\})$ all countries except country i choose these emission levels but country i is free to choose either e_i^{max} or any other emission level in order to maximize its deviation payoff.

34. The following two points may seem 'overcritical' but are due to my ambition for a critical analysis of all assumptions. I will take up these points in subsection 3.3.6. See also the next note.

35. The credibility of sanctions is an important issue in C-models and readers particularly interested in this issue may want to return to this subsection after reading section 4.

36. Recall that in the case of global pollutants all transportation coefficients are one, which explains why they do not appear in equation (3.2).

37. For instance, suppose that for some reason a country does not value environmental damages from global pollution. Hence, $\phi_i' = 0$, and the second term in (3.2) is zero. Thus, if this country reduces its emissions in the social optimum compared to the Nash equilibrium, then it is compensated for its loss of benefits and would therefore break even compared to the *status quo*.

38. Alternatively, the payoff structure may be viewed as a differential game, except that there is no structural dependence of emissions.

39. In Kaitala et al. (1995) stability of the particular example is not proved but it is claimed that the theoretical results of Chander and Tulkens (1991, 1992) apply. This conclusion seems premature given that the assumptions of the transportation coefficients in the latter are less general than in the former.

40. It can be shown that it is a sufficient condition that not only global emissions but also individual emissions of each country are lower in the social optimum than in the Nash equilibrium.

41. Roughly speaking, a local game is the game as it looks at time t for the rest of the game.

42. In the case of linear damage cost functions, as assumed in Germain et al. (1998a) and Germain et al. (1998b), reaction functions are orthogonal, implying that countries choose their non-cooperative emission strategies independently of those of other countries (dominant strategy) and hence there is no strategic independence anyway.

43. In the case of closed-loop strategies they consider Markov perfect strategies: at each point in time, strategies in the local games are chosen according to the present state (stock of pollutants) and must constitute a best reply (Nash equilibrium) for the rest of the game.

44. This may be interpreted as some weak form of strategic dependence of membership: membership can be revised at each point in time. However, there is no full dependence since decisions are not related to previous membership strategies.

45. This includes the trivial case of a coalition comprising only one member (singleton).

46. The similarity derives from the fact that a coalition reducing emissions (output) has not only a positive effect on coalition members but also on outsiders via a reduction of global emission (aggregate output), which reduces damages (increases the market price).

47. In some papers (for example, Carraro, 1997 and Carraro and Siniscalco, 1998) profitability is stated as an extra condition, though it is weaker than the condition of internal stability (Finus and Rundshagen, 2001b, 2002).

48. Note 34 applies. See also the remark in note 35.

49. See Appendix 3.2 for more background information on the properties of best-reply functions.

50. Leakage effects have been studied in the energy market by Bohm (1993), Felder and Rutherford (1993) and Golombek et al. (1995). Countervailing measures are discussed in Bohm and Larsen (1993) and Hoel (1994).

51. All results of this section are proved in Finus (2001, ch. 13). Note that for other payoff functions of types 1 and 2, the number of participants will be different, though small compared to N. For any payoff function of type 3 the result of Table 3.2 holds.

52. Internal stability follows from the fact that in the case of symmetric countries any

externally unstable coalition of $n - 1$ countries implies an internally stable coalition of n countries (see subsection 3.3.4 for details). Thus, if the coalition of $N - 1$ countries is externally unstable, the grand coalition must be internally stable. Trivially, the grand coalition is always externally stable since there are no outsiders. Of course, the grand coalition cannot assume a Stackelberg leader position since no followers are left and all members simply maximize aggregate payoffs to all coalition members. For details see Finus (2001), ch. 13.

53. I measure the degree of externality in relative (Finus and Rundshagen, 1998b) and not in absolute terms (Barrett, 1994b) since this index applies to a large group of payoff functions.

54. Of course, only in a model can N be regarded as a parameter; it is fixed in reality.

55. This assumption may be defended as follows. First, by varying the parameter γ, any value of the slope of the best-reply function between -1 and 0 (including the bench-mark case -1 ($\gamma \to 0$) and 0 ($\gamma \to \infty$)) can be captured. Second, in both agreements participants assume a strong position compared to non-participants. Under the Montreal Protocol participants have the possibility of sanctioning non-participants through trade measures, and the participants (non-participants) of the Kyoto Protocol comprise all important industrialized countries (developing countries). Of course, the withdrawal of the USA from the Kyoto Protocol has changed the balance of power, which would also justify the Nash–Cournot assumption. The reader is encouraged to interpret the empirical evidence under the Nash–Cournot assumption in the case of the Kyoto Protocol.

56. This is not to say that emission reductions under the Montreal Protocol are not large, but simply that they more or less reflect what countries would have done anyway by pursuing a non-cooperative strategy on their own.

57. Those countries with a higher payoff in the Nash equilibrium receive a higher weight since they have a better bargaining position should negotiations break down. For details on the Nash bargaining solution and the Shapley value see, for instance, Eichberger (1993).

58. Of course, the Stackelberg assumption is only relevant in the case of payoff function of type 2. See subsection 3.3.2.

59. Petrakis and Xepapadeas (1996) also consider the moral hazard problem of transfer if emissions of bribed countries cannot be completely observed. See also Hübner and Dröttboom (1999) on this problem.

60. Jeppesen and Andersen (1998) assume symmetric countries, payoff function of type 2, participants acting as Stackelberg leaders whereas Hoel and Schneider (1997) assume that countries differ with respect to the disutility of being a non-participant and a payoff function of type 1, which renders the distinction between Nash–Cournot and Stackelberg assumption irrelevant (see subsection 3.3.2).

61. I do not include Kroeze-Gil and Folmer (1998) in the review since it is the only contribution in the context of M-models that is based on the characteristic function and applies core-stability.

62. For excellent surveys, including many examples of industrial economics and trade theory, see Bloch (1997) and Yi (1997, 1999). All concepts of these surveys are illustrated in the context of IEAs in Finus (2001, ch. 15).

63. Recall the example of Botteon and Carraro (1997) discussed in section 3.3.4 under the heading '*Ex ante* transfers'.

64. Modifications of Chwe's original definition are discussed in Mariotti (1997).

65. See the evaluation of these concepts in subsections 3.2.1 and 3.3.1.

66. In differential games non-compliance is immediately discovered and sanctioned. Therefore, only the play of non-cooperative strategies at each point in time can be self-enforcing. For an introduction to differential games in the context of IEAs, see de Zeeuw (1998) and for applications Kaitala et al. (1992), Mäler and de Zeeuw (1998) and Tahvonen (1994).

67. For an excellent introduction to difference games see de Zeeuw and van der Ploeg (1991).

68. A discussion of finite repeated games is provided in Finus (2001).

69. The Nash equilibrium goes back to Nash (1950). The subgame-perfect equilibrium was invented by Selten (1965). The concept of weak and strong renegotiation-proof equilibrium that has been applied in the literature on IEAs goes back to Farrell and Maskin (1989), though other scholars have developed similar concepts. The concept of a strong subgame-perfect equilibrium was formalized for dynamic games by Rubinstein (1980). For a full account of all concepts and modifications see Finus (2001) and the literature cited there.
70. Only Stähler (1996) extends the notion of a WRPE to multiple deviations. However, he restricts attention to three countries, which makes his model less suitable for studying coalition formation.
71. This positive effect can be measured in many ways. For details see Finus (2002a).
72. A similar line of reasoning can be applied to explain the difference between the positive role of transfers in all M-models discussed in section 3, except in Hoel and Schneider's model.
73. The practical implications are discussed in Finus (2001, ch. 8 and 2002a).
74. The monitoring issues and the first four punishment issues can easily be accommodated in a standard model (Finus, 2001, ch. 12; 2002 and Finus and Rundshagen, 1998a). The last two punishment issues require departing from the assumption of stationary strategies and standard punishment profiles (Finus, 2001, ch. 12).

REFERENCES

Abreu, D. (1986), 'Extremal Equilibrium of Oligopolistic Supergames', *Journal of Economic Theory*, **39**, 191–225.
Abreu, D. (1988), 'On the Theory of Infinitely Repeated Games with Discounting', *Econometrica*, **56**, 383–96.
Abreu, D., D. Pearce and E. Stacchetti (1986), 'Optimal Cartel Equilibrium with Imperfect Monitoring', *Journal of Economic Theory*, **39**, 251–69.
Aumann, R. (1959), 'Acceptable Points in General Cooperative N-Person Games', in A.N. Tucker and R.D. Luce (eds), *Contributions to the Theory of Games, Vol. IV, (Annals of Mathematics Studies 40)*, Princeton, NJ: Princeton University Press, 287–324.
Ausubel, J.H. and D.G. Victor (1992), 'Verification of International Environmental Agreements', *Annual Review of Energy and Environment*, **17**, 1–43.
Avenhaus, R. (1992), 'Monitoring the Emissions of Pollutants by Means of the Inspector Leadership Method', in R. Pethig (ed.), *Conflicts and Cooperation in Managing Environmental Resources. Microeconomic Studies*, Berlin: Springer, ch. 9, 241–69.
Barrett, S. (1991), 'The Paradox of International Environmental Agreements', mimeo, London: London Business School.
Barrett, S. (1992a), 'Alternative Instruments for Negotiating a Global Warming Convention', in OECD (ed.), *Convention on Climate Change. Economic Aspects of Negotiations*, Paris: OECD, ch. 1, 11–48.
Barrett, S. (1992b), 'International Environmental Agreements as Games', in R. Pethig (ed.), *Conflicts and Cooperation in Managing Environmental Resources. Microeconomic Studies*, Berlin: Springer, ch. 1, 11–37.
Barrett, S. (1992c), 'Cooperation and Competition in International Environmental Protection', invited paper, Economics of the Environment Session, International Economic Association Meeting, Moscow, 24–28 August.

Barrett, S. (1994a), 'The Biodiversity Supergame', *Environmental and Resource Economics*, **4**, 111–22.

Barrett, S. (1994b), 'Self-Enforcing International Environmental Agreements', *Oxford Economic Papers*, **46**, 804–78.

Barrett, S. (1997a), 'Toward a Theory of International Environmental Cooperation', in C. Carraro and D. Siniscalco (eds), *New Directions in the Economic Theory of the Environment*, Cambridge: Cambridge University Press, ch. 8, 239–80.

Barrett, S. (1997b), 'Heterogeneous International Agreements', in C. Carraro (ed.), *International Environmental Negotiations: Strategic Policy Issues*, Cheltenham, UK and Lyme, USA: Edward Elgar, 9–25.

Barrett, S. (1997c), 'The Strategy of Trade Sanctions in International Environmental Agreements', *Resource and Energy Economics*, **19**, 345–61.

Barrett, S. (1998), 'On the Theory and Diplomacy of Environmental Treaty-Making', *Environmental and Resource Economics*, **11**, 317–33.

Barrett, S. (1999a), 'Montreal Versus Kyoto, International Cooperation and the Global Environment', in: I. Kaul, I. Grunberg and M. Stern (eds), *Global Public Goods: International Cooperation in the 21st Century*, Oxford: Oxford University Press, 192–219.

Barrett, S. (1999b), 'A Theory of Full International Cooperation', *Journal of Theoretical Politics*, **11**, 519–41.

Barrett, S. (2000), 'Consensus Treaties', preliminary draft of unpublished manuscript, Johns Hopkins University, Washington, DC.

Bauer, A. (1992), 'International Cooperation Over Greenhouse Gas Abatement', mimeo, Seminar für empirische Wirtschaftsforschung, University of Munich, Munich.

Bennett, L., S.E. Ragland and P. Yolles (1998), 'Facilitating International Agreements Through an Interconnected Game Approach: The Case of River Basins', in R. Just and S. Netanyahu (eds), *Conflict and Cooperation on Trans-Boundary Water Resources*, Boston, MA: Kluwer, 61–85.

Bernheim, D., B. Peleg and M.D. Whinston (1987), 'Coalition-Proof Nash Equilibria. I. Concepts', *Journal of Economic Theory*, **42**, 1–12.

Bloch, F. (1995), 'Endogenous Structures of Associations in Oligopolies', *Rand Journal of Economics*, **26**, 537–56.

Bloch, F. (1996), 'Sequential Formation of Coalitions in Games with Externalities and Fixed Payoff Division', *Games and Economic Behavior*, **14**, 90–123.

Bloch, F. (1997), 'Non-Cooperative Models of Coalition Formation in Games with Spillovers', in C. Carraro and D. Siniscalco (eds), *New Directions in the Economic Theory of the Environment*, Cambridge: Cambridge University Press, ch. 10, 311–52.

Bohm, P. (1993), 'Incomplete International Cooperation to Reduce CO_2 Emissions: Alternative Policies', *Journal of Environmental Economics and Management*, **24**, 258–71.

Bohm, P. and B. Larsen (1993), 'Fairness in a Tradable-Permit Treaty for Carbon Emissions Reductions in Europe and the Former Soviet Union', *Environmental and Resource Economics*, **4**, 219–39.

Bothe, M. (1996), 'The Evaluation of Enforcement Mechanisms in International Environmental Law', in R. Wolfrum (ed.), *Enforcing Environmental Standards: Economic Mechanisms as Viable Means?* Berlin: Springer, 13–38.

Botteon, M. and C. Carraro (1997), 'Burden-Sharing and Coalition Stability in

Environmental Negotiations with Asymmetric Countries', in C. Carraro (ed.), *International Environmental Negotiations: Strategic Policy Issues*, Cheltenham, UK and Lyme, USA: Edward Elgar, ch. 3, 26–55.

Botteon, M. and C. Carraro (1998), 'Strategies for Environmental Negotiations: Issue Linkage with Heterogeneous Countries', in: N. Hanley and H. Folmer (eds), *Game Theory and the Global Environment*, Cheltenham, UK and Northampton, USA: Edward Elgar, ch. 9, 180–200.

Brown Weiss, E. and H.K. Jacobson (1997), 'Compliance with International Environmental Accords', in M. Role, H. Sjöberg and U. Svedin (eds), *International Governance on Environmental Issues*, Dordrecht: Kluwer, 78–110.

Carraro, C. (1997), 'The Structure of International Environmental Agreements', working paper, Fondazione Eni Enrico Mattei, Milan, April.

Carraro, C. (2000), 'Roads towards International Environmental Agreements', in H. Siebert (ed.), *The Economics of International Environmental Problems*, Tübingen: Mohr Siebeck, 169–202.

Carraro, C. and C. Marchiori (2001), 'Endogenous Strategic Issue Linkage in International Negotiations', paper presented at the Workshop on Coalition Theory, Louvain-la-Neuve, Belgium, January.

Carraro, C., C. Marchiori and S. Oreffice (2001), 'Endogenous Minimum Participation in International Environmental Treaties,' mimeo, Fondazione Eni Enrico Mattei, Milan.

Carraro, C. and C. Marchiori (2002), 'Stable Coalitions', working paper No. 5.2002, Fondazione Eni Enrico Mattei, Milan. Forthcoming in C. Carraro, (ed.), *Endogenous Formation of Economic Coalitions*, Cheltenham, UK and Northampton, USA: Edward Elgar.

Carraro, C. and F. Moriconi (1998), 'International Games on Climate Change Control', working paper 56.98, Fondazione Eni Enrico Mattei, Milan.

Carraro, C. and D. Siniscalco (1991), 'Strategies for the International Protection of the Environment', Working Paper, Fondazione Eni Enrico Mattei, Milan, March.

Carraro, C. and D. Siniscalco (1992), 'The International Dimension of Environmental Policy', *European Economic Review*, **36**, 379–87.

Carraro, C. and D. Siniscalco (1993), 'Strategies for the International Protection of the Environment', *Journal of Public Economics*, **52**, 309–28.

Carraro, C. and D. Siniscalco (1997), 'R&D Cooperation and the Stability of International Environmental Agreements', in C. Carraro (ed.), *International Environmental Negotiations: Strategic Policy Issues*, Cheltenham, UK and Lyme, USA: Edward Elgar, 71–96.

Carraro, C. and D. Siniscalco (1998), 'International Environmental Agreements: Incentives and Political Economy', *European Economic Review*, **42**, 561–72.

Cesar, H. and A. de Zeeuw (1996), 'Issue Linkage in Global Environmental Problems', in A. Xepapadeas, *Economic Policy for the Environment and Natural Resources: Techniques for the Management and Control of Pollution*, Cheltenham, UK and Brookfield, USA: Edward Elgar, ch. 7, 158–73.

Chander, P. and H. Tulkens (1991), 'Strategically Stable Cost Sharing in an Economic–Ecological Negotiation-Process', CORE Discussion Paper No. 9135, Center for Operations, Research and Econometrics, Louvain: Université Catholique de Louvain, revised version in A. Ulph (ed.), *Environmental Policy, International Agreements, and International Trade*, Oxford: Oxford University Press, 2001, 66–80.

Chander, P. and H. Tulkens (1992), 'Theoretical Foundations of Negotiations and

Cost Sharing in Transfrontier Pollution Problems', *European Economic Review*, **36**, 388–98.

Chander, P. and H. Tulkens (1995), 'A Core-Theoretic Solution for the Design of Cooperative Agreements on Transfrontier Pollution', *International Tax and Public Finance*, **2**, 279–93.

Chander, P. and H. Tulkens (1997), 'The Core of an Economy with Multilateral Environmental Externalities', *International Journal of Game Theory*, **26**, 379–401.

Chayes, A.H. and A. Chayes (1993), 'On Compliance', *International Organization*, **47**, 175–205.

Chayes, A.H. and A. Chayes (1995), *The New Sovereignty*, Cambridge, MA and London: Harvard University Press.

Chichilnisky, G. (2000), 'An Axiomatic Approach to Choice Under Uncertainty with Catastrophic Risks', *Resource and Energy Economics*, **22**, 221–31.

Chichilnisky, G. and G. Heal (1998), 'Global Environmental Risks', in G. Chichilnisky, G. Heal and A. Vercelli (eds), *Sustainability: Dynamics and Uncertainty*, Dordrecht: Kluwer, 23–46.

Chwe, M.S.-Y. (1994), 'Farsighted Coalitional Stability', *Journal of Economic Theory*, **63**, 299–325.

Congleton, R.D. (1996), 'Political Institutions and Pollution Control', in R.D. Congleton (ed.), *The Political Economy of Environmental Protection. Analysis and Evidence*, Ann Arbor, MI: The University of Michigan Press, ch. 12, 273–89.

Courtois, P., J.C. Péreau and T. Tazdait (2001), 'An Evolutionary Approach to the Climate Change Negotiation Game', working paper 81.2001, Fondazione Eni Enrico Mattei, Milan.

D'Aspremont, C., A. Jacquemin, J.J. Gabszeweiz and J.A. Weymark (1983), 'On the Stability of Collusive Price Leadership', *Canadian Journal of Economics*, **16**, 17–25.

Dockner, E., S. Jorgenson, N. van Long and G. Sorger (2000), *Differential Games and Management Sciences*, Cambridge: Cambridge University Press.

Ecchia, G. and M. Mariotti (1997), 'The Stability of International Environmental Coalitions with Farsighted Countries: Some Theoretical Observations', in C. Carraro (ed.), *International Environmental Negotiations: Strategic Policy Issues*, Cheltenham, UK and Lyme, USA: Edward Elgar, ch. 10, 172–92.

Ecchia, G. and M. Mariotti (1998), 'Coalition Formation in International Environmental Agreements and the Role of Institutions', *European Economic Review*, **42**, 573–82.

Eichberger, J. (1993), *Game Theory for Economists*, San Diego, CA: Academic Press.

Endres, A. (1996), 'Designing a Greenhouse Treaty: Some Economic Problems', in E. Eide and R. van den Bergh (eds), *Law and Economics of the Environment*, Oslo: Juridisk Forlag, 201–24.

Endres, A. (1997), 'Negotiating a Climate Convention – The Role of Prices and Quantities', *International Review of Law and Economics*, **17**, 201–24.

Endres, A. and M. Finus (1998), 'Renegotiation-Proof Equilibria in a Bargaining Game over Global Emission Reductions – Does the Instrumental Framework Matter?', in N. Hanley and H. Folmer (eds), *Game Theory and the Global Environment*, Cheltenham, UK and Northampton, USA: Edward Elgar, ch. 7, 135–64.

Endres, A. and M. Finus (1999), 'International Environmental Agreements: How the Policy Instrument Affects Equilibrium Emissions and Welfare', *Journal of Institutional and Theoretical Economics*, **155**, 527–50.

Endres, A. and M. Finus (2002), 'Quotas May Beat Taxes in a Global Emission Game', *International Journal of Tax and Public Finance*, vol. 9, 687–707.

Endres, A. and C. Ohl (2001), 'International Environmental Cooperation in the One Shot Prisoners' Dilemma', *Journal of Applied Social Science Studies*, 1, 1–26.

Endres, A. and C. Ohl (2002), 'Introducing "Cooperative Push": How Inefficient Environmental Policy (Sometimes!) Protects the Global Commons Better', *Public Choice*, 111, 285–302.

Eyckmans, J. (1999), 'Strategy proof uniform effort sharing schemes for transfrontier pollution problems', *Environmental Resources Economics*, 14, 165–89.

Eyckmans, J. (2000), 'Endogenous Coalition Formation in Global Warming, a General Framework and Some Preliminary Simulation Results', preliminary version, January.

Eyckmans, J. (2001), 'On the Farsighted Stability of the Kyoto Protocol', working paper series, Faculty of Economics and Applied Economic Sciences, University of Leuven, No. 2001–03.

Eyckmans, J. and H. Tulkens (1999), 'Simulating with RICE Coalitionally Stable Burden Sharing Agreements for the Climate Change Problem', CES ifo working papers series, No. 228, Munich.

Farrell, J. and E. Maskin (1989), 'Renegotiation in Repeated Games', *Games and Economic Behavior*, 1, 327–60.

Felder, S. and T.F. Rutherford (1993), 'Unilateral Reductions and Carbon Leakage: The Consequences of International Trade in Oil and Basic Materials', *Journal of Environmental Economics and Management*, 25, 162–76.

Finus, M. (2001), *Game Theory and International Environmental Cooperation*, Cheltenham, UK and Northampton, USA: Edward Elgar.

Finus, M. (2002a), 'Game Theory and International Environmental Cooperation: Any Practical Application?', in C. Böhringer, M. Finus and C. Vogt (eds), *Controlling Global Warming: Perspectives from Economics, Game Theory and Public Choice*, Cheltenham, UK and Northampton, USA: Edward Elgar, ch. 2., 9–104.

Finus, M. (2002b), 'New Developments in Coalition Theory: An Application to the Case of Global Pollution', forthcoming in M. Rauscher (ed.), *The International Dimension of Environmental Policy*, Dordrecht: Kluwer.

Finus, M. and B. Rundshagen (1998a), 'Toward a Positive Theory of Coalition Formation and Endogenous Instrumental Choice in Global Pollution Control', *Public Choice*, 96, 145–86.

Finus, M. and B. Rundshagen (1998b), 'Renegotiation-Proof Equilibria in a Global Emission Game When Players Are Impatient', *Environmental and Resource Economics*, 12, 275–306.

Finus, M. and B. Rundshagen (2000), 'Strategic Links between Environmental and Trade Policies if Plant Location is Endogenous', working paper No. 283, University of Hagen.

Finus, M. and B. Rundshagen (2001a), 'Endogenous Coalition Formation in Global Pollution Control', working paper No. 43.2001, Fondazione Eni Enrico Mattei, Milan.

Finus, M. and B. Rundshagen (2001b), 'Endogenous Coalition Formation in Global Pollution Control. A Partition Function Approach', working paper No. 307, University of Hagen. Revised version forthcoming in C. Carraro (ed.), *Endogenous Formation of Economic Coalitions*, Cheltenham, UK and Northampton, USA: Edward Elgar.

Finus, M. and B. Rundshagen (2001c), 'Sequential Move Unanimity Equilibria in a Public Good Model', working paper No. 308, University of Hagen.

Finus, M. and B. Rundshagen (2002), 'How the Rules of Coalition Formation Affect the Outcome in Positive Externality Games', preliminary draft, University of Hagen.

Finus, M. and S. Tjøtta (2002), 'The Oslo Protocol on Sulfur Reduction: The Great Leap Forward?', *Journal of Public Economics*, forthcoming.

Folmer, H. and P. van Mouche (1994), 'Interconnected Games and International Environmental Problems II', *Annals of Operations Research*, **54**, 97–117.

Folmer, H. and P. van Mouche (2000), 'Transboundary Pollution and International Cooperation', in T. Tietenberg and H. Folmer (eds), *The International Yearbook of Environmental and Resource Economics*, Cheltenham, UK and Northampton, USA: Edward Elgar, ch. 6, 231–67.

Folmer, H. and P. van Mouche (2002), 'The Acid Rain Game. A Mathematically Rigorous Analysis', in P. Dasgupta, B. Kriström and K.-G. Löfgren (eds), *Festschrift in Honor of Karl-Göran Mäler*, Cheltenham, UK and Northampton, USA: Edward Elgar.

Folmer, H., P. van Mouche and S. Ragland (1993), 'Interconnected Games and International Environmental Problems', *Environmental and Resource Economics*, **3**, 313–35.

Folmer, H. and A. de Zeeuw (2000), 'International Environmental Problems', in H. Folmer and H.L. Gabel (eds), *Principles of Environmental and Resource Economics*, Cheltenham, UK and Northampton, USA: Edward Elgar, ch. 16, 447–78.

Friedman, J.W. (1986), *Game Theory with Applications to Economics*, Oxford and New York: Oxford University Press.

Fudenberg, D. and D. Levine (1992), 'Maintaining a Reputation When Strategies Are Imperfectly Observable', *Review of Economic Studies*, **59**, 561–79.

Fudenberg, D., D. Levine and E. Maskin (1994), 'The Folk Theorem with Imperfect Public Information', *Econometrica*, **62**, 997–1039.

GAO (1992), 'International Environmental Agreements Are Not Well Monitored', Washington, DC: United States General Accounting Office, RCED-92-43.

Germain, M., P.L. Toint and H. Tulkens (1996a), 'International Negotiations on Acid Rains in Northern Europe: A Discrete Time Iterative Process', in A. Xepapadeas (ed.), *Economic Policy for the Environment and Natural Resources*, Cheltenham, UK and Brookfield, USA: Edward Elgar, ch. 10, 217–36.

Germain, M., P.L. Toint and H. Tulkens (1996b), 'Calcul économique itératif et stratégique pour les négociations internationales sur les pluies acides entre la Finlande, la Russie et l'Estonie', *Annales d'Économie et Statistique*, **43**, 101–27.

Germain, M., P.L. Toint and H. Tulkens (1998a), 'Financial Transfers to Sustain Cooperative International Optimality in Stock Pollutant Abatement', in S. Faucheux, J. Gowdy and I. Nicolai (eds), *Sustainability and Firms: Technological Change and the Changing Regulatory Environment*, Cheltenham, UK and Northampton, USA: Edward Elgar, ch. 11, 205–19.

Germain, M., H. Tulkens and A. de Zeeuw (1998b), 'Stabilité stratégique en matière de pollution internationale avec effet de stock: Le cas linéaire', *Revue Économique*, **49**, 1435–54.

Germain, M., P.L. Toint, H. Tulkens and A. de Zeeuw (2000), 'Transfers to Sustain Core-Theoretic Cooperation in International Stock Pollutant Control', revised version of CORE discussion paper No. 9832, Centre for Operations Research and Econometrics, Université Catholique de Louvain.

Germain, M. and J.-P. van Ypersele (1999), 'Financial Transfers to Sustain International Cooperation in the Climate Change Framework', preliminary draft, Université Catholique de Louvain.

Gibbons, R. (1992), *A Primer in Game Theory*, New York: Harvester Wheatsheaf.

Golombek, R., C. Hagem and M. Hoel (1995), 'Efficient Incomplete International Agreements', *Resource and Energy Economics*, **17**, 25–46.

Green, E. and R. Porter (1984), 'Noncooperative Collusion Under Imperfect Price Information', *Econometrica*, **52**, 87–100.

Greene, O. (1998), 'The System for Implementation Review in the Ozone Regime', in D. G. Victor, K. Raustiala and E.B. Skolnikoff (eds), *The Implementation and Effectiveness of International Environmental Commitments: Theory and Practice*, Laxenburg: IIASA and MIT Press, ch. 3, 89–136.

Güth, W. and R. Pethig (1992), 'Illegal Pollution and Monitoring of Unknown Quality – A Signaling Game Approach', in R. Pethig, (ed.), *Conflicts and Cooperation in Managing Environmental Resources. Microeconomic Studies*, Berlin: Springer, ch. 10, 275–330.

Hart, S. and M. Kurz (1983), 'Endogenous Formation of Coalitions,' *Econometrica*, **51**, 1047–64.

Heister, J. (1997), *Der internationale CO2-Vertrag: Strategien zur Stabilisierung multilateraler Kooperation zwischen souveränen Staaten*, Tübingen: J.C.B. Mohr.

Heister, J. (1998), 'Who Will Win the Ozone Game? On Building and Sustaining Cooperation in the Montreal Protocol on Substances that Deplete the Ozone Layer', in P. Michaelis, and F. Stähler (eds), *Recent Policy Issues in Environmental and Resource Economics*, Heidelberg and New York: Physica, ch. 7, 121–54.

Helm, C. (2001), 'On Coalitional Games with Multilateral Environmental Externalities', *International Journal of Game Theory*, **30**, 141–6.

Hillman, A. L. and H.W. Ursprung (1994), 'Greens, Supergreens, and International Trade Policy: Environmental Concerns and Protectionism', in C. Carraro (ed.), *The International Dimension of Environmental Policy*, Dordrecht: Kluwer, 75–108.

Hoel, M. (1991), 'Global Environmental Problems: The Effects of Unilateral Actions Taken by One Country', *Journal of Environmental Economics and Management*, **20**, 55–70.

Hoel, M. (1992), 'International Environment Conventions: The Case of Uniform Reductions of Emissions', *Environmental and Resource Economics*, **2**, 141–59.

Hoel, M. (1994), 'Efficient Climate Policy in the Presence of Free Riders', *Journal of Environmental Economics and Management*, **27**, 259–74.

Hoel, M. and K. Schneider (1997), 'Incentives to Participate in an International Environmental Agreement', *Environmental and Resource Economics*, **9**, 153–70.

Hübner, M. and M. Dröttboom (1999), 'Environmental Consciousness and Moral Hazard in International Agreements to Protect the Environment: A Note', working paper No. 264, University of Hagen, Hagen.

IPCC (2001), 'Climate Change 2001: Mitigation', contribution of Working Group III to the Third Assessment Report of the Intergovernmental Panel on Climate Change, Cambridge: Cambridge University Press.

Jeppesen, T. and P. Andersen (1998), 'Commitment and Fairness in Environmental Games', in N. Hanley and H. Folmer (eds), *Game Theory and the Environment*, Cheltenham, UK and Northampton, USA: Edward Elgar, ch. 4, 65–83.

Jordan, A. and J. Werksman (1996), 'Financing Global Environmental Protection', in J. Cameron, J. Werksman and P. Roderick (eds), *Improving Compliance with International Environmental Law*, London: Earthscan, 247–55.

Kaitala, V., K.-G. Mäler and H. Tulkens (1995), 'The Acid Rain Game as a Resource Allocation Process with an Application to the International Cooperation among Finland, Russia and Estonia', *Scandinavian Journal of Economics*, **97**, 325–43.

Kaitala, V., M. Pohjola and O. Tahvonen (1992), 'Transboundary Air Pollution and Soil Acidification: A Dynamic Analysis of an Acid Rain Game between Finland and the USSR', *Environmental and Resource Economics*, **2**, 161–81.

Katsoulacos, Y. (1997), 'R&D Spillovers, Cooperation, Subsidies and International Agreements', in C. Carraro (ed.), *International Environmental Negotiations: Strategic Policy Issues*, Cheltenham, UK and Lyme, USA: Edward Elgar, ch. 6, 97–109.

Keohane, R.O. (1995), 'Compliance with International Standards: Environmental Case Studies', in J. L. Hargrove (ed.), *Proceedings of the Eighty-Ninth Annual Meeting of the American Society of International Law*, Buffalo, NY: Hein & co., 206–24.

Kolstad, C.D. (2000), *Environmental Economics*, New York and Oxford: Oxford University Press.

Kroeze-Gil, J. and H. Folmer (1998), 'Linking Environmental Problems in an International Setting: The Interconnected Games Approach', in N. Hanley and H. Folmer (eds), *Game Theory and the Global Environment*, Cheltenham, UK and Northampton, USA: Edward Elgar, ch. 8, 165–80.

Krutilla, J.V. (1975), 'The International Columbia River Treaty: An Economic Evaluation', in A.V. Knesse and S.C. Smith (eds), *Water Research*, Baltimore, MD: Johns Hopkins University Press, 68–97.

Kummer, K. (1994), 'Providing Incentives to Comply with Multilateral Environmental Agreements: An Alternative to Sanctions?', *European Environmental Law Review*, **3**, 256–63.

Mäler, K.-G. (1989), 'The Acid Rain Game', in H. Folmer and E. van Ierland (eds), *Valuation Methods and Policy Making in Environmental Economics*, Amsterdam: Elsevier, ch. 12, 231–52.

Mäler, K.-G. (1990), 'International Environmental Problems', *Oxford Review of Economic Policy*, **6**, 80–108.

Mäler, K.-G. (1994), 'Acid Rain in Europe: A Dynamic Perspective on the Use of Economic Incentives', in E.C. van Ierland (ed.), *International Environmental Economics. Developments in Environmental Economics 4*, Amsterdam: Elsevier, 351–72.

Mäler, K.-G. and A. de Zeeuw (1998), 'The Acid Rain Differential Game', *Environmental and Resource Economics*, **12**, 167–84.

Marauhn, T. (1996), 'Towards a Procedural Law of Compliance Control in International Environmental Relations', *Zeitschrift für ausländisches öffentliches Recht und Völkerrecht*, **56**, 696–731.

Mariotti, M. (1997), 'A Model of Agreements in Strategic Form Games', *Journal of Economic Theory*, **74**, 196–217.

van Mouche, P. (2000), 'Théorie Formelle des Jeux Tensoriels', preliminary draft, University of Wageningen.

van Mouche, P. (2001), 'Formal Transboundary Pollution Games: A Non-cooperative Analysis', preliminary draft, University of Wageningen.

Murdoch, J.C. and T. Sandler (1997a), 'Voluntary Cutbacks and Pretreaty Behavior: The Helsinki Protocol and Sulfur Emissions', *Public Finance Review*, **25**, 139–62.

Murdoch, J.C. and T. Sandler (1997b), 'The Voluntary Provision of a Pure Public Good: the Case of Reduced CFC Emissions and the Montreal Protocol', *Journal of Public Economics*, **63**, 331–49.

Musgrave, P. (1994), 'Pure Global Externalities: International Efficiency and Equity', in L. Bovenberg and S. Cnossen (eds), *Public Economics and the Environment in an Imperfect World*, Boston: Kluwer, ch. 12, 237–59.

Nash, J. (1950), 'Equilibrium Points in N-Person Games', *Proceedings of the National Academy of Sciences*, **36**, 48–9.

Nordhaus, W. and Z. Yang (1996), 'A Regional Dynamic General-Equilibrium Model of Alternative Climate-Change Strategies', *American Economic Review*, **86**, 741–65.

Osborne, M.J. and A. Rubinstein (1994), *A Course in Game Theory*, Cambridge, MA and London: MIT Press.

Petrakis, E. and A. Xepapadeas (1996), 'Environmental Consciousness and Moral Hazard in International Agreements to Protect the Environment', *Journal of Public Economics*, **60**, 95–110.

Ragland, S.E. (1995), 'International Environmental Externalities and Inter-connected Games', Ph.D. dissertation, University of Colorado, Boulder.

Ray, D. and R. Vohra (1997), 'Equilibrium Binding Agreements', *Journal of Economic Theory*, **73**, 30–78.

Ray, D. and R. Vohra (1999), 'A Theory of Endogenous Coalition Structures', *Games and Economic Behavior*, **26**, 286–336.

Rubinstein, A. (1980), 'Strong Perfect Equilibrium in Supergames', *International Journal of Game Theory*, **9**, 1–12.

Rubio, S. and A. Ulph (2001), 'A Simple Dynamic Model of International Environmental Agreements with a Stock Pollutant', preliminary version, University of Southampton.

Rundshagen, B. (2002), 'On the Formalization of Open Membership in Coalition Formation Games', working paper No. 318, University of Hagen.

Russell, C.S. (1992), 'Monitoring and Enforcement of Pollution Control Laws in Europe and the United States', in R. Pethig (ed.), *Conflicts and Cooperation in Managing Environmental Resources. Microeconomic Studies*, Berlin: Springer, ch. 7, 195–213.

Sand, P.H. (1996), 'Compliance with International Environmental Obligations: Existing International Legal Agreements', in J. Cameron, J. Werksman and P. Roderick (eds), *Improving Compliance with International Environmental Law*, London: Earthscan, 48–82.

Sand, P.H. (1997), 'Commodity or Taboo? International Regulation of Trade in Endangered Species', in H.O. Bergensen and G. Parmann (eds), *The Green Globe Year Book 1997*, New York: Oxford University Press, 19–36.

Scarf, H. (1971), 'On the Existence of a Cooperative Solution for General Class of N-Person Games', *Journal of Economic Theory*, **3**, 169–81.

Selten, R. (1965), 'Spieltheoretische Behandlung eines Oligopolmodells mit Nachfrageträgheit', *Zeitschrift für die gesamte Staatswissenschaften*, **12**, 301–24.

Siebert, H. (1985), 'Spatial Aspects of Environmental Economics', in A.V. Kneese, and J.L. Sweeney (eds), *Handbook of Natural Resource and Energy Economics. Vol. I*, Amsterdam: North Holland, ch. 3, 125–64.

Spagnolo, G. (1996), 'Issue Linkage, Delegation and International Policy Coordination', working paper: Economics, Energy, Environment, No. 49.96, Fondazione Eni Enrico Mattei, Milan.

Stähler, F. (1996), 'Reflections on Multilateral Environmental Agreements', in A. Xepapadeas (ed.), *Economic Policy for the Environment and Natural Resources: Techniques for the Management and Control of Pollution*, Cheltenham, UK and Brookfield, USA: Edward Elgar, ch. 8, 174–96.

Széll, P. (1995), 'The Development of Multilateral Mechanisms of Monitoring Compliance', in W. Lang, (ed.), *Sustainable Development and International Law*, London: Graham and Tritman, 97–109.

Tahvonen, O. (1994), 'Carbon Dioxide Abatement as a Differential Game', *European Journal of Political Economy*, **10**, 685–705.

Tulkens, H. (1979), 'An Economic Model of International Negotiations Relating to Transfrontier Pollution', in K. Krippendorff (ed.), *Communication and Control in Society*, New York: Gordon and Breach, 199–212.

Tulkens, H. (1998), 'Cooperation Versus Free-Riding in International Environmental Affairs: Two Approaches', in N. Hanley and H. Folmer (eds), *Game Theory and the Environment*, Cheltenham, UK and Northampton, USA: Edward Elgar, ch. 2, 30–44.

Ulph, A. (1998), 'Learning About Global Warming?', in N. Hanley and H. Folmer (eds), *Game Theory and the Global Environment*, Cheltenham, UK and Northampton, USA: Edward Elgar, ch. 13, 255–86.

Victor, G. (1998), 'The Operation and Effectiveness of the Montreal Protocol's Non-Compliance Procedure', in D.G. Victor, K. Raustiala and E.B. Skolnikoff (eds), *The Implementation and Effectiveness of International Environmental Commitments: Theory and Practice*, Laxenburg: IIASA and MIT Press, ch. 4, 137–76.

Welsch, H. (1993), 'An Equilibrium Framework for Global Pollution Problems', *Journal of Environmental Economics and Management*, **25**, 64–79.

Werksman, J. (1997), 'Five MEAs, Five Years since Rio: Recent Lessons on the Effectiveness of Multilateral Agreements', London: FIELD (Foundation for International Environmental Law and Development), special focus report.

Yi, S.-S. (1997), 'Stable Coalition Structures with Externalities', *Games and Economic Behavior*, **20**, 201–37.

Yi, S.-S. (1999), 'Endogenous Formation of Economic Coalitions: A Survey on the Partition Function Approach', preliminary draft, Sogang University, Seoul. Revised version forthcoming in C. Carraro, (ed.), *Endogenous Formation of Economic Coalitions*, Cheltenham, UK and Northampton, USA: Edward Elgar.

Yi, S.-S. and H. Shin (1995), 'Endogenous Formation of Coalitions in Oligopoly', mimeo, Department of Economics, Dartmouth College.

de Zeeuw, A. (1998), 'International Dynamic Pollution Control', in N. Hanley and H. Folmer (eds), *Game Theory and the Global Environment*, Cheltenham, UK and Northampton, USA: Edward Elgar, ch. 12, 237–54.

de Zeeuw, A.J. and F. van der Ploeg (1991), 'Difference Games and Policy Evaluation: A Conceptual Framework', *Oxford Economic Papers*, **43**, 612–36.

APPENDIX 3.1

Table 3A.1 Selection of important international environmental agreements*

Protocol	Objectives	Status of membership
Framework Convention on Climate Change (FCCC)	Framework convention preceding the Kyoto Protocol; expresses concern about climate change due to greenhouse gases; no binding emission ceilings were set	Signed at the Earth Summit in Rio de Janeiro in 1992 by 166 countries; entered into force in 1994; presently numbers 186 parties
Kyoto Protocol	Targets a reduction of greenhouse gas emissions of 5.2 per cent based on 1990 emission levels to be achieved in the period 2008–12; emission reduction of major emitters between 6 and 8 per cent	Signed in Kyoto in 1997 by 38 countries; has not yet entered into force; USA withdrew from the protocol in 2001
Vienna Convention	Framework convention preceding the five subsequent protocols; expresses concern about the depletion of the ozone layer through CFCs and halons, no binding emission ceilings were set	Signed in Vienna in 1985 by 28 countries, entered into force in 1988, currently numbers 182 parties
Montreal Protocol	CFCs to be cut to half of 1986 levels by 1999, starting with a freeze of production and consumption within one year after the protocol comes into force; freeze of halons at 1986 levels	Signed in Montreal in 1987 by 46 countries; entered into force in 1989, currently numbers 181 parties
London amendment to the Montreal Protocol	Further reduction of CFCs; complete phase-out by 2000; new substances were included in the list of harmful substances	Signed in London in 1990; entered into force in 1992; currently numbers 153 parties
Copenhagen amendment to the Montreal Protocol	Tightening of the timetable for the reduction of ozone-depleting substances; most substances to be eliminated by 1996	Signed in Copenhagen in 1992; entered into force in 1994; presently numbers 128 parties

Table 3.4.1 (continued)

Protocol	Objectives	Status of membership
Montreal amendment to the Montreal Protocol	Tightening of the timetable for the phase-out of methyl bromide; establishment of a new licensing system for controlling trade ozone-depleting substances	Signed in Montreal in 1997; entered into force in 1999; currently numbers 63 parties
Beijing amendment to the Montreal Protocol	Establishment of monitoring system to control bromochloromethane and new trade rules for hydrochlorofluorocarbons (HCFCs) that were developed as replacements for CFCs	Signed in Beijing in 1999; not in force yet, presently 11 signatories
Convention on Long-Range Transboundary Pollution (LRTAP)	Framework convention preceding the four subsequent protocols (and other protocols); expresses concern about transboundary pollution problems (e.g., acidification of lakes and soils)	Signed in Geneva in 1979 by 33 countries; entered into force in 1983; currently numbers 48 parties
Helsinki Protocol	Targets 30 per cent reduction of sulphur emissions based on 1980 levels by 1993	Signed in Helsinki in 1985 by 19 countries; entered into force in 1987; currently numbers 22 parties
Sofia Protocol	Targets uniform freeze of nitrogen oxides at 1987 levels by 1995	Signed in Sofia in 1988 by 25 countries; entered into force in 1991; currently numbers 28 parties
Geneva Protocol	Targets 30 per cent reduction of volatile organic compounds based on 1998 levels by 1999	Signed in Geneva in 1991 by 23 countries; entered into force in 1997; currently numbers 21 parties; 5 signatories have not yet ratified the treaty; 3 countries acceded later

Oslo Protocol	Follow-up protocol to the Helsinki Protocol; sets tighter non-uniform sulphur ceilings to be achieved by 2000 so that critical loads are not exceeded	Signed in Oslo in 1994 by 28 countries; entered into force in 1998; currently numbers 24 parties; 4 signatories have not yet ratified the treaty
Gothenburg Protocol	Follow-up protocol to the Oslo and Helsinki Protocols (sulphur), the Sofia Protocol (nitrogen oxides) and Geneva Protocol (volatile organic compounds); sets tighter non-uniform emission ceilings including regulations of ammonia, not regulated so far.	Signed in Gothenburg in 1999 by 31 countries; ratified by 4 countries; has not yet entered into force
Convention on International Trade in Endangered Species of Wild Fauna and Flora (CITES)	Banning of commercial international trade with endangered species	Signed in Washington DC in 1973 by 47 countries; entered into force in 1975; currently numbers 152 parties
International Convention for the Regulation of Whaling (ICRW)	Establishment of a system of international regulations to ensure the conservation and development of whale stocks	Signed in Washington DC in 1946 by 15 countries; entered into force in 1948; currently numbers 48 parties
Columbia River Treaty	Coordination of flood control and electrical energy production in the Columbia River Basin between the USA and Canada	Signed in 1961 by the USA and Canada; further negotiations resulted in a protocol signed and ratified in 1964
Convention on Biological Diversity	Convention with three main goals: conservation of biological diversity; sustainable use of its components; and fair and equitable sharing of the benefits from the use of genetic resources; no binding targets were set	Earth Summit in Rio de Janeiro in 1992 by 168 countries, entered into force in 1993, currently numbers 183 parties

Note: *Legal terminology as explained in note 3 applies.

APPENDIX 3.2

If a country individually maximizes its payoff as given in (3.1) in the text, the first-order conditions for an interior optimum are given by

$$\beta_i'(e_i) = a_{ii}\phi_i'\left(a_{ii}e_i + \sum_{j\neq i}^{N} a_{ij}e_j\right).\qquad(3A.1)$$

If all countries choose Nash equilibrium emissions, the first-order conditions are satisfied for each country. From (3A.1) it is evident that a country's optimal choice depends on external emissions e_j. Hence (3A.1) can also be interpreted as an implicit best-reply function. The word 'implicit' means that no exact relation of dependence can be established as long as no particular payoff function (as for instance in Table 3.2 in the text) is assumed. From (3A.1) we can conclude that the higher emissions e_j, the higher will be marginal damages if $\phi_i'' > 0$ and hence an optimal response calls on country i to lower its emissions e_i, in order to lower ϕ_i' and to raise β_i' (recall that $\beta_i'' \leq 0$) so as to restore equality in (3A.1). Only in three cases will there be no response: (a) $a_{ii} = 0$, (b) $a_{ij} = 0$ and (c) ϕ_i' is constant. Case (a) implies that all emissions are transported abroad and case (b) that no foreign emissions are deposited in coutry i. In reality cases (a) and (b) may simultaneously apply if country i is a pure upwind country and only case (b) may apply if pollution is of the pure local type, in which case $a_{ii} = 1$. Case (c) applies to linear damage cost functions, in which case $\phi_i' = 0$. Cases (a), (b) and (c) imply that countries have a dominant strategy.

An alternative way of analysing the optimal reaction of countries to external changes of emissions is possible if the first-order conditions in (3A.1) are totally differentiated. Then we have (using shorthand notation):

$$\beta_i''\cdot de_i = a_{ii}^2\phi_i''\cdot de_i + a_{ii}a_{ij}\phi_i''\cdot de_j\qquad(3A.2)$$

or, rearranging terms,

$$\frac{de_i}{de_j} = \frac{a_{ii}a_{ij}\phi_i''}{\beta_i'' - a_{ii}^2\phi_i''}.\qquad(3A.3)$$

(3A.3) is the slope of a country's best-reply function and thus approximates an optimal change of emissions e_i if foreign emissions of country j, e_j, change. It is evident that cases (a), (b) and (c) imply a zero slope, also called an orthogonal best-reply function. This explains that a dominant strategy is equivalent to an orthogonal best-reply function. In all other cases, the slope will be negative.

In the context of coalition formation a similar analysis can be conducted.

The only difference is that coalition members jointly maximize the payoff to their coalition and hence act as one single player. For concreteness, I briefly illustrate the case of symmetric countries and global pollution discussed in subsection 3.3.2, but the extension to the more general case is straightforward. In this case, all transportation coefficients are one and the optimal choice of emissions depends only on the size of a coalition, which I denote c_i. Then, the first-order conditions of coalition c_i (using shorthand notation) reads:

$$\beta' = c_i \phi', \qquad (3A.4)$$

where derivatives are not indexed because of symmetry. Total differentiation and rearranging terms gives the slope of coalition's best-reply function:

$$\frac{de^i}{de^r} = \frac{c_i \phi''}{(1/c_i)\beta'' - c_i \phi''} \qquad (3A.5)$$

where e^i denotes aggregate emissions of coalition i, and e^r are total emissions of all other countries. Thus, it is evident that for linear damage cost functions $\phi'' = 0$ (payoff function of type 1 in subsection 3.3.2), and hence the slopes of the best-reply functions are zero. Moreover, slopes are -1 if $\beta''_i = 0$ (and $\phi'' > 0$), which applies to linear benefit functions (payoff function of type 3 in subsection 3.3.2). In all other cases it is easily checked that the slopes are between 0 and -1 (payoff function of type 2 in subsection 3.3.2). For the example in Table 3.2, $\beta''_i = b$ and $\phi'' = c$. Inserting these values in (3A.5) and using $\gamma = b/c$, it is easily checked that the absolute value of the slopes of the best-reply functions decrease with γ.

APPENDIX 3.3

Table 3A.2 Historical development of models applying the concept of the core

Paper	Payoff structure					Pollution		Core
	Static	Dynamic				Global	Transb.	
		Discrete	Cont.	Flow	Stock			
Tulkens (1979)								—
Chander and Tulkens (1991)			•				•	α, d, t
Chander and Tulkens (1992)			•				•	α, d, t
Kaitala et al. (1995)			•				•	α, d, t
Chander and Tulkens (1995)			•			•		γ, s, t
Chander and Tulkens (1997)			•			•		γ, s, t
Germain et al. (1996a)	•	•		•			•	γ, d, t
Germain et al. (1996b)	•	•		•			•	γ, d, t
Germain et al. (1998a)			•		•	•		γ, s, t, o
Germain et al. (1998b)			•		•	•		γ, d, t, o
Germain et al. (2000)			•		•	•		γ, d, t, c
Eyckmans and Tulkens (1999)					•	•		γ, s, e, o
Germain and van Ypersele (1999)			•		•	•		γ, d, e, c

Note: In the 'Core' column: d = dynamic stability test along the entire time path, s = static stability test, t = core properties theoretically established, e = core properties empirically established, c = closed loop strategies, o = open loop strategies.

158

4. Managing environmental risk through insurance

Paul K. Freeman and Howard Kunreuther

Risk is inherent in all human activities, both personal and professional. While the number and variety of risks have grown and changed dramatically throughout history, the basics remain the same: risk of loss of life, limb, health, livelihood, or property due to predictable events (reduced income upon reaching the mandatory retirement age) or to unpredictable events (loss of life in an earthquake).

There are some risks that governments, corporations and individuals choose to retain, consenting to pay for any losses that result from those risks. There are many more risks that exposed parties would prefer not to retain. Insurance can often be used as a policy tool to transfer these risks to another party. It has the added advantage that it can encourage the entity through premium reductions to invest in cost-effective risk reduction measures.

Increasingly, policy-makers have been exploring the proactive use of insurance as a tool to manage environmental risk effectively. In particular, five attributes of insurance exist that make it an effective risk management tool: its ability to spread risk; its role in variance reduction; its ability to segregate risk; its encouragement of loss reduction measures; and its ability to monitor and control behavior. The precondition for utilizing insurance as a policy tool is that the risk in question must meet a set of preconditions that make it insurable.

This chapter explores the role that insurance can play in managing environmental risk. We define environmental risk rather broadly to include natural hazards as well as technological risks. Section 1 explores the nature of environmental risk and the role that the public sector and private insurance can play in managing it. Section 2 then discusses the conditions that make a risk insurable. Section 3 focuses on two examples using insurance to address environmental problems: the role it can play as part of a national strategy for coping with natural hazards and how it can be used in conjunction with third-party inspections to enforce government regulations. The chapter concludes by discussing both the strengths and limitations of insurance as well as suggesting directions for future research.

1.   MANAGING ENVIRONMENTAL RISK

Environmental risks are particularly challenging because they are normally low-probability events that can produce severe consequences. Natural hazards, such as earthquakes and hurricanes, can cause mass destruction and take many lives; technological risks, such as chemical accidents, can adversely impact the environment and cause human health problems.

With respect to natural hazards, Figure 4.1 depicts the losses due to *great natural catastrophes* from 1950 to 2001 throughout the world.[1] The figure includes data on the overall economic and insured losses worldwide (in 2001 dollars) from earthquakes, floods, windstorms, volcanic eruptions, droughts, heat waves, freezes and cold waves.[2]

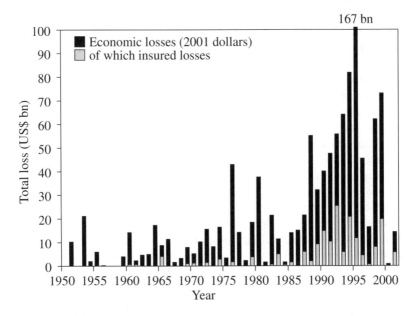

Source: Munich Re (2002).

Figure 4.1   Losses due to great natural catastrophes worldwide

A few interesting points emerge from the graph. First, there is an upward trend in both economic losses and insured losses worldwide over the course of these 50 years. This trend will likely continue into the future due to the higher concentration of population and built environment in areas susceptible to natural hazards worldwide. Next, a jump in both the economic losses and the insured losses took place within the last decade of the century. Since 1990, worldwide losses were over $40 billion each year with few exceptions. Losses were as high as $167 billion in 1995 alone. As a result of an increase in the insured property value, the insured losses also grew during this same timeframe (Kunreuther and Grossi, in press).

Despite the concentration of capital assets in the developed world compared to emerging economies, the economic impacts of catastrophes are relatively evenly split between these two groups of countries. The developed world primarily bears the costs of windstorms (hurricanes and tsunamis) while the developing world bears the brunt of economic damage from flooding. The cost of earthquakes tends to be equally divided between the developed and developing world (Freeman, 2000). However, based on the enormous disparity in the gross domestic product between the two, the per capita impact of natural disasters in the developing world is dramatically higher. According to the World Bank, the impact in the developing world is 20 times greater on a per capita basis (Gilbert and Kreimer, 1999).

The financial implications of environmental damage from commercial activity are also enormous. The accrued liability for environmental risk related to real property in the USA alone is estimated at $2 trillion, or approximately 20 per cent of the total value of all property in the country (Wilson, 1991). This environmental liability primarily arises from the imposition of standards of care arising from governmental regulation. Since the 1960s, the USA and Europe have seen the creation of hundreds of federal, state and local statutes that assign liability for the contamination of air, water and soil resources.

Role of the Public Sector

When the federal government is the entity that absorbs a particular risk, there is the implicit assumption that this type of disaster is the responsibility of all residents in the country. The government has the ability to transfer these risks to each citizen through the power of taxation (Arrow, 1992). If the number of taxpayers is large, and/or the cost of the risk is small relative to the economy, the risk faced by each taxpayer is likely to be sufficiently small that it will not be of concern to citizens.

The government assumption of risk creates an enormous incentive for policy makers to design public sector programs. In dealing with natural hazards, there are abundant examples of governments assuming a portion of the risk of others. The creation of a government-subsidized insurance scheme is the most common example. The natural hazard programs in France and Spain and the National Flood Insurance Program (NFIP) in the USA illustrate these approaches (Pollner, 2000).

The creation of the Turkish Catastrophe Insurance Pool (TCIP) in 2000 is an example of a new program developed in an emerging economy. Under the TCIP, all existing and future privately owned property is required to contribute to the TCIP. The payments made will contribute to a fund that will pay homeowners up to $28 000 in the event that a catastrophe damages their homes (Gulkan, 2000). Proposals are now being explored in Mexico, the Caribbean, Central America and Africa to engage the government in providing risk-transfer options for farmers, homeowners and businesses in case of natural-catastrophe losses (World Bank, 2000).

All of these proposals are balancing the appropriate role of the government in emerging and developing countries to assist in the creation of market mechanisms to manage risk from natural hazards more efficiently. These proposals build on the active role played by the World Bank in helping Turkey establish the TCIP.

In the USA, government benefit programs have also been created to absorb risk from environmental contamination. State Guarantee Funds were established by states to absorb liability placed on property owners due to the enactment of new regulations governing underground storage tanks. In these programs, taxes are collected on the sale of gasoline to create a fund to pay for the cleanup of contamination caused by leaking tanks. To the extent that the fund is inadequate, other tax sources are used to supplement the required funds (Boyd and Kunreuther, 1997).

There are disadvantages to relying on government-assisted programs to cope with risk. Government programs generally treat all disaster victims identically without regard to their need for benefits or their ability to pay. The question normally asked before providing disaster relief benefits is whether the claimant resided within the designated disaster area, not whether the claimant should have avoided living or working in that region in the first place (Priest, 1996). For example, federal government benefits to those damaged by wildfires is dependent on whether the claimant lived in the fire zone. The fact that the claimant made a deliberate decision to expose himself to damage by consciously living in a high-risk zone does not impact his ability to receive assistance after the disaster.

Transferring risk to the government implies that citizens are willing to have the risk borne by them through some form of taxation. For most developing countries, the losses associated with some catastrophic natural disasters are beyond their ability to absorb these costs (Ferranti *et al.*, 2000). A graphic example is Hurricane Mitch, which caused direct and indirect damages in Honduras equivalent to $6 billion, or one year's gross domestic product. With a population of 6.2 million and 53 percent of the population below the poverty line, the cost of $1000 per person is beyond the ability of the government to absorb by relying on taxation.

It is thus not surprising that Honduras and other developing countries now place considerable reliance on transferring risk outside the country to finance post-disaster reconstruction (Pollner, 2000). These risk transfers are provided either in the form of grants or loans by the governments of the developed world or through international financial institutions such as the World Bank, the regional development banks and UN agencies. The funding for post-disaster reconstruction has substantially increased in recent years. During the past four years, the Inter American Development Bank has increased its disaster-related lending by a factor of 10 compared to the previous 15 years (Clarke, 2000). The increasing demands of post-disaster reconstruction funding drive the interest of the international aid and financing community in exploring catastrophe hedges, including insurance, to transfer the risk of loss from natural catastrophes from governments in poorer countries to professional risk bearers: either insurance companies or the capital markets.

Role of Private Insurance

Two issues drive the interest of policy-makers to shift the burden of environmental risk from the government to other parties. The first concern is the limitation of public sector programs to encourage *ex ante* risk-reducing behavior. If residents in hazard-prone areas believe, sometimes incorrectly, that they will receive federal assistance following a disaster, they have less economic incentive to invest in loss prevention measures or insurance than if they knew they were going to have to bear the recovery costs themselves. Second, the assumption of risk by the government may be inappropriate, either as a matter of public policy or because the government is not in a position to absorb the risk. For example, in many developing countries the government assumption of homeowner risk provides a disincentive for homeowners to manage the risk on their own, either through private insurance or by risk mitigation strategies. Furthermore, the risk assumed by the government may be beyond its ability to finance the loss after a disaster. A major earthquake in some countries would be so destructive that the government commitment to fund housing reconstruction would be beyond its resources (Freeman et al., 2002). If the government is not the appropriate entity to absorb risk, the natural question is how may the risk be transferred? Increasingly, policy makers are exploring the voluntary shifting of environmental risk through insurance.

Historical perspective

Insurance has long played a role in developed societies as a risk-reducing and risk-spreading tool. The Code of Hammurabi, issued about 1950 BC, laid the basis for the institutionalization of insurance by formalizing the concept of bottomry (Covello and Mumpower, 1985). Bottomry was the basis for maritime contracts on vessels, cargo, or freight that charged risk premiums between 10 and 25 percent of shipping costs to cover the chance of loss. Around 750 BC, the concept of risk sharing was formalized when all parties engaged in a shipping arrangement agreed to share proportionately in any loss suffered during the voyage.

Insurance temporarily disappeared from western civilization after the fall of the Roman Empire, but re-emerged in the form of marine insurance in Italian port cities around AD 1000. Insurance became more highly developed between the twelfth and fourteenth centuries as an integral component of the Hanseatic League's activities. Fire insurance, developed in London following the Great Fire of 1666, became extremely popular in England.

The best example of using private insurance as a viable means of spreading and reducing societal risk comes from the factory mutual insurance companies, founded in early nineteenth-century New England (Bainbridge, 1952). These mutual companies offered factories protection against potentially large losses from fire in return for a small premium. In order to reduce risk, the mutuals required inspections of a factory both before issuing a policy and after one was in force. Customers who were regarded as poor risks had their policies canceled; factories that instituted loss prevention measures received premium reductions.

As the mutual companies gained experience with fire risks, they set up research departments to determine what factors caused fires and how to reduce losses by concentrating on those factors. For example, the Boston Manufacturers' Mutual Company worked with lantern manufacturers to encourage them to develop safer designs and required policyholders to purchase lanterns only from companies whose products met their specifications. Manufacturers' Mutual hired researchers to find ways of reducing the risk of fire, for example developing non-flammable lubricating oils. It then shared these findings with key trade associations, and distributed educational pamphlets on preventing fires to textile mill owners.

In many cases, mutual companies would only offer insurance to companies that adopted specific loss prevention methods. For example, Spinners Mutual only insured factories that installed automatic sprinkler systems. Manufacturers' Mutual in Providence, Rhode Island, developed specifications for fire hoses and advised mills to buy only from companies whose hoses met those specifications. By researching and requiring loss prevention techniques and inspecting facilities before issuing or renewing a policy, nineteenth-century insurers were able to reduce losses dramatically and provide coverage against risks for which there had previously been no protection.

Historically, insurance has blended risk transfer with incentives to reduce risk. It is a unique policy tool in that it rewards individuals before a disaster for investing in loss reduction measures through lower premiums, as well as paying these same people for damages suffered from a disaster.

Characteristics of insurance

Insurance has five specific characteristics that make it effective in managing risk: ability to spread risk; capacity to reduce the variance of risk; segregation of risk; encouragement of loss reduction; and ability to monitor and control the behavior of the insured.

Risk spreading If a business bears the entire cost of losing its property to fire, the impact of such a loss on that business can be severe. If the business owns multiple properties, the damage to one facility diminishes the loss severity somewhat, because the business only loses part of its holdings. If the business pools its risk with other businesses through the purchase of fire insurance, it can experience a further reduction in the financial impact from a fire. As a result, insurance enables activities to take place that might not otherwise occur if the business were forced to bear individually the risk associated with the activity itself.

As the above discussion illustrates, insurance spreads the economic consequences of individual events (fire) across broader groups (many businesses). In so doing, it reduces the potentially catastrophic consequences of unforeseen events on an individual or business by having those consequences absorbed by a third party. The third party, usually an insurance company, collects premiums from many to pay for the unexpected losses of a few. Insurance tends to be self-funding, with the collected premiums held in reserve to pay future claims (Rejda, 1982).

Variance reduction Insurance markets normally exist because companies issue a large number of policies whose losses are independent of each other so that an insurer's expected losses can be characterized by 'the law of large numbers'. In simple terms, this law states that, as the number of independent events (here, losses) under consideration increases, the frequency distribution of those events tends toward the normal distribution. Therefore, the mean or expected value of the events (losses) and their variance (or measure of dispersion) are sufficient to describe the distribution of events. Furthermore, the variance of the mean value decreases as the number of events increases. If we view the variance as a measure of volatility or risk of loss, then the risk associated with the loss reduces as the number of policies grows.

As long as the number of policies issued is reasonably large, an insurer can charge premiums for disaster events that are independent of each other by estimating their mean loss or expected loss. Fire and automobile coverage are two examples of risks that tend to be independent. Notable exceptions include the 1991 Oakland fire that destroyed 1941 single-unit dwellings and damaged 2069 others or a major accident on a freeway involving many cars. Natural hazards, however, create problems for insurers because the losses arising from these events are rarely independent. The law of large numbers does not apply here (Kunreuther and Grossi, in press).

For example, if a severe earthquake occurs in Los Angeles, there is a high probability that many structures will be damaged or destroyed simultaneously. If an insurer had 1000 policies in this one region, then the estimated variance of its losses would be much larger than if these policies were written in 1000 different cities across the USA.

Segregation of risks   Insurance works best when it segregates risk. This involves discriminating between different classes of potential policyholders, using such identifying features as characteristics of the individual (good drivers versus bad drivers), classes of business (trucks versus recreational automobiles), or groups with different risk exposure (general contractors versus hazardous waste removal contractors).

Segregation enables insurance providers to separate the lowest risk category (good drivers) from a risk pool (all drivers) and to price and sell policies separately to members of that category. Safe drivers, for example, would pay an amount based on their risk profile rather than being charged a rate that subsidizes those drivers with accident records.

Encouraging loss reduction measures   In the process of creating uniform risk categories, insurance companies have adopted techniques for modifying the behavior of potential insureds. The insurer, taking a cue from the nineteenth-century mutual companies, will often require its potential policyholders to undertake specific loss reduction activities before receiving insurance coverage. In fact, insurance companies have often been the driving force behind the implementation of safety procedures. As discussed in the section on the history of insurance, as new protective measures reduced the incidence of fire in the workplace during the nineteenth century, fire risk was reduced, as were the overall costs to society (Bainbridge, 1952).

Insurers also offer premium reductions to individuals and businesses who have taken actions to reduce their risks or have better-than-average records regarding their past performance. Life insurance, for example, costs less for nonsmokers than for smokers. Security systems, burglar-proof safes, and other loss prevention devices lower insurance premiums (Greene and Trieschmann, 1988). Auto insurance costs less for drivers who have not had an accident in several years. Insurers design these forms of experience rating to encourage behavior that reduces overall risk exposure.

Monitoring and control   Insurers also provides a valuable function by monitoring the activities of their policyholders. Insurance providers generally undertake this monitoring function to verify that the insured operates in a manner consistent with underwriting standards. Monitoring may be as simple as verifying driving records, or as complicated as inspecting manufacturing facilities.

The insurer will not always undertake the inspection or audit itself but may hire certified inspectors or experts for this purpose. For example, after some serious accidents involving steam boilers in the nineteenth century, insurers used certified inspectors to monitor and approve boiler designs. Once these inspectors performed their work, insurers offered policies to cover any losses from a boiler explosion. The insurer knew the probability of such an event was low given the certification process. In fact, the monitoring of operations by the insurance provider can have significant benefit for other parties, such as the government, interested in having the behavior of others reviewed. For nearly 100 years, operators of steam boiler vessels in the USA have met government regulations by securing insurance certificates for those boilers.

Insurance has a number of inherent qualities that promise to reduce future risks and provide compensation if a loss occurs. Policy-makers have expressed significant interest in the use of insurance as a policy tool to complement the existing use of government benefit programs as a tool to transfer risk. However, the risks in question have to meet the conditions of insurability for this policy tool to be applicable.

2.   INSURABILITY OF RISKS[3]

What does it mean to say that a particular risk is insurable? This question must be addressed from the vantage point of the potential supplier of insurance who offers coverage against a specific risk at a stated premium. The policyholder is protected against a prespecified set of losses defined in the contract.

Two conditions must be met before insurance providers are willing to offer coverage against an uncertain event. Condition 1 is the ability to identify and quantify the chances of the event occurring, and the extent of losses likely to be incurred when providing different levels of coverage.

Condition 2 is the ability to set premiums for each potential customer or class of customers. This requires some knowledge of the customer's risk in relation to others in the population of potential policyholders.

If Conditions 1 and 2 are both satisfied, a risk is considered to be insurable. But it still may not be profitable. In other words, it may impossible to specify a rate for which there is sufficient demand and incoming revenue to cover the development, marketing and claims costs of the insurance and yield a net positive profit. In such cases the insurer will opt not to offer coverage against this risk.

Condition 1: Identifying the Risk

To satisfy this condition, estimates must be made of the frequency at which specific events occur and the extent of losses likely to be incurred. Such estimates can use data from previous events, or scientific analyses of what is likely to occur in the future. One way to reflect what experts know and do not know about a particular risk is to construct a loss exceedance probability (EP) curve.

A loss EP curve depicts the probability that a certain level of loss will be exceeded on an annual basis. The loss can be reflected in terms of dollars of damage, fatalities, illness or some other measure. To illustrate with a specific example, suppose one was interested in constructing an EP curve for dollar losses from a catastrophic chemical accident. Using probabilistic risk assessment one combines the set of events that could produce a given dollar loss and then determines the resulting probabilities of exceeding losses of different magnitudes.

Based on these estimates, one can construct the mean EP depicted in Figure 4.2. By its nature, the EP curve inherently incorporates uncertainty in the probability of an event occurring and the magnitude of dollar losses. This uncertainty is reflected in the 5 percent and 95 percent confidence interval curves in Figure 4.2.

The EP curve is the key element for evaluating a set of risk management tools. The accuracy of the EP curves depends upon the ability of the scientific and engineering community as well as social scientists to estimate the impact of events of different probabilities and magnitudes using the different units of analysis. These units normally include quantifiable measures such as dollar damage, number of people injured or killed and business interruption losses.

When dealing with extreme events, the key question that needs to be addressed when constructing an EP curve is the degree of uncertainty with respect to both the probability and the consequences of the event. It is much easier to construct an EP curve for natural disasters and chemical or

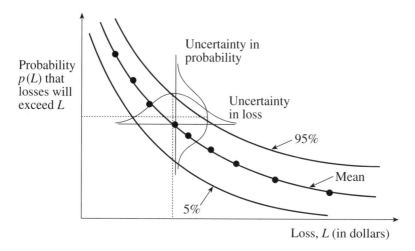

Figure 4.2   Example of exceedance probability curves

nuclear power plant accidents than it is for terrorist activities. But even for these more predictable events there is considerable uncertainty with respect to both the probability of occurrence and the resulting losses. Here are a few questions in this regard to ponder:

- What are the chances that there will be a chemical accident that kills more than 100 people somewhere in the world during the next year and what will be the resulting damage and indirect losses?
- What is the likelihood of a major hurricane striking the most populated portions of the Florida coastline in the next ten years and what would be the damages from this event?
- What are the chances that there will be a cancer epidemic due to leakages from underground storage tanks in the next five years and how many people would be affected?

Condition 2: Setting Premiums for Specific Risks

Once the risk has been identified, the insurer needs to determine what premium it can charge to make a profit while not subjecting itself to an unacceptably high chance of a catastrophic loss. There are a number of factors that influence this decision. In the discussion which follows we are assuming that insurers are free to set the premiums at any level they wish. In reality, state regulations often limit insurers in their rate-setting process.

Ambiguity of risk

Not surprisingly, the higher the uncertainty regarding the probability of a specific loss and its magnitude, the higher the premium will be. As shown by a series of empirical studies, actuaries and underwriters are so averse to ambiguity and risk that they tend to charge much higher premiums than if the risk were well specified. Kunreuther et al. (1995) conducted a survey of 896 underwriters in 190 randomly chosen insurance companies to determine what premiums would be required to insure a factory against property damage from a severe earthquake. The survey results examine changes in pricing strategy as a function of the degree of uncertainty in either the probability and/or loss.

A probability is considered to be well specified when there is enough historical data and/or scientific information on the nature of the event that all experts agreed that the probability of a loss is p. When there is wide disagreement about the estimate of p among the experts, this ambiguous probability is referred to as Ap. L represents a known loss – that is, there is a general consensus about what the loss will be if a specific event occurs. When a loss is uncertain, and the experts' estimates range between L_{min} and $L_{max,}$ this uncertain loss is denoted as UL.

Combining the degree of probability and loss uncertainty leads to four cases that are shown in Table 4.1 along with a set of illustrative examples of the types of risks that fall in each category.

Table 4.1   Classification of risks by degree of ambiguity and uncertainty

Probability	Loss	
	Known	Unknown
Well specified	*Case 1* p, L Life, auto, fire	*Case 3* p, UL Playground accidents
Ambiguous	*Case 2* Ap, L Satellite	*Case 4* Ap, UL Earthquake, bioterrorism

To see how underwriters reacted to different situations, four scenarios for an earthquake risk were constructed as shown in the columns of Table 4.2. Where the risk is well specified, the probability of the earthquake is either 0.01 or 0.005; the loss, should the event occur, is either $1 million or $10 million. The premium set by the underwriter is standardized at 1 for the non-ambiguous case; one can then examine how ambiguity affects pricing decisions.

Table 4.2   Ratios of underwriters' actuarial premiums for ambiguous and/or uncertain earthquake risks relative to well-specified risks

Scenario	Cases			
	1 p, L	2 Ap, L	3 p, UL	4 Ap, UL
$p = 0.005$ $L = \$1$ million $pL = \$5,000$	1	1.28	1.19	1.77
$p = 0.005$ $L = \$10$ million $pL = \$50\,000$	1	1.31	1.29	1.59
$p = 0.01$ $L = \$1$ million $pL = \$10\,000$	1	1.19	1.21	1.50
$p = 0.01$ $L = \$10$ million $pL = \$100\,000$	1	1.38	1.15	1.43

Source: Kunreuther et al. (1995).

Table 4.2 shows the ratio of the other three cases relative to the non-ambiguous case (p, L) for the four different scenarios, which were distributed randomly to underwriters in primary insurance companies. For the highly ambiguous case (Ap, UL), the premiums were between 1.43 to 1.77 times higher than if underwriters priced a non-ambiguous risk. The ratios for the other two cases were always above 1, but less than the (Ap, UL) case.

These concerns with the ambiguity and uncertainty of the risks have been brought to the fore since 11 September 2001, when insurers have been concerned with providing coverage against terrorism because they feel that the probability of another attack is highly ambiguous and the losses very uncertain. During the fall of 2001 it was not unusual for investors to require an annual return as high as 20 percent to invest in terrorist coverage because they were so concerned with the ambiguity of the risk (Kunreuther, 2002).

Adverse selection[4]
If the insurer sets a premium based on the average probability of a loss, using the entire population as a basis for this estimate, those at the highest risk for

a certain hazard will be the most likely to purchase coverage for that hazard. In an extreme case, the poor risks will be the only purchasers of coverage, and the insurer will lose money on each policy sold. This situation, referred to as adverse selection, occurs when the insurer cannot distinguish between the probabilities of a loss for good- and poor-risk categories.

The assumption underlying adverse selection is that purchasers of insurance have an informational advantage by knowing their risk type. Insurers, on the other hand, must invest considerable expense to collect information to distinguish between risks. For example, suppose some homes have a low probability of suffering damage (the good risks), and others have a higher probability (the poor risks). The good risks stand a 1 in 10 probability of loss, and the poor risks a 3 in 10 probability. For simplicity, assume that the loss is $100 for both groups and that there is an equal number of potentially insurable individuals in each risk class.

Since there is an equal number in both risk classes, the expected loss for a random individual in the population is $20.[5] If the insurer charges the actuarially fair premium across the entire population, only the poor-risk class would normally purchase coverage, since their expected loss is $30 (0.3 × $100), and they would be pleased to pay only $20 for the insurance. The good risks have an expected loss of $10 (0.1 × $100), so they would have to be extremely risk-averse to want to pay $20 for coverage. If only the poor risks purchase coverage, the insurer will suffer an expected loss of −$10 (that is, $20 − $30) on every policy it sells.

There are three principal ways that insurers can deal with this problem. The insurer can raise the premium to at least $30 so that it will not lose money on any individual purchasing coverage. In reality, where there is a spectrum of risks, the insurer may only be able to offer coverage to the worst-risk class in order to make a profit. Hence, raising premiums in this way is likely to deprive a large segment of the population from buying insurance because the going rate will be too high. This is a type of market failure.

Rothschild and Stiglitz (1976) proposed a second way for the insurer to deal with adverse selection. It could offer two different price-coverage contracts. For example, contract 1 could be offered at Price = $30 and Coverage = $100, while contract 2 might be Price = $10 and Coverage = $40. If the poor risks preferred contract 1 over 2, and the good risks preferred contract 2 over 1, this would be one way for the insurers to market coverage to both groups while still breaking even.

A third approach is for the insurer to require some type of audit or examination to determine the nature of the risk more precisely. However, inspections and audits are expensive and will raise the premium charged unless the potential policyholder pays for the audit.

Moral hazard[6]

Providing insurance protection to an individual may lead that person to behave more carelessly than before he or she had coverage. If the insurer cannot predict this behavior and relies on past loss data from uninsured individuals to estimate rates, the resulting premium is likely to be too low to cover losses.

Moral hazard refers to an increase in the probability of loss caused by the behavior of the policyholder. Obviously, it is extremely difficult to monitor and control behavior once a person is insured. How do you monitor carelessness? Is it possible to determine if a person will decide to collect more on a policy than he or she deserves by making false claims?

The numerical example used above to illustrate adverse selection can also demonstrate moral hazard. With adverse selection the insurer cannot distinguish between good and bad risks, but the probability of a loss for each group is assumed not to change after a policy is sold. With moral hazard the actual probability of a loss becomes higher after a person becomes insured. For example, suppose the probability of a loss increases from $p = 0.1$ before insurance to $p = 0.3$ after coverage has been purchased. If the insurance company does not know that moral hazard exists, it will sell policies at a price of $10 to reflect the estimated actuarial loss ($0.1 \times \$100$). The actual loss will be $30 since p increases to 0.3. Therefore, the firm will lose $20 ($30 - $10) on each policy it sells.

One way to avoid the problem of moral hazard is to raise the premium to $30 to reflect the known increase in the probability, p, that occurs once a policy has been purchased. In this case there will not be a decrease in coverage as there was in the adverse selection example. Those individuals willing to buy coverage at a price of $10 will still want to buy a policy at $30 since they know that their probability of a loss with insurance will be 0.3.

Another way to avoid moral hazard is to introduce deductibles and co-insurance as part of the insurance contract. A sufficiently large deductible can act as an incentive for the insureds to continue to behave carefully after purchasing coverage because they will be forced to cover a significant portion of their loss themselves. With co-insurance the insurer and the insured share the loss together. An 80 percent co-insurance clause in an insurance policy means that the insurer pays 80 percent of the loss (above a deductible), and the insured pays the other 20 percent. As with a deductible, this type of risk-sharing arrangement encourages safer behavior because those insured want to avoid having to pay for some of the losses.[7]

Another way of encouraging safer behavior is to place upper limits on the amount of coverage an individual or enterprise can purchase. If the insurer will only provide $500000 worth of coverage on a structure and contents worth $1 million, then the insured knows he or she will have to incur any residual costs of losses above $500000. This assumes that the insured will not be able to purchase a second insurance policy for $500000 to supplement the first one and hence be fully protected against a loss of $1 million, except for deductibles and co-insurance clauses. One could also discourage moral hazard by restricting the number of claims before one canceled or refused to renew one's policy. If the claims have been very costly the insurer could also raise the premiums from what they were in the previous year.[8]

Even with these clauses in an insurance contract, the insureds may still behave more carelessly with coverage than without it simply because they are protected against a large portion of the loss. For example, they may decide not to take precautionary measures that they would have adopted had they been uninsured. The cost of adopting mitigation may now be viewed as too high relative to the dollar benefits that the insured would receive from this investment. If the insurer knows in advance that an individual will be less interested in loss reduction activity after purchasing a policy, then it can charge a higher insurance premium to reflect this increased risk or it can require specific mitigation measures as a condition of insurance. In either case this aspect of the moral hazard problem will have been overcome.

Correlated risk
The simultaneous occurrence of many losses from a single event raises the possibility of insurer insolvency and/or a severe financial crisis to the firm. As pointed out earlier, natural disasters such as earthquakes, floods and hurricanes produce highly correlated losses: many homes in the affected area are damaged and destroyed by a single event.

If a risk-averse insurer faces highly correlated losses from one event, it may want to set a high enough premium not only to cover its expected losses but also to protect itself against the possibility of experiencing catastrophic losses. An insurer will face this problem if it has many eggs in one basket, such as providing earthquake coverage mainly to homes in Los Angeles County rather than diversifying across the entire state of California.

To illustrate the impact of perfectly correlated risks on the distribution of losses, assume that there are two policies sold against a risk where $p = 0.1$, $L = \$100$. The actuarial loss for each policy is $10. For perfectly correlated losses, there will be either two claims with probability of 0.1 or no claims with a probability of 0.9. On the other hand, if the losses are independent of each other, then the chance of two losses decreases to 0.01 (that is, 0.1×0.1), with the probability of no losses being 0.81 (that is, 0.9×0.9).

There is also a 0.18 chance that there will be only one loss (that is, $0.9 \times 0.1 + 0.1 \times 0.9$).

In this example the expected loss for both the correlated and uncorrelated risks is $20.[9] However, the variance will always be higher for correlated than uncorrelated risks if each have the same expected loss. Thus risk-averse insurers will always want to charge a higher premium for the correlated risk (Hogarth and Kunreuther, 1992).

Insurability Conditions and Demand for Coverage

The above discussion suggests that in theory insurers can offer protection against any risk that they can identify, and for which they can obtain information to estimate the frequency and magnitude of potential losses as long as they have the freedom to set premiums at any level. However, due to problems of ambiguity, adverse selection, moral hazard and highly correlated losses, they may want to charge premiums that considerably exceed the expected loss.

For some risks the desired premium may be so high that there would be very little demand for coverage at that rate. In such cases, even though an insurer determines that a particular risk meets the two insurability conditions discussed above, it will not invest the time and money to develop the product. More specifically, the insurer must be convinced that there is sufficient demand to cover the development and marketing costs of the coverage through future premiums received.

If there are regulatory restrictions that limit the price insurers can charge for certain types of coverage, then companies will not want to provide protection against these risks. In addition, if an insurer's portfolio leaves them vulnerable to the possibility of extremely large losses from a given disaster due to adverse selection, moral hazard and/or high correlation of risks, then the insurer will want to reduce the number of policies in force for these hazards.

3. EXAMPLES OF MANAGING ENVIRONMENTAL RISK THROUGH INSURANCE

This section illustrates how insurance has been utilized to manage environmental risk. The first example looks at the use of insurance as a component of a comprehensive risk management program for natural disasters. The second examines a current proposal to use insurance and third-party inspections to enforces one of the provisions of the Clean Air Act amendments of 1990 in the USA.

Insurance and Natural Hazard Management in Developing Countries[10]

A fundamental distinction between the risk management policies in the developed world and in developing countries is the role of risk transfer. The developed countries use risk transfer through the insurance mechanism as a major component of their natural disaster risk strategy. As shown in Figure 4.3, 29 percent of their losses from natural hazards are insured. In the poorest countries, insurance covers 1 percent of the losses from natural hazards.

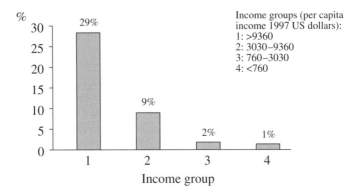

Source: Munich Re (2002), pp. 24–5.

Figure 4.3   Ratio of insured losses to total losses according to country income groups for period 1985–99

There is considerable worldwide activity in promoting different government-based programs for shifting the risk to those who reside in hazard-prone areas. As mentioned above, Turkey has a recent insurance program to transfer risk from earthquakes to property owners residing in seismically active parts of the country. Proposals are being explored in Mexico, the Caribbean, Central America and Africa to engage the government in providing risk-transfer options for farmers, homeowners and businesses in case of natural-catastrophe losses (World Bank, 2000). The Caribbean Disaster Mitigation Project (CDMP) commissioned a study to explore insurance options for small states in the region (Pollner, 2000). The World Bank has proposed the creation of a new insurance program for Honduras. As a component to the recently announced Puebla to Panama initiative sponsored by Mexico, the Inter American Development Bank is considering regional insurance options for Central America (IDB, 2002).

The use of insurance as an effective policy tool to enable countries to deal with risk more efficiently is a major theme in the current development literature. The 2000/2001 *World Development Report* on Poverty devotes considerable attention to the role of insurance in enabling countries to deal better with risk, including the risk from natural catastrophes (World Bank, 2000).

Barriers to supplying catastrophe insurance

It is no coincidence that insurance is an economic tool used by wealthy countries. It requires sophisticated financial institutions to operate. Insurance requires a complex series of laws, regulations and administrative agencies. Those include the proper financial structure of insurance companies to ensure their financial capacity to pay future claims and the actuarial science (including the required information base) that underpins the setting of premiums and reserves. One also needs legal knowledge about insurance contracts and proper legal institutions to enforce sophisticated contractual agreements. To market coverage and settle claims one needs a distribution network and qualified loss adjustors.

Designing major institutional reforms to permit the proper operation of financial institutions is very difficult. For example, the financial crises suffered by Mexico in 1995 can be traced to a weak banking system, its fragility traced to the privatization process used for the banks, some aspects of the financial liberalization program, and weak regulatory institutions (World Bank, 2000).

In addition to the need for institutional reforms, there are issues related to the fundamental structure of the market for insurance. For example, many countries may be too small to provide adequate risk diversification to properly support a national insurance scheme. Proposals to create regional insurance markets hope to increase risk diversification and potential market size, thereby making the market more attractive for the insurance industry and lowering the cost of insurance. For example, proposals exist to create a regional natural-hazard insurance market for the eastern Caribbean. Since the region is populated with small island countries with high covariant risk, the pooling of each country's risk into a regional pool is likely to increase the availability of insurance (Pollner, 2000).

A larger potential market subject to a uniform regulatory scheme may encourage the international insurance industry to help develop viable markets. To the extent that small countries in a region have varied regulatory policies, it provides a barrier to insurance companies offering coverage for similar risks in the region. The costs associated with developing premiums and marketing coverage may make it prohibitively expensive for firms to market insurance for what is likely to be limited demand for the product. Regional proposals like the Puebla to Panama catastrophe in-surance initiative for all of Central America and Mexico are partially based on overcoming impediments to the supply of insurance. Since Central America is populated with small countries each with high natural-hazard risk, the creation of a regional market that offers insurance to anyone within the region is viewed as an alternative for diversifying risk across the region. In so doing, it is hoped that the availability of insurance against natural-hazard risk for each country will be increased over what is now offered to each individual country in the region. Since the regional market is larger and more diversified than each separate-country market, there should be more incentive for insurance companies to develop and offer natural-hazard insurance in the region.

Demand for insurance in poorer countries

In truth, the problem with developing risk transfer as an effective policy tool is more related to a lack of demand for catastrophe insurance. In poorer countries, large-scale businesses can and do buy catastrophe in-surance. In Mexico, nearly 100 percent of industrial enterprises buy insu-rance (Kreimer et al., 1999). Worldwide, the strongest demand for insurance is from medium-sized businesses and homeowners. Since most developing countries do not have either a substantial middle class (who are homeowners) or many medium-sized businesses, there is a small natural clientele for insurance.

Professional risk bearers, like insurance companies, are fully capable of modifying their products to adapt to local needs. However, there will be little willingness on their part to do so if limited demand exists for the modified products. One direct approach to creating demand is to make insurance mandatory. Turkey has adopted this strategy in requiring home-owners to purchase earthquake insurance. France and Spain also make participation in their natural-disaster insurance programs mandatory (Gulkan, 2000).

Because of the relatively high administrative costs associated with mar-keting insurance and budget constraints facing the low-income residents in developing countries, this type of protection is not a viable option for this group. There is much that can be done to support the poor outside the establishment of a formal insurance program. The main strategy for the poor to deal with external shocks requires a poverty-sensitive policy that focuses on the following components:

- Helping poor households maintain their consumption.
- Ensuring that poor people do not lose whatever access they have to basic social services.

- Preventing permanent reversals in the accumulation of human and physical capital.
- Averting self-defeating behavior, such as criminal activity, prostitution, and exploitative forms of child labor (World Bank, 2000).

Among the most effective programs are workfare programs introduced or expanded in the disaster area in conjunction with post-disaster reconstruction.

Disaster management in Fiji

One developing country that looked to tie insurance as a major component of its risk management strategy for natural hazards is Fiji. Fiji is a developing country with extensive natural-catastrophe exposure from cyclones, floods, droughts, earthquakes and tsunamis. Fiji has moved remarkably towards an integrated system for disaster risk management that includes a strong national program and plan, involvement by private insurers, and a keen awareness that non-governmental organizations (NGOs) and local efforts are an integral part of the system (Benson, 1997).

Fiji's national disaster management program began as an *ad hoc* governmental committee for emergency response, but by 1990, the national program was restructured to make it more comprehensive, covering prevention, mitigation, preparedness and rehabilitation activities in addition to emergency response. In 1995 the government published the National Disaster Management Plan (Government of Fiji, 1995), which laid out a comprehensive policy and detailed the supporting roles of NGOs in all the functions of disaster management.

For a poor country, private insurance plays an important role in Fiji's national strategy. Since Fiji has a thriving tourism industry, it is not surprising that private insurance has a very high uptake in the business sector, whereas there is less but still significant insurance cover for private urban dwellings. The purchase of insurance is a key strategy to permit the tourism industry to remain in business despite the likelihood of recurrent tsunamis.

Insurers take a proactive role in mitigation and prevention. After particularly severe cyclones in 1984, the Commissioner of Insurance established the Fiji Building Standards Committee, made up mainly of private insurers. This committee had the responsibility to oversee the preparation of a national building code that would set minimum standards to reduce disaster-related losses and help achieve a stable or reduced hurricane insurance premium (Government of Fiji, 1985). Upgraded homes are inspected by a structural engineer and issued a certificate; they are required to obtain cyclone insurance cover. Most urban areas have adopted the building code (Rokovada and Vrolijks, 1993).

A number of other emerging and developing countries have integrated insurance into their national strategies to cope with natural-hazard risk. Barbados and Mexico both require that all government-owned buildings be insured (Freeman et al., 2001). Mexico has a fund for natural disasters that reimburses local governments and private property owners for a portion of their losses from natural catastrophes (Kreimer et al., 1999).

While the challenges to using insurance to cope with natural-hazard risk are difficult, the limited successes of a number of developing and emerging countries to initiate new programs has created greater interest in the role that insurance can play in managing natural-hazard risk.

Insurance coupled with third-party inspections[11]

The passage of Section 112(r) of the Clean Air Act Amendments (CAAA) of 1990 offers an opportunity to utilize insurance coupled with third-party inspections to encourage firms to reduce their risks from accidents and disasters. This legislation created two new federal regulatory programs aimed at preventing releases of hazardous chemicals: the Occupational Safety and Health Administration (OSHA) Process Safety Management (PSM) standard and the US Environmental Protection Agency (EPA) Risk Management Program.

The PSM standard was enacted in 1992 and requires facilities containing large quantities of highly hazardous chemicals to implement accident prevention and emergency response measures to protect workers. The EPA Risk Management Program regulation, published in 1996, borrowed the same accident prevention concepts and language from PSM but went beyond the OSHA program. It also required facilities to perform a hazard assessment, estimate consequences from accidents and submit a summary report to EPA by 21 June 1999 called the Risk Management Plan (RMP) (Belke, 2001). The challenge is how to encourage compliance of these regulations.

Use of insurance with third parties to enforce regulation
Consider an industrial facility that has a relatively high probability (p_h) of causing an accident which results in a loss (L), where L is a multidimensional vector reflecting direct impacts, which include lives lost or injured and damage to physical property. In addition there may be negative externalities in the form of environmental and social impacts (for example decreases in property values and disruptions in community life) that are not borne by the firm.[12]

The firm has an opportunity to reduce L as well as these negative externalities arising from accidents by implementing an RMP that will reduce the probability of an accident to $p_l < p_h$ at a fixed cost C. The magnitude of

C is based on the expenditures in both time and money in implementing a strategy for reducing the risks of future accidents.

EPA and other regulatory agencies have been searching for ways to ensure a high compliance level with respect to their regulations and standards. Consider the case of enforcing Section 112(r) of the CAAA of 1990. Given the potentially severe negative externalities associated with accidents and EPA's limited personnel and funds for providing technical guidance and auditing regulated facilities,[13] there is some urgency for a type of decentralized procedure with appropriate incentives.

Chemical firms, particularly smaller ones, may have little financial incentive to follow centralized regulatory procedures if they estimate that the chances that they will be inspected by a regulatory agency are very small and/or they know the fine should they be caught will be low. To see this, suppose that the cost of investing in an RMP is *C* and the discounted expected benefits are $E(B)<C$, so that the firm perceives that the net expected loss to them of investing in an RMP will be $E(L)=C-E(B)$. Suppose that the chance that a regulatory agency will inspect a firm is *p*. If the firm is found not to have implemented an RMP, then it will be fined *F* and be required to incur the investment cost *C*. The expected cost to the firm of not implementing an RMP is thus $p(F+C)$. A risk-neutral firm will not want to invest in an RMP if $p(F+C)<E(L)$. Smaller firms with asset levels $A<F+C$ will have even less reason to invest in an RMP, preferring to declare insolvency should they be caught.[14]

The combination of a mandatory private insurance in conjunction with third-party inspections is a powerful combination of two market mechanisms that can convince many firms of the advantages of implementing RMPs to make their plants safer and encourage the remaining ones to comply with the regulation to avoid being caught and fined. Such a program would reduce societal risk due to the negative externalities associated with accidents, while providing a tool for the government to help ensure compliance at minimal regulatory cost.

To show the conditions under which third parties can be effective, Kunreuther et al. (2002) have developed a simple model where there are two types of firms – high and low risk. Firms are assumed to maximize their expected profits. The probability of an accident is p_l for a low-risk firm and p_h for a high risk firm $(p_l<p_h)$. The losses from an accident are *L* whether the firm is low or high risk.

In this model firms are required to have insurance to cover their losses should a catastrophic accident occur. Financial institutions may require insurance as a condition for a mortgage to protect the bank's investment. The regulatory agency could require this coverage, so that the firm will not declare insolvency should it suffer a severe loss from an accident.

If a firm agrees to be audited, the third party will charge C for the inspection and the insurer will charge a premium that reflects the outcome of the inspection. A low-risk firm will be charged $p_l L$ and a high risk firm will be charged $p_h L$. If the firm refuses to be audited, it will be presumed to be high risk and will be charged a higher premium.

The intuition behind using third parties and insurance to support regulations can be stated in the following way. One of the biggest concerns of a regulatory agency (RA) is that it doesn't have enough resources to audit all firms in the industry. Low-risk firms, which the RA has no need to audit, cannot credibly distinguish themselves from the high-risk ones without some type of inspection. By delegating part of the inspection process to the private sector through insurance companies and third parties, the RA provides a channel through which the low-risk firms can speak for themselves. If a firm chooses not to be inspected by third parties, it is more likely to be a high- rather than a low-risk one. Therefore this mechanism not only substantially reduces the number of firms the RA has to audit, but it also makes their audits more efficient.

The Kunreuther et al. (2002) paper suggests that the government fine associated with a regulatory audit needs to be carefully considered as a part of the policy process. If there is a small chance that a firm will be audited, then F has to be much larger than if p were relatively high. There is likely to be political pressure from the regulated industry for low fines, since small firms may have to declare insolvency if F is too high. To the extent that third parties provide other risk management services, then voluntary inspection becomes a more attractive option for any given (p, F) combination.

Success of insurance and third-party inspections

Steam boiler insurance and inspections provide a convincing illustration of the use of these two policy tools for reducing risks of explosions. The Hartford Steam Boiler Inspection and Insurance Company (HSB) initiated inspections coupled with insurance in the 1860s after a severe boiler explosion on the Mississippi River. HSB has always stressed that insurance was secondary to loss prevention, with engineering and inspection services making up a large part of the insurance premium. In an effort to reduce future risks, HSB undertook studies of boiler construction, which eventually led to boilermakers adopting safer designs (Er, 1996).

One of the key elements leading to the reduction in the number of boiler accidents is that all the states in the USA require annual inspections of pressure vessels by a representative licensed by the state, county or municipality in which the facility is located. Inspectors are qualified by either a formal examination or through a certificate of competency issued by the National Board of Boiler and Pressure Vessel Inspectors.[15]

Workers' compensation provides a second example of the role that insurance and third-party inspections can play in improving the safety of the workplace. Today almost every worker in the USA is covered by a workers' compensation program, which provides cash benefits and medical care for work-related injuries and diseases. Since premiums for many employers are linked by experience rating formulas to benefits paid to their employees, firms have financial incentives to reduce risk levels.[16] Moore and Viscusi (1990) provide evidence that workers' compensation creates substantial incentives for firms to promote safety. However, other scholars do not find similar results and Burton (2001) concludes that the evidence that experience rating improves safety is only mildly persuasive.

The workers' compensation mechanism has some similarities to the model described above for those who choose to purchase coverage from insurers. Insurance companies normally undertake an inspection, although it is not mandatory that they do so. The insurer may offer risk management services, often at a fee, to reduce a company's losses and its premium. The types of accidents considered in this paper (for example, chemical explosions, chemical fires, or chemical releases) usually generate more costs to the external world than do workplace hazards. Large-scale industrial accidents often impact on the whole neighborhood and surrounding area, while the consequences of workers' accidents are normally confined to the employees in the firm.

Delaware and Pennsylvania pilot experiments
During 1999 and 2000 two pilot studies on third parties and insurance were undertaken by a task force convened by the Wharton Risk Management and Decision Processes Center consisting of the EPA's Chemical Emergency Preparedness and Prevention Office (CEPPO), EPA Region III and the State of Delaware's Department of Natural Resources and Environmental Control (DNREC).[17]

Third-party auditors have been used to examine RMPs and ensure compliance with Section 112(r) of the CAAA in Delaware and Pennsylvania at both water chlorination and ammonia refrigeration facilities.[18] Ammonia and chlorine were the chemicals selected in the experiment because they represent 50 percent of the hazardous chemicals that facilities report under section 112(r) of the CAAA and because the task force was confident that the third-party auditors could be trained to conduct audits in chlorine and ammonia facilities in a two-day training period.

In both Delaware and Pennsylvania the owners and operators of facilities were sympathetic to having third-party inspections and would be inclined to use them if they yielded certain benefits. More specifically, facility owners said they would be especially interested if the EPA or a regulatory agency gave them a seal of approval based on the results of the inspection, if economic benefits were offered them by the insurance companies in undertaking the inspection, and if the community viewed positive results from an inspection as a signal that the firm was operating safely.

These pilot experiments indicate some of the additional actions that EPA must consider if it modifies the provisions of section 112(r) of the Clean Air Act Amendments to allow for third-party auditors to be used on a national basis. For one thing the agency needs to establish a certification mechanism for the selection and training of third-party auditors. It also needs to expand the selection and training of third-party auditors to include all chemicals listed on the EPA list, not just ammonia and chlorine. The agency also has to address the issue as to actions that need to be taken if an inspector discovers that the firm is operating in ways that may be hazardous to employees and/or residents in the region.[19]

Where do we go from here?

By linking a required insurance policy with a third-party inspection there is an opportunity to convince both large and small firms that it is worthwhile for them to undertake an RMP and submit voluntarily to an inspection. This action will be particularly attractive if the inspector can provide special risk management services in addition to its audit function.

In addition, it is important for the regulatory agency to be able to charge an appropriate penalty if a firm is not in compliance. For example, if the US EPA imposes the maximum allowable fine of $27 500 per day should it discover that a firm does not have an RMP, then this may be an added incentive for industrial facilities to undertake a third-party inspection voluntarily.

The implicit assumption is that if a high-risk firm undertakes an inspection and does not want to incur the costs associated with investing in a process to make it a low-risk enterprise, then it not be required to do so. Furthermore, there is no obligation by the firm or the third party to report the results of the inspection to the regulatory authority. In practice there may need to be exceptions to this rule. For example, if an inspector finds that a facility poses a hazard where employees in the firm are in imminent danger, then he would be torn between maintaining confidentiality with the client and exposing individuals to possible injury or death.

One way to deal with this situation would be to require the inspector to reveal this information to the relevant regulatory authority if the firm refuses to take any remedial action within a prespecified period of time. Such a procedure would be in line with current OSHA policy for consultants to the agency who discover such a situation (Occupational Safety and Health Administration, 1989). More studies need to be undertaken to determine in what situations inspectors have an obligation to reveal the results of their findings to employees, citizens and/or the regulatory authority.[20]

The use of third-party inspections has had very beneficial effects on reducing the risks associated with different activities. Steam boiler accidents have been very rare ever since it was required that boilers be inspected. If the safety incentives of workers' compensation were removed, there would be an increase of over 30 percent in fatality rates in the USA. This translates into an increase of 1200 workers who would die from job-related accidents (Viscusi, 1991).

5. CONCLUSIONS

This chapter makes the case for using insurance coupled with other policy tools for reducing future losses from environmental risks. Our focus has been on losses from natural hazards and risks associated with catastrophic accidents from industrial facilities, although these concepts can be applied to other areas as well. To date the public sector provides some relief to victims of natural disasters in all parts of the world and assumes much of the burden in emerging economies. With respect to reducing losses from large-scale industrial accidents, there have been regulations passed to reduce these losses, but the relevant agencies do not have sufficient person power to enforce them.

Insurance is a risk transfer instrument that has the added benefit of encouraging those seeking financial protection to take steps to reduce future losses since this will lower their annual premium. We discussed the conditions for making a risk insurable and the challenges in obtaining sufficient data to quantify the risk. In addition, the resulting premium has to be low enough to be attractive to a large enough group of potential policyholders for insurers to incur the costs of developing and marketing the product.

With respect to future research, there is a set of issues that should be addressed with respect to natural-hazard risk. While the use of insurance to handle natural-hazard risk is well understood, its application to the needs of developing countries is an area of increasing focus. As the losses from disasters continue to escalate, additional sources of funding for reconstruction and recovery will be needed. In addition, the reduction of vulnerability to natural-hazard losses is a central policy concern. Insurance provides a tool to both reduce losses by encouraging *ex ante* risk-reducing behavior and by providing post-disaster reconstruction funding. Complex issues related to both the supply and demand of natural-hazard catastrophe insurance for the poorest of countries need to be resolved.

There is a number of open issues that have to be explored in future research in the area of insurance and third-party inspections for industrial accidents. These include the ability of inspectors to determine how safe a firm actually is, the asymmetry of information between firms, insurers and inspectors and the ability to estimate the risk of chemical accidents and the costs of preventive actions.

In the Kunreuther et al. (2002) model the authors assume that third-party inspections can perfectly distinguish high-risk firms from low-risk ones. It is important to examine how firms would behave if misclassification exists. We also assume an asymmetry of information between firms, regulatory agencies and third parties. Only the firms know their own risk levels. But firms may not have a clear idea as to how safe their operations are. How will firms behave when the asymmetry has been removed? Further research on these questions is needed to shed light on the opportunities and challenges of utilizing third-party inspection in concert with insurance, government regulations and/or well-defined standards.

The 11 September 2001 terrorist attack has stimulated considerable interest throughout the world in how we can better manage risk for extreme events. Insurance is a potentially powerful policy tool for addressing this issue, but as we have shown in this chapter, it needs to be combined with other programs. It is uncertain what types of strategies will emerge in the coming months and years. What is much clearer is that there is a need to rethink the role of the public and private sectors in dealing with these types of risks.

NOTES

1. Developed by the Geoscience division of Munich Re.
2. A *great natural catastrophe* is defined as one where the affected region is 'distinctly over-taxed, making interregional or international assistance necessary. This is usually the case when thousands of people are killed, hundreds of thousands are made homeless, or when a country suffers substantial economic losses, depending on the economic circumstances generally prevailing in that country' (Munich Re, 2000).
3. A more detailed discussion of insurability conditions and their relationship to environmental and natural hazards protection can be found in Freeman and Kunreuther (1997) and Kunreuther and Roth (1998). Gollier (2000) examines the various factors that may make certain risks uninsurable.
4. For a survey of adverse selection in insurance markets see Dionne and Doherty (1992).
5. This expected loss is calculated as follows: $[50(0.1 \times \$100) + 50(0.3 \times \$100)]/100 = \$20$.
6. See Winter (1992) for a survey of the relevant literature on moral hazard in insurance markets.
7. For more details on deductibles and co-insurance in relation to moral hazard, see Pauly (1968).
8. We are grateful to Henk Folmer for this suggestion.
9. For the correlated risk the expected loss is $0.9 \times \$0 + 0.1 \times \$200 = \$20$. For the independent risk the expected loss is $(0.81 \times \$0) + (0.18 \times \$100) + (0.01 \times \$200) = \$20$.
10. This section is based on Freeman et al. (2001).
11. This section is based on Kunreuther et al. (2002).
12. We could also include indirect impacts in this analysis so that the loss is a function of

time (L_t), but this complicates the analysis without changing any of the qualitative results. Indirect impacts include business interruption should the plant be damaged or destroyed, the effect on property values in the community, social and emotional stress to the community as well as long-term impacts on the industry.

13. For example, EPA's Region III has only five auditors for inspecting its many facilities.
14. Of course, if managers of firms are held criminally liable for failure to comply with regulations, there will be added incentives for them to take the regulations seriously.
15. For more details on the role of insurance and inspection in the context of steam boilers, see Er (1996).
16. Many large companies self-insure their workers' compensation programs, which is another version of experience rating. In addition, many insurance policies have deductibles that require the employers to pay 100 percent of the benefits up to a specified amount, which strengthens the financial incentives for these employers to reduce injuries and diseases. In recent years, benefits paid by self-insured employers plus benefits paid under deductibles have accounted for over 30 percent of all workers' compensation benefits (Mont, Burton, Reno and Thompson 2001, Table 6).
17. State of Delaware, Department of Natural Resources and Environmental Control (DNREC) is the state agency that is the implementing agency for the Extremely Hazardous Substances Risk Management Act.
18. Delaware was selected as one location to carry out experiments because it has had a state regulation for inspecting chemical facilities since 1990. Pennsylvania was selected to conduct third-party audits because state officials in Pennsylvania do not routinely inspect chemical facilities for their risk management programs.
19. For more details on the experiments in Delaware see McNulty et al. (1999). The Pennsylvania project is discussed in US Environmental Protection Agency (2001).
20. See Collins et al. (2002) for a more detailed discussion on how much legal liability third-party auditors would acquire by participating in this program.

REFERENCES

Arrow, K.J. (1992), 'Insurance, Risk and Resource Allocation', in G. Dionne and S.E. Harrington (eds), *Foundations of Insurance Economics: Readings in Economic and Finance*, Boston: Kluwer Academic Publishers, 220–29.

Bainbridge, John (1952), *Biography of an Idea: The Story of Mutual Fire and Casualty Insurance*, Garden City, NY: Doubleday & Co.

Belke, J. (2001), 'The case for voluntary third party risk management program audits', paper presented at the 2001 Process Plant Safety Symposium of the American Institute of Chemical Engineers, 23 April.

Benson, C. (1997), 'The Economic Impact of Natural Disasters in Fiji', London: Overseas Development Institute.

Boyd, James and Howard Kunreuther (1997), 'Retroactive Liability or the Public Purse?', *Journal of Regulatory Economics*, **11**, 79–90.

Burton, John F., Jr. (2001), 'Economics of Safety', in Neil J. Smelser and Paul B. Baltes (editors-in-chief), and Orley Ashenfelter, (economics section editor), *International Encyclopedia of the Social and Behavioral Sciences*, Elsevier Science.

Clarke, C. (2000), 'Facing the challenge of natural disasters in Latin American and the Caribbean: An IDB Action Plan', Washington, DC: Inter-American Development Bank.

Collins, L. et al. (2002), 'The Insurance Industry as a Qualified Third Party Auditor', *Professional Safety*, **47**(4).

Covello, V.J. and J. Mumpower (1985), 'Risk Analysis and Risk Management: An Historical Perspective', *Risk Analysis*, **5**, 103–20.

Dionne, Georges and Neil Doherty (1992), 'Adverse Selection in Insurance Markets: A Selective Survey', in Georges Dionne (ed.), *Contributions to Insurance Economics*, Boston: Kluwer, 97–140.

Er, J.P. (1996), 'A Third Party Approach To Environmental Regulation And Possible Roles For Insurance Companies', PhD dissertation, University of Pennsylvania.

Ferranti, D., G.E. Perry et al. (2000), *Securing Our Future in a Global Economy*, Washington, DC: World Bank.

Freeman, Paul K. (2000), 'Infrastructure, Natural Disasters and Poverty', in A. Kreimer and M. Arnold (eds), *Managing Disaster Risk in Emerging Economies*, Washington, DC: World Bank.

Freeman, Paul K. and Howard Kunreuther (1997), *Managing Environmental Risk through Insurance*, Washington DC: AEI Press (softback), Norwell, MA: Kluwer Academic Publishers (hardback).

Freeman, Paul K., Leslie Martin, Joanne Linnerooth-Bayer, Koko Warner, Alan Lavell, Omar D. Cardona and Howard Kunreuther (2001), 'National Systems and Institutional Mechanisms for the Comprehensive Management of Disaster Risk', working paper, Natural Disasters Regional Policy Dialogue, Inter-American Development Bank, Washington, DC.

Freeman, Paul K., Leslie Martin, Georg Pflug, Reinhard Mechler, Joanne Linnerooth-Bayer, Koko Warner and Omar D. Cardona (2002), 'National Systems for Comprehensive Disaster Management: Financing Reconstruction', working paper, Natural Disasters Regional Policy Dialogue, Inter-American Development Bank, Washington, DC (http://www.iadb.org/int/drp/)

Gilbert, R. and A. Kreimer (1999), *Learning from the World Bank's Experience of Natural Disaster Related Assistance*, Washington, DC: Urban Development Division, World Bank.

Gollier, Christian (2000), 'Towards an economic theory of the limits of insurability', *Assurances*, January, 453–74.

Government of Fiji (1985), *Budget 1986*, Suva: Government of Fiji.

Government of Fiji (1995), 'Fiji National Disaster Management Plan', Suva: Government of Fiji National Disaster Management Council.

Greene, Mark and James Trieschmann (1988), *Risk and Insurance*, Cincinatti, OH: South-Western Publishing Co.

Gulkan, Polat (2000), 'Rebuilding the Sea of Marmara Region: Recent Structural Revisions in Turkey to Mitigate Disasters', A Wharton–World Bank Conference on Challenges in Managing Catastrophic Risks: Lessons for the US and Emerging Economies, Washington, DC.

Hogarth, Robin and Howard Kunreuther (1992), 'Pricing Insurance and Warranties: Ambiguity and Correlated Risks', *The Geneva Papers on Risk and Insurance Theory*, **17**, July, 35–60.

IDB America, magazine of the Inter-American Development Bank (2002), 'A New Vision for Mesoamerica', 24 January.

Kreimer, A., M. Arnold, C. Barham, P. Freeman, R. Gilbert, F. Krimgold, R. Lester, J.D. Pollner and T. Vogt (1999), 'Managing Disaster Risk in Mexico: Market Incentives for Mitigation Investment', Washington, DC: World Bank.

Kunreuther, Howard (2002), 'The Role of Insurance in Managing Extreme Events: Implications for Terrorism Coverage', *Risk Analysis*, **22**, June, 427–38.

Kunreuther, H. and R.J. Roth (eds) (1998), *Paying the Price: The Status and Role of Insurance Against Natural Disasters in the United States*, Washington, DC: Joseph Henry Press.

Kunreuther, Howard and Patricia Grossi (in press), 'Introduction' Chapter 1 in

Howard Kunreuther, and Patricia Grossi (eds), *New Approaches to the Management of Natural Hazards*, Norwell, MA: Kluwer Academic Publishers.

Kunreuther, Howard, Patrick McNulty and Yong Kang (2002) 'Improving environmental safety through third party inspection', *Risk Analysis*, **22**, 309–18.

Kunreuther, Howard, Jacqueline Meszaros, Robin Hogarth and Mark Spranca (1995), 'Ambiguity and underwriter decision processes', *Journal of Economic Behavior and Organization*, **26**, 337–52.

McNulty, P.J., R.A. Barrish, R.C. Antoff and L.C. Schaller (1999), 'Evaluating the use of third parties to measure process safety management in small firms', 1999 Annual Symposium, Mary Kay O'Connor Process Safety Center, Texas A&M University, 26 October.

Mont, Daniel, John F. Burton, Jr., Virginia Reno, and Cecili Thompson (2001), *Workers' Compensation: Benefits, Coverage, and Costs, 1999 New Estimates and 1996–1998 Revisions*, Washington, DC: National Academy of Social Insurance.

Moore, Mark and K. Viscusi (1990), *Compensation Mechanisms for Job Risks: Wages, Workers' Compensation and Product Liability*, Princeton, NJ: Princeton University Press.

Munich Reinsurance Company (2000), *Topics: Natural Disasters. Annual Review of Natural Disasters 1999*, Munich: Munich Reinsurance Group.

Munich Reinsurance Company (2001), *Topics: Natural Disasters. Annual Review of Natural Disasters 2000*, Munich: Munich Reinsurance Group.

Munich Reinsurance Company (2002), *Topics: Natural Disasters. Annual Review of Natural Disasters 2001*, Munich: Munich Reinsurance Group.

Occupational Safety and Health Administration (OSHA) (1989), 29 CFR Part 1908, Consultation Agreements, Final Rule, 49 FR 25094, 19 June 1984, as amended at 54 FR 24333, 7 June 1989.

Pauly, Mark (1968), 'The Economics of Moral Hazard: Comment', *American Economic Review*, **58**, 531–7.

Pollner, John (2000), 'Catastrophe Risk Management Using Alternative Risk Financing & Insurance Pooling Mechanisms: The Insurance Market and the Case of the Caribbean Region', Washington, DC: World Bank.

Priest, George L. (1996), 'The Government, the Market, and the Problem of Catastrophic Loss', *Journal of Risk and Uncertainty*, **12**, 219–37.

Rejda, George (1982), *Principles of Insurance*, Glenview, IL: Scott, Foresman & Co.

Rothschild, Michael and Stiglitz, Joseph (1976), 'Equilibrium in Insurance Markets: An Essay on the Economics of Imperfect Information', *Quarterly Journal of Economics*, **90**, 629–49.

Rokovada, J. and L. Vrolijks (1993), 'Case Study Fiji: Disaster and development linkages', *South Pacific Workshop*, Apia: Western Samoa.

US Environmental Protection Agency (2001), 'Third Party Audit Pilot Project in the Commonwealth of Pennsylvania', final report US EPA Region III, Philadelphia, PA, February.

Viscusi, W. Kip (1991), *Reforming Products Liability*, Cambridge, MA: Harvard University Press.

Wilson, Albert R. (1991), *Environmental Risk: Identification and Management*, Chelsea, MI: Lewis Publishers.

Winter, Ralph (1992), 'Moral Hazard and Insurance Contracts', in Georges Dionne (ed.), *Contributions to Insurance Economics*, Boston, MA: Kluwer, pp. 61–96.

World Bank (2000), 'Chapter 9: Managing Economic Crises and Natural Disasters', *World Development Report 2000/2001: Attacking Poverty*, Washington, DC: Oxford University Press and World Bank, 161–76.

5. Motor vehicles and the environment

Winston Harrington and Virginia McConnell

1. INTRODUCTION

One hundred years ago the new horseless carriage was hailed as a clean technology for urban transportation. And so it was, at least compared to the technology it eventually replaced, namely horses and horse-drawn carriages (Bettman, 1988). Since then, the growth in the number and use of motor vehicles, together with the ramifications of that growth, has been among the most conspicuous features of the modern industrial economy, as well as one of the most influential forces on the natural and built environment.

It is easy to understand why motor vehicles are so popular: they bring rapid, reliable and convenient mobility on demand to those lucky enough to have access to them. And increasingly, even in some developing and transitional economies, the lucky ones are not just the élites. The automobile is truly a mass transportation medium, in precisely the same way radio or television is a mass communication medium.

And yet, as one acute observer wrote a generation ago, 'Today, everyone who values cities is disturbed by automobiles' (Jacobs, 1961). Throughout the world motor vehicles are a major source of pollution, especially in urbanized areas, where most vehicles are found and where pollution from all sources is most severe. They cause congestion and accidents, although, compared with their predecessor technology, it is not clear that motor vehicles are any less safe. Certainly there are more traffic deaths today than a century ago, but there is vastly more traffic. As major users of fossil fuels, motor vehicles are collectively a significant contributor to greenhouse gas emissions. Not least, by reducing the cost of transportation they have contributed to the decentralization of urban areas, which is generally thought to be a bad thing, although there is no consensus on the reasons why.

Our purpose here is to examine the environmental effects of automobiles and the policies undertaken to manage those effects. We make this enormous area of study manageable in one chapter in several ways. First, we do not try to be comprehensive, especially on policy. Second, we focus primarily, though not exclusively, on the household sector. To an extent uncommon in environmental policy, policy outcomes depend on the behavioral responses of consumers. For example, to what extent do drivers change travel decisions or vehicle choice in response to changes in the costs or provision of alternative travel modes, and do these responses vary with different land-use configurations? There is a considerable literature that models these decisions, with application to vehicle use and mode choice, and we examine these in some detail. Third, we ignore off-road transport and vehicle use (for example railroads, water transport, construction equipment), even though they are also an important part of the air pollution problem. Finally, we focus on only a few major topic areas, and, by necessity, give short shrift to others.

The different strands of the literature that are the focus of this study on vehicles and the environment include fuel demand models, vehicle ownership models, general environmental policy, environmental policy for motor vehicles including alternative policy instruments, energy use in motor vehicles, and transportation and land-use modeling. There are already many reviews of these individual literatures, and we won't attempt a comprehensive review of them all. Neither is this a 'review of reviews', although we will mention several that we think are particularly useful. Rather it is our assessment of the state of knowledge in certain areas and with respect to certain problems. These are not necessarily the most important environmental problems associated with motor vehicles but, arguably, the ones that have received the most attention from politicians and policy analysts.

In the remainder of this section, we examine current levels and rates of growth of vehicle ownership and use in countries around the world. Next, we consider what it is about motor vehicles that, from an economic and policy perspective, sets them apart from other environmental issues and makes them worthy of special consideration.

In section 2 we categorize the private and social costs of vehicle ownership and use. The private costs (and benefits) provide some insight into motorists' behavior. As for social costs, we describe some estimates that help put environmental damages from motor vehicles in perspective. Section 3 provides an overview of empirical models of consumer behavior with regard to transportation choices. The next three sections review economic aspects of three major environmental problems frequently associated with motor vehicle use: local air pollution, global climate change, and land use. Finally, we examine trends and possibilities for vehicles and vehicle use in the future.

1.1 Vehicle Holdings

The total stock of vehicles in the world is growing at about 3 percent per year. Figure 5.1 tracks the growth rate of cars and trucks and buses separately

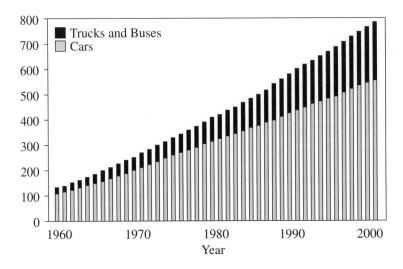

Source: World Resources Institute, based on AAMA data.

Figure 5.1   Global motor vehicle registration (millions), 1960–2001

since 1960 and shows that the total stock of vehicles is close to 800 million, up from about 100 million in 1960. Although holdings of both have been increasing, the growth rate of trucks and buses has been higher than that for cars in recent years, and is expected to continue to grow at rapid rates worldwide. In Europe alone, the European Commission forecasts truck traffic to increase by more than 50 percent in the next ten years (Walsh, 2002).

The aggregated nature of these fleet data conceal the dramatic differences in vehicle holding and use among countries and regions of the world. Table 5.1 shows the average vehicle holdings of vehicles of all types per 1000 of population for selected countries. Vehicle holdings in developing countries are many times smaller than they are in more developed economies. Holdings in the USA, Canada and most of Europe were above 500 vehicles per 1000 population by 1998, while holdings in China and India were less than ten vehicles per 1000. Overall, the developed countries hold about 78 percent of the cars and 66 percent of buses and trucks (AAMA, 1996). However, the growth rates of vehicle ownership are very high in developing countries and are likely to remain so for many years.[1]

The last column of Table 5.1 shows that the average age of the vehicle fleet varies a great deal across countries. The age of the fleet is determined by the rate of new and used additions to the fleet and the rate at which vehicles are scrapped. Japan has the lowest average age, at just over five years,

Table 5.1 Vehicle holdings, gross domestic product and vehicle age in selected countries

Country	Average vehicle holdings per 1000 population 1980	Average vehicle holdings per 1000 population 1998	% change in vehicle holdings (1980–1998)	GDP per capita $1999	Average age of the car fleet[d] (years) 2000
South America					
Argentina	155	176	14%	10,300	11+
Chile	61	110	80%	12,500	–
North America					
Canada	548	560	2%	22,400	6.7
U.S.	660	783	20%	31,500	6.8
Asia					
China	2	8	300%	3,600	–
India	2	7	250%	1,720	15*
Indonesia	8	22	175%	2,830	9.4
Japan	323	560	73%	23,100	5.3
Europe					
Finland	288	448	56%	20,100	10.8
Italy	334	591	77%	20,800	8.1
Poland	86	273	217%	6,800	10
Middle East					
Turkey	23	81	252%	6,600	9.3
Africa					
Nigeria	4	26	550%	960	12+

Notes:
[d] Data from Pemberton Associates, International Automotive Research, Analysis, Forecasting and Consultancy, London.
– data not available.
*Data obtained informally through research organizations.

Sources: *World Development Indicators*, World Bank (2000), CIA *World Factbook* (1999), Eurostat Statistical Compendium (2001).

in part because of the high costs of getting older vehicles through the tight inspection system. In contrast, India is estimated to have a fleet with an average age of about 15 years. One factor that causes developing countries to have an older fleet is that they import many used vehicles from countries in the developed world. Another reason is that vehicles tend to be driven until they are much older before they are scrapped. Older vehicles tend to have higher emissions of both greenhouse gases and conventional pollutants.

Over 60 percent of vehicles in the world are held in the developed countries, and their sheer numbers in places like the USA and parts of Europe mean their influence on the environment is pervasive. However, the rapidly growing size of fleets in developing countries and their relatively older age indicate the growing role of vehicles and policies toward the vehicle in these countries in the coming years.

1.2   The Special Characteristics of Mobile Sources

Few real-world situations fit perfectly the conditions of the standard economic approach to environmental externalities learned in one's first graduate environmental economics course and presented, for example, in Baumol and Oates (1988). However, motor vehicles are quite likely an especially poor fit. Their distinctive features offer opportunities and – more commonly – create difficulties for fashioning approaches to environmental policy, especially policy respecting conventional pollutants.

The users are primarily households, rather than firms. This means there are millions of potential polluters, rather than thousands as in the case of stationary sources. This obvious fact has had several ramifications that have profoundly shaped policy. First, emissions and emission reductions cannot be directly measured for every vehicle, nor, for that matter, can vehicle use. Vehicle use and vehicle emissions can only be determined indirectly by inferences from surveys of households or (for emissions) of vehicles.[2] Planners and regulators have had to rely heavily on modeled rather than measured emissions. In the USA, for example, EPA's MOBILE model is now used not only for planning but for enforcement as well, a development that has had unfortunate consequences both for the model itself and for policy. Second, these millions of motorist–polluters vote, which has made it very difficult to implement effective emission regulations directly on vehicles. Instead, most of the work in reducing emissions has been done by emission standards for new vehicles.

Responsibility for emissions is shared among a number of parties. The actions of many different parties can affect motor vehicle emissions. Manufacturers design and install the engine and emission control system. Refiners can produce fuel with highly variable emission potential, particularly with regard to hydrocarbon (HC) emissions for gasoline engines and sulfur for diesel fuel. Actual emissions vary greatly with how the vehicle is driven. Responsibility for vehicle maintenance and emission system repair is shared between mechanics and motorists.

The advantage of this diffusion of responsibility is that there are many potential regulatees, and many possible interventions in the system. On the other hand, the more policies, the greater the difficulty of choosing among them. Various actors can more easily point to others as the real problem. And actions taken by one actor can be undone by the behavior of others. For example, motorists' failure to maintain their vehicles can compromise the integrity of manufacturer-installed emission control systems. The observed pattern of responsibility is in part a product of the institutional structure that governs motor vehicle production, ownership and use. Thus, one possible approach to motor vehicle emission policy is to consider ways to alter this structure. For example, manufacturers could be required to maintain pollution control over the lifetime of their vehicles; or in-use vehicle emission control could be bid on and contracted by one party, who would then be responsible for a target level of emissions reductions. These approaches have been suggested (Harrington and McConnell, 2000, have reviewed alternative property rights structures) but have not been tried.

Variation in emission rates. The variation in emission rates shows up in many different ways.

(1) *Among various models and vintages.* In the USA, because of the gradual tightening of emission standards between 1973 and the present, emissions from new vehicles in 1995 were less than 5 percent of the average emissions of uncontrolled vehicles from the early 1970s. 'Engine out' emissions (that is, emissions produced by the engine before abatement) have declined by about 70 percent. The emission control system reduces the remaining emissions by about 85–90 percent (Ross et al., 1995). Light-duty truck emissions standards have not been as strict as car emission requirements, but are required to be equivalent by 2005. However, heavy-duty engines have hardly been regulated at all through this period in the USA. Recent legislation has changed this, and huge reductions in both NO_x and particulate emissions from heavy-duty diesel engines will be required by the 2007 model year.

Emission rates also increase with vehicle mileage, probably a consequence of the gradual deterioration of the emission control equipment and other systems on the vehicle that affect emissions. In addition, emissions appear to vary by manufacturer (Ross, 1994; Ross et al.; 1995, Bishop and Stedman, 1996). Also, for some makes, emission rates of the more expensive models are lower on average than in less expensive models. It is not known whether this variation arises from differences in manufacture or differences in owner characteristics (Harrington and McConnell, 2000).

(2) *Among vehicles of the same model and vintage.* Emission rates of vehicles of the same model and year of manufacture can vary. Emissions systems break down in some random pattern over time, and some vehicles are better maintained over time than others. As evidence of this variation, randomly selected models at emission inspection stations in Arizona during 1995/1996 were found to have a range of emission rates (Harrington et al., 2000). At the time Arizona used the 'IM240' emission test, which probably gives the most accurate and replicable test results among those feasible for use in emission inspection programs.

(3) *Under different operating conditions for the same vehicle.* Emissions vary widely depending on speed and acceleration. At very high rates of acceleration, gasoline vehicles enter an 'enrichment' cycle that sends more fuel to the engine than can be burned, and more than can be oxidized by the catalytic converter. The resulting emissions of CO and HC are extremely high, perhaps hundreds of times greater than under normal operating conditions (Ross et al., 1995).

(4) *At different times for the same vehicle and same operating conditions.* Some vehicles, especially those with underlying emission control system malfunctions, have emissions that vary substantially even under the same conditions. Bishop and Stedman (1996) call these vehicles 'flippers' and estimated that they were responsible for a substantial share of fleet emissions in Colorado in the early 1990s.

It has long been well understood (and recently formalized by Newell and Stavins, 2000) that emission variation across sources strongly increases the potential benefits of economic incentive approaches to environmental policy. If so, mobile sources ought to offer a promising application of economic incentive programs. Despite this potential, few market-based policies for motor vehicles have been implemented. Several have been suggested, as we discuss below.

2.   THE PRIVATE AND SOCIAL COSTS OF AUTOMOBILE OWNERSHIP AND USE

Every year the American Automobile Association publishes an estimate of the cost of driving. In its most recent publication,[3] the AAA estimate for a late-model mid-size vehicle (2001 Ford Taurus) traveling 15000 miles per year is 51 cents per mile ($\cent$/mi). Note that the AAA estimate is for a new vehicle; for older vehicles the average driving cost is much less. For example, we estimate the cost of driving a ten-year-old Ford Taurus to be 20 to 30

¢/mi. In older cars, lower depreciation is countered by higher repair and maintenance costs. For a given age, cost declines with use, because there are more units over which to spread the fixed costs. These costs are, of course, only the private costs and don't include the costs imposed on others, which are rarely paid by the motorist.

Before turning to the external costs of auto use, we will take note of a couple of interesting aspects of private costs. First, the cost of owning and using an automobile is evidently quite high – so high, in fact, that vehicular transportation now accounts for 18 percent of expenditure among American households (BLS, 2001). But no one forces people to buy cars, and the fact that the average American household owns 1.9 cars suggests that the benefits of auto ownership and use are also very high. In fact, the average benefits per mile must exceed the average costs.

For a new vehicle, about 50–70 percent of the average private costs are fixed costs, which are costs that do not vary with miles traveled. The importance of fixed costs declines with age and intensity of use, but even for the ten-year-old Taurus, fixed costs still comprise 38–55 percent of our estimate of overall costs. The variable costs of using a Taurus are about the same – 11–15¢/mi – regardless of age. For other vehicles, the variable cost may differ (it depends strongly on fuel economy), but except for extremely old vehicles, the variable cost of vehicle use is much less than the average total cost, and *a fortiori* much less than average benefit as well. This disparity suggests what the review of empirical studies below will bear out: the short-run elasticity of vehicular travel with respect to its marginal cost of additional mileage is very low.

Motorist costs include fuel taxes, vehicle excise taxes, registration fees and other payments to governments. These vary tremendously in structure, magnitude and purpose from one jurisdiction to another (Sterner, 2002). In the USA nearly all vehicle-related taxes are revenue-raising instruments earmarked for roads and other transportation investments. According to AAA estimates the average annual registration fee is only about $200, or 0.6 to 1.2 ¢/km.[4] Gasoline taxes also vary to some extent from state to state, but in all cases are very low, averaging only about one cent per km. In Europe, both fuel taxes and vehicle taxes are much higher and not only pay for transportation facilities but also contribute revenues to the general fund. There are also great differences among European countries. Both points are shown in Table 5.2, which compares lifetime fuel and ownership taxes for the USA and selected European Union countries. The low diesel fuel taxes relative to gasoline taxes in Europe reflect a desire to keep commercial transport costs low.

Table 5.2   Lifetime ownership and fuel taxes in Europe and the USA

	Ownership taxes as a percentage of net vehicle price		Fuel taxes as a percentage of net fuel cost	
	Diesel	Gasoline	Diesel	Gasoline
Belgium	43	35	188	311
Finland	155	127	184	347
France	25	24	293	428
Germany	32	22	234	334
UK	29	49	509	487
USA	18	18	21	33

Note: Fuel prices used in calculation: gasoline $1.13; diesel $1.36.

Sources: European countries: Mayeres and Proost (2001); USA: authors' calculations based on data in *Ward's Communications* (1999) and US DOE (2001).

External Cost

Traditionally, transportation infrastructure was regarded as a public good, one that can be supplied to users at zero marginal cost. Over time, it became clear that marginal costs can be positive – sometimes positive for all vehicles and always positive for some vehicles. For example, at high levels of use a highway or bridge becomes congested, and then each additional user imposes costs on every other user. Roadway congestion was first studied extensively by Vickery (1963) and his work led to an extensive literature on congestion externalities and congestion pricing. In a study of road wear in the USA, Small et al. (1989) pointed out that vehicles cause road damage at a rate (and cost) that is a sharply increasing function of the weight per axle, so that virtually all damage is attributed to heavy-duty commercial vehicles. They recommend replacement of the current fuel taxes and weight-based license fees by a mileage fee sharply increasing with vehicle weight.

The accounting so far leaves out many other potential cost components of motor vehicle use, and since about 1990 transportation researchers as well as transit and environmental advocates have been trying to describe and if possible quantify those external social cost components (for example Delucchi et al., 1996; Litman, 1994; Lee, 1995; McKenzie et al., 1992; Miller and Moffet, 1993; and Kågeson, 1993). A survey of cost-of-driving studies commissioned by the Metropolitan Washington Council of Governments identified nearly 40 such studies (K.T. Analytics, 1997). An excellent introduction to the issues involved can be found in several of the papers in Greene et al. (1997). Although some of these studies are careful to define 'external costs' as economists might understand the term, others seem to use it to include all costs not associated with vehicle ownership and operation, such as infrastructure costs and parking.

These studies have been undertaken primarily with at least three questions in mind. One concerns the marginal costs of transportation use: are ground transportation modes properly priced, so that the socially optimal level of transport is demanded and supplied and is distributed properly among the various transport modes? To meet the efficiency objective these prices must equal the marginal social costs. The second is a question about total costs, and thus is concerned not only with efficiency, but also with cost recovery and fairness: are the total social costs of transport fully paid by the users? Are transportation users unfairly subsidized? Third, it is recognized that transportation markets and behavior interact with other markets, notably housing and land use, but also the labor market. Government policies, including fees and subsidies, have been developed in transport, land use, housing and other policy areas without taking these interactions into account. In Europe, transport cost studies are increasingly being used to examine policy interactions as part of the EU drive toward harmonization of national policies (Quinet, 1997).

The scope and variety of transportation impacts within this framework are quite large, and include parking costs, losses from accidents, national expenditures associated with defending international oil trade, and such environmental impacts as air pollution, greenhouse gas emissions, and damage to wetlands and other sensitive areas from road construction. Table 5.3 provides the range of estimates in each of these categories from US and European studies. As is common practice, researchers express costs in cents per passenger or vehicle mile (or kilometer) traveled. This is true regardless of whether the cost category is truly a component that varies with distance or is a fixed cost component that is averaged over some standard distance.

The estimates differ so much both because they reflect different assumptions about the kinds of trips and mileage, and because different methods are used in evaluation. In some cases there is controversy about whether the effects cited are truly externalities, for example with infrastructure, accidents or parking.

In addition, the differences in objectives affect what is included, and things that may be inappropriate to the discussion of whether transportation is priced efficiently may be quite germane to the discussion of whether it is priced fairly or whether road transportation covers its costs. On this last issue, the studies cited broadly agree that the revenues from motorists – primarily gasoline taxes and vehicle registration fees – approximately

Table 5.3   Range of reported external costs in cost-of-driving studies[a]
(cents per mile)

	Low[b]	High[b]
Infrastructure	3.0	7.0
Congestion	4.0	15.0
Air pollution	1.0	14.0
Climate change	0.3	1.1
Noise	0.1	6.0
Water	0.1	3.0
Accidents (external)	1.0	10.0
Energy security	1.5	2.6
Parking	2.0	9.0

Notes:
[a] Combination of the studies surveyed by K.T. Analytics (1997) and Gomez-Ibanez (1997).
[b] 'Low' and 'High' are respectively the second lowest and the second highest estimates reported in the articles surveyed.

cover costs. However, if ancillary costs of operating the highway system – road police, signals, the court system – are included, many authors find that the system cannot cover costs.[5] Gomez-Ibanez (1997) reviews the differences in assumptions and definitions in some of the studies and shows how they can affect the estimates.

As comprehensive as the social costing framework appears, it is actually incomplete in two ways. First, the external cost calculation only begins when the vehicle rolls out of the showroom and ends when it is retired. But plainly, there are also environmental impacts associated with vehicle and fuel production and with vehicle/parts disposal. The internal costs of these activities are of course included in the owner's costs, but any external costs are omitted. To get at external production and disposal costs, researchers have begun to apply life cycle analysis (LCA), a systematic attempt to catalog and value the full womb-to-tomb range of impacts of consumer products, to the motor vehicle. LCA was developed initially for analysis of the fate and toxicological effects of hazardous substances, and guidelines for producing and using LCA have been adopted by the International Standards Organization (ISO 14040–3). So far, however, LCAs of motor vehicles have been largely limited to construction of inventories of impacts, with few if any attempts at valuation.[6]

Research into the life cycles of conventional gasoline- and diesel-powered vehicles indicates that by far the majority of environmental impacts occur during vehicle use (MacLean and Lave, 2002). Thus results of LCA for conventional vehicles would not give results much different from those in Table 5.3. The situation is very different for vehicles with different fuel or propulsion systems, a point to which we return in section 7, when we consider alternatives to current motor vehicle technologies.

The social cost framework also does not integrate the analyses of various impacts, but instead treats them independently. Individual cost components are computed and simply added together. Furthermore, displaying the results in costs per mile of travel encourages the interpretation that these are marginal costs, but in many cases they are average costs of elements where the marginal cost of an additional mile of travel is essentially zero. The estimates are best viewed as a rough estimate of the current costs of vehicle use under particular assumptions; they are not very useful for designing environmental policy to reduce pollution from vehicles.

Nonetheless, some of the various estimates of social costs have been used as inputs to more comprehensive studies that put all these externalities in a consistent optimizing framework. One such model is the TRENEN model developed by researchers in Europe (Proost and van Dender, 1999). TRENEN is a welfare maximization model of the urban transport sector in the presence of environmental and congestion externalities. In a partial equilibrium framework, it solves for a set of welfare maximizing policy instruments, such as externality fees or quantity restrictions, allowing for various political, practical or technological constraints. TRENEN has been calibrated for a number of different European cities and used to examine local transport issues. For examples of its use in policy analysis, see Proost and van Dender (1999), Calthrop et al. (2000), and Roson (1998).

Proost and van Dender (1999) compare a range of possible vehicle policies for Europe using a partial equilibrium model calibrated for Brussels in the year 2005. They report net benefits for a number of policies, including fuel policies, external cost pricing and mandates for improved emission technology. They find, not surprisingly, that the full external cost pricing policy provides the greatest net benefits. This policy has motorists pay the marginal cost of driving, including congestion, pollution, accidents and noise costs. They acknowledge that this policy is not feasible to implement, and compare it to more feasible policies such as parking fees and cordon pricing. Cordon pricing results in about 50 percent of the welfare gain of full marginal cost pricing. Another interesting finding of this analysis is that the mandatory emission control technology scenario fares better in terms of air pollution reduction than the full marginal cost pricing case. This is because the technology controls assumed reduce VOCs (volatile organic compounds), NO_x, and CO but not the more damaging particulate emissions such as SO_2, and the marginal costs of additional controls increase as controls become tighter.

Another such model is found in the recent paper by Parry and Small (2001), which attempts to estimate welfare-maximizing gasoline taxes for Britain and the USA. From a simple general equilibrium model containing a population of identical households using vehicular transportation and a numeraire consumption good, together with a simple production sector employing labor from the household sector, Parry and Small derive a formula for the optimal taxes to maximize social welfare in the presence of transport externalities, costly infrastructure and a distortionary tax on labor. The transport externalities they include in the model are congestion, air pollution and accidents; as shown by the range of estimates in Table 5.3, those three categories are probably the most significant.

What they find is that the optimum gasoline tax for the USA is $1.01 per gallon, more than double the average combined state and federal gasoline tax throughout the country (37¢/gallon), and the optimum tax for the UK is $1.34, less than half its current value. However, each tax is estimated under the constraint that it is the only available instrument. They also argue that in both countries the welfare is greatly increased if, instead of a fuel tax, a tax on vehicle miles travelled (VMT) is used. The reason is that the external effects that are assumed in their model to vary with mileage (accidents, congestion and conventional pollutants) dominate those that vary with fuel use (global climate change). One of the inefficiencies of the tax on fuel consumption is that fuel use declines much more than vehicle use because of switching to more efficient vehicles.

Parry and Small also show that the optimum fuel tax and VMT tax each differ considerably from the 'naïve' rates found by combining the social cost components on the basis of fuel and mileage, respectively. It is of particular interest that the optimum VMT tax is 40 percent greater than the naïve VMT tax in the USA but 14 percent less in the UK.

One possible surprise from Table 5.3 is the relative unimportance of externalities affecting the natural environment, except for conventional air pollution. The social cost of global warming attributed to motor vehicles is small relative to other costs, only 0.3 to 1.1¢ per mile. It is also surprising to find little mention of urban sprawl, an important part of the environmentalist indictment against motor vehicles in the USA. The low ranking of these environmental effects seems strangely at odds with the high value the public places on environmental matters. For accidents, at least, this disparity may reflect public awareness that this externality is partially internalized by insurance payments. Another possible explanation is the difference in the parties affected in the transactions. The congestion and accident externalities primarily affect other drivers; when one uses a vehicle, it is with the understanding that accidents are possible and congestion is likely, and that both are part of the price one has to pay to enjoy the benefits of driving. Environmental effects are in a different category, affecting the general population, not just motorists. Perhaps this is another example of the very different attitudes toward voluntary versus involuntary risk.

A third explanation for these attitudes could be that the actual damages from global warming and the effects of sprawl are poorly understood and not reflected in the damage estimates. In some cases, the estimates of social costs associated with global climate change are based not on damage estimates, but on the estimated marginal cost of emission reductions from stationary sources sufficient for complying with the Kyoto Accords. It is worth noting that most observers agree that if the concerns about anthropogenic climate change turn out to be justified (as the evidence increasingly suggests they are), the requirements agreed to in Kyoto are but a small first step. The damages associated with climate change are just the kind that benefit–cost analysis has trouble dealing with: damages that are uncertain but potentially very large and very far in the future.[7]

Likewise, few analysts have ventured an estimate of the social costs of sprawl that are attributable to the automobile. In part this is because there is little consensus on what sprawl is and what its effects are. And whatever they are, the social costs of sprawl cannot entirely be laid at the tires of motor vehicles. Brueckner (2001), for example, puts part of the blame on land-use development impact fees that are below the marginal cost, requiring a taxpayer subsidy. Pietro Nivola (1999) discusses several other factors contributing to suburbanization and low-density development, including home mortgage subsidies, school desegregation and federal highway subsidies. In any case, because many of the policies now being used or considered to combat sprawl directly affect urban transportation, we will examine the urban transportation and land-use connection below.

To sum up, then, the social costs of automobile use are potentially large and, at 13 to 67 cents per mile, comparable in magnitude to the private costs in some situations. The main implication is that the internalizing of these social costs requires an increase in the cost of driving. Contrary to what some authors seem to think, however, finding the optimum policy is more than just a matter of summing the costs and imposing a tax. For one thing, even though the social costs are customarily expressed on a per-mile basis, they actually affect several different margins, including miles, VMT, and emissions. This means that the optimum policy will require several different instruments, one for each margin. Because of the interrelatedness of these externalities, very likely it would not be the optimum policy to set each instrument at the marginal damages. Finding the optimum taxes requres a comprehensive modeling framework like that of Proost and Van Dender that takes into account

the interrelations. Most likely, a policy of this sort would be too complicated to be enacted. For this reason, researchers continue to look for
simpler policies, such as Parry and Small's VMT tax, that can capture
most of the benefits of an optimum instrument. We return to these points
frequently in later sections.

3.   MODELING VEHICLE OWNERSHIP AND USE

Let's say you are a policy analyst charged with examining both the likely
consequences and the wisdom of policies at the nexus of environment and
transport. These could include, for example, highway or transit investments, policies to encourage or discourage certain technologies, vehicle
emission policies, even land-use policies. What would you like to know?
What resources are at your disposal? What are you unlikely to know, given
current data and methods?

To illuminate the ways economists have approached issues raised by the
automobile, we will center the discussion on three environmental problems
in which motor vehicle use has been widely implicated: (i) conventional
emissions (particulates and ozone); (ii) global climate change; and (iii) land
use and sprawl. In the first two cases, economic models have been used
extensively to examine the properties and likely consequences of various
policy options and to make judgments about their relative merits. Detailed
economic analysis has made less headway in analysis of sprawl, but it shows
considerable promise for doing so in the future.

Before turning to those specific issues, in this section we discuss some
matters that are common to all environmental problems involving motor
vehicles. There is a class of models that have been extensively used in
the transportation literature to examine how vehicle characteristics and
patterns of use change when operating costs or incomes change. For
example, when regulations or market-based policies change the relative
costs of driving, it is critically important to know how vehicle owners
will respond to these changes. Knowledge of such price elasticities is
essential for understanding both the response to particular policies and
their impacts on affected parties (motorists and potential motorists).
Knowledge of income elasticities is less important for policy evaluation,
but with world population heading for 11 digits, most of whom will live
in currently poor countries striving for higher living standards, it is vital
for understanding the scale and scope of future problems associated with
auto use.

We distinguish between two subclasses of models: (i) models using aggregate data that are primarily (but not exclusively) concerned with fuel

demand, and (ii) models using household data that attempt to model household decision-making explicitly.

3.1 Aggregate Models

Several fuel price elasticities appear in these models: elasticity of gasoline use (G), vehicle use (VMT) and fuel economy in miles per gallon (MPG).[8] These three variables are related thus: $G = VMT/MPG$.[9] VMT is a function of c, the price per mile of travel, which in turn depends on the price p of fuel and the fuel economy, that is, $c = p/MPG$. If we write these relationships as logarithmic functions of logarithms, we have

$$\ln G = \ln(VMT(\ln c)) - \ln MPG(p). \tag{5.1}$$

Now if we differentiate (5.1), we get

$$\varepsilon_{G \cdot p} = \varepsilon_{VMT \cdot c}(1 - \varepsilon_{MPG \cdot p}) - \varepsilon_{MPG \cdot p}. \tag{5.2}$$

This formula says that the price elasticity of gasoline is the same as the elasticity of VMT with respect to its cost if fuel economy is fixed. If $\varepsilon_{MPG \cdot p} \geq 0$ and $\varepsilon_{VMT \cdot c} < 0$, then $\varepsilon_{G \cdot p} \leq \varepsilon_{VMT \cdot c} < 0$. Fuel economy can respond to price in the short run by means of a reallocation of trips to more fuel-efficient vehicles in the existing fleet. In the long run it can result from stock turnover, as consumers turn to more efficient vehicles.

Ordinarily we would think of vehicle fuel economy as a dependent variable, but in the USA it has become an independent variable by statute. The Energy Policy and Conservation Act of 1975 mandated for each vehicle manufacturer a minimum 'corporate average fuel economy' (CAFE) under which the average fuel economy of the vehicles sold by each manufacturer had to meet minimum requirements, beginning with the 1979 model year. We discuss CAFE again below, but for now we merely observe that the elasticity of a vehicle's fuel use with respect to MPG, with fuel price unchanged, is

$$\varepsilon_{G \cdot MPG} = -1 - \varepsilon_{VMT \cdot c}. \tag{5.3}$$

If vehicle use remained constant, then this elasticity would be unity. But with better fuel economy, the fuel cost per mile declines, leading to greater vehicle use. This effect, whereby a part of the effectiveness of CAFE is given back, has been called the rebound effect. As shown in (5.3), the rebound effect is the elasticity of VMT to the fuel cost per mile, and most studies find it to be rather small, at about 10 to 20 percent.

The empirical literature on fuel demand models is vast. Ten years ago a review of studies of fuel price elasticity (Dahl and Sterner, 1991a and 1991b)[10] found nearly one hundred studies, with more than 300 separate elasticity estimates using a wide variety of econometric approaches and data sources and representing some twenty countries. Subsequently Dahl (1995) surveyed an additional 39 studies that appeared after the earlier review. This later survey was limited to studies using data from the USA.

In all cases, the main dependent variable is gasoline demand. The dependent variables always include gasoline price and some measure of average household income. Nearly all the studies examined in the two reviews are aggregate studies. Several types of models are discussed:

- *Static models*. Usually based on non cross-sectional data, these models estimate a single price and income elasticity parameters.
- *Lagged endogenous models*. Estimated on time series or panel data, these models contain a lagged dependent variable to distinguish between short- and long-run elasticities. The duration of the lag strongly affected the estimates, with short lags (one month or one quarter) producing very low elasticities, especially in the long run. Dahl and Sterner discounted these estimates as being confounded with seasonal effects.
- *Models with other lags*. Other lag structures don't require the same rate of adjustment to price and to income changes.
- *Models with vehicles and vehicle characteristics*. These models included the number of vehicles or average vehicle characteristics, such as fuel economy.

Examination of the results of these studies suggests that gasoline demand is still moderately responsive to both price and income. However, in recent years the elasticities have fallen substantially. This conclusion is illustrated in Table 5.4, which compares elasticity estimates in the two time periods for simple static models and for lagged endogenous models. The decline in responsiveness extended to other related phenomena. For example, Dahl (1995) reported that the mean price elasticity of average fuel economy (MPG) declined from about 0.4 to about 0.2.

Several explanations have been suggested for the decline, including improved data, rising incomes in many countries in the world, and the much lower fuel prices in the 1980s, which made gasoline a smaller portion of the cost of driving. Moreover, the studies surveyed by Dahl (1995) used data from the 1980s, a period when energy prices declined substantially. At the same time, Gately (1992) found that the response of gasoline demand to both price and income is asymmetric; that is, sensitivity to price declines

Table 5.4   Median price and income elasticities of gasoline demand

		Price		Income	
Static models – fuel use					
Dahl and Sterner (1991a, 1991b)		−0.51		1.24	
Dahl (1995)		−0.18		0.39	
Lagged endogenous models	Short-run	Long-run	Short-run	Long-run	
Dahl and Sterner (1991a, 1991b)	−0.26	−0.86	0.48	1.21	
Dahl (1995)	−0.13	−0.65	0.19	0.72	

Note: In Dahl and Sterner (1991a and 1991b) few studies contain data after 1980; in Dahl (1995) most studies contain data at least to 1985.

is much lower than to price increases. This asymmetry has suggested to some observers that the US CAFE standards have been responsible for the decline in elasticity. When prices decline, mandatory CAFE standards reduce fuel costs as a share of the cost of driving; they have also reduced the availability of larger, less efficient vehicles.

Most of the studies examined in Dahl and Dahl and Sterner were reduced-form models using aggregate data. In some models fuel demand was estimated directly from aggregate data on prices and transportation fuel use; in other models, energy demand is estimated indirectly by estimating the separate effects of fuel price on vehicle use, usually measured by vehicle kilometers traveled (VKT), and on fuel economy. Because fuel use is the product of fuel economy and vehicle use, its elasticity is the sum of these elasticities.

Income elasticity

It is clear from Table 5.1 that higher GDP per capita is associated with larger per capita vehicle holdings. Many of the studies discussed above also compute income elasticities, but most have been limited to one or at most a few countries and have a limited range of years and incomes. Recently Dargay and Gately (1999) examined vehicle ownership patterns (measured in vehicles per 1000 people) in 26 countries with widely varying per capita incomes, over a period that usually extended from 1960 to 1992. They found that income was by far the most important variable explaining vehicle ownership – more important than fuel price, vehicle price, infrastructure, or population density. They also found that the relationship of vehicle ownership to income in each country tended to be nonlinear and in fact S-shaped.[11] (In no country was the historical record so complete as to see the entire S. In a country like the USA they observed the upper part, and in China the the lower part.) Between 1992 and 2015, the long-run ownership elasticity falls from 0.24 to 0.04 in the USA and from1.92 to 0.40 in a middle-income country like Korea, but increases from 1.34 to 2.16 in China.

3.2   Structural Models Using Microdata

Thanks to their high level of aggregation, the reduced-form models considered in section 3.1 can be used to simulate responses to changes in policy. However, their use is limited to aggregate outcomes: changes in the total size of the fleet and average vehicle use. Evaluation of environmental policies usually requires more detailed information. Vehicles differ greatly in their characteristics, and these differences can affect both their attractiveness to motorists and their impact on the environment. Often the performance of a proposed policy will have very different effects on cars versus small trucks, old vehicles versus new vehicles, the number of vehicles owned by various types of households, the level of vehicle use, and the implications of all these outcomes on various fuels.

To examine those effects we need more detailed models that explicitly represent individual choices among types of vehicles and their use. We now turn briefly to these more detailed models.

In the past couple of decades there have also been numerous attempts to build structural models of transportation behavior using microdata from household surveys. These models attempt explicitly to account for all kinds of transportation choices made by households, applying the discrete and discrete-continuous modeling frameworks pioneered by Daniel McFadden and colleagues. McFadden brought together two fairly new ideas in the social science of the time: the idea of random utility, which had appeared in the psychological literature about thirty years before, and the logit model, which economists, transportation planners and psychologists had borrowed from biostatistics in the early 1960s and begun to use in empirical studies of processes with discrete outcomes. In McFadden (1973) it was shown that under particular assumptions about the structure of the error term, the empirically convenient multinomial logit model applied to individual decisions was equivalent to a random utility model (RUM).

In a random utility model it is acknowledged that most important household or individual decisions depend on many variables, not all of which can be observed by the researcher. Thus, the utility V_i of alternative i can be written as the sum of components depending on observable and unobservable variables:

$$V_i = W_i + \varepsilon_i. \tag{5.4}$$

If the unobservable component ε_i has an appropriate distribution,[12] then the probability that alternative i will be chosen is

$$P(i) = \frac{e^{W_i}}{\sum_j e^{W_j}} \qquad (5.5)$$

Most commonly the observable utility function W is assumed to be a linear function of observed variables, but occasionally other utility functions have also been used.

The multinomial logit model was not, unfortunately, a 'flexible' functional form; that is, its use imposed strong structural assumptions. In particular, it had the property of 'independence of irrelevant alternatives' (IIA). If an additional choice is introduced, the probabilities of choosing each of the previously available choices are changed by the same multiple. If the new alternative is very similar to one of the existing alternatives, this assumption is obviously untenable.

An important theme in the recent history of discrete choice models has been the efforts to get away from the IIA assumption while maintaining the connection to utility theory. Until recently the most successful and still the most widely used alternative was the nested logit model, introduced by Ben-Akiva (1972) and given a RUM justification by Ben-Akiva and Lerman (1979) and McFadden (1979). A nested logit model consists of a decision tree of multinomial logit submodels, each linked sequentially by an 'accessibility' or 'inclusive value' term that indicates the overall attractiveness of the alternatives in the next lower nest. For example, an individual decides whether to take a trip for a given purpose, and if so, to which destination, and finally, by which mode. Nested logit is a natural fit for hierarchical decision-making, which is common in transportation decisions.[13]

Discrete choice models are well suited to models of household decision-making, and not least those decisions affecting transportation, because so many transportation choices are discrete. In particular they have been used in the following ways.

Urban travel demand
Predicting urban travel demand, and particularly mode choice, was one of the earliest applications of the random utility model (Domencich and McFadden, 1975; McFadden, 1978). Today, transportation planners generally use nested (and non-nested) logit models to predict mode choice and, less commonly, trip destination parameters for use in detailed, spatially disaggregated urban travel models. (For example, the Washington DC metropolitan area model has 2100 zones and 18000 travel links.) However,

commercially available transportation planning packages still rely on a mix of behavioral and heuristic devices. For example, many use a 'gravity' model for distributing trips among possible destination zones. Rather than rely on assumptions about individual behavior, a gravity model bases its estimate of trips between zones A and B on aggregate productions and attractions in each zone, plus some measure of the distance or travel time between them. The distance parameter is then altered to fit the observed number of trips between the zones.

Locally, these models now produce official estimates of total travel, levels of congestion, mode share and, when coupled with a mobile-source emissions factor model, aggregate vehicle emissions in US metropolitan areas over the duration of the transportation planning cycle, which is generally 20 years or more. These uses have made transportation planning models local sources of controversy among planning officials and interested parties, especially the environmental and business communities.

Empirical models of urban travel behavior that are fully based on individual behavior have been developed but are still largely research tools (Ben-Akiva and Bowman, 1998). These models are entirely 'bottom-up' in their reliance on individual behavior. In addition, recent work has attempted to be more explicit about the manner in which transportation contributes to household utility. For example, recent work has moved beyond 'trips' as a unit of analysis. Newer models are 'activity-based', with utility-producing activities outside the home organized into 'tours'.

Integrated land-use and travel models
These models aspire to a fully integrated model of urban transportation and land use. Unlike the pure transportation model, in which housing and employment locations are taken to be exogenous, these models endogenize housing location decisions. For example, Watterson (1993) attempt to link commercially available transportation and land-use modeling tools in an interactive framework. Ben-Akiva and Bowman (1998) and Eliasson and Mattsson (2000) link models in a coherent microeconomic framework. These models could help sort out the causal relationships between highways and land use (discussed in detail in section 6), provide insight into the social costs of various types of land-use development, and assist in evaluation of land-use and transportation policies intended to curb suburban sprawl.

Vehicle ownership and use decisions
RUM models have been extensively used to study vehicles holdings and use by households. These models generally rely on the discrete-continuous model developed by Dubin and McFadden (1984) and, in the motor vehicle

context, Train (1986). In these models, households are generally assumed to have an observable conditional utility function

$$W_\theta = W\left(p_{i_1}, ..., p_{i_n}, \left(Y - \sum_{i \in \theta} c_i\right); s, z(\theta)\right), \tag{5.6}$$

where the p_i are the per-mile operating costs (the price of fuel divided by fuel economy), the c_i are the annualized fixed costs associated with each vehicle in the set θ, Y is household income, s is a vector of household characteristics affecting vehicle ownership and use decisions (for example number of household members, number of workers, age of children) and $z(\theta)$ is a vector of characteristics of both individual vehicles and the set as a whole (for example the crashworthiness of each vehicle, the maximum cargo capacity of all vehicles, whether the set contains a truck).

For a household that owns the set of vehicles $\theta \in \Theta$, Roy's Identity is used to obtain the level of use of each. If annual usage is measured in miles, the demand for miles traveled in the *j*th vehicle in θ is

$$VMT_\theta^j = -\frac{\partial W_\theta / \partial p^j}{\partial W_\theta / \partial Y} = f^j\left(p_1, ..., p_m, Y - \sum_{j \in \theta} c_i, s, z(\theta)\right). \tag{5.7}$$

VMT for a given vehicle in the household is thus a function of the cost of driving each vehicle owned by the household but not of vehicles not owned. This is in contrast to the vehicle holdings decision, which is a function of the operating costs and prices of all vehicles.

The equations (5.6) and (5.7) constitute the system to be estimated, (5.6) by one of the discrete models discussed earlier. Estimation of (5.7) requires a selectivity correction based on the estimated probability of owning the particular vehicle combination observed and obtained from estimation of (5.6), because the number and type of vehicles owned are endogenous.

This setup has been used in numerous environmental policy studies requiring detailed characterization of vehicles and their use. For example,

- Demand for alternate-fuel vehicles: Train (1986), Bunch et al. (1993), Brownstone et al. (1996), Leiby and Rubin (1997), Rubin and Leiby (2000).
- Effect of density, transit availability and other land-use characteristics on vehicle ownership: Kockleman (1997), Schimek (1996), Walls et al. (2002), Bento et al. (2002).
- Simulations of CAFE policy: Goldberg (1998).

The discrete-continuous models of vehicle ownership and use also produce elasticities of vehicle ownership and use with respect to vehicle and

fuel price, income and fuel economy. Short-run fuel price and income elasticities can be determined directly from the conditional VMT equation; in
a log–log specification they are simply the coefficients. However, determination of the long-run elasticities is more complex, requiring computation
of expected vehicle use and ownership using the conditional probabilities
estimated in each nest of the conditional logit model.

When the short-run elasticities are compared with the elasticities estimated using aggregate data and the simpler methods of section 3.1, the
RUMs tend to have, with some exceptions, higher fuel price elasticities. A
possible explanation for the disparity is that many of the studies using
RUMs have used cross-section household survey data, including those by
Train (1986), Berkovec (1985), Walls et al. (1993), Bento et al. (2002). The
elasticity estimates in cross-sectional RUMS are probably a blend of the
short and long run – short-run because vehicle holdings and other household characteristics are effectively held constant, but long-term since there
are some adjustments, such as in household location and commute length.
Therefore they are likely to have higher elasticities than estimates using time
series aggregate data.[14]

Notwithstanding the hundreds of studies of fuel and vehicle demand
that have been done over the last several decades, there is still no consensus
on the responsiveness of fuel use to price changes. There are still questions
about whether the data and various methods have identified the true underlying elasticities.

4.   CONVENTIONAL POLLUTANTS

Vehicle emissions contribute to a range of local and regional air pollution
problems. We summarize the major pollutants and what is known about
their damages, and then present evidence about the extent and causes of
these air quality problems in regions around the world. Although vehicle
ownership and use have been increasing in all parts of the world and there
is some commonality in pollution issues, the variations in the levels and
causes of pollution, and the extent of controls among countries, are striking. There are differences in the pollution problems themselves, in the use
of policy tools, in enforcement and institutional settings, and in the penetration of new technologies. We briefly review the extent of pollution
problems and experience with regulatory and control policies in different
parts of the world. Finally, we examine policies for controlling emissions
with a focus on the opportunities for market-based policies.

4.1   Vehicle Pollutants, Air Quality and Damages

Some of the damaging pollutants from vehicles come directly from fuel that is not completely combusted, others are formed by chemical processes during combustion or other vehicle processes and then released, and still others are formed by chemical processes that occur in the atmosphere. The processes are complex and can vary with types of fuels and engines, and other factors including temperature conditions and natural background levels of chemical compounds.

The emissions patterns of gasoline and diesel engines are quite different. For gasoline engines, the pollutants of most concern are carbon monoxide (CO), volatile organic compounds (VOCs), oxides of nitrogen (NO, N_2O, and NO_2 – collectively NO_x), and airborne lead. From diesel engines emissions of CO and VOCs are low, but NO_x emissions are comparatively higher than with gasoline engines. Diesel engines are also major emitters of fine particulates.

The link between vehicle emissions, pollution formation and damages to human health, vegetation and materials is fairly well understood for some pollutants (ozone and CO) and not for others (fine particulates). We briefly describe the major air quality problems associated with vehicle emissions.

Ozone (O_3) is not discharged from vehicles but is formed on hot sunny days through a series of complex chemical reactions involving many atmospheric contaminants, in particular NO_x and VOCs. Vehicle emissions of both hydrocarbons (HC) and NO_x can contribute to ozone formation, but the effects on air quality vary with weather conditions and total emissions of both HC and NO_x from all sources, including natural sources. In general though, ozone or urban smog is one of the most prevalent vehicle-induced pollution problems, and can form locally, or down-wind of the sources of the emissions. Damages to human health include changes in pulmonary function, especially during exercise, and impaired defense against bacterial and viral infections. Short-term effects can include eye, nose and throat irritation, coughing and chest tightness. Asthmatics appear to be particularly affected (Romieu, 1992; Krupnick et al., 1990, NRC, 2002b).

Total suspended particulates (TSP) from vehicles fall into two categories of concern: coarse particles (PM-10) are those with a diameter of 10–2.5µm, and fine particles (PM-2.5) with a diameter of 2.5 µm or less. PM-2.5 has more serious health consequences than PM-10 because it can reach lung tissue (PM-10 tends to be deposited higher in the respiratory tract) and can remain imbedded in the lungs for long periods. Most of the PM emitted directly by diesel vehicles falls in the latter category of fine particles, with a diameter of less than 1 μm.

PM-2.5 can also be formed indirectly by chemical reactions in the atmosphere involving other pollutants such as SO_2, NO_x and HC. Sulfate aerosols, particulates formed from SO_2, appear to be especially harmful and have been linked to such respiratory diseases as pneumonia, asthma and bronchitis. In general, long-term exposure to PM-2.5 in the USA has been associated with higher mortality rates in epidemiological studies (Dockery et al., 1993). However, there is still incomplete understanding of how vehicle emissions contribute to various types of PM-2.5 formation, and which is more damaging (Onursal and Gautam, 1997).

Lead is added to gasoline to raise octane levels. When gasoline engines use leaded fuel, much of the lead is released through the exhaust and forms fine particles (PM-10) in the ambient air. Lead is absorbed in human tissues and organs, and, in levels found in urban areas where leaded gas is the primary fuel, has been shown to have adverse health effects on both children and adults (Romieu et al., 1992). For example, epidemiological studies have found evidence linking higher blood levels of lead and reduced IQ test performance in children (US EPA, 1990). The share of leaded gasoline in total gasoline fuel has declined in many parts of the world in recent years (in the USA and some countries in Europe it is no longer used), but in some countries it remains a major component of the gasoline fuel supply.[15]

All of these air quality problems are most severe in large urban areas, and their severity and extent vary greatly both within and among countries. Table 5.5 summarizes what is known about the severity of various pollution problems for many of the world's largest cities. Particulates (TSP) appear to be the most severe problem. More than half of the cities have levels that exceed World Health Organization (WHO) guidelines by more than a factor of 2. In recent years, it has become clear that health damages from exposure to particulate levels are relatively greater, on average, than exposure to ambient ozone levels. Of course, it depends on the city and current exposure levels, but a recent study concluded that across a sample of US cities, acute PM-10-related mortality appears to be about four to five times greater than ozone-related mortality (TRB, 2002). Lead exposure presents a serious health problem in several of the cities in Table 5.5, because lead gasoline is still used exclusively in most parts of Africa and in the Middle East. Los Angeles, Mexico City and Tokyo have the most serious ozone problems.

For each of these pollution issues, vehicles are one of many factors influencing local air quality. Emissions of the underlying pollutants can

Table 5.5   Air pollution levels in selected world megacities

	Population	SO$_2$	TSP	Lead	CO	NO$_2$	O$_3$
Bangkok	10.3	*	***	**	*	*	*
Beijing	11.5	***	***	*	–	*	**
Buenos Aires	13.0	–	**	*	–	–	–
Cairo	11.8	–	***	***	**	–	–
Calcutta	15.9	*	***	*	–	*	–
Jakarta	13.2	*	***	**	**	*	**
London	10.8	*	*	*	**	*	*
Los Angeles	10.9	*	**	*	**	**	***
Manila	11.5	*	***	**	–	–	–
Mexico City	24.4	***	***	**	***	**	***
Moscow	10.1	–	**	*	**	**	–
New York	16.1	*	*	*	**	*	**
Rio de Janeiro	13.0	**	**	*	*	–	–
Seoul	13.0	***	***	*	*	*	*
Shanghai	14.7	**	***	–	–	–	–
Tokyo	21.3	*	*	–	*	*	***

Notes:
–   Inadequate data.
*   Low pollution, WHO guidelines are normally met (short-term guidelines may be exceeded occasionally).
**   Moderate to heavy pollution, WHO guidelines exceeded by up to a factor of 2 (short-term guidelines exceeded on a regular basis at certain locations).
*** Serious problem, WHO guidelines exceeded by more than a factor of 2.

Source: ARIC (1996).

come from transport, power, industrial or residential sources. In fact, the contribution of vehicles to total emissions varies considerably. For example, the percentage of NO$_x$ contributed by vehicles is higher in developing than developed countries for a number of reasons: diesel vehicles make up a large share of the fleet; there are large numbers of two-wheeled vehicles such as motorcycles that tend to have high NO$_x$ emissions; and the stock gasoline vehicles tend to be older and therefore without catalysts to reduce NO$_x$ emissions. Table 5.6 shows the shares contributed by motor vehicles to total emissions of the pollutants listed for a range of countries and cities.

4.2   Vehicle Emissions: Experience and Policy

We briefly examine vehicle emission policies in the USA, Europe and selected developing countries.

Table 5.6   *Contribution of motor vehicles to urban air pollution (% of total air emissions by pollutant)*

	SO_2	TSP	CO	HC	NO_x
By country					
USA	–	–	66	48[a]	43
Germany	6	–	74	53[a]	65
UK	2	–	86	32[a]	49
By city					
Budapest	12	–	81	75	57
Cochin, India	–	–	70	95	77
Delhi	13	37	90	85	59
Lagos, Nigeria	27	69	91	20	62
Mexico City	22	35	97	53	75
Santiago	14	11	95	69	85
São Paulo	64	39	94	89	92

Note: [a] Data are for volatile organic compounds (a component of HC).

Sources: Small and Kazimi (1995); World Resources Institute (1997).

4.2.1   Developed countries

The USA was the first country to take serious steps to reduce air pollution from motor vehicles, and billions of dollars have been invested trying to reduce emissions of certain vehicular pollutants since the mid-1970s. California, often acting independently, has led efforts to impose strict controls on vehicle emissions. For the most part, the regulations in the USA have been technology-based, with only occasional cases of the use of market-based policies.

The focus in the 1970s and 1980s was on a handful of pollutant emissions considered in the Clean Air Act of 1970 to be the most important. These included HC (VOCs), lead, particulates, NO_x and CO.

First in California and then the rest of the country, the primary policy has been to require increasingly stringent new-car controls on light-duty vehicles, focusing initially on HC and CO, and then in more recent years on NO_x.[16] The requirements were in the form of new-car standards that had to be met by all vehicles in the fleet, with light-duty trucks having more lenient standards than cars (reductions of 80 to 95 percent over uncontrolled levels of 1970 vehicles were required). Figure 5.2 shows that over that period emissions of several pollutants have declined despite an average annual increase in VMT of more than 3 percent. Lead has been phased out completely, and CO and VOC emissions have fallen. However, these controls are uniform across vehicles and regions of the country and target only

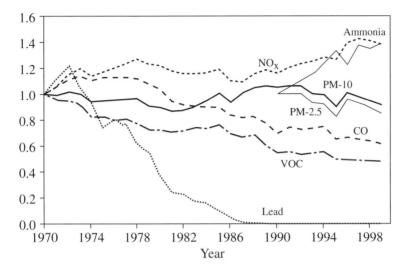

Source: US EPA Office of Air Quality Planning and Standards, *National Air Pollutant Trends.*

Figure 5.2 *Index of air pollutants from transportation, USA 1970 = 1.00 (for PM-2.5 and ammonia 1990 = 1.00)*

emissions from new vehicles, and as such, they may have relatively high costs and some unintended consequences.

For example, Gruenspecht (1980) argued that imposing strict controls on new cars may create a 'new source bias' that could actually increase emissions in the short run. If new vehicles cost more – by some estimates up to $1000 more per vehicle, or 5 percent of the cost in the early 1980s (McConnell et al., 1995) – then motorists are likely to hold on to their old vehicles longer, thereby increasing the average age of the fleet. Depending on the elasticity of demand for new vehicles and the rate of substitution of old for new vehicles, emissions could initially increase as a result of this policy. Gruenspecht (2001) and Kazimi (1997) have both argued that this could also occur if zero-emission vehicles or alternative-fuel vehicles are introduced, depending on the cost of the new vehicles relative to the existing gasoline fleet.

The Clean Air Act (1970) and its initial amendments (1977) focused primarily on pushing manufacturers to produce cleaner new cars. By the late 1980s, however, there was growing evidence that the vehicle emissions problem would not be solved by new-car controls alone. The standards for emissions levels of HC, CO and NO_x were not being maintained throughout the life of the vehicle, and in fact, average emissions of the fleet on the road were roughly two to three times higher than the new-car standards

(Crandall et al., 1986; Harrington et al., 2000). Further, evidence began to accumulate that emissions from the on-road fleet were skewed, with a small number of high-emitting vehicles contributing a disproportionate share of the total emissions (Beaton et al., 1992).

To deal with in-use emissions, vehicle emissions inspection and maintenance (I/M) programs were required under the 1990 Clean Air Act amendments for the most polluted urban areas. However, these programs have met with mixed success over the past decade. Motorists have little incentive to comply with the requirements, and enforcement is difficult because of the large number of vehicles. Further, the high-emitting vehicles appear to have the highest repair costs and therefore their owners have the greatest incentive to avoid compliance. Nevertheless, I/M has been found relatively cost-effective (Harrington et al., 2000), and there are likely ways to better target such programs (Harrington and McConnell, 2000; NRC, 2001). This is important because in-use vehicle emissions are perhaps the most important component of air pollution problems in developing countries (see below).

With the most recent 1990 amendments to the Clean Air Act, policies have become more regionally targeted. I/M programs are required only in the more polluted urban areas. In general, urban areas are identified for stricter regulation of specific pollutants according to the severity of the local pollution levels. This is consistent with the costs and benefits of additional controls and how they vary by region (Oates and Schwab, 1988), and reflects recognition of steeply increasing marginal costs once substantial reduction has been achieved. For many regions, the first 80 percent of vehicle emissions reductions have been reached, and the marginal cost of reducing the last 20 percent may be quite high. Additional reductions in HC should be targeted to areas where the associated benefits are high – in areas that have high pollution or exposure levels.

Another early focus of the Clean Air Act of 1970 was leaded gasoline, which interfered with efficient working of the new pollution control equipment.[17] Starting in 1974, lead was to be phased out of gasoline. The costs of the phase-out were high, so the policy evolved into a market-based program in which refineries could trade or bank 'credits' for exceeding some prescribed level for lead reduction, with required total reductions in lead increasing over time (Kerr and Maré, 1997; Kerr and Newell, 2001). Lead was completely phased out by 1989, and the trading mechanism was estimated to have saved $226 million of the transition cost.

After the intense efforts to reduce lead in fuel and remove HC and CO from vehicle exhaust, attention has gradually turned toward other pollution issues. There was growing evidence that early efforts to reduce ozone were too simplistic, and reductions in HC in certain areas were said to have actually increased ozone levels when NO_x was the limiting pollutant (NRC,

1991). Policies in the 1990s have focused more on NO_x reductions for ozone control. And, recent years have witnessed growing concern over emissions of particulates and toxics, which, until now, have been virtually ignored in regulatory policies. Diesel-fueled vehicles are the major source of PM-2.5, but they have been relatively unregulated compared to gasoline-fueled vehicles.

Recent legislation in the USA, however, has focused on diesel engines and diesel fuels. New regulations on both heavy-duty trucks and on light-duty gasoline vehicles require the use of catalysts to reduce NOx (and particulates on trucks) to very low levels. However, to operate effectively, these controls require fuels with very low-sulfur levels (MECA, 2000). The engine technology and the fuel type must thus change in tandem.[18] This is, as in past regulations of vehicle emissions in the USA, a uniform technology-based regulation for new engines. It calls for a 90 percent reduction in particulates and 95 percent reduction in NO_x over current levels by 2007 models, and requires an 80 percent conversion to low-sulfur diesel fuel in all regions by 2006 (sulfur levels must be less than 15 ppm compared with 500 ppm currently).[19] We discuss alternative, more market-based policies to achieve the emission reduction goals of the diesel program below.

In Europe, policy developments have paralleled those of the USA. The primary tool has been strict new-car standards, which were implemented coincident with US policy. Europe has also relied heavily on new-car standards, and although they have been slower to implement requirements with equivalent stringency, standards are now being gradually harmonized between the USA and the EU.

There are some important differences in transport policies, however. Europe has had a larger public sector role in transportation, with much higher tax rates in general, and higher taxes on fuels in particular, as shown in Table 5.2 above. Over the years, the higher taxes have been used, in part, to subsidize rail transport. Nevertheless, rail use has been declining as a share of transportation in kilometer miles traveled (KMT), for both passengers and freight, and in some countries it has been declining in absolute levels (US DOT, 1996).

The use of diesel-fuel vehicles has increased in Europe in recent years. Although much of this increase was for freight transport, diesel passenger car registrations rose from 14 percent of all car registrations in Europe in 1990 to 21 percent by 1993 (Schipper et al., 2001). In part, this growth reflects lower tax rates for diesel fuel than for gasoline in many countries (Mayeres and Proost, 2001). Diesel fuel use has grown, in response to these policies, at a much faster rate than gasoline use through the 1980s and 1990s. The problem is that diesel engines, with current technology, have both higher particulate and higher NO_x emissions than gasoline engines. Mayeres and Proost (2001) have argued that the relatively low taxes on diesel fuel and the higher taxes on gasoline are inefficient because these external effects are not taken into account.

In the EU as in the USA, recent regulatory efforts have been directed toward making diesel engines and fuels cleaner. Diesel engines manufactured after 2006 in the USA and 2005 in Europe are mandated to be more than 90 per cent cleaner in emissions of NO_x and particulates, but these levels can be achieved only if diesel fuel is very low in sulfur content. Countries in Europe have taken the lead in moving to low-sulfur diesel by implementing differential environmental taxes on low- and high-sulfur fuels (Arthur D. Little, 1998). Sulfur levels in Sweden and Finland have been reduced from about 300 ppm to 50 ppm in more than 90 percent of the fuel, through the introduction of differential taxes of about 5 cents (euros equivalent) per liter through the middle 1990s. Sweden's tax was designed to be revenue-neutral, but to date revenues have decreased because the conversion to low-sulfur fuel has been more rapid than expected (Arthur D. Little, 1998). The UK and Germany are now following suit, and introducing their own versions of the differential tax.

In part the willingness to initiate new policies is prompted by the increasing levels of NO_x and TSP in many European cities over the past decade (US DOT, 1996). Some cities have used innovative policies to try to reduce transport-related urban pollution. Stockholm uses a toll system to steer traffic around the city and away from the central district. Milan restricts driving in the downtown area on days when air quality exceeds certain levels. Other cities are considering similar policies, by which only certain vehicles can drive in the downtown areas (only vehicles equipped with specified level of pollution control equipment), or all except certain exempt vehicles are restricted from entering on high-pollution days. In various forms, these so-called low emission zone policies have already been implemented in Germany, Sweden and Switzerland (Rapaport, 2002). Sweden currently has four cities with environmental zones, including Stockholm, where diesel trucks and buses of a certain size are not allowed to travel in the zone without advanced emissions and noise control systems (Rapaport, 2002). Analyses of such policies in Stockholm (Rapaport, 2002) and London (Carslaw and Beevers, 2002) find that they are likely to have only very small effects on ambient NO_2 concentrations, in part because of the non-linear chemistry of NO_2 formation, and also because traffic will be displaced to other parts of the city where pollution levels may become worse.

As in the USA, the type and severity of pollution problems in Western Europe vary regionally. The southern countries tend to be poorer, with a somewhat older vehicle fleet, less stringent control policies, and weather conditions that make certain pollutants (ozone) more severe.

4.2.2 Developing countries

The nations referred to here as the developing countries actually differ a great deal in income and level of economic development. They include countries as economically diverse as Brazil and Bolivia in South America to Senegal and South Africa in Africa. As the data above showed, many of the world's most polluted cities are in the developing world. The general policy tools available and the problems of regulating such large numbers of emissions sources are the same as in the developed world, but the developing countries have a different fleet mix – larger shares of older vehicles, of diesel buses and trucks, and many more motorized bikes. Although data on vehicle emissions in most developing countries are scarce, there is some evidence that vehicle emissions of particulates and SO_2 are a significant source of air pollution problems in major cities and present the most serious health hazards (see Table 5.5 above). Lead in gasoline remains an important health issue in the relatively small number of countries that still use leaded gasoline.

The average annual rate of growth of vehicle ownership in these countries was about 6.5 percent through the last three decades, compared with 2.5 percent in the USA. During this period, the share of the world's vehicle fleet held by countries outside the Organisation for Economic Co-operation and Development (OECD) increased from 14 percent to 24 percent.[20] Most of this growth in vehicle holdings comes from imports of used vehicles. As a result, the average age of the fleet is 12 to 15 years in many developing countries, compared with 6 to 8 years in the OECD (US DOT, 1996). Emissions per kilometer traveled tend to be high in developing countries, both because older fleets mean that more vehicles were built to lower design standards, and because vehicle emissions tend to increase with vehicle age. The share of motorcycles in many developing countries, particularly in certain countries of Asia, is very large (WBCSD, 2001), and the two-stroke engines on most motorcycles have high emissions of particulates.

Fuels are a major issue in the developing world. Although leaded gasoline is being phased out in most countries, it is still the primary gasoline fuel in some areas such as the Middle East and Africa. Sulfur in fuel, particularly diesel fuel, poses one of the greatest health risks for many developing countries (Onursal and Gautam, 1997). Sulfur levels in diesel fuels were increasing in many parts of the world during the 1980s and early 1990s (US DOT, 1996), and diesel fuel is heavily subsidized in many places (such as in Manila; see Shah and Nagpal, 1997). If policies to introduce lower-sulfur fuels result in higher prices or reduced supplies, drivers may switch to even higher-sulfur heating fuels and emissions could actually go up (Harrington and Krupnick, 1997). In general, it is not yet well understood how policies to promote low-sulfur fuel in some markets or in some grades may simply shift the sulfur in fuel to other markets and other grades.

Developing countries have implemented many policies to cope with worsening vehicle pollution in urban areas. Some have learned from the lessons and mistakes of the developed nations, and there are many examples of innovations not seen in the developed world. Many countries have attempted to subsidize retrofitting of diesel trucks and buses with particulate traps and other technologies. However, the success of current retrofit programs for diesel engines apparently depends on the sulfur content of diesel fuel. At sulfur levels between about 30 and 150 ppm, ceramic particulate filters reduce emissions only slightly, and at high sulfur levels (2000 ppm and higher, the levels of sulfur in diesel fuel in most developing countries), sulfate emission levels actually increase substantially with these traps (US DOE, 2002).

In Mexico, ambient ozone levels are among the highest in the world, and particulate levels are also very high.[21] Most of the PM-10, HC and NO_x emissions come from cars, trucks, buses and taxis (Onursal and Gautam, 1997). Average vehicle emissions rates are high, primarily because an estimated 50 percent or more of the vehicles were built before 1991, and lack catalytic converters. Older vehicles tend to remain in circulation, and the increase in newer vehicles has been very high in recent years (close to 10 percent per year), creating a fleet of more than 3 million in Mexico City.

Mexico has tried to deal with its severe air pollution by an array of regulatory policies, from incentives for retrofitting truck and bus engines, to fuel taxes and fuel regulations, to transportation management policies. One of the best known and controversial is the *hoy no circula* (don't drive today) policy implemented in 1989, under which each nonexempt vehicle is barred from the city on one day of the week.[22] Exemptions from this requirement have provided an incentive for retrofitting some truck and bus engines with pollution control equipment, but the policy has also had unexpected consequences. Many households purchased a second (often older) vehicle to circumvent the restriction, and there is evidence that vehicles kilometers traveled may have actually increased as a result of the policy (Eskeland, 1997).

Singapore has imposed high fees on vehicle ownership and use (the fees are often greater than the cost of a vehicle). Despite these high prices, vehicle ownership continues to grow rapidly, so Singapore is now considering a quota system to limit vehicle ownership (see section 4.2.3 below). The introduction of mass transit systems has also not been as effective for reducing vehicle use in developing countries as many had hoped. For example, the new underground rail system in Seoul, South Korea, has not attracted as many riders as expected (OECD, 1995). It has also been argued that policies in some countries have tended to promote auto use and discouraged non-motorized and low-cost forms of private transit (Hamer and Linn, 1987).

4.3 Market-based Policies for Pollution Control in Urban Transport: Theory and Evidence

Market-based policies for vehicles have long been suggested, starting with White (1982), who proposed an ideal system of effluent fees, or an alternative marketable emissions rights system. However, few market-based policies to reduce vehicle pollution have been implemented anywhere in the world. Difficulties of implementation and enforcement, and political resistance to price or tax policies, at least in the USA, might explain why such instruments are missing from the regulatory toolkit for fighting urban air pollution. Interest in such policies is increasing around the world, however, and some initial applications look promising.

Although the main attraction of emission fees or tradable permit systems is their efficiency properties, they have other useful properties. One of the most important is cost revelation (Johansson-Stenman, 1999). In a regulatory or command-and-control system it is very difficult to determine the true cost of environmental regulations, but with economic incentives the marginal cost of compliance is the tax rate or the permit price.[23]

Market-based policies can be either broadly applied or narrowly targeted. Policies narrowly targeted to a specific environmental problem will be the most efficient if there are no monitoring and enforcement costs, since they provide the most direct incentive to reduce emissions. If the goal is to reduce NO_x emissions, for example, a tax on each vehicle's on-road NO_x emissions would be the most efficient. However, it is difficult to monitor vehicle-by-vehicle NO_x emissions for millions of vehicles,[24] so broader tax policies have been suggested, such as a tax on fuel, or a tax on vehicle type that varies with pollution control equipment. These taxes are more feasible, but not as efficient. They provide the incentive to use less fuel or install pollution control devices, respectively, but do not tax the vehicle's total NO_x emissions over time. Various studies have considered how broader taxes could be designed and how policies could be combined to yield results that mimic efficient outcomes; we discuss their results below.

Market policies can also be implemented as price-based or quantity-based instruments (that is, a system of tradable permits, now often called 'cap-and-trade' programs). Weitzman (1974) showed that price and quantity instruments give equivalent results only when abatement costs are known with certainty. If costs are uncertain, then taxes are more efficient if and only if the marginal benefits of abatement are elastic. When marginal benefits are inelastic – for example, when increasing levels of pollution cause little damage up to a threshold beyond which damages suddenly become very large – a quantity instrument is preferred. Weitzman's results further suggest that a quantity-based command-and-control standard could easily be more efficient than an emissions fee if the possibility of catastrophic damages exists.

The costs of controlling most conventional pollutants, such as NO_x, HC and particulates from diesel engines are probably known with a fair degree of certainty. However, the lifetime effectiveness of controls on, for example, diesel engines is uncertain at this point, suggesting some uncertainty in the costs per unit of control. The marginal benefit of controlling particulates is widely found to be relatively elastic, suggesting that price controls may be preferred to quantity-based controls for diesel vehicles. Europe has moved toward price-based policies for reducing sulfur in diesel fuel as a way of reducing NO_x and particulates from diesel vehicles (see discussion above). The USA has opted for a quantity-based regulatory approach, requiring refineries to convert a certain percentage of their fuel to low-sulfur by a target date (note that this is not a pure quantity standard), with some allowances for trading fuels by sulfur level among refineries (US EPA, 2000).

4.3.1 Tax policies

Direct taxes based on the damages from vehicle emissions would be an efficient instrument for pollution control. Polluters (drivers) would respond efficiently to the direct signal about the external costs of the pollution they cause. However, taxing emissions directly is both technically and politically very difficult. Emissions vary by individual vehicle (size and type of vehicle), and over time (control equipment ages or breaks down), by how the vehicle is maintained, by fuel use and type, and by miles driven. There is no proven technique yet to monitor emissions as vehicles are driven.[25] Even if emissions could be measured and taxed, enforcement would be difficult and unpopular given the millions of vehicles in every urban area.

There has been a good deal of theoretical attention to defining an optimal tax, and then examining second-best alternatives to it. Eskeland (1994) derives a first-best emissions tax, and examines combinations of possible taxes and mandates that can mimic this tax. Eskeland and Devarajan (1996), in an application of the analysis to Mexico City, show how combining a vehicle I/M program and new-car controls with certain taxes can get very close to the optimal emissions tax. They also show that the mandated controls then being suggested for Mexico City could be 25 percent more expensive if not implemented with a gasoline tax.

Innes (1996) and Fullerton and West (2002) both use general equilibrium models to derive an optimal emissions tax, and explore alternatives. Fullerton and West (2002) assume a single pollutant that is affected by engine size, pollution control equipment, and fuel quality. They derive the optimal emissions tax under two assumptions: first that consumers are homogeneous, and then that they have differing preferences over both how much they drive and their vehicle characteristics (engine size, and pollution control levels). Given that pure emissions taxes are not feasible, they also examine a range of other tax schemes, including different taxes on each of the choice variables. They find that a gasoline tax that varies with the vehicle at the pump (engine size and pollution characteristics) can yield results similar to the optimal emissions tax, assuming either homogeneous or heterogeneous preferences. They then examine the welfare implications of alternative, more politically feasible second-best policies. How closely these more politically acceptable policies come to the first-best emissions tax depends on key parameters of the model, which must be empirically determined.

Harrington et al. (1998) compare emissions taxes with alternative policies, focusing on different aspects of the problem. Although some of the analyses described above allow for variation in engine size and pollution control equipment, they do not account for variation in emissions or emissions measurements within these categories. In fact, on-road emissions vary a great deal, even for vehicles with the same pollution control equipment. Harrington et al. (1998) focused on policies currently in use, specifically I/M programs, including uncertainty in how well emissions are measured, and in how well repairs reduce emissions. They find that fees are significantly less costly than I/M alternatives when drivers are well informed about the effectiveness of potential repairs. However, when there is uncertainty about repair effectiveness and the associated improvements in fuel economy, fees fared little better than the mandatory I/M program.

Harrington et al. (2000), using a different model, examine the relative importance of factors that might cause emissions fees to look either more or less similar to current mandatory policies, such as I/M. They look at the effect of factors such as transactions costs, consumer myopia, and uncertainty about the effectiveness of repair of the effectiveness of different programs. Oates et al. (1989) derived more general results that the efficiency differences between command-and-control policies and market-based regulation are quite complex, and depend on a number of different factors.

Sveigny (1998) also examines alternative second-best emissions tax policies, in which the emissions tax depends on measured emissions rates of the vehicle and miles driven. Harvey (1994) compared distance and emissions-based pollution fees with a gasoline tax in a study of alternative pollution reduction policies in the Los Angeles and San Francisco regions.

In another applied welfare analysis, Jansen and Denis (1999) broaden the scope of the analysis to examine tax and other policies for reducing both CO_2 emissions and conventional pollutants in an application to the European case. They find that the best policy for CO_2 emissions is a fuel tax, with a supplementary differential fee on vehicles of different sizes (the latter tax is to correct for myopia on the part of drivers about the value of better fuel efficiency). For conventional pollutants, they find that the best combination is an emissions-based kilometer tax and a new vehicle purchase tax based on the emissions equipment of the vehicle. Their results show substantial joint benefits for reducing both pollutants for some policies, such as the straight fuel tax, and emission-based road pricing. Considering joint benefits and synergistic effects of different policies on the different external margins of vehicle use appears important for comparing alternative policies.

Another European analysis, by Mayeres and Proost (2001), compares actual and optimal taxes on gasoline and diesel vehicles. They find that taxes on current diesel vehicles are too low, and conclude that the tax mix is best altered through a revenue-neutral change in diesel and non-diesel vehicle ownership taxes.

Sterner and Hoglund (2000) also make the case for two-part pricing instruments. With a tax on the pollution-causing input – fuel, for example – polluters can reduce their tax liability if they can show that they are using a cleaner fuel than some average required level. Eskeland (1994) suggests such policies in developing countries to reduce vehicle emissions. For example, fleet operators would be required to pay a tax, but if they use compressed natural gas vehicles, their tax is reduced or eliminated. This type of two-part tax still provides incentives for pollution reduction, and may lower administrative costs by shifting the reporting responsibilities to the polluters. Harrington et al. (1998) find that a two-part tax on emissions, where the tax on some baseline allowable emissions is zero, results in welfare levels very close to those under a pure emissions tax. This may be the result of the particular focus of their study, but two-part taxes and combined quantity- and price-based instruments (see discussion below) need to be examined in more detail.

4.3.2 Trading policies

Obviously, it would be very difficult to devise a pure quantity instrument for individual vehicles. Even the emission standards that have done most of the work of emission reduction in the past 30 years fall far short of being true quantity instruments for two reasons: they affect only new vehicles, and they affect only emissions rates. Fixing the quantity of total emissions would require restrictions on individual vehicle use, which would be difficult to implement and enforce. Instead, quantity instruments for vehicles take two forms.

What comes closest, perhaps, to a pure quantity instrument for individual vehicles is the complex system of vehicle use permits suggested by

Goddard (1997) for Mexico City. The three types of permits in Goddard's scheme are a base permit that allows the driver on the road on any given day of the week, an interruptible permit that can be revoked on high-pollution days, and a visitor permit for a vehicle in the city temporarily. These permits would be distributed and could then be bought and sold in many locations in and around the city. The issuance of additional permits or the buy-back of permits would give regulators another tool to achieve pollution reduction goals. The scheme also has the advantage of being able to address severe short-term pollution problems, which most other policies do not have.

Other quantity instruments have been directed at vehicle emission rates or the number of vehicles. For example, Kling (1994) compared the possibility of trading emissions certification on new cars with the existing system in the USA, uniform certification requirements. Vehicles could have different emissions certification rates as long as the sales-weighted average of each manufacturer's fleet meets the required emissions rate. Manufacturers can reach the target rate by averaging within their own fleet or by trading with other manufacturers. The model is applied using data from California on vehicle fleet and emission rates, and cost functions for different levels of control. Allowing emissions trading in lieu of the existing uniform requirements results in cost savings of 1 to 18 percent, depending on the functional form of the cost function, the pollutants considered, and certain technology assumptions. These costs savings are relatively small because the existing vehicle mix under the current policy was already weighted in the direction of small vehicles, so allowing trading from this command-and-control baseline does not have much impact. The results might be different in today's market, which includes many sport utility vehicles and light-duty trucks.

Singapore uses a quota policy for the purchase of new cars. To limit the growth in vehicles, the government has set a quota on the number of new cars that can be brought into the country. The quota of new vehicles is auctioned off each year in a sealed bid auction, allowing for a maximum fleet growth rate of 4 percent (Koh and Lee, 1994).

It is also possible to devise quantity instruments 'upstream' by establishing markets for commercial fleets or for fuel constituents. The leaded gasoline phase-out discussed in section 4.2.1 above is an example. Another example is provided by the regional clean air incentives market (RECLAIM) in Los Angeles. This program was established in 1994 to reduce the high cost of compliance with clean air requirements in the Los Angeles region. It allowed sources to trade emissions of either NO_x or SO_2 emissions. For NO_x reductions, private companies in the Long Beach area were allowed to buy old vehicles around the Los Angeles basin and retire them in exchange for having the right to emit greater levels of NO_x at the plant sites. Such scrappage programs have been examined by Alberini et al. (1995, 1996), who found that the vehicles scrapped tend to be older and in worse condition than other vehicles in that same age class. Although emissions from these vehicles are high, their remaining useful life on the road is low. The cost-effectiveness of such policies ranges from $3500 to $6500 per ton of HC removed, which makes them attractive in some contexts and not others. Dill (2001) provides a summary of many different scrappage programs and finds a range of cost-effectiveness results.

Accelerated vehicle scrappage is an example of trading mobile source for stationary source pollution, which until recently has not been allowed by the EPA. It is not a cap-and-trade program as considered by Weitzman, but an 'offset' program, in this case allowing regulated sources to substitute emission reductions from existing unregulated sources for emission reductions at their own facilities.

Another upstream policy was established in the USA under the Energy Policy Act of 1992. Fleet operators must purchase a proportion of their new vehicles as alternative-fuel vehicles, to reduce dependence on foreign energy supplies. Under the rule, government or private sector fleet owners can obtain credits for buying more alternative-fueled vehicles than required and sell those credits to other fleet owners. Winebrake and Farrell (1997) discuss the program and its potential to reduce emissions, but there has been no analysis of its potential or actual cost savings to date.

Combinations of quantity- and tax-based instruments, as suggested in the general environmental literature, are also possible. One such policy was suggested by Roberts and Spence (1976). In their analysis, an initial distribution of permits is made and permits are traded, but sources can purchase more at some trigger price. These options have not been examined in the context of vehicles.

5. MOBILE SOURCES AND GLOBAL WARMING

Growing concern about global climate change has directed the attention of policy-makers and analysts worldwide to all major sources of greenhouse gases (GHGs). The transportation sector is one such source, and within this sector motor vehicles are now coming under particularly careful scrutiny. In the USA, which leads the world in motor vehicle use both in total and per capita, motor vehicles account for about 20 percent of CO_2 emissions. In other countries motor vehicle use is growing rapidly, especially in the developing world. Accordingly, the search is on for efficient and equitable policies to reduce emissions of greenhouse gases from motor vehicles.

Reducing CO_2 emissions essentially means reducing fossil fuel use in vehicles, and there are only three ways to do that:

1. Reduce the amount of vehicular travel.
2. Improve fuel economy in vehicles.
3. Switch to alternative fuels with lower greenhouse gas potential.

5.1 Fuel Taxes versus Fuel Economy Standards

As in the case of conventional pollutants, the question of price versus quantity instruments is relevant for global climate change. Newell and Pizer (forthcoming) has examined price and quantity regulation in this context, finding that an optimal tax policy generates welfare gains that are several times higher than a permit policy. Because carbon is a stock pollutant, they argue that the marginal benefits of abatement are relatively elastic. Their analysis did not focus on the transportation sector specifically.

The relevant price instrument is a fuel tax. Nearly all the carbon in gasoline is emitted as CO_2, and most of the rest is emitted as carbon monoxide (CO), an even more potent greenhouse gas. This, together with the fact that the location and timing of greenhouse gas emissions do not matter, means that a tax on the carbon content of fuel would be an almost ideal Pigouvian instrument against global warming – 'almost' because other GHGs are present in vehicle emissions, including methane, and because a fuel tax would provide no incentives for abatement technology. It would, however, provide incentives to reduce emissions in the three ways mentioned above.

The familiar gasoline tax, which is in use in nearly every country, could be easily converted to a carbon tax. Since motor fuel is already taxed at varying rates, achieving a reduction in fuel use would require even higher fuel taxes. In Europe, there appears to be an acceptance of high tax rates, although the civil disturbances in the summer and fall of 2000 may have shown there are limits to high fuel prices even in Europe. At any rate, the European approach to reducing greenhouse emissions in the long run is to rely on alternative propulsion systems. In the short run, it is apparently to encourage the use of diesel-powered engines, which are considerably more fuel-efficient than spark-ignition engines of comparable power.

In the USA, however, gasoline taxation to mitigate global warming has very little purchase with politicians, and little wonder, considering how unpopular gas taxes are with the general public. These taxes are widely perceived as unfair to the poor and to those whose circumstances and life choices have locked them into a high-mileage lifestyle. And their effectiveness is challenged, not only by the public but also by some economists, who argue that the low price elasticity of motor fuel will require very large tax increases to have the desired effect (for example Greene, 1991). As noted in section 2 above, recent studies find the elasticity of motor fuel to be low, especially since 1980.

Resistance to high fuel prices would make it just as difficult to implement a quantity instrument as it would a price. A pure quantity instrument for GHG emissions from vehicles would very likely be an upstream instrument, whereby refineries would need carbon permits to sell fuel. At the retail level, prices of fuels would rise and fall depending on the availability of permits.[26]

Instead, the favored approach in the USA is likely to be mandated fuel economy standards for new vehicles powered by fossil fuels. Since 1979 motor vehicles in the USA have been subject to sales-weighted corporate fuel economy (CAFE) standards. At the time of enactment, the principal justification was a concern about a scarcity of motor fuel and fear of a reliance on imported oil. Today these concerns have abated somewhat, but the policy is still strongly favored by environmentalists as a way of curbing emissions of greenhouse gases. Since 1991 the CAFE standards have required fuel economy in new cars and trucks to be 27.5 and 20.7 mpg, respectively. Pressure is growing to raise these standards substantially. In 2001 the National Research Council issued a report examining the cost and technical feasibility of raising the CAFE standards, and at this writing there are bills before Congress to raise the standard for cars and trucks to 36 miles per gallon by 2013. These deliberations will be guided in part by the past performance of the CAFE policy.

Because CAFE stands out as the principal alternative policy to higher fuel prices to control greenhouse gas emissions in the transport sector, and because it offers so many examples of the unintended consequences of policies, it will be the focus of the discussion below. In addition, other countries are considering policies that resemble CAFE. For example, the UK has recently imposed on new vehicles a variable excise duty based on CO_2 emission rates.

5.2 CAFE Effectiveness

Between 1978 and 1991 the CAFE standards increased from 18 to 27.5 mpg for cars and from 17.2 (in 1979) to 20.7 mpg for trucks. Over that same period, the fuel economy of new vehicles sold in the USA increased from 19.9 to 25.1 (US DOE, 2001). Most observers agree that this increase was caused by CAFE (NRC, 2002a), but for dissenting views see Nivola and Crandall (1995) and Sykuta (1996). One of the points of contention is the 'rebound effect,' which prevents an increase in fuel economy from causing a proportional decrease in fuel use. The idea is that as fuel economy improves, the cost per mile of driving declines, causing an increase in the demand for travel. The size of the rebound effect thus equals the elasticity of VMT: $\varepsilon_{G \cdot mpg} = -1 - \varepsilon_{VMT \cdot cpm}$. As noted earlier, the elasticity of travel is well studied, and the consensus estimate of the size of the rebound effect is between -0.10 and -0.2 (NRC, 2002). The rebound effect is real but fairly small.

There is less consensus concerning other effects of CAFE, including its effect on highway safety and its role in several profound changes in the US motor vehicle market since 1980. These controversies are due partly to problems inherent in fuel economy standards in general, and partly to the details of the particular CAFE standards adopted.

5.4 Details of CAFE Policy

The most important of these details was that separate standards were specified for cars and light trucks. And the timetable of gradually increasing car standards was specified in the legislation itself. For trucks, standards were established later by regulation. At the time, most trucks were commercial and farm vehicles, and business and agricultural groups argued successfully that severe restrictions would adversely affect profits and productivity. Federal policy also favored light trucks by exempting vehicles exceeding 8500 pounds from any CAFE standards, and by exempting trucks from the 'gas-guzzler' tax imposed on cars. The upshot was that the CAFE standards for trucks were much more lenient and remain so today.

The difference between car and truck standards was rendered especially important by another aspect of the CAFE policy, little noticed at the time: the definition of 'car' and 'light truck.' Manufacturers managed to get trucks defined in a very liberal way, such that a vehicle was considered a truck if it had no hump behind the front seat and if its rear seats could be removed without the use of tools.

The fuel economy standards were also 'fleet-weighted' by manufacturer. This approach allowed manufacturers much more flexibility than a set of model-specific standards – and hence lowered the costs – of meeting a particular fuel economy standard. Thus a manufacturer could still sell gas-guzzlers as long as their sales were offset by sales of enough subcompacts that the average fuel economy met the standards. To prevent manufacturers from shifting production (and employment) abroad, where small-vehicle capacity and expertise were high, a manufacturer's imports (from outside North America) were considered separately from domestic production.

5.4 Effects on Market Structure[27]

Several writers have pointed out that the CAFE policy, in principle at least, creates some unusual and even perverse incentives. Vehicle manufacturers have three general strategies for meeting the CAFE standards: (i) adopt fuel-saving innovations in new vehicles; (ii) modify vehicle characteristics to reduce fuel use (mainly, reduce vehicle weight); and (iii) use pricing to affect the mix of vehicles sold. That is, a manufacturer can improve its CAFE rating by raising the price of big cars and lowering the price of small cars. This third alternative was not much discussed during the legislative deliberations over CAFE, but it is the only alternative available in the short run. Kwoka (1983) observed that such a fleet-mix strategy would affect not only the mix of vehicles but also the number of vehicles sold, and if sales increased, then aggregate fuel use would rise even as average fuel economy improved.[28]

In Kwoka's model the firm is a monopolist. Kleit (1990) develops a similar model for a competitive firm, giving conditions under which output and energy use will rise when a CAFE standard is imposed. Then, using plausible assumptions together with empirically determined initial conditions and parameter values, he solves a market simulation model with five types of vehicles. He finds that a CAFE standard below 28.1 mpg causes fuel consumption to increase. At higher rates, CAFE does reduce fuel use, but very inefficiently. He concludes that even modest changes in the fuel economy standards could be costly.

Greene (1991) calibrates a multinomial logit model of consumer vehicle choice with 1986 sales data and uses it to estimate the efficient set of price changes required to achieve a given improvement in fuel economy. He asserts that the consumer surplus change approximates the maximum cost to firms, assuming that firms were made to bear the entire cost of the policy. This gives him an upper bound on the cost to manufacturers, which turns out to be small for small changes in the CAFE standard, but which increases rapidly as the standards become successively tighter. Compared with the estimated cost of new technology and design changes, Greene (1991) concludes that a pricing strategy is not economically attractive except for short-run changes.

A more serious market structure question involves cars and light trucks. Between 1980 and 1998, the sales of new light-duty vehicles that were classified as trucks increased from 21.4 to 47.3 percent. Part of the growth could be attributed to the growing popularity of pickup trucks in both commercial and household applications. But far more important was the introduction of mini-vans and sport utility vehicles (SUVs) – new families of vehicles that were classified as trucks for regulatory purposes but had many of the characteristics and appeal of passenger cars. By 1990 what had been only a farm or commercial vehicle had become a household vehicle as well.

The growth of the light-truck market is a fact; the role of CAFE in that growth is less certain. The disparity between car and light-truck CAFE standards is certainly a strong incentive for manufacturers to look for ways to sell trucks to car buyers, and the loose definition of a truck certainly created opportunities to do that. However, other events were occurring simultaneously. As the recent NRC report points out, during the 1980s the full-size light-duty truck category was dominated by domestic US manufacturers, and they naturally sought to expand sales in that category.

Thorpe (1997) constructed a CGE model consisting of a light-duty vehicles sector, with the rest of the economy treated as a single remaining sector. Thorpe's motor vehicle model has 17 vehicle classes, differing by vehicle type, vintage and country of origin. His conclusion was that CAFE reduces fuel economy by encouraging motorists to shift to less fuel-efficient vehicles (for example from Japanese small cars to American cars and from big cars to light trucks).

Godek (1997) examined the trend in the light-truck share of the passenger vehicle market and found that the abrupt rise that began in 1981 could be explained by a CAFE dummy variable and a CAFE variable interacted with a time trend, results consistent with an upward rotation of the trend line. During this same period, the small-car market declined slightly while the large-car market declined substantially – it was a mirror image of the truck trend. On the other hand, the truck share of the market was growing in the decade before 1978, though not quite as fast as the two decades after 1981, and it declined drastically, from 29 to 26 percent, between 1978 and 1981. Because of these puzzles in the trend line, the National Research Council committee report refrained from assigning all the blame for the shift to trucks to the CAFE policy.

5.5 Effects of CAFE on Conventional Pollutants

The conventional wisdom is that CAFE policy has no effect on conventional pollutants. This is by design, for the US emissions standards for light-duty vehicles are written in terms of grams of pollutant per mile, regardless of fuel economy. However, various observers have noted several disparate effects of CAFE on emissions. First, the CAFE standards and the vehicle emissions standards interact at the design stage, but not in a simple way. Certain technologies, such as electronic fuel injection, both improved fuel economy and reduced vehicle emissions. But emissions controls add weight to vehicles, and stringent emissions standards have also precluded the use of lean-burn engines, which are desirable from a fuel-economy standpoint, but which cannot meet emission standards for NO_x (NRC, 2001).

Second, to the extent that CAFE reduces fuel use, it also reduces all the

VOC emissions from upstream petroleum industry operations. Delucchi et al. (1994) have estimated these emissions and found them to be large. Perhaps not coincidentally, the two American cities with the worst air quality – Los Angeles and Houston – both have substantial refinery operations.

Third, although gas-guzzlers may discharge pollutants at the same rate as more efficient cars, they generate pollutants at a much higher rate. To avoid higher discharges they must have more efficient emission control systems. If, over time, the systems' performance deteriorates, then the vehicle's emissions profile will grow to resemble its generation rate. Using 1990 remote sensing data, Harrington (1997) found that CO and VOC emissions did depend on fuel economy. The effect was small for the first five years or so but increased with vehicle age, so that at age 12, a 20-mpg car had 60 percent more emissions of VOC and HC than did a 40-mpg car. With more recent vintages, however, that effect is likely to be attenuated because of the improvements in the durability of control equipment.

Finally, the rebound effect implies that higher CAFE standards will induce greater vehicle use, which in turn will raise emissions of conventional pollutants (Khazzoom et al. 1990). As noted above, this effect will be small – a 10 percent increase in CAFE will generate at most a 2 percent increase in travel in new vehicles subject to it – and will in any case be countered by the improved emission rates over time as vehicles with improved technology make up a larger share of the fleet.

To our knowledge no one has examined the net impact of these effects.

5.6 CAFE and Highway Safety

Probably the most important and controversial issue involving CAFE is its putative effect on highway safety, an issue discussed at length by two National Research Council reports (1992, 2002). The mechanism is weight. Numerous studies, reviewed in both reports, have found a significant negative correlation between vehicle weight and the probability that an accident will result in serious injury or death. Crandall and Graham (1989) connected these results to CAFE in a quantitative way. They developed a model explaining vehicle weight as a function of the expected prices of gasoline and steel four years hence (the estimated lead time for design and production), and estimate it on vehicle weights for new vehicles in 1970–85. Over this period the elasticity of weight to fuel price is only −0.14. When restricted to 1970–77, however, they found an elasticity of −0.54. They interpreted this result as evidence that CAFE was binding after the fall in oil prices in 1982, and use their results to construct counterfactual vehicle weights in the 1978–85 period. They estimate that CAFE reduced vehicle weights by an average of 18 percent, or about 500 pounds. Using Evans's

(1985) study of the role of vehicle size in traffic fatalities, Crandall and Graham estimate that the 500-pound reduction in average vehicle weight caused a 14 to 27 per cent increase in occupants' fatality risk. As Godek (1997) points out, however, the increased accident incidence may have been counteracted by the shift from cars to trucks.

Crandall and Graham's work was criticized by Khazzoom (1994) and Ledbetter (1989), primarily for equating vehicle size with vehicle weight. These authors argued that vehicle length or volume might be the crucial variable, but because weight and volume are highly correlated in vehicles, volume is usually discarded in studies of vehicle characteristics and accidents. This issue is still largely unresolved. Two physical principles are at work. When two vehicles of different weights collide head-on, the deceleration is proportionately lower in the heavier vehicle.[29] Deceleration is also lower in more spacious vehicles, because the greater volume provides greater 'crush space' – the ability of vehicle components to absorb the energy of impact and not transmit it to the driver. The simple physics implies that (i) in one-vehicle collisions mass doesn't matter but crush space does, and (ii) in multi-vehicle collisions it is not mass *per se* but the disparity in the masses of the vehicles that kills.

The realization that weight disparity was important gave new significance to the observed shift in fleet composition toward trucks. Whereas vehicle safety studies had hitherto concentrated on the safety of the occupants of the truck, concern was growing over the fate of occupants of the other vehicle in a crash. The recognition of this externality, together with the controversial article by Crandall and Graham, motivated new work by the National Highway Traffic and Safety Administration on the question (NHTSA, 1997). In this study, the effects of weight on accident severity were categorized by vehicle type. A 100-pound weight reduction increased fatalities by about the same amount for cars and trucks (actually, slightly more for trucks) in accidents involving stationary objects, a confirmation of intuition. A 100-pound reduction in car weight increased the fatality risk by 2.63 percent in a collision with a light truck. However, a similar reduction in trucks reduces fatality risk by 1.39 percent in a collision with a car. Taking all types of accidents and their incidence into account, the study found that reducing car weight increases fatality risk by 1.13 percent per 100 pounds, while reducing truck weight reduces fatality risk by 0.26 percent per 100 pounds. These results remain controversial, and NRC was not able to achieve unanimity on this point.

In its discussions of safety, the NRC committee considered only the effects of differences in weight. But the rebound effect also has obvious safety implications. Indeed, the rebound effect may look small when only fuel consumption is considered, but once its effects on conventional pollutants, accidents and traffic congestion are brought into the discussion, they might no longer look so small.

5.7   Looking Ahead

As far as we know, the CAFE policy is in use in only one country, the USA. Nonetheless, the importance of the USA as a fuel consumer – 27 percent of the world's motor vehicles and 22 percent of the world's petroleum consumption in 1996 – means that the CAFE policy is of interest to policy-makers throughout the world. Not only does CAFE influence vehicle design throughout the world; it also offers a policy alternative to countries that wish to reduce transportation fuel use without raising transportation fuel prices. Also, as mentioned above, countries that do not adopt CAFE may nonetheless levy taxes on the potential CO_2 emissions of vehicles.

To that end it is worth noting that in addition to its apparent effectiveness in improving fuel economy and reducing the rate of growth in fuel use, CAFE may have had several unanticipated consequences. (We say 'may' because confounding variables make it difficult to draw conclusions.) Early on, its effectiveness may have been compromised by manufacturers' use of pricing policies that changed fleet mix to improve fuel economy, yet led to greater vehicle sales and possibly higher fuel use. CAFE may also have caused the down-weighting of vehicles, which in turn may have increased the severity of accidents and fatalities. Finally, CAFE may have encouraged the shift in vehicle markets from cars to light trucks and SUVs.

It is important to keep in mind, however, that except for the use of pricing strategies, the unanticipated consequences of CAFE could be traced to the details of policy design; they were not inevitable consequences of the policy. Chief among these details was the disparity between truck and car standards and the loose definition of trucks. In the next few years the US Congress is likely to revise and render more stringent the CAFE policy, which has remained unchanged for a decade. Much of the discussion will center on these unanticipated consequences and what can be done about them.

6.   VEHICLES AND THE URBAN ENVIRONMENT

For some time it has been clear to urban planners and policy analysts that (i) patterns of land use exhibit very large and measurable differences from one urban area to another, and (ii) some urban forms are associated with high levels of vehicle ownership and use, others with low – even controlling for household income. Low-VMT areas tend to be densely settled, have good access to transit, and offer a mix of residential and commercial uses, so residents can walk to work and to the shops. In high-VMT areas, density is lower, transit access is poor and inconvenient, the 'jobs–housing balance' (ratio of jobs to workers in a neighborhood) is far from unity, and land uses are segregated, so nearly every errand requires a car trip. On the other hand, many if not most US households choose to live in suburban areas when they have a chance, and sprawl is just a reflection of these preferences and, in fact, a solution to congestion (Gordon and Richardson, 1999).

Theory shows that the failure of motor vehicles to pay either the full or the marginal social costs of travel is a potential cause of sprawl, which is defined for these purposes as urban development that is less dense than the optimum. Using the traditional model of urban form, Brueckner (2001) has argued that one of the major market failures that lead to sprawl is unpriced congestion externalities from vehicle use. Because the congestion externality is not accounted for in road pricing, the cost of driving is too low, resulting in urban areas that are too dispersed. Using a simulation, Wheaton (1998) finds that developed areas could be roughly 10 percent too large. In an earlier paper, McConnell and Straszheim (1982) examine the case with both unpriced pollution and congestion externalities from vehicle use in a city. They simulate an urban area using parameter values from the literature, and find that the joint externalities cause the city to be too dispersed, and that the congestion externality dominates the pollution externality.

The evidence is strong that lower-density development is associated with higher VMTs. Newman and Kenworthy (1989) have made this case with data assembled from a number of cities around the world. Figure 5.3 shows the association with data from 1960 and 1990, using average household VMT and average density for 19 cities. Over time density has fallen and VMT has increased. This evidence of the inverse relationship between aggregate VMT and average urban density has led researchers to search for, and in some cases claim, a causal relationship.

These results have found their way into the policy realm. Under the banner of 'smart growth' or 'transit-oriented development', policies to promote transit-friendly, compact development are making their way on to the agenda of numerous planning boards and city councils in developed countries, especially in the USA. In part, such developments are advocated for their own sake. Environmentalists and 'new urbanists' believe they are more pleasant and 'livable' for residents, and the fact that some such developments have succeeded in the marketplace provides a bit of supporting evidence. But they are also advocated because they are thought to further other environmental goals. For example, if more compact development reduces VMT, then it will *pari passu* reduce emissions of conventional pollutants and greenhouse gases.

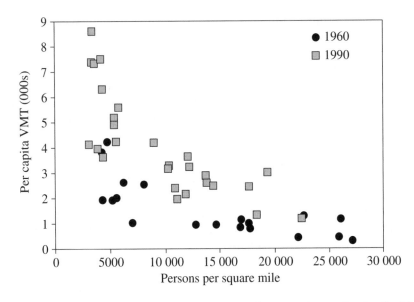

Figure 5.3   Per capita VMT (cars) versus urban population density for 19 cities

6.1   Do Land-use Patterns Affect the Demand for Travel?

Much of the evidence invoked to support the proposition that land-use patterns reduce travel demand is descriptive. We won't review these studies here (see Crane, 1999 for an excellent review), but many are based on hypothetical maps of land-use developments, showing that some designs are much better than others at reducing the distance residents must travel to get to employment or shopping opportunities. In addition, besides Newman and Kenworthy's (1989) aggregate study of density, transit availability and auto use, other researchers have observed the same tendencies in microdata.

Holtzclaw (1994) added detail to Newman and Kenworthy's work by using data from specific neighborhoods in four California cities. His estimation results show vehicle ownership and VMT to be a function of density, public transit availability, neighborhood shopping availability, and a constructed measure of 'pedestrian friendliness'. For example, his results suggest that a doubling of density should lead to a 25 to 30 percent drop in average VMT per household. Holtzclaw did not have individual household-level data, however, and he omitted prices, income and other factors besides the land-use measures that might explain vehicle use.

Using the US Nationwide Personal Transportation Survey (NPTS),[30] Dunphy and Fischer (1996) found evidence of greater transit use and lower

VMTs in autos in higher-density communities. However, they also found that underlying demographic characteristics influenced both. Residents of higher-density communities tended to be those with less need for autos and with greater dependence on transit systems. This also raised the issue that location itself was endogenous and that both travel demand and location were affected by other underlying variables. For example, those with an aversion to auto travel choose residential locations that cater to their travel tastes and capabilities. This endogeneity is a serious obstacle to sorting out the relationship between land use and travel demand.

Several other studies using microdata have failed to find clear empirical evidence for a large land-use effect once other factors are accounted for. These studies are based on discrete-continuous models of travel choice, as described in section 3.2 above. Individuals or households are assumed to make decisions based on an underlying utility function, in which the demand for travel is derived from the demand for activities and goods that require travel.

Cervero and Kockelman (1997) used travel diary data for individuals in San Francisco neighborhoods to examine the link between travel decisions, land-use variables, and other socioeconomic variables. In separate equations, VMT and mode choice (car versus transit) were regressed on such land-use variables as population and employment densities, the extent of mixed-use development, and street design measures, and such sociodemographic variables as education, gender and age. Some of the land-use variables were significant but tended to have smaller effects on the travel measures than the sociodemographic variables. In a similar analysis, Kitamura et al. (1997) found that the personal attitudes of the diary respondents about driving, the environment and other factors were more important in explaining travel behavior than the land-use variables.

Bento et al. (2002) estimated both a commute mode choice model in which commuters chose to drive, walk, or take some form of transit, and a model of vehicle ownership and use. This study is distinguished in part by its careful attention to the definition of exogenous land-use variables – measures of land use that are clearly exogenous to individuals making commuting, vehicle ownership, and driving decisions. The measure of density was city-wide (more than 7000 households drawn from 119 Metropolitan Statistical Areas from the 1990 NPTS), and the transit supply measure is of transit miles supplied normalized by city area. The land-use variables are found to be significant, but to have relatively small effects on mode choice and on vehicle ownership. There is little effect on miles traveled per vehicle. While sensible, the search for exogenous land-use variables comes at a cost, for if the important land-use variables are local, then their analysis will overlook them.

Walls et al. (2002) also estimated a model of vehicle choice and use with data from the 1990 NPTS, but they took the opposite strategy on the land-use variables, accepting the possibility of endogeneity but offering more nuanced land-use variables. To the extent that the data permitted, their land-use variables were local: population density in the respondent's zip code and self-reported transit availability. The paper specified a sequential choice model, in which respondents first chose how many vehicles to own (one, two or three) and the type of vehicle, and then how many miles to drive each vehicle. The paper found that the major effect of the land-use variables was on vehicle ownership, not on use per vehicle, and that the effect on vehicle ownership was very small except at high densities, above roughly 5000 people per square mile (they estimated that 72 percent of urban households lived at lower densities). Finally, they found that proximity to a transit stop reduced the likelihood of vehicle ownership only if transit stops were less than ¼ mile away from the respondent's residence.

In an earlier study using multivariate techniques, Schimek (1996) found similar results: that residential density had a significant effect on household vehicle use and vehicle trips, but only when density levels reached 4000 people per square mile. At 7000 per square mile, the effect was more pronounced (the mean density of the urban areas in his study was 2500 per square mile).

Other researchers have examined directly whether the jobs–housing balance affects commute times or the journey to work. This question has in fact been studied in urban economics for 20 years, ever since Hamilton's (1982) 'wasteful commuting' article, a comparison of actual commute times in Baltimore and the efficient level of commuting based on a monocentric model. Hamilton found that actual commuting exceeded 'efficient commuting' by a factor of 5 to 8. Giuliano and Small (1993) also examined commuting patterns in travel analysis zones in Los Angeles, focusing on the jobs–housing balance throughout the city. They found that jobs and housing were reasonably well balanced, but as in Hamilton's results, hypothetical minimum commutes are much lower than actual commutes. These results lend support to the notion that in US cities, long commutes are attributable to other factors, such as two-worker households, frequency of job changes, and the demand and supply of particular worker skills at different sites.

Crane and Crepeau (1998) estimated several equations using data from travel diaries in San Diego. The dependent variables for the first equation were the number of nonwork trips, and for the second, choice of mode (walk, vehicle, or other). These travel measures were assumed to depend on economic variables such as price and income, on tastes and other household variables, and on various land-use measures. The trip costs were found to be highly significant in the number of nonwork trips: if trips were longer or slower, there were fewer of them. Also, the greater the share of commercial land use, the greater the number of trips; however, VMT could rise or fall depending on the length of the trips.

Boarnet and Crane (2001) extended that analysis and found conflicting evidence in the results. Some of the land-use measures had an impact on the travel demand variables only at the larger zip code levels (comparable to Census tracts) and only when residential location was treated as endogenous. They also examined whether trip costs had a separate impact on travel decisions. The results show that when land-use variables have an impact on the number of trips, it is through the effect on trip price (speed and distance in their model). They found that for areas with a higher proportion of commercial land use, people have both shorter nonwork trip distances and slower trip speeds. The net effect on trip costs was ambiguous. Overall, these authors found very little conclusive evidence about the effect of land uses on travel behavior because of the complexity of the interrelationships.

In summary, what do we know about the effect of land uses on travel demand from this research? Decisions about travel are complex and are made jointly with other decisions about residential and employment location. It is not clear that the existing studies have fully captured these decisions and identified the role of economic variables relative to others. Several conclusions do emerge, however.

First, most studies find either none or only small effects of land-use variables compared with other variables on travel measures, such as VMT or vehicle ownership. As with any negative finding, it is impossible to say whether the effect really does not exist or whether the land-use variable has not been modeled correctly.

Second, there is fairly consistent evidence over a number of studies that measures of urban form tend to have more impact on vehicle ownership than on VMT, and the effect on vehicle holdings tends to be at high density (Walls et al., 2002; Bento et al., 2002).

Third, even though the effects of certain land uses on travel measures are small but significant in these studies, it is not clear that we can take the next step and assume that policies to change existing land uses over time would have the predicted effect.

Finally, some evidence suggests that differences in land uses have an impact through the effect on the price (time and distance) of trips, at least for nonwork trips. This suggests that it is prices and costs that drive travel decisions, and changing costs directly would have more impact on urban travel than more indirect methods of changing urban design and land use.

6.2   Transportation Cost and Urban Travel Demand

Accessibility and the cost of transportation have always played a central role in theoretical models of urban form. Households are assumed to trade off higher commuting costs for housing cost savings at locations distant from employment centers (see classic articles by Muth, 1969 and Mills, 1972). As the cost of transportation falls, whether because of improvements in vehicles themselves or improved transport infrastructure, households are able to purchase more housing farther away, causing the density of development to fall. In general, lower transportation costs tend to disperse employment locations as well, particularly if jobs follow the outward movement of workers. Firms' locations also depend on the costs of transporting raw materials and finished goods, and thus transport technology, which varies by industry and type of product, has affected industry dispersion. For a good review of this literature, see Pickrell (1999).

For the USA, Pickrell (1999) argues that travel time per mile fell by 50 percent in the early part of the twentieth century and has fallen tenfold in the past 200 years, since the time many eastern cities were first developed. Little wonder urban densities have also fallen with each subsequent decade (McDonald, 1989). A decline in costs of urban mass transit did not occur, so these results also provide some explanation for replacement of transit by motor vehicles as the principal transportation mode in most urban areas of the USA. McDonald (1989) and Jordan et al. (1998), in empirical studies of density patterns and the determinants of density across cities, conclude that transportation cost differences have contributed to density differences.

In a study of motorization and road provision in countries with widely varying income levels, Ingram and Liu (1999) argue that another explanation for urban decentralization is the combination of congestion and the high cost of road building in existing cities. They find that at the national level, vehicle ownership and roadway length both tend to increase in proportion to income. In constrast, in most urban areas, the amount of roadways tends to increase much more slowly than vehicle ownership or income. The resulting higher congestion levels tend to increase pressure to build more roads, but new roads in already urbanized areas are expensive to build. It is less expensive to build new roads at the outer edge of cities, leading to more decentralization.

Noland and Lem (2002) have examined whether increasing urban road infrastructure increases VMT and therefore congestion, and possibly urban decentralization. They conclude that the induced travel effects of road building are real, but some empirical questions remain. It is not clear, for example, that the endogeneity of road capacity has been fully accounted for in these models on induced travel demand. In addition, the implications for urban form and infrastructure investment need to be drawn out.

One final point we wish to make is that transportation costs have not fallen everywhere. In downtown Manhattan, for example, vehicular transportation costs are very high, even though the costs of vehicles and fuel are not much different than in other places. But other transportation costs in New York City are very high: principally traffic congestion and the cost of vehicle storage (which can run into hundreds of dollars per month and helps explain why the observed effects of density on VMT operate through the number of vehicles and not the level of use of each vehicle). In addition, there is a cheap, reliable, and fast transit system. Note that the traffic congestion and high vehicle storage costs in New York City are inevitable, given its density. But that makes vehicular transportation costs endogenous also, if density levels are high enough.

6.3 Vehicle Policies and the Urban Environment

The competing hypotheses presented above generate competing policy strategies for reducing private vehicle use. One strategy aims to reduce the need for car travel by more compact development that mixes housing, shopping and employment so that the same errands can be accomplished with less travel, or by improving alternatives to private vehicles, such as pedestrian- or bicycle-friendly development or cheaper and improved mass transit. Policies that implement this strategy can be carrot-based, such as subsidized transit fares, investment subsidies for desired commercial and office development near transit stops, and provision of bicycle or pedestrian facilities; or they can be stick-based, such as zoning, use of 'growth boundaries', or limits on the number of building permits issued in a given period. The goal of these policies is not to reduce vehicle use directly but to encourage development that makes it easier to get by without a vehicle. They cannot be evaluated simply by their effects on vehicle use.

Casual evidence suggests that these land-use strategies may work better if transportation prices are already reasonably high. At least in Europe, where fuel prices are high, cities appear to have made more effective use of transit and have been better able to control land use than US urban areas. Also, car ownership and use are much lower in Europe. Multicollinearity makes it difficult to sort out the relative strength of fuel prices and land-use measures in achieving these objectives, though. In the USA, there have been several periods since the 1920s when a consensus emerged favoring the reining-in of suburban growth, and we are apparently in one now. Thus we find smart-growth initiatives, first in Maryland but now spread to other states, that use a mix of regulation, taxes and government investment to channel growth into favored areas. And then there is Portland, Oregon, the cynosure for those attempting to apply land-use tools to control development and reduce dependence on automobiles. Portland has implemented a growth boundary that severely limits all development outside until development within the line reaches a certain level.

It is too early to evaluate these programs, but the results so far of Portland's growth boundary have in some ways fulfilled the hopes of its supporters and the fears of its opponents. Despite rapid economic and population growth in the region, the rate at which rural land is converted to urban uses has slowed, a new transit system is thriving, and the city has enhanced its reputation for livability. On the other hand, traffic congestion and housing prices have increased impressively.

The other strategy is to discourage auto travel directly by making it more costly to users. The policies that implement this strategy include higher fuel taxes, mileage-based registration fees, high-occupancy vehicle (HOV) lanes, congestion or time-of-day pricing of roads, and parking fees. Fuel taxes are used almost universally, but only as a revenue-raising instrument. Although congestion pricing is highly regarded by economists for its efficiency properties, it faces formidable political barriers (Giuliano, 1992; Goodwin 1994) and is not often used in practice. Interest in high-occupany toll (HOT) lanes is high, and some experiments are under way in other cities. Only in Singapore and a few Norwegian cities (for example Trondheim) is it used extensively to ration access to scarce roadway capacity.

Far more common are regulatory methods to restrict vehicle use. The auto-free zone, which prohibits motor vehicles in the city core (except perhaps for residents), is an example of a regulatory policy that directly discourages vehicle use. Another is 'traffic calming', the use of barriers and speed bumps to reduce the impact of traffic in residential neighborhoods. These measures may have beneficial local effects, but whether traffic is shunted to other areas is not well understood.

7.   TOWARD MORE SUSTAINABLE TRANSPORT

7.1   Trends

Predicting the future is always difficult, but there are some predictions that inspire more confidence than others. One thing that appears so likely that it is almost considered a fact is that world population will be much greater in the future. The United Nations' medium projection of world population in 2030 is 8.1 billion, nearly a 35 percent increase over the present. Substantial per capita income growth is also expected, and combined population and income growth will very likely produce unprecedented increases in vehicle ownership and use. Dargay and Gately (1999) applied their model of income elasticities (see section 3.1) to World Bank GDP growth estimates, extrapolated to 2015, and found that the world vehicle fleet would nearly double between 1992 and 2015. Similarly, a doubling of worldwide vehicle travel was forecast by Schafer (1998), using travel budgets. Even then there will be plenty of room for further growth. China, for example, is both the world's most populous country as well as an economic dynamo, with current and projected growth rates exceeding those of almost every other country. By 2015, vehicle ownership in China, for example, is projected to increase from 2 to 60 vehicles per 1000 population, for a total of 78 million vehicles (Dargay and Gately, 1999).

At the other end of the certainty spectrum, there will almost certainly be surprises: new and unanticipated developments in markets, technologies and environmental impacts. Motor vehicles have encountered their share of such surprises. When tetra-ethel lead was introduced into fuel for octane enhancement in the 1920s, no one dreamed that the health of three generations of children would be put at risk. Just recently something similar has happened for methyl *t*-butyl ether (MTBE), which serves as both an octane enhancer and an oxygenate in gasoline. More soluble than gasoline, MTBE has begun to show up in community drinking water, presumably from groundwater supplies contaminated by leaking underground storage tanks. California has recently announced plans to outlaw MTBE in fuel; if the oxygenate is to be replaced, ethanol will have to be used. That MTBE was put into fuel initially for environmental reasons adds irony to environmental distress.

The possibilities for problems of this sort are always present, given that fuels and additives are complex mixtures of organic compounds, few of which have been completely tested for health or ecological effects. But even the common air pollutants we think we are bringing under control – CO, NO_x, SO_2 – have the potential for causing hitherto unsuspected problems. Recently, scientists have discovered a significant decline in the concentration of hydroxyl radical in the atmosphere. This ion is one of the principal agents for cleansing the atmosphere (Madronich, 1993). If hydroxyl levels continue to drop, the lifetime of many atmospheric constituents will increase and could turn smog from a moderately serious local or regional issue into a life-threatening global problem.[31]

Putting aside the catastrophic implications of that scenario, the resource and environmental implications of the trends in vehicle ownership and use are sobering enough. For conventional pollutants, the problems are probably manageable. The effectiveness and durability of vehicle emissions control systems are driving emissions rates to very low levels. Certainly, many dirty cars will remain in world fleets, but over time they will be replaced by much cleaner, if not always state-of-the-art vehicles.

Even for diesel-powered vehicles, which continue to lag behind the best achievements of gasoline-powered engines, substantial emissions reductions are expected in the new generation of diesel engines to be produced in the USA and Europe by 2006. These engines will require ultra-low-sulfur fuel, and policies designed to assure adequate supplies have already been promulgated. Of course, emissions from existing vehicles will remain an issue in the intermediate term, especially since diesel vehicles in commercial applications tend to have long lifetimes.

It is more difficult to be sanguine about emissions of greenhouse gases. Because there is no known abatement technology for CO_2, emissions are determined by the amount of carbon in the fuel. Reductions in GHG emissions from motor vehicles, therefore, would seem to require a large reduction in use of fossil fuels, which in turn requires some combination of reduced vehicle travel, better fuel economy, and alternative fuels that cause no net increase in carbon use.

The trends of urbanization and suburbanization will very likely continue. That is, larger and larger shares of the population will live in urbanized areas, and within those areas, at lower and lower population densities. The resulting spatial arrangement of activities will be more and more difficult to serve by transit, and mode share will continue to move toward the automobile. At the same time, there will be difficulties everywhere, but especially in developing countries, in coping with the increased traffic. If the recent past is any guide, lack of funds, environmental concerns, and difficulty of securing rights-of-way in already built-up areas will make it extremely difficult to build enough highway infrastructure to keep up. This appears to be a worldwide phenomenon. Even in the USA, which has a dedicated source of transportation funds, rates of VMT growth have exceeded rates of highway expansion by a factor of 2 in recent years (Shrank and Lomax, 2002).

7.2 Technologies

We briefly consider three technological effects: technology that produces substitutes for travel; technology that improves management and use of transportation infrastructure; and new transportation technology that addresses the environmental implications of increased demand for transportation.

7.2.1 New technology and transportation substitution

For some time policy-makers and the public have been beguiled by the idea that advances in communications technology will enable people to conduct more of their work and personal business without leaving their homes. 'Telecommuting' and more recently 'e-shopping' have been put forward as potential replacements for urban travel. Although the latter is too new for researchers to gauge its long-term effect on travel, telecommuting has been a noticeable phenomenon since the 1980s.[32] Most telecommuting is home-based, but some companies and local governments in the USA have set up telecommuting centers offering office space to workers of many companies. For both home-based and center-based telecommuters, it is difficult to identify the determinants of telecommuting and their effect on travel demand. It is even difficult to estimate how many home-based telecommuters there are. Surveys of home-based work in the USA conducted between 1980 and 1997 (Mokhtarian and Henderson, 1998) variously estimated between 2 million and 55 million home workers, with most of the variation due to differences in definitions and the categories included. Only a small fraction of these workers are telecommuters; the rest work out of the home or engage in uncompensated after-hours work. A congressionally mandated study of the effect of telecommuting on transport (US DOT, 1992) asserted that 2 percent of the workforce was telecommuting one to two days per week in 1992 and predicted that, within a decade, 7 to 15 percent would be telecommuting three to four days per week. Drawing on evidence from several sources, Mokhtarian (1998) estimated that in California in 1997, 6 percent of the population telecommuted 1.2 days per week.

Although telecommuting offers flexibility and convenience to those able to take advantage of it, its effects on transportation are likely to remain minor. To be sure, telecommuting does appear to reduce daily VMT. In a survey of California workers Mokhtarian and Henderson (1998) found that among telecommuters, trips and time spent traveling were 18 and 16 percent less, respectively, than among ordinary commuters. But when we multiply this by the fraction of telecommuters and their frequency of telecommuting (about 6 percent and 20 percent, respectively), the effects on travel are small. Similarly, Eash (2001) analyzed the 1995 Nationwide Personal Transportation Survey and found that VMT by home-based workers did not differ from that of on-site workers, but the distribution by time and trip purpose did differ. Even one optimistic study (US DOT, 1992) found that even if 15 percent of the workforce were telecommuting three to four days per week, total VMT would be reduced by only 1.4 percent (4.5 percent during rush hour).

Finally, Mokhtarian and Salomon (1997) point out that telecommuting cannot be taken out of context because other aspects of the information revolution may encourage more travel, not less. At the very least, cell-phones, car faxes, and wireless Internet may make it more bearable to be stuck in traffic, and many workers can now begin their workday while still commuting. These opportunities are not limited to personal travel. Just-in-time inventory systems, made possible in part by computerized management of inventories and electronic links between factories and suppliers, have allowed manufacturers to substitute transportation for inventory. More generally, better communications technology has always meant the expansion of markets and trade over longer distances. No doubt, the rapid growth in world trade in the past few decades is primarily the result of falling trade barriers, but certainly better information flows about products and developments in electronic banking have played important roles. When all aspects are considered, say these authors, the weight of evidence suggests that the relationship between transport and telecommunications is one of complementarity, not substitution.

7.2.2   Technology and management of infrastructure

Telecommunications and information technologies also provide many opportunities for improving travel itself, through what are called intelligent transportation systems (ITS).[33] These technologies are being applied in myriad ways, such as better emergency response, incident information to allow motorists to alter routes, information about wait duration at transit stops, and dynamically optimized signal control. Their main purpose, however, is to improve productivity of roads and hence increase the capacity of a given amount of concrete. The environmental effects of these innovations will therefore resemble those of capacity additions. In the short run, we can expect smoother traffic flow, less stop-and-go traffic, and lower emissions. Long-run effects are ambiguous, since capacity expansion will reduce the costs of travel and attract latent demand to the roadways.

From an environmental perspective, probably the most significant application of ITS is to electronic metering and electronic toll collection (ETC). With ETC, vehicles are equipped with a transponder that communicates with a roadside device and allows metering of road use. The first application of this technology has been to freeways, and worldwide, an estimated 8800 freeway lanes have been equipped with ETC (Fourchet, 2001). ETC systems can reduce congestion by replacing tollbooths on major highways, but their real environmental significance is that they remove most of the technical barriers to something approaching true social cost road pricing, as discussed in section 2. That is, with electronic road pricing, the toll rates can vary by time of day, type of road, location, and eventually vehicle emissions rate and driver characteristics. So far, these capabilities have only begun to be exploited; with rare exceptions (for example congestion pricing in Singapore, Norway, and a few other places), ETC is being used to collect revenue tolls. The Netherlands may be about to take a further step (Pieper, 2001). Road pricing is a central element of the Dutch National Transport

Plan, and late in 2002 the government will decide whether to implement an ambitious program of social cost pricing – congestion and air quality – on all roadways, not simply expressways. Rollout of this system would begin in 2004, with mandatory use of transponders by 2006 for the 8 million vehicles of the Dutch fleet.[34]

Also using transponders, London is implementing a congestion tax. The 250 000 motorists who drive into the eight square miles of the City between 7:00 a.m. and 6:30 p.m. will have to pay £5 ($7) a day. Those who fail to do so will face an automatic £80 penalty unless they fall into one of several exempt categories, such as taxi drivers or nurses on duty.

Elsewhere, there is more resistance, not only to road pricing but to electronic toll payments. In the USA, which currently has about half of worldwide ETC lane installations, use of transponders in vehicles is voluntary almost everywhere. Despite the large time savings that the use of electronic tollgates provides, market penetration of transponders is less than 50 percent for most US systems (ETTM, 2002). According to one observer, the ETC market in the USA has 'peaked' and is approaching a replacement market (Fourchet, 2001).

It is not clear why participation in electronic tolling is so low. In part, it could be the lack of coordination among different tolling agencies, requiring multiple transponders (which can interfere with each other's operation). Significantly, in the northeast, where the EZ-Pass system is used in the New York City region south to Delaware, transponder penetration is much higher, at 50 to 70 percent. Concerns about privacy and fraud may also be holding back transponder use. On expressways with ETC in Japan, only about 2 percent of commuters use ETC transponders.[35] One reason is their high cost – about $300, ten times or more than is charged in the USA and Europe (where transponder fees are often credited against future tolls).

Despite the slow acceptance of electronic tolling, pressures will be strong for expanding its use in the long run. Given the political, financial, and environmental opposition to new highways, authorities everywhere are on the lookout for methods to raise revenues and ration access to existing roads. These pressures will intensify in the future if gasoline tax revenues, everywhere one of the major sources of revenue for new transportation infrastructure, fall as alternative vehicles and more fuel-efficient conventional-fuel vehicles achieve greater fleet penetration.

7.2.3 Environmentally benign vehicles
If alternative vehicles do not achieve more prominence, it will not be for lack of effort, for the environmental problems associated with the current technology of motor vehicles have inspired an intensive search for alternatives. This search has been two-pronged, directed at both new fuels and new

propulsion technologies. Within limits, it is possible to mix and match these technologies. For example, either compressed natural gas or methanol can be used to power either a spark-ignition engine or a fuel cell. The coupling of an engine with different fuels can have very different environmental characteristics – and vice versa.

As mentioned in section 2, when comparing technologies we must compare life-cycle emissions – emissions during vehicle and fuel production, vehicle use and final disposal. For motor vehicles, by far the most important stages are fuel production and vehicle use. Numerous researchers have now constructed life-cycle estimates comparing fuel propulsion configurations. These studies cover a wide range of alternative assumptions about future technology, and they consider a wide range of vehicle characteristics and performance. This breadth is useful for some purposes, but it complicates the making of comparisons across studies. Costs are rarely considered, largely because of the uncertainties in costing out products and technologies not yet available on a commercial scale. Energy-efficiency and GHG emissions rates are the metrics used for comparison, and some studies also pay attention to performance characteristics, including acceleration, range and refueling time. For an excellent review of these studies, see MacLean and Lave (2002).

For our brief treatment of the issue, we focus on one such study, conducted by General Motors, Argonne National Laboratories, British Petroleum, Exxon/Mobil, and Shell (GMC/Argonne 2001).[36] This study held vehicle characteristics constant – the specimen vehicle was a Silverado full-size truck – and considered 75 fuel pathways applied to spark-ignition (SI) engines (common gasoline engines), compression-ignition (CI) engines (diesel), fuel cell vehicles, battery-powered vehicles, hybrid electric vehicles (HEV), and fuel cell HEV. The full report is accessible on the Internet.

Table 5.7 summarizes the main results of this study for a representative set of fuel-propulsion combinations. The table displays three performance characteristics: acceleration, fuel economy, and GHG emissions. The fuel economy is a measure of the energy-efficiency of the vehicle itself: the so-called tank-to-wheel (TTW) efficiency. GHG emissions are more or less an indicator of the efficiency of the entire fuel-vehicle system, the well-to-wheel (WTW) efficiency.

For fuel economy we show both mpg and an index of performance that indicates the amount of fuel in percentage terms required to travel a fixed distance, relative to the baseline, conventional gasoline spark-ignition vehicle. Likewise, we show two measures of GHG emissions: grams per mile and an index of emissions emitted while traveling a fixed distance. As indicated by the fuel economy index, a diesel vehicle provides about a 15 percent reduction in fuel requirements, diesel plus HEV a 31 percent reduc-

Table 5.7   Fuel economy and GHG emissions of vehicle propulsion technologies

	Feedstock	Fuel economy		Zero to 60 mph (seconds)	GHG emissions	
		mpg	index		g/mi	index
Conventional gasoline SI	Fossil	20.2	100	7.9	544	100
Conventional diesel CI	Fossil	23.8	85	9.2	472	87
Ethanol (85%) SI	Renewable	20.2	100	7.9	172	32
Gasoline SI HEV	Fossil	24.4	83	6.3	454	83
Diesel HEV	Fossil	29.4	69	7.2	384	71
Gasoline fuel cell	Fossil	27.2	74	10.0	408	75
Methanol fuel cell	Fossil	30.3	67	9.4	371	68
Ethanol (100%) fuel cell	Renewable	28.6	71	10.0	35	6
Hydrogen fuel cell	Fossil	43.2	47	8.4	330	61
Hydrogen fuel cell HEV	Fossil	48.1	42	10.0	296	54

Notes:
SI: spark ignition.
CI: compression ignition.
HEV: hybrid electric vehicle.

Source: GMC/Argonne (2001) Tables 2.1 and Appendix 3C.

tion, gasoline and alcohol fuel cells about 30 percent, and hydrogen fuel cells about 53 to 58 percent.

Now compare the GHG index. For fossil hydrocarbon fuels, the GHG index tracks the fuel economy index quite closely, reflecting the high and relatively uniform conversion efficiency of hydrocarbon fuels at the fuel production stage. For hydrogen-fueled vehicles the two indices diverge, mainly because of the low efficiency of converting fossil fuels to hydrogen. They diverge even more strikingly for ethanol, the only renewable fuel process considered here. As shown, a conventional vehicle with 85 percent ethanol fuel has the same fuel economy as a gasoline-powered conventional vehicle, yet its GHG emissions are only one-third as high.[37] Comparison of the ethanol SI with the various fuel cell vehicles shows that fuel is a more important determinant of GHG emissions than engine type. When renewable ethanol is combined with a fuel cell propulsion system, GHG emissions approach zero.

Considering that these new vehicle technologies have not yet been produced for commerce, and in fact are barely available at a demonstration scale, it should not be surprising that their costs are very uncertain. Toyota's Prius is the first HEV available in the consumer market, and its purchase price is $3000 greater than a comparable vehicle, the conventionally powered Toyota Corolla.[38] According to Lave and MacLean (2002), the Prius becomes economically preferable to the Corolla only when fuel prices exceed $3.55 per gallon. That makes the Prius attractive to buyers in Europe but not in the USA. As for fuel cell technologies, the consensus seems to be that the price premium over conventional vehicles will be even greater for the foreseeable future.

What, then, would constitute a cost-effective GHG reduction strategy for the USA? Taking the Kyoto Accords as representative of climate policies in the short term, meeting the proposed targets would cost $30 per ton: about 0.3 cents per mile, or about 7.5 cents per gallon (see section 2). But a 7.5-cents-per-gallon gasoline tax would have only minimal effects on vehicle use, purchase patterns, or technology. In other words, motor vehicles have only a small role to play in any cost-effective near-term strategy adopted by the USA, and no doubt other countries as well.

When we turn to long-term strategies, however, motor vehicles can no longer be ignored, especially in light of the prospects for a vast expansion in worldwide motor vehicle ownership and use. Table 5.7 suggests that in the long run, use of renewable fuels will be essential. Cellulosic ethanol was the most attractive alternative for Lave et al. (2001), for several reasons. First, it provides a very large reduction in net GHG emissions, considerably larger even than a fuel cell vehicle with a natural gas feedstock. Second, the existence of large numbers of flexible-fuel vehicles means that the USA already has an installed user base for ethanol fuel. Third, although ethanol production would require considerable land resources, marginally productive lands that would not impinge on current food production could be used. It would not be cheap, however. Current estimates suggest that ethanol could be produced for the gasoline equivalent of $2.70 per gallon, equivalent to a carbon price of $300 per ton.

Meeting the current gasoline demand with ethanol would require 300 million to 600 million acres of land – up to a quarter of the total US land area. Demand, of course, will continue to grow, at least in the short run, but increases in productivity both on the land and in the factory will increase the fuel output per acre. According to Lave et al. (2001), growing energy crops will have much smaller impacts on the environment than other agricultural or urban uses of land. But even if this is true, the ability of the land to service increasing demands for both fuel and food is not guaranteed.

8. CONCLUSION

Collectively, motor vehicles contribute significantly to several important environmental problems. We have discussed three here: air pollution, global warming and urban sprawl. We have also tried to look to the future, to see what is on the horizon for vehicles and their effects on the environment. We will close with a few observations about what will be most important in the coming years as the world grapples with its need for mobility and the effect of vehicles on the environment.

8.1 The Shifting Focus of Environmental Concern

In the past 20 years, enormous resources have been spent to reduce ambient ozone pollution in the USA, Mexico, Europe, and other places. Although ozone continues to be a serious problem, recent and growing evidence about the health effects of particulate exposure is quickly becoming the major environmental problem associated with vehicle use worldwide. The formation of particulates and the health effects of different particulate types are still not well understood, but there is enough evidence, particularly about diesel particulates, to make diesel fuel and diesel engines the focus of serious regulatory efforts in the coming decade. Already, there are new regulations in the USA, Europe and other countries to reduce diesel NO_x and particulate levels. These regulations will begin to take effect around the middle of this decade, and they purport to reduce diesel emissions as much as the legislation of the 1970s and 1990s reduced light-duty vehicle emissions.

This represents a major new effort in reducing emissions, and it is useful to learn from past successes and failures. What are the opportunities for incentive-based policies? This is an important area for future research. In Europe, differential fuel taxes on high- and low-sulfur fuel have already been effective in bringing about the early introduction of low-sulfur diesel (which reduces particulates both directly and indirectly, in the latter case by enabling the pollution control equipment that captures NO_x and particulates before they are released).

Even after new diesel engines and lower-sulfur diesel fuels are introduced, however, the trucks built through the middle part of this decade will remain on the roads for many years, particularly in developing countries, where average vehicle age will continue to be very high. The ability to design and compare policy alternatives for a diverse fleet across many different external margins will be crucial, especially in developing countries.

8.2 The Importance of Transaction Costs

While collectively significant, individual motor vehicles don't make much of an impact, and yet there are very great differences in those impacts from one vehicle to another. Just as with larger sources that are heterogeneous, efficiency would be served by policies that can target those vehicles for which the payoff is high relative to the cost. This sort of targeting is just what well-conceived economic instruments do, but targeting small sources can have very high transaction costs. The role for incentive policies in regulating motor vehicles, we believe, lies in devising instruments and finding applications whose transaction costs are likely to be low. For example, the gasoline tax (or more generally, carbon content taxes) are nearly the perfect Pigouvian instrument for mitigating global warming. They also have very low transaction costs, since they can be (and are) easily collected at the point of sale. Pollution fees for motor vehicles are more difficult, since they require knowledge of vehicle emissions, which cannot be easily observed. This is, after all, why authorities opted for a policy of increasingly stringent new vehicle standards: they are much more easily enforced.

However, emerging technologies are allowing for new possibilities for emissions fees. There are now means for identifying vehicle type and therefore pollution control equipment as part of electronic pricing systems, and such technologies are being used in Hong Kong and will be tried in London and in the Netherlands.

8.3   The Importance of a Comprehensive Approach

As we have noted, a variety of fee instruments can be used to address different policy goals, including pollution reduction, congestion mitigation, and reduction in greenhouse gas emissions. That is in addition to the use of fuel taxation to raise revenue. Rather than a piecemeal approach, it makes sense to consider these instruments in a comprehensive framework, such as the TRENEN framework of Proost and van Dender (1999) or that of Parry and Small (2001).

The importance of a comprehensive approach extends to the use of instruments that are not economic incentives. For example, we noted above that the CAFE policy was most likely responsible for the improvement in fuel economy in the USA in the early 1980s, and may yet again be used for this purpose. Implementing that policy while fuel prices were low created a hardship for vehicle manufacturers, which were in the untenable position of making vehicles that consumers had little interest in. The combination of CAFE and low fuel prices may also have accelerated the fleet shift from cars to trucks.

8.4   Continuing Importance of Advanced Technology

Since 1970, virtually all emissions reductions in motor vehicles have come about because of technology-based emissions standards imposed first in the USA, and soon afterward in Europe. Regulation forced the development of new abatement technologies that by 2000 had reduced emissions rates of new vehicles by two orders of magnitude. These regulations may also have had an indirect role in introducing technology that improved overall vehicle performance. Fuel injectors, for example, were found on only a few high-performance vehicles in 1970. Emissions control systems, which required much more precise distribution of fuel to the engine, helped hasten the diffusion of fuel injectors to all vehicles. A similar story could be told with respect to the spread of digital technology monitoring every aspect of engine performance.

The pace of technological improvement has not slowed and is still responding to regulatory pressure. Concerns have expanded to include not only conventional pollutants but also global warming. Strenuous efforts are under way around the world to develop vehicle propulsion technologies that reduce the use of fossil fuels, either by improving fuel economy or by switching to renewable fuels. Some researchers are already thinking about the replacement of the internal combustion engine, in the usual scenario by fuel cells.

Clearly, motor vehicle emissions policies will continue to affect vehicle and fuel technologies. But now, causality may begin to go the other way as well. Rapidly improving remote sensing and telecommunications technology promises to enable nonintrusive determination of vehicle travel and emissions in ways that protect the privacy of individual motorists. This will finally make it feasible to charge motorists the true marginal social costs of travel – that is, fees based on fuel use, distance traveled, and possibly emissions. However, just having this technology is not sufficient. The technologies and the policy ideas have to be sold to a skeptical citizenry. So far, motorists have demonstrated considerable resistance not only to economic incentive policies but also to the electronic metering technologies themselves.

8.5 Overcoming Political Opposition to Economic Instruments

Several times we have noted the political opposition to such economic instruments as congestion fees, pollution fees and gasoline taxes. This is an issue that needs to be revisited and considered in greater detail, we believe. It is possible that much of the opposition arises from the context in which these instruments ordinarily are discussed, where it is understood that there will be a tax increase. If the purpose of the fee is to change behavior rather than to raise revenue, these instruments should be revenue-neutral. That means that the discussion is incomplete without consideration of which existing taxes or fees should be cut. So far, to the extent to which other taxes have been discussed at all in discussions of economic instruments, the goal has been to have the most beneficial possible effect on preexisting tax distortions. That is a worthy objective, but perhaps it would be equally worthy to ask, 'What package of tax reductions would most reduce political opposition?' There is no obvious reason to expect the package with the best performance on one goal would also be the best performer on the other.

ACKNOWLEDGEMENTS

The chapter has been greatly improved by the helpful comments of the editors, Henk Folmer and Tom Tietenberg, and by reviewers Haynes Goddard and Lester Lave. We also appreciate comments and suggestions by George Eads, Ian Parry and Elena Safirova. We are grateful to Elizabeth Kopits and Na Li for excellent research assistance, and to RFF for financial support.

NOTES

1. Aggregate world holdings are predicted to go up roughly in proportion to increases in the population over the next 20 years. Population is forecast to increase by 50 percent between 1990 and 2020 (Schafer, 1998).
2. Until the advent of universal inspection and maintenance (I/M) programs, it had proved almost impossible to recruit a random sample of vehicles for emissions testing. Owners of dirty vehicles would have an incentive to avoid testing, for fear that test results might be used to require repair.
3. 'Your Driving Costs 2001: Figuring It Out', American Automobile Association.
4. These fees are set at the state level so they vary, but some states with high fees have begun to eliminate them. For example, in 1998 Virginia began to phase out an annual personal property tax for household motor vehicles which is allocated to local government revenues. Local governments set the rate as a percentage of Blue Book value. For a new vehicle this tax could easily reach $1000 per year.
5. There is very little information on the costs of roads and who pays those costs for developing countries. It is even difficult to find data on the number of lane miles and road capacity for most countries.
6. For a discussion of the promise and potential pitfalls of LCA, see Portney (1993–94). Among the difficulties that have been encountered in applying LCA is the boundary problem. That is, we may examine the impacts of inputs to vehicle production, but what of the impacts of the processes producing those inputs? Where is the line to be drawn? One approach, developed by researchers at Carnegie Mellon University, is to link the analysis to an input–output model of the national or world economy (Lave et al., 1995). The researchers make available on the web an I/O model of the US economy, linked to a matrix of environmental effect coefficients (EIOLCA, 2001). The Carnegie Mellon University model is an application of an approach initially suggested by Ayres and Kneese (1969).
7. Parry and Small's (2001) concise survey of damage studies finds a range of marginal damage estimates from a low of $0.70/ton carbon to $560/ton.
8. In the USA the unit of vehicle use is vehicle miles traveled (VMT) and the unit of fuel economy is miles per gallon (mpg). Note that this measure of fuel economy is the inverse

of that used in Europe, where fuel economy is typically expressed in units of liters of fuel per 100 km of travel.

9. This relationship is obviously true for individual vehicles. It is also used in aggregate studies, where G and VMT are understood to be total fuel and vehicle use, respectively, and MPG is taken to be the average fuel efficiency (AFE) of the fleet. Average fuel economy of two vehicles is calculated assuming each travels the same distance, which requires the harmonic mean of the MPG of individual vehicles, not the arithmetic mean.

10. Dahl and Sterner (1991a) tabulate results of individual studies, categorized by type of study. The paper also contains an extensive bibliography of studies. Dahl and Sterner (1991b) present a summary of the review and an interesting and useful discussion of the implications of various studies.

11. Dargay and Gately (1999) used a Gompertz function in their estimation procedure.

12. The required distribution is the extreme value distribution: $P(X < x) = \exp(e^{-ax})$. See, for example, Maddala (1983) for details.

13. The focus of travel demand research now appears to be the mixed multinomial logit model (MMNL), which is still more flexible than the nested logit model, and which in fact can approximate any random utility model. MMNL is only now beginning to be used in applications. McFadden (2001) surveys the historical development of qualitative choice models up to the present day. Also, Maddala (1983, ch. 3) provides an extensive and accessible treatment of the logit and nested logit models.

14. Two exceptions can be found in articles by Brownstone et al. (1996) and Goldberg (1998). Using RUMs they find low elasticities, but this is likely because they use transactions on new vehicles rather than vehicle holdings as the dependent variable. Goldberg's data set was the US Consumer Expenditure Survey for the years 1984–90.

15. Reductions in the use of lead were achieved by designing engines to be tolerant of lower-octane fuels and by substituting other additives to raise octane.

16. Although NO_x reductions were required through the 1970s and 1980s, the reductions were not as strict as for HC and CO, in part because the technology that reduced HC and CO tended to increase NO_x. With the advent of the three-way catalysts in the early 1990s, reducing all three pollutants became more feasible. Also, the chemical reactions leading to ozone formation were complex and not well understood. VOC had been considered the limiting pollutant for ozone formation through the 1980s, but new evidence – that VOC emissions were higher than originally believed – made it clear that NO_x was the key in many jurisdictions (NRC, 1991).

17. Only later did evidence emerge that lead in gasoline was a major contributor to elevated blood concentrations of lead. See US EPA (1990).

18. In the past, policies toward the vehicle and the fuel have been made independently, although there was likely some interdependence, as evidenced by the fact that the fuel companies have always lobbied hard for strict controls on engines, and auto makers were strong advocates of the cleanest, highest-quality fuel.

19. Trading of sulfur credits is to be allowed within each of five major petroleum regions to achieve the 80 percent reduction.

20. See US DOT (1996).

21. SO_2 and lead pollution were problems in the past, but levels of these two pollutants have improved in the past decade.

22. The program operates by issuing color-coded decals that contain vehicle license numbers. Five colors are issued, and cars must be parked on the day the color is prohibited. Cars from outside the control area do not have to follow these rules.

23. It is telling that economic incentive policies comprise only a small fraction of all regulatory programs in the USA and Europe but nonetheless account for a large share of the *ex post* economic studies of regulatory policies. Perhaps this is due to the fact that economists, who conduct these *ex post* studies, have an avuncular interest in economic instruments, but surely the relative ease of determining costs also is important. See Harrington et al. (2000).

24. It is possible to monitor individual vehicle emissions using remote sensors on the roadside, but these readings provide only a snapshot of emissions, not a continuous monitor-

ing. It is important to get a number of readings for each vehicle and while it is in a mode of travel that best reflects its true emissions (mild acceleration). It is also difficult to get readings on an entire fleet of vehicles because the sensors work only for one lane of traffic and in good weather. Finally, remote sensors tend to work better for CO and VOC emissions, and less well for NO_x. Research is under way to develop ways to read vehicle emissions continuously using on-board devices.

25. On-board devices that measure emissions may be feasible in the future, but capability does not yet exist. Currently, remote sensors can measure pollutant levels for CO and HC at a specific time, and under certain driving conditions.

26. Kopp et al. (1997) have resurrected an idea first proposed by Roberts and Spence (1976): a hybrid instrument, that is, a carbon emission permit market in which sources could purchase additional permits at some ceiling price.

27. There were also some major disparities in firms' impacts that are beyond our scope. See Kwoka (1983), Kleit (1990), and Yun (1997) for a discussion and some results. Kleit's simulation, for example, separates results for Ford, GM, Chrysler, 'Asian', and 'other'.

28. Kwoka also noted that domestic manufacturers in 1978, CAFE's first year, sharply raised the ratio of big-car to small-car prices, evidence that in that year at least, manufacturers did adopt a fleet-mix strategy.

29. Conservation of momentum requires that, for example, if two vehicles, one twice the mass of the other, collide head-on while traveling at 45 mph, the velocity immediately after the crash will be 15 mph in the direction traveled by the heavier vehicle. Thus the change in velocity in the heavier vehicle is 30 mph; in the lighter, 60 mph.

30. The NPTS is a national survey of daily household travel patterns. It is conducted every five years by the Federal Highway Administration, Department of Transportation.

31. A special issue in the popular UK science magazine *New Scientist* (22 April 2001) used Madronich's results to develop a scenario of global catastrophe from a runaway reaction involving conventional pollutants.

32. Most observers see telecommuting as a desirable trend. However, Safirova (2002) argues that it can also reduce welfare by interfering with agglomeration economies in cities.

33. Massive web resources are devoted to ITS. A good introduction to the possibilities can be found on the US DOT site, www.its.dot.gov.

34. From a presentation by M.M.D. van Eeghen, Director-General of Passenger Transport of the Ministry of Traffic, Public Works and Water Management, 'Road Pricing in the Netherlands', at the Kickoff Road Pricing Event, 20 March 2002. http://www.roadpricing.nl/item.asp?categoryID=23&itemId=70

35. 'Prices Keep Electronic Toll Collection System from Catching On', *The Japan Times*, 9 May 2002.

36. Examples of other such comparisons are those by Delucchi (1998) and Wang (1999).

37. Conventional gasoline engines can use mixed ethanol fuel (15 percent gasoline) with some minor modifications. In the USA there are now substantial numbers of flexible-fuel vehicles capable of using 'E85' fuel. The Alternative Motor Fuels Act of 1988 (P.L. 100.494) provides a CAFE credit for such vehicles, even though gasoline is now used with these vehicles almost exclusively.

38. Even at that price, Toyota is said to be providing substantial subsidies for each Prius sold (Lester B. Lave, personal communication, 5 June 2002).

REFERENCES

AAMA (American Automobile Manufacturers Association) (1996), *Motor Vehicle Fact and Figures 1996,* Washington, DC: AAMA.

Alberini, Anna, Winston Harrington and Virginia D. McConnell (1995), 'Determinants of Participation in Vehicle Retirement Programs', *Rand Journal of Economics*, **26**(1), 93–112.

Alberini, Anna, Winston Harrington and Virginia McConnell (1996), 'Estimating an Emissions Supply Function from Accelerated Vehicle Retirement Programs', *Review of Economics and Statistics*, **78**(2), 251–65.

Ando, Amy, Virginia McConnell and Winston Harrington (2000), 'Costs, Emission Reductions and Vehicle Repair: Evidence from Arizona', *Journal of Air and Waste Management*, **50**, 509–21.

ARIC (Atmospheric Research and Information Centre) (1996), 'Urban Air Pollution in World Cities Series: World Megacities', factsheet.

Ayres, Robert U. and A.V. Kneese (1969), 'Production, Consumption and Externalities', *American Economic Review*, **59**(3), 282–7.

Baumol, William and Wallace Oates (1988), *The Theory of Environmental Policy*, Cambridge: Cambridge University Press.

Beaton, S.P., G.A. Bishop and D.H. Stedman (1992), 'Emission Characteristics of Mexico City Vehicles', *Journal of the Air and Waste Management Association*, **42**(11), 1424–9.

Ben-Akiva, M.E. (1972), 'The Structure of Travel Demand Models', Ph.D. dissertation, Department of Civil Engineering, MIT.

Ben-Akiva, M.E. and J. Bowman (1998), 'Activity-based Travel Demand Model Systems', in P. Marcotte and S. Nguyen (eds), *Equilibrium and Advanced Transportation Modelling*, Montreal: Kluwer, 27–46.

Ben-Akiva, M.E. and S. Lerman (1979), 'Disaggregate Travel and Mobility Choice Models and Measures of Accessibility', in D. Hensher and P. Stopher (eds), *Behavioural Travel Modeling*, London: Croom Helm, 654–79.

Bento, Antonio M., Maureen L. Cropper, Mushfiq Mobarak and Katja Vinha (2002), 'The Impact of Urban Spatial Structure on Travel Demand in the U.S.', paper presented at the American Economic Association meetings, Atlanta, GA.

Berkovec, James (1985), 'New Car Sales and Used Car Stocks: A Model of the Automobile Market', *Rand Journal of Economics*, **16**(2), 195–214.

Bettmann, Otto L. (1988), *The Good Old Days: They Were Terrible*, New York: Random House.

Bishop, Gary A. and D.H. Stedman (1996), 'Motor Vehicle Emissions Variability', *Journal of the Air and Waste Management Association*, **46**(7), 667–75.

Boarnet, Marlon G. and Randall Crane (2001), 'The Influence of Land Use on Travel Behavior: Specification and Estimation Strategies', *Transportation Research Part A*, **35**, 823–45.

Brownstone, D., D.S. Bunch, T.F. Golob and W. Ren (1996), 'A Vehicle Transactions Choice Model for Use in Forecasting Demand for Alternative-fuel Vehicles', *Research in Transportation Economics*, **4**, 87–129.

Brueckner, Jan K. (2001), 'Urban Sprawl: Lessons from Urban Economics', in William G. Gale and Janet Rothenberg Pack (eds), *Brookings–Wharton Papers on Urban Affairs*, Washington, DC: Brookings Institution Press, 65–89.

Bunch, D.S., M. Bradley, T.F. Golob, R. Kitamura and G.P. Occhiuzzo (1993), 'Demand for Clean-fuel Personal Vehicles in California: A Discrete-choice Stated Preference Study', *Transportation Research*, **27A**, 237–53.

Bureau of Labor Statistics (2001), 'Consumer Expenditures in 1999', Report 949, US Department of Labor, http://stats.bls.gov/cex/csxann99.pdf.

Calthrop, Edward, Stef Proost and Kurt van Dender (2000), 'Parking Policies and Road Pricing', *Urban Studies*, **37**(1), 63–76.

Carslaw, David C. and Sean D. Beevers (2002), 'The Efficacy of Low Emission

Zones in Central London as a Means of Reducing Nitrogen Dioxide Concentrations', *Transportation Research Part D: Transport and Environment*, **17**(1), 49–64.

Central Intelligence Agency (1999), *CIA World Factbook*, Washington, DC.

Cervero, Robert and Kara Kockelman (1997), 'Travel Demand and the 3Ds: Density, Diversity and Design', *Transportation Research Part D: Transport and Environment*, **2**(2), 199–219.

Crandall, R.W. and J.D. Graham (1989), 'The Effect of Fuel Economy Standards on Automobile Safety', *Journal of Law and Economics*, **32**, 97–118.

Crandall, Robert, Howard K. Gruenspecht, Theodore E. Keeler and Lester B. Lave (1986), *Regulating the Automobile*, Washington, DC: Brookings Institution.

Crane, Randall (1999), 'The Impacts of Urban Form on Travel: A Critical Review', working paper WP99RC1, Cambridge, MA: Lincoln Institute of Land Policy.

Crane, Randall and Richard Crepeau (1998), 'Does Neighborhood Design Influence Travel? A Behavioral Analysis of Travel Diary and GIS Data', *Transportation Research Part D Transport and Environment*, **3**, 225–38.

Dahl, Carol A. (1995), 'Demand for Transportation Fuels: A Survey of Demand Elasticities and Their Components', *The Journal of Energy Literature*, **1**(2), 3–27.

Dahl, Carol and Thomas Sterner (1991a), 'Analyzing Gasoline Demand Elasticities: A Survey', *Energy Economics*, **13**, 203–10.

Dahl, Carol and Thomas Sterner (1991b), 'A Survey of Econometric Gasoline Demand Elasticities', *International Journal of Energy Systems*, **11**(2), 53–76.

Dargay, Joyce and Dermot Gately (1999), 'Income's Effect on Car and Vehicle Ownership, Worldwide: 1960–2015', *Transportation Research*, **33A**, 101–38.

Delucchi, Mark (1998), 'Lifecycle Energy Use, Greenhouse-Gas Emissions and Air Pollution from the Use of Transportation Fuels and Electricity', Institute of Transportation Studies, University of California, Davis.

Delucchi, Mark A., D.L. Greene and Q. Wang (1994), 'Motor Vehicle Fuel Economy: The Forgotten NMHC Control Strategy?', *Transportation Research A*, **28A**, 223–44.

Delucchi, Mark et al. (1996), 'Annualized Social Cost of Motor Vehicle Use in the United States, Based on 1990–91 Data', Institute of Transportation Studies, University of California, Davis. Summarized in Mark Delucchi, 'Total Cost of Motor-Vehicle Use', *Access*, **8**, 7–13.

Dill, Jennifer (2001), 'Design and administration of accelerated vehicle retirement programs in the U.S. and abroad', *Transportation Research Record*, 1750.

Dockery, D.W., C.A. Pope, X. Xu, J.D. Spengler, J.H. Ware, M.E. Fay, B.G. Ferris and F.E. Speizer (1993), 'An association between air pollution and mortality in six U.S. cities', *New England Journal of Medicine*, **329**(24) 1753–9.

Domencich, Tom and Daniel McFadden (1975), *Urban Travel Demand*, Amsterdam: North-Holland.

Dubin, Jeffrey and Daniel McFadden (1984), 'An Econometric Analysis of Residential Electric Appliance Holdings and Consumption', *Econometrica*, **52**(2): 53–76.

Dunphy, Robert T. and Kimberly Fischer (1996), 'Transportation, Congestion and Density: New Insights', *Transportation Research Record*, **1522**, 89–96.

Eash, W. Ronald (2001), 'Home-based Worker and Telecommuter Travel Behavior Reported in the 1995 Personal Transportation Survey', presented at the 80th Annual Meeting of the Transportation Research Board (TRB).

EIOLCA (2001), 'Carnegie Mellon University Green Design Initiative. Economic Input Output Life Cycle Analysis Model', http://www.eiolca.net.

Eliasson, J. and L.-G. Mattsson (2000), 'A Model for Integrated Analysis of Household Location and Travel Choices', *Transportation Research*, **34A**(5), 375–94.

Eskeland, Gunnar S. (1994), 'A Presumptive Pigovian Tax: Complementing Regulation to Mimic an Emissions Fee', *World Bank Economic Review*, **8**(3), 373–94.

Eskeland, Gunnar S. (1997), 'Rationing Can Backfire: The "Day without a Car" in Mexico City', *World Bank Economic Review*, **11**(3), 383–408.

Eskeland, Gunnar S. and Shantayanan Devarajan (1996), 'Taxing Bads by Taxing Goods: Pollution Control with Presumptive Charges', Washington DC: International Bank for Reconstruction and Development, World Bank.

ETTM (2002), 'United States Toll Facilities', ETTM on the web, www.ettm.com.

Eurostat (2001), *Eurostat Statistical Compendium*.

Evans, Leonard (1985), 'Fatality Risk for Belted Drivers Versus Car Mass', *Accident Analysis and Prevention*, **17**(3), 251–71.

Fourchet, Laurence (2001), 'What Does the Future Hold for the Electronic Toll Collection Market in North America?', http://www.ettm.com/na_future.html.

Fullerton, Don and Sarah E. West (2002), 'Can Taxes on Cars and on Gasoline Mimic an Unavailable Tax on Emissions?', *Journal of Environmental Economics and Management*, **43**(1), 135–57.

Gately, Dermot (1992), 'Imperfect Price-Reversibility of U.S. Gasoline Demand: Asymmetric Responses to Price Increases and Decreases', *The Energy Journal*, **13**(4), 179–207.

General Motors Corporation/Argonne National Laboratory (2001), 'Well-to-Wheel Energy Use and Greenhouse Gas Emissions of Advanced Fuel/Vehicle Systems – North American Analysis', Argonne National Laboratory.

Giuliano, Genevieve and Kenneth A. Small (1993), 'Is the Journey to Work Explained by Urban Structure?', *Urban Studies*, **30**(9), 1485–500.

Giuliano, Genevieve (1992), 'An Assessment of the Political Acceptability of Congestion Pricing', *Transportation*, **19**, 335–58.

Goddard, Haynes C. (1997), 'Using Tradable Permits to Achieve Sustainability in the World's Largest Cities: Policy Design Issues and Efficiency Conditions for Controlling Vehicle Emissions, Congestion and Urban Decentralization with an Application to Mexico City', *Environmental and Resource Economics*, **10**(1), 63–99.

Godek, Paul E. (1997), 'The Regulation of Fuel Economy and the Demand for "Light Trucks"', *Journal of Law and Economics*, **40**, 495–509.

Goldberg, Pinelopi (1998), 'The Effects of the Corporate Average Fuel Efficiency Standards in the U.S.', *Journal of Industrial Economics*, **46**(1), 1–33.

Gomez-Ibanez, Jose A. (1997), 'Estimating Whether Transport Users Pay Their Way: The State of the Art', in David L. Greene, Donald W. Jones and Mark A. Delucchi (eds), *The Full Costs and Benefits of Transportation*, Heidelberg, Germany: Springer-Verlag, Ch. 3.

Goodwin, Phil B. (1994), 'Road Pricing or Transport Planning?', in Borje Johansson and Lars-Goran Mattsson (eds) (1995), *Road Pricing: Theory, Empirical Assessment and Policy. Transportation Research, Economics and Policy*, vol. 3, Boston, MA and Dordrecht: Kluwer Academic.

Gordon, Peter and Harry Richardson (1999), 'Are Compact Cities a Desirable Planning Goal?', in *Environment, Land Use and Urban Policy*, vol. 2, Northampton, MA: Edward Elgar, 516–27.

Greene, David L., Donald W. Jones and Mark A. Delucchi (eds) (1997), *The Full Costs and Benefits of Transportation*, Heidelberg, Germany: Springer-Verlag.

Greene, David (1991), 'Short-run Pricing Strategies to Increase Corporate Average Fuel Economy', *Economic Inquiry*, **29**(1), 101–14.

Gruenspecht, Howard (1980), 'Differentiated Regulation: The Case of Auto Emissions Standards', *American Economic Review*, **72**(2), 328–31.

Gruenspecht, Howard (2001), 'Zero Emissions Vehicles: A Dirty Little Secret', *Resources*, **142**, 7–10. Washington, DC: Resources for the Future.

Hamer, A.M. and J.F. Linn (1987), 'Urbanization in the Developing World', in Edwin Mills (ed.), *Handbook of Urban Regional Economics*, vol. 2, Amsterdam: North Holland, 1255–84.

Hamilton, Bruce (1982), 'Wasteful Commuting', *Journal of Political Economy*, **90**(5), 1035–51.

Harrington, Winston (1997), 'Fuel Economy and Motor Vehicle Emissions', *Journal of Environmental Economics and Management*, **33**(3), 240–52.

Harrington, Winston and Alan J. Krupnick (1997), 'Energy, Transportation and Environment: Policy Options for Environmental Improvements', Washington, DC: The World Bank.

Harrington, Winston and Virginia McConnell (2000), 'Coase and Car Repair: Who Should be Responsible for Emissions of Vehicles in Use?', in Michael D. Kaplowitz (ed), *Property Rights, Economics and the Environment*, Stamford, CT: JAI Press, 201–37.

Harrington, Winston, Virginia McConnell and Anna Alberini (1998), 'Economic Incentive Policies under Uncertainty: The Case of Vehicle Emission Fees', in Kenneth Small and Roberto Roson (eds), *Environment and Transport in Economic Modelling*. Amsterdam: Kluwer Academic Publishing.

Harrington, Winston, Virginia McConnell and Amy Ando (2000), 'Are Vehicle Emission Inspection Programs Living Up to Expectations?', *Transportation Research Part D*, **5**(3), 153–72.

Harvey, Greg W. (1994), 'Transportation Pricing and Travel Behavior', in *Curbing Gridlock: Peak-Period Fees To Relieve Traffic Congestion, Volume 2*, National Research Council, 89–114.

Holtzclaw, J. (1994), 'Using Residential Patterns and Transit to Decrease Auto Dependence and Costs', San Francisco, CA: Natural Resources Defense Council.

Ingram, Gregory K. and Zhi Liu (1999), 'Determinants of Motorization and Road Provision', in Jose A. Gomez-Ibanez, William B. Tye and Clifford Winston (eds), *Essays in Transportation Economics and Policy*, Washington, DC: The Brookings Institution, ch. 10.

Innes, R. (1996), 'Regulating Automobile Pollution Under Certainty, Competition and Imperfect Information', *Journal of Environmental Economics and Management*, **31**, 219–39.

Jacobs, Jane (1961), *The Death and Life of Great American Cities*, New York: Vintage Books.

Janson, Heinz and Cecile Denis (1999), 'A Welfare Cost Assessment of Various Policy Measures to Reduce Pollutant Emissions from Passenger Road Vehicles', *Transportation Research, Part D*, **4**(6), November, 379–96.

Johansson-Stenman, Olof (1999), 'Regulating Road Transport Externalities: Pricing v. Command and Control,' in Thomas Sterner (ed.), *The Effectiveness of Market-Based Policy Instruments for Environmental Reform*, Cheltenham, UK and Northampton, USA: Edward Elgar, 134–57.

Jordan, Stacy, John P. Ross and Kurt G. Usowski (1998), 'U.S. Suburbanization in the 1980s', *Regional Science and Urban Economics*, **28**, 611–27.

Kågeson, Per (1993), 'Getting the Prices Right: A European Scheme for Making Transport Pay Its True Costs', report T&E 93/6, Brussels: European Federation for Transport and Environment.

Kazimi, Camilla (1997), 'Valuing Alternative Fueled Vehicles in Southern California', *American Economic Review, Papers and Proceedings*, **87**(2), 265–71.

Kerr, Suzi and David Maré (1997), 'Efficient Regulation Through Tradeable Permit Markets: The United States Lead Phasedown', Department of Agricultural and Resource Economics, University of Maryland College Park.

Kerr, Suzie and Richard Newell (2001), 'Policy-Induced Technology Adoption: Evidence from the U.S. Lead Phasedown', discussion paper 01–14. Washington, DC: Resources for the Future.

Khazzoom, J. Daniel (1994), 'Fuel Efficiency and Automobile Safety: Single-Vehicle Highway Fatalities for Passenger Cars', *The Energy Journal*, **15**(4), 49–101.

Khazzoom, J. Daniel, Michael Shelby and Rob Wolcott (1990), 'The Conflict Between Energy Conservation and Environmental Policy in the US Transportation Sector', *Energy Policy*, **18**(5), 456–8.

Kitamura, Ryuichi, Patricia Mokhtarian and Laura Laidet (1997), 'A Micro-Analysis of Land Use and Travel in Five Neighborhoods in the San Francisco Bay Area', *Transportation*, **24**, 125–58.

Kleit, Andrew N. (1990), 'The Effect of Annual Changes in Auto Fuel Economy Standards', *Journal of Regulatory Economics*, **2**, 151–72.

Kling, C.L. (1994), 'Emission Trading versus Rigid Regulations in the Control of Vehicle Emissions', *Land Economics*, **70**, 174–88.

Kockelman, Kara Maria (1997), 'Travel Behavior as a Function of Accessibility, Land Use Mixing, and Land Use Balance: Evidence from the San Francisco Bay Area', *Transportation Research Record*, **1607**, 116–25.

Koh, W. and D. Lee (1994), 'The Vehicle Quota System in Singapore: An Assessment', *Transportation Research Part A*, **28A**, 31–47.

Kopp, R. (1997), 'Something for Everyone: A Climate Policy That Both Environmentalists and Industry Can Live With' (with Richard Morgenstern and William Pizer), Weathervane, url http://www.weathervane.rff.org/features/feature015.html October 1997.

Krupnick, Alan, Winston Harrington and Bart Ostro (1990), 'Ambient Ozone and Acute Health Effects: Evidence from Daily Data', *Journal of Environmental Economics and Management*, **18**, 1–18.

Krupnick, Alan, Dallas Burtraw and Anil Markandya (2000), 'The Ancillary Benefits and Costs of Climate Change: A Conceptual Framework', in *The Ancillary Benefits and Costs of Greenhouse Gas Mitigation*, Paris: OECD/RFF/WRI/CI, 53–94.

K.T. Analytics, Inc. and Victoria Transport Policy Institute (1997), 'Review of Cost of Driving Studies', paper prepared for The Metropolitan Washington Council of Governments.

Kwoka, John E. (1983), 'The Limits of Market-Oriented Regulatory Techniques: The Case of Automotive Fuel Economy', *Quarterly Journal of Economics*, **98**, 695–704.

Lave, Lester B. and Heather L. MacLean (2002), 'An Environmental-Economic Evaluation of Hybrid Electric Vehicles: Toyota's Prius vs. Its Conventional Internal Combustion Engine Corolla', *Transportation Research*, **7D**(2), 155–62.

Lave, Lester B., W. Michael Griffin and Heather MacLean (2001), 'The Ethanol Answer to Carbon Emissions', *Issues in Science and Technology*, **18**(2), 73–8.

Lave, Lester B., E. Cobas-Flores, C.T. Hendrickson and F.C. McMichael (1995), 'Using Input–Output Analysis to Estimate Economy-wide Discharges', *Environmental Science and Technology*, **29**, 420A–426A.

Ledbetter, Marc (1989), 'Automobile Safety and Fuel Economy: A Critique of "The Effect of Fuel Economy Standards on Automobile Safety"', ACEEE research report, Washington, DC: American Council for an Energy Efficient Economy.

Lee, Douglas (1995), 'Full Cost Pricing of Transportation', paper presented at meetings of the Eastern Economic Association, March, Cambridge, MA: US DOT/VNTSC.

Leiby, Paul and Jonathan D. Rubin (1997), 'The Transitional Alternative Fuels and Vehicles Model', *Transportation Research Record*, **1587**, 10–18.

Litman, Todd (1994), *Transportation Cost Analysis: Techniques, Estimates, and Implications*, Victoria, BC: Todd Litman.

Little, Arthur D. (1998), 'Case Study: The Introduction of Improved Transport Fuel Qualities in Finland and Sweden', final report.

MacLean, Heather L. and Lester B. Lave (forthcoming), 'Evaluating Automobile Fuel/ Propulsion System Technologies', *Progress in Energy and Combustion Science*.

Maddala, G.S. (1983), *Limited Dependent Variables in Economics*, New York: Oxford University Press.

Madronich, Sasha (1993), 'Tropospheric Photochemistry and Its Response to UV Changes', in M.-L. Chanin (ed.), *The Role of the Stratosphere in Global Change*, Vol. 18, NATO–ASI Series, Amsterdam: Springer-Verlag, 437–61.

Mayeres, Inge and Stef Proost (2001), 'Should Diesel Cars in Europe be Discouraged?', *Regional Science and Urban Economics*, **31**(4), 453–70.

McConnell, Virginia D. and Mahlon Straszheim (1982), 'Auto Pollution and Congestion in an Urban Model: An Analysis of Alternative Strategies', *The Journal of Urban Economics*, **11**(1), 11–31.

McConnell, Virginia D., Margaret Walls and Winston Harrington (1995), 'Evaluation of the Costs and Emissions Reductions from Compliance with Mobile Source Emission Control Requirements: Retrospective Analysis', working paper 95–36, Washington, DC: Resources for the Future.

McDonald, John F. (1989), 'Econometric Studies of Urban Population Density: A Survey', *Journal of Urban Economics*, **26**, 361–85.

McFadden, D. (1973), 'Conditional Logit Analysis of Qualitative Choice Behavior', in P. Zarembka (ed.), *Frontiers in Econometrics*, New York: Academic Press.

McFadden, Daniel (1978), 'Modelling the Choice of Residential Location', in A. Karlquist et al. (eds), *Spatial Interaction Theory and Residential Location*, Amsterdam: North-Holland, 75–96.

McFadden, Daniel (1979), 'Quantitative Methods for Analyzing Travel Behavior of Individuals: Some Recent Developments', in David Hensher and P. Stopher (eds), *Behavioral Travel Modeling*, London: Croom Helm, 279–318.

McFadden, Daniel (2001), 'Disaggregate Behavioural Travel Demand's RUM Side: A 30-Year Retrospective', in David Hensher (ed), *Travel Behavior Research: The Leading Edge*, London: Pergamon, 17–64.

McKenzie, James J., Roger C. Dower and Donald D.T. Chen (1992), *The Going Rate: What It Really Costs to Drive*, New York: World Resources Institute.

MECA (Manufacturers of Emission Controls Association) (2000), 'Catalyst-Based

Diesel Particulate Filters and NO$_x$ Adsorbers: A Summary of the Technologies and the Effects of Fuel Sulfur', Washington, DC.

Miller, Peter and John Moffet (1993), *The Price of Mobility: Uncovering the Hidden Cost of Transportation*, New York: National Resources Defense Council.

Mills, E.S. (1972), *Studies in Structure of Urban Economy*, Baltimore, MD: Johns Hopkins Press.

Mokhtarian, Patricia L. (1998), 'A Synthetic Approach to Estimating the Impacts of Telecommuting on Travel', *Urban Studies* **35**(2): 215–241.

Mokhtarian, Patricia L. and Dennis K. Henderson (1998), 'Analyzing the Travel Behavior of Home-Based Workers in the 1991 Caltrans Statewide Travel Survey', *Journal of Transportation and Statistics*, **1**(3), 25–41.

Mokhtarian, Patricia L. and Ilan Salomon (1997), 'Emerging Travel Patterns: Do Telecommunications Make a Difference?', invited resource paper for the 8th Meeting of the International Association for Travel Behavior Research, Austin, TX, 21–25 September.

Muth, R.F. (1969), *Cities and Housing*, Chicago: University of Chicago Press.

Newell, Richard G. and William A. Pizer (forthcoming), 'Regulating Stock Externalities Under Uncertainty', *Journal of Environmental Economics and Management*.

Newell, Richard G. and Robert N. Stavins (2000), 'Cost Heterogeneity and the Potential Savings from Market-Based Policies', RFF discussion paper 00-10, Washington, DC: Resources for the Future.

Newman, P.W.G. and J.R. Kenworthy (1989), *Cities and Auto Dependence: A Source Book*, Aldershot, UK: Gower.

NHTSA (National Highway Traffic Safety Administration) (1997), 'Relationship of Vehicle Weight to Fatality and Injury Risk in Model Year 1985–93 Passenger Cars and Light Trucks', NHTSA Summary Report DOT HS 808 569, Springfield, VA: National Technical Information Service.

Nivola, Pietro (1999), 'Fit for Fat City: A "Lite" Menu of European Policies to Improve Our Urban Form', policy brief No. 44, Washington, DC: The Brookings Institution.

Nivola, Pietro and Robert Crandall (1995), *The Extra Mile: Rethinking Energy Policy for Automotive Transportation*, Washington, DC: The Brookings Institution.

NRC (National Research Council) (1991), *Rethinking the Ozone Problem in Urban and Regional Air Pollution*, Washington, DC: National Academy Press.

NRC (National Research Council) (1992), *Automotive Fuel Economy: How Far Should We Go?*, Washington, DC: National Academy Press.

NRC (National Research Council) (2001), *Evaluating Vehicle Emissions Inspection and Maintenance Programs*, Washington, DC: National Academy Press.

NRC (National Research Council) (2002a), *Effectiveness and Impact of Corporate Fuel Economy (CAFE) Standards*, Washington, DC: National Academy Press.

NRC (National Research Council) (2002b), *Estimating the Public Health Benefits of Proposed Air Pollution Regulations*, Washington DC: National Academy Press.

Noland, R.B. and L.L. Lem (2002), 'A Review of the Evidence for Induced Travel and Changes in Transportation and Environmental Policy in the US and the UK', *Transportation Research*, **7D**(1) January.

Oates, Wallace and Robert Schwab (1988), 'Economic Competition Among Jurisdictions: Efficiency Enhancing or Distortion Inducing?', *Journal of Public Economics*, **35**(3), 333–54.

Oates, Wallace, Paul Portney and Albert McGartland (1989), 'The Net Benefits of

Incentive-Based Regulation: A Case Study of Environmental Standard Setting', *American Economic Review*, **79**(December), 1233–42.

OECD (Organisation for Economic Co-operation and Development) (1995), 'Urban Travel and Sustainability', Paris: European Conference of Ministers of Transport.

OECD (Organisation for Economic Co-operation and Development) (1996), 'Energy Prices and Taxes', Paris: International Energy Agency.

OECD (Organisation for Economic Co-operation and Development) (1999), 'Older Gasoline Vehicles in Developing Countries and Economies in Transition: Their Importance and the Policy Options for Addressing Them', OECD/UNEP.

Onursal, Bekir and Surhid P. Gautam (1997), 'Vehicular Air Pollution: Experiences from Seven Latin American Urban Centers', technical paper No. 373, Washington, DC: World Bank Group.

Parry, Ian and Kenneth Small (2001), 'Does Britain or The United States Have the Right Gasoline Tax?', discussion paper, Washington, DC: Resources for the Future.

Pickrell, Don (1999), 'Transportation and Land Use', in Jose A. Gomez-Ibanez, William B. Tye and Clifford Winston (eds), *Essays in Transportation Economics and Policy*, Washington, DC: The Brookings Institution, ch. 12.

Pieper, Roel (2001), 'Mobimiles: Conscious on the Road', report prepared for the Dutch Minister of Transport, Public Works and Water Management.

Portney, Paul (1993–94), 'The Price is Right: Making Use of Life-Cycle Analyses', *Issues in Science and Technology*, **10**(2), 69–75.

Proost, Stef and Kurt van Dender (1999), 'Effectiveness and Welfare Impacts of Alternative Policies to Address Atmospheric Pollution in Urban Road Transport', discussion paper, Center for Economic Studies, Katholieke Universiteit, Leuven, Belgium.

Quinet, Emile (1997), 'Full Social Cost of Transportation in Europe', in David L. Greene, Donald W. Jones and Mark A. Delucchi (eds), *The Full Costs and Benefits of Transportation*, Heidelberg, Germany: Springer-Verlag, ch. 3.

Rapaport, Eric (2002), 'The Stockholm Environmental Zone: A Method to Curb Air Pollution from Bus and Truck Traffic', *Transportation Research*, **7**(3D), 213–24.

Roberts, Marc and Michael Spence (1976), 'Effluent Charges and Licenses Under Uncertainty', *Journal of Public Economics*, **5** (3–4), 193–208.

Romieu, Isabelle (1992), 'Epidemiologic Studies of the Health Effects of Air Pollution due to Motor Vehicles', in David E. Mage and Oliver Zali (eds), *Motor Vehicle Air Pollution: Public Health Impact and Control Measures*, Geneva: World Health Organization and Department of Public Health.

Romieu, Isabelle, H. Weitzenfeld and J. Finkelman (1992), 'Urban Pollution in Latin America and the Caribbean: Health Perspective', *World Health Statistics Quarterly*, **43**, 153–67.

Roson, Roberto (1998), 'Revealed Preferences, Externalities and Optimal Pricing for Urban Transportation', in Roberto Roson and Kenneth Small (eds), *Environment and Transport in Economic Modeling*, Boston, MA: Kluwer Academic Publishers.

Ross, Marc, Rob Goodwin and Rick Watkins (1995), 'Real World Emissions from Model-Year 1993, 2000, and 2010 Vehicles', American Council for an Energy-Efficient Economy.

Ross, Marc (1994), 'Automobile Fuel Consumption and Emissions: Effects of

Vehicle and Driving Characteristics', *Annual Review of Energy and the Environment*, **19**, 75–112.

Rubin, Jonathan and Paul Leiby (2000), 'An Analysis of Alternative Fuel Credit Provisions of US Automotive Fuel Economy Standards', *Energy Policy*, **28**(9), 589–602.

Safirova, Elena (forthcoming), 'Telecommuting, traffic congestion, and agglomeration: a general equilibrium model', *Journal of Urban Economics*.

Schafer, Andreas (1998), 'The Global Demand for Motorized Mobility', *Transportation Research A*, **32**(6) 455–77.

Schimek, Paul (1996), 'Household Vehicles Ownership and Use: How Much Does Residential Density Matter?', *Transportation Research Record*, **1552**, 120–30.

Schipper, Lee, Celine Marie-Lilliu and Lew Fulton (2001), 'Diesels in Europe: Analysis of Characteristics, Usage Patterns, Energy Savings and CO_2 Emission Implications', Paris: International Energy Agency.

Shah, J.J. and T. Nagpal (eds) (1997), 'Urban Air Quality Management Strategy in Asia – Metro Manila Report', World Bank technical paper No. 380, Washington, DC: International Bank for Reconstruction and Development/World Bank.

Shrank, David and Tim Lomax (2002), 'The 2002 Urban Mobility Report', Texas Transportation Institute, Texas A&M University.

Small, Kenneth A. and Camilla Kazimi (1995), 'On the Costs of Air Pollution from Motor Vehicles', *Journal of Transport Economics and Policy*, **29**, 7–32.

Small, Kenneth A., Clifford Winston and Carol A. Evans (1989), *Road Work*, Washington, DC: The Brookings Institution.

Sterner, Thomas (2002), *Policy Instruments for Environmental and Natural Resource Management*, Washington, DC: Resources For the Future/World Bank/Swedish International Development Cooperation Agency.

Sterner, Thomas and Lena Hoglund (2000), 'Output-Based Refunding of Emission Payments: Theory, Distribution of Costs and International Experience', discussion paper 00-29, Washington, DC: Resources for the Future.

Sveigny, Maureen (1998), *Taxing Automobile Emissions for Pollution Control*, Cheltenham, UK and Northampton, USA: Edward Elgar.

Sykuta, Michael (1996), 'Do Automotive Fuel Economy Standards Work?', St. Louis, MO: Washington University Center for the Study of American Business.

Thorpe, Steven (1997), 'Fuel Economy Standards, New Vehicle Sales, and Average Fuel Efficiency', *Journal of Regulatory Economics*, **11**, 311–26.

Train, Kenneth (1986), *Qualitative Choice Analysis: Theory, Econometrics, and an Application to Automobile Demand*, Cambridge, MA: MIT Press.

Transportation Research Board, National Research Council (2002), 'Surface Transportation Environmental Research: Long-Term Strategy', special report 268, Washington, DC: National Academy Press.

US Department of Energy (2001), 'Transportation Energy Data Book', edition 21, http://www-cta.ornl.gov/data/Index.html.

US Department of Energy (2002), 'Evaluating the Effects of Sulfur on Diesel Particulate Filters. Heavy Vehicle Technologies Research', Washington, DC, http://www.trucks.doe.gov/research/fuel/decse-filterphase1.html.

US Department of Transportation (1992), *Transportation Implications of Telecommuting*, http://ntl.bts.gov/DOCS/telecommute.html.

US Department of Transportation (1996), 'Transportation Statistics Annual

Report, An International Comparison of Transportation and Air Pollution', Chapter 9, Washington, DC: US DOT Bureau of Transportation Statistics.

US Environmental Protection Agency, Office of Air Quality Planning and Standards, *National Air Pollutant Trends*, http://www.epa.gov/ttn/chief/trends/index.html.

US Environmental Protection Agency (1990), 'Air Quality Criteria for Lead: Supplement to the 1986 Addendum', Washington, DC: US EPA Office of Research and Development.

US Environmental Protection Agency (2000), 'Regulatory Impact Analysis of Diesel Fuel Sulfur', http://www.epa.gov/otaq/diesel.htm#hd2007.

van Eeghan, Maarten (2001), 'Road Pricing in the Netherlands', CPB Netherlands Bureau for Economic Policy Analysis, working paper 107, http://www.cpb.nl/eng/pub/werkdoc/107.

Vickery, William (1963), 'Pricing in Urban and Suburban Transport', *American Economic Review Papers and Proceedings*, **53**, 452–65.

Walls, Margaret, Alan Krupnick and C. Hood (1993), 'Estimating the Demand for Vehicle-Miles-Traveled Using Household Survey Data: Results from the 1990 Nationwide Personal Transportation Survey', discussion paper ENR 93–25, Washington, DC: Resources for the Future.

Walls, Margaret, Alan Krupnick and Winston Harrington (2002), 'Population Density, Transit Availability, and Vehicle Travel: Results from a Nested Logit Model of Vehicle Use', paper presented at the American Economic Association Meetings, Atlanta, GA.

Walsh, Michael P. (2002), *Carlines*, Washington, DC, April.

Wang, M.Q. (1999), 'GREET 1.5 – Transportation Fuel-Cycle Model. Volume I: Methodology, Development, Use and Results', Argonne National Laboratory, Center for Transportation Research, ANL/ESD-39.

Ward's Communications (1999), 'Ward's Motor Vehicle Facts and Figures', Southfield, MI.

Watterson, W.T. (1993), 'Linked Simulation of Land Use and Transportation Systems: Developments and Experience in the Puget Sound Region', *Transportation Research*, **27A**(3), 193–206.

WBCSD (World Business Council on Sustainable Development) (2001), 'Mobility 2001: World Mobility at the End of the 20th Century and its Sustainability', Switzerland (www.wbcsdmobility.org).

Weitzman, Martin (1974), 'Prices and Quantities', *Review of Economic Studies*, **41**(4), 477–91.

Wheaton, William C. (1998), 'Land Use and Density in Cities with Congestion', *Journal of Urban Economics*, **43**, 258–72.

White, Lawrence J. (1982), *The Regulation of Air Pollutant Emissions from Motor Vehicles*, Washington, DC: American Enterprise Institute.

Winebrake, James J. and Alex Farrell (1997), 'The AFV Credit Program and its Role in Future AFV Market Development', *Transportation Research* D, **2**(2), 125–32.

World Bank (2000), *World Development Indicators 2000*, Washington, DC.

World Resources Institute (1997), *World Resources*, Washington, DC.

World Resources Institute (1998–99), *World Resources*, Washington, DC, http://www.wri.org/wr-98-99/autos.htm.

Yun, John M. (1997), 'Measuring the Unintended Effects and Costs of Fuel Economy Regulation', Department of Economics, Emory University.

6. Recreation demand models

Joseph A. Herriges and Catherine L. Kling

The first and second welfare theorems assure us that goods traded in well-functioning markets will be produced in an efficient quantity. In contrast, goods that are public in nature, and for which well-functioning markets do not exist, may need government provision in order to be efficiently provided. The efficient level of provision in turn depends on the value consumers place on the good. Unfortunately, while the price of a market good can be interpreted as its marginal value, no such marginal value information is available for nonmarket goods such as water quality or hunting success at a marsh; thus the problem of nonmarket valuation arises. Recreation demand models have played a central role in the nonmarket valuation literature since its inception by linking environmental quality with a market-like good (that is, the use of recreational resources) for which value information does exist. A subject search in ECONLit of 'recreation demand' and related terms yields 171 distinct articles on the topic during the last decade alone. The prevalence of recreation demand studies in the literature attests to a public policy need to understand efficient provision levels of these goods.

In addition to the policy relevance of recreation demand models, researchers have also found recreation data sets to be a rich source for empirical and econometric research. This is due in part to the unique characteristic of price variation in recreation demand data. Specifically, the price of the good varies across individuals even within a particular time period, making cross-section analysis both possible and productive. Many other goods for which empirical demand studies have been undertaken have a uniform price in any given period that all consumers face. To gain the necessary price variation for econometric estimation, researchers must collect and employ time series data and techniques. Recreation demand data, which are generally based on individual observations and for which varying distances from the sites generate price variation, avoid the need for time series treatments. This makes it an appealing case study for applying econometric techniques and microeconomic behavioral models. Despite the econometric advantage that the price variability provides, however, it should also be clearly noted that 'price' in this context is notoriously difficult to measure. For example, accounting for and appropriately integrating the opportunity cost of time into models of recreation demand remains an elusive goal. Defining the commodity of interest itself and the set of available substitutes (that is, the choice set) can likewise be a challenge. More will be said on these topics later.

In this chapter, we outline the historical development of the theory and empirical implementation of recreation demand models that rely on revealed preference data. Revealed preference data and approaches are those that are based on observed behavior, with surveys typically used to collect information from individual recreators on their use of various recreation sites. The value placed in a site, or in changes to specific attributes of a site, is then inferred from how visitation patterns change with changing site characteristics. Freeman (1993) refers to these as a type of 'indirect' method, as value is indirectly inferred from the associated behavior, with the term 'travel cost' model also commonly used. In contrast, stated preference data and methods, referred to by Freeman (1993) as 'direct' since values are directly elicited, have also been extensively used to estimate the demand and surplus. While we do not discuss this alternative, and sometime complementary, line of research, excellent reviews of both the theory and practice of stated preference methods can be found in Bateman and Willis (1999) and Carson (2002).

We begin by identifying two distinct, but equally valuable, approaches to modeling revealed preference choices to which almost all of the current models can trace their beginnings. We will refer to these as participation and site selection models, respectively. The first efforts to estimate recreation demand with revealed preference data were participation models, based on standard Marshallian demand theory; they used data on the quantity of visits to a recreation area to fit a demand function. The models, at least initially, treated the number of visits to a given site as a continuous variable, ignoring the integer (or count) nature of trips. In contrast, the more recent random utility maximization (RUM) models focused on the site selection decision using 'discrete' choice models as to which of several recreation sites to visit on a particular choice occasion. Although many variations of these approaches can be found in the modern recreation demand literature, these two broad categories still capture the essential focus of and distinction between alternative methods.

In tracking the historical development of these approaches from their beginnings to their modern-day versions, we note that each has become more rigorous and more accurately reflects the underlying data-generating process of recreation data. Consequently, the models have, in some respects, become more similar over time. However, they retain the distinctive features of their beginnings and have different advantages relative to one another. Although neither approach can clearly be said to dominate the other, we offer our assessments of their relative strengths and the areas in which additional improvements would be most beneficial.

In the second major section of this chapter, we address a number of difficult empirical issues that all recreation demand models must address, regardless of whether they focus primarily on the participation or site selection aspect of the decision. These issues include valuing the opportunity cost of time (critical for accurately measuring the 'price' of recreation), defining the extent of the market (also referred to as choice set definition in RUM models), the choice of functional form and error structure, and the dynamic nature of recreation demand (for example, habit formation, variety seeking and information gathering).

An important caveat is in order. Although we provide the reader with many citations to the relevant literature, our list is far from exhaustive. Many excellent papers appear in the published literature that are not cited here and a rich literature in the unpublished and gray literatures also exists. Further, we do not attempt to provide details of the many econometric methods for estimation, prediction and model selection. An excellent source for the econometrics of both continuous and discrete choice models is Haab and McConnell (2002). The chapters in Herriges and Kling (1999b) are a useful resource as well. Finally, there are a number of other valuable review articles and books on this subject (Ward and Loomis, 1986; Bockstael et al., 1991; Freeman, 1993; Smith, 1989, 1993 and 1997; and Phaneuf and Smith, 2002).

HISTORICAL DEVELOPMENT: BEGINNINGS AND INITIAL REFINEMENTS

As noted earlier, current recreation demand models can trace their origins to one of two fundamental approaches to the modeling problem: the standard neoclassical demand model of participation or the random utility maximization model of site selection.[1] Since the continuous demand approaches were the first on the scene, we begin our discussion with them.

Participation Models

While most environmental and resource economists know the Hotelling rule for resource extraction, fewer may realize that he is credited with being the first to propose an empirical strategy for estimating recreation demand. In a now famous letter to the Park Service in the 1940s, Hotelling suggests using aggregate visitation data combined with distance to the site of interest to generate a recreation demand curve. Although Hotelling's letter is dated 1947, the first actual implementation of his suggestion did not occur until Wood and Trice (1958), followed by Clawson (1959), Clawson and Knetsch (1966), Brown and Nawas (1973), and Cesario and Knetsch (1976). These models used the per capita numbers of visitors from arbitrarily defined zones of origin (sharing about the same distance from, and hence costs of travel to, a single recreation site) to estimate a 'zonal' demand. A standard form for estimation of a simple zonal model was

$$y_i = f(p_i, z_i) + \varepsilon_i, \tag{6.1}$$

where y_i is the per capita number of visitors from zone i to the site in question, p_i is the distance or the travel costs from zone i to the site, z_i consists of summary characteristics for individuals living in zone i (for example age, income, and so on), and ε_i is an additive error. Early applications focused on single recreation sites, but were later extended to multiple sites. Other early examples of this approach are Wetzstein and McNeely (1980), Sutherland (1982), Smith and Kopp (1980), Bowes and Loomis (1980) and Huppert and Thomson (1984).

A significant conceptual and empirical step took place in the development of recreation demand models when researchers began to recognize that more information could be obtained by using individual observations as the unit of measurement rather than zonal aggregates. Early examples include Vaughan and Russell (1982), Smith et al. (1983a) and Smith and Desvousges (1985). Although there was some debate about the value of this approach (Hellerstein, 1995; and Brown et al., 1983), individual observations ultimately won the day. In this formulation, the model specification in (6.1) is still a natural starting point, except that the subscript i now refers to the individual observation instead of the zone.

The increased richness associated with individual observation data does not come without costs. The most obvious of these, of course, are the survey data collection costs themselves. Moreover, the use of individual survey responses raises, or at least make more transparent, a number of important econometric issues, making the analysis itself more complex. We highlight three of these issues. First, when the analysis relies upon data collected through household-level surveys, sampling issues must be carefully addressed. Specifically, if data are collected on site, only observations with positive numbers of trips will be represented in the sample. Application of OLS to such data will yield biased coefficient estimates (Smith, 1988; Shaw, 1988; and Laitila, 1999). Similarly, nonresponse to the survey itself can cause the available data to underrepresent a segment of the population, such as those who have little or no interest in the recreational activity being studied.

Second, if a random population survey is used instead to collect the data, the simple regression model in (6.1) is likely to be a poor representation of individual behavior due to the abundance of 'zeros' in such data; that is, a large percentage of the general population typically will not visit a particular site. Hence, a survey data set will contain many corner solutions. This problem of zeros has motivated the application of Tobit, Heckman and Cragg estimators to recreation data (Bockstael et al., 1990; Smith, 1988; Shaw, 1988; and Hellerstein, 1992). The Tobit model, for example, replaces (6.1) with

$$y_i = \begin{cases} f(p_i, z_i) + \varepsilon_i & f(p_i, z_i) + \varepsilon_i > 0 \\ 0 & f(p_i, z_i) + \varepsilon_i \le 0 \end{cases} \tag{6.2}$$

Thus the frequency of corners (or 'zeros') is determined by $\Pr[\varepsilon_i \le -f(p_i, z_i)]$, which in turn depends upon the distributional assumptions regarding ε_i and the individual characteristics p_i and z_i. Note that the source of the error term in this model is vague, potentially capturing a myriad of 'sins', including measurement error, optimization errors by the individual, omitted variables and model misspecification. In turn, the correction for the abundance of zeros is largely statistical in nature, with little in the way of behavioral underpinnings. The Cragg and Heckman approaches are similar in spirit to the Tobit model, except that they allow the factors that determine participation (that is, whether y_i is zero or positive) to differ from those that determine the level of consumption *given* participation.

Third, individual-level observations make it clear that recreation demand data are almost always 'count' in nature; that is, recreationists can choose only an integer-valued number of trips. The econometric literature has developed models to correctly account for this massing of probability and numerous authors have employed these models in a recreation demand setting (Smith, 1988; Shaw, 1988; Creel and Loomis, 1990; Hellerstein, 1991; Hellerstein and Mendelsohn, 1993; Englin and Shonkwiler, 1995; and Haab and McConnell, 1996).

The Poisson regression model is perhaps the simplest of the count specifications. It assumes that the number of trips taken by an individual (y_i) is drawn from a discrete Poisson distribution, with

$$\Pr[y_i = k] = \frac{e^{-g(p_i, z_i)} g(p_i, z_i)^k}{k!} \qquad k = 0, 1, 2, \ldots, \tag{6.3}$$

where $g(p_i, z_i)$ denotes the average number of trips taken by individuals with trip costs p_i and characteristics z_i. Typically, it is also assumed that

$$g(p_i, z_i) = \exp(\beta_p p_i + \beta_z' z_i), \tag{6.4}$$

insuring that the average number of trips is positive. One of the limitations of the Poisson model is that it restricts the conditional mean and variance of the number of trips taken to be the same, a property known as equidispersion. In practice, this assumption is often violated, with the conditional variance exceeding the mean (overdispersion) and there being more zeros than is consistent with the Poisson specification. A variety of generalizations to the Poisson model have been developed that allow for overdispersion, such as the negative binomial model. Other generalizations allow the factors that determine the participation decision to differ from those that determine the quantity decision, much like the Cragg approach does for continuous models.[2]

The emphasis in the early recreation demand analysis was clearly on modeling the quantity decision (that is, how many trips were taken) for a given recreational site, with relatively little consideration given to the site selection issue (that is, the tradeoffs among sites and their characteristics). A number of early exceptions are worth noting, however. These studies generalized the single-site demand equation to a system:

$$y_{ij} = f(p_{ij}, z_{ij}) + \varepsilon_{ij} \qquad j = 1, ..., J, \qquad (6.5)$$

where J denotes the total number of sites available in the choice set, y_{ij} denotes the number of trips taken by individual i to site j ($j = 1, ..., J$), and $p'_{ij} = (p_{i1}, ..., p_{iJ})$ denotes the vector of travel costs to the various sites, thus allowing for potential cross-price effects as well as error terms that are correlated across sites. Burt and Brewer (1971), for example, estimated a system of demands for a set of lakes in southern Missouri. In addition to being remarkable for its use of a large data set at a time when data were not easily manipulated, their paper also tested for and imposed symmetry of the cross-price effects to assure the path independence of their consumer surplus measures. Another early application of a system was Cichetti et al. (1976).

In a subsequent series of papers, Morey (1981, 1984, 1985) took the systems approach one step further, accounting for both censoring and the discrete nature of recreation demand using a system of trip share equations. An individual's share of total trips allocated to a single site ($s_{ij} = y_{ij}/T$) was modeled as drawn from a multinomial distribution

$$f(s_{i1}, ..., s_{iJ}; T, \theta_{i1}, ..., \theta_{iJ}) = \frac{T!}{\prod\limits_{j=1}^{J} y_{ij}!} \prod\limits_{j=1}^{J} \theta_{ij}^{x_{ij}}, \qquad (6.6)$$

where $\theta_{ij} = E(s_{ij})$ and T is the total number of trips taken by the individual. The mean shares were derived from a specific utility function, such as the generalized CES in the case of Morey (1984). The advantage of this approach is that the resulting share equations were restricted to lie in the unit interval and to sum to one over the choice set. There are, however, a number of disadvantages as well. First, the total number of trips (T) must be specified *a priori* by the analyst and is typically assumed to be constant across individuals. Second, the distributional assumptions regarding s_{ij} impose considerable structure on the pattern of correlation (substitution) among sites. In particular, the structure imposes that $\text{cov}(s_{ij}, s_{ik}) = -(\theta_{ij}\theta_{ik})/T < 0$, precluding positive correlation (complementarities) among sites.[3] Nonetheless, Morey's system of shares represents one of the earliest efforts to model the site selection and participation decisions in a unified framework.

Site Selection Models

While early continuous recreation demand analysis emphasized modeling the quantity of trips taken to an individual site, the discrete choice branch of the literature evolved in large part to analyze the substitution possibilities among competing sites and the influence of site characteristics on site selection. Interest in the decision as to where to recreate on a given choice occasion led some researchers, notably Michael Hanemann in his Ph.D. thesis in 1978, to investigate the use of discrete choice models formalized and popularized by McFadden (1974, 1981, 2001).

In the simple discrete choice framework, instead of focusing on the decision of how often to visit a given recreation site, the emphasis is on modeling which site to visit. Most of this work is based on McFadden's (1981) random utility maximization (or RUM) hypothesis, which assumes an individual receives utility (U_j) from a visit to site j and chooses that site yielding the highest level of utility. Thus an individual visits site j on a particular choice occasion if $U_j > U_k$ for all $k \neq j$. The individual's utility is assumed to depend upon individual- and site-specific characteristics (s and x_j, respectively); that is,

$$U_j = U(x_j, s). \tag{6.7}$$

It is important to note that in this framework the decision-making process is not random from the point of view of individuals. They are assumed to know all of the factors (that is, s and x_j) influencing their utility and to have a clear preference ordering among the alternatives. The uncertainty arises, instead, from the point of view of the analyst, who does not observe all of the relevant individual and site characteristics and does not know the specific way in which they influence preferences. For example, suppose that the analyst observes only a subset of the relevant characteristics ($\tilde{x}_j, \tilde{s}$), while the remaining characteristics, $(\check{x}_j, \check{s})$ are unobserved.[4] They must then make some assumption about how these observed factors influence utility, in most cases assuming that they affect utility in a linear fashion, so that

$$U_j = V_j(\tilde{x}_j, \tilde{s}) - \varepsilon_j$$
$$= \beta'\tilde{x}_j + \gamma_j\tilde{s} + \varepsilon_j. \tag{6.8}$$

Comparing (6.7) and (6.8), it is clear that

$$\varepsilon_j = U(\tilde{x}_j, \tilde{s}, \check{x}_j, \check{s}) - V(\tilde{x}_j, \tilde{s}). \tag{6.9}$$

Thus the error term in this framework has a clear interpretation, capturing that portion of the consumer's preferences unobserved by the analyst or due to model misspecification. Consequently, it represents a part of the consumer's utility derived from the site and should be taken into account in conducting welfare analysis. The representative utility function $V_j = V(\tilde{x}_j, \tilde{s})$ captures only that portion of utility reflected through the observed characteristics. Furthermore, understanding potential sources of omitted variables (for example boat ownership) may suggest patterns of correlation that need to be accounted for in specifying the error distribution (for example, allowing for correlation among sites with boat ramps).[5]

The earliest applications of the RUM framework to site selection models assumed that the errors were independently and identically distributed extreme value terms, resulting in multinomial logit (MNL) choice probabilities. In this case, the probability that an individual would choose to visit site j on a given choice occasion is given by

$$P_j = \frac{e^{V_j}}{\displaystyle\sum_{k=1}^{J} e^{V_k}}. \tag{6.10}$$

The attraction of the MNL specification lies not only in the convenient closed form choice probabilities, making maximum likelihood estimation straightforward, but also in the correspondingly simple formulas for computing the welfare consequences associated with price and/or quality changes (Small and Rosen, 1981; Hanemann, 1999). For example, if households have a constant marginal utility of income, as is typically assumed, then the compensating variation associated with a change in either site availability or characteristics is simply given by:

$$CV = \beta_y^{-1}\left[\ln\sum_{j\in J^0}\exp(V_j^0) - \ln\sum_{j\in J^1}\exp(V_j^1)\right], \tag{6.11}$$

where βy denotes the marginal utility of income, J^m denotes the available choice set ($m = 0$ for the initial conditions and 1 for the new conditions), and $V_j^m = V(\tilde{x}_j^m, \tilde{s}^m)$ denotes the representative utility for site j under conditions m. Because of its ease of use, the MNL specification remains popular, especially in situations when there are large numbers of alternatives in the choice set. (See, for example, Hanemann, 1978; Caulkins et al., 1986; Kling, 1988a, 1988b; Bockstael et al., 1989; and Morey et al., 1991).

Although estimation ease gave the logit specification a head start in modeling site selection, its ease of use comes at a cost in terms of realism. In particular, the standard logit models suffers from the well-known independence of irrelevant alternatives (IIA) assumption. The IIA property is a direct outcome of the form of the logit distribution and results in the ratio of any two choice probabilities being independent of any of the remaining alternatives (and their characteristics). This, in turn, implies a rigid pattern for how choice probabilities change with changing site characteristics. The elasticity vector of site j's choice probability with respect to a change in site k's characteristics vector $\tilde{x}_k$ becomes:

$$\eta_{jk} = \frac{\partial \ln P_j}{\partial \ln \tilde{x}_k} = (\delta_{jk} - P_k)V_{kk}, \tag{6.12}$$

where $V_{kk} = (\partial \ln V_k)/(\partial \ln \tilde{x}_k)$ and $\delta_{jk} = 1$ if $j = k; = 0$ otherwise. Thus, all cross-site responses are the same, $\eta_{jk} = \eta_{j'k} \forall j,\ j' \neq k$ see (Herriges and Phaneuf, 2002 for more detail). This would preclude, for example, complementary relationships among sites.

In an effort to relax the IIA assumption inherent in the standard logit model, McFadden (1978) proposed a class of models based on the generalized extreme value (GEV) distribution. The GEV models retain much of the simplicity of MNL, but allow for correlations among the error components associated with each alternative (that is, the ε_j's in equation (6.8)). This in turn partially relaxes the IIA assumption and reduces, although does not eliminate, the rigid response elasticities of MNL. The most frequently used GEV model is the nested logit (NL) specification (see, for example Morey et al., 1993; and Milon, 1988).

The nested logit model begins by assuming that the set of alternatives (or sites) can be grouped (that is, nested) into mutually exclusive subsets such that alternatives within the same nest are more similar (that is, better substitutes) than sites that are in different nests. For example, in modeling recreational fishing, one might assume that all sites with boat ramps belong in the same nest, whereas sites allowing only shore fishing comprise a second nest. Each nest can, in turn, be divided into subsets, allowing for a complex pattern of correlations and substitution among sites.

To better understand the NL model, consider a simple example in which the available J alternatives are subdivided into G nests.[6] Let $n(j)$ denote the nest to which alternative j belongs and N_g be the set of alternatives in nest g.[7] This nested logit model results if the utility associate with visiting site j is given by

$$U_j = V(\tilde{x}_j, s) + \varepsilon_j, \tag{6.13}$$

where $\varepsilon_j \equiv (\varepsilon_1, ..., \varepsilon_J)'$ is drawn from a GEV distribution with a cumulative distribution function

$$F(\varepsilon_j) = \exp\left(-\sum_{g=1}^{G}\left[\sum_{j \in N_g} \exp\left(-\frac{\varepsilon_j}{\theta_g}\right)\right]^{\theta_g}\right), \tag{6.14}$$

where θ_g is known as the dissimilarity coefficient for nest g.[8] While a detailed discussion of the implications of the above error structure is beyond the scope of this review, several important features of the NL are worth noting.[9]

1. The nested logit model defined by equations (6.13) and (6.14) implies that the probability of choosing alternative j has two components; that is,

$$P_j = P_{j|n(j)}Q_{n(j)}, \tag{6.15}$$

where

$$P_{j|n(j)} = \frac{\exp\left[\dfrac{V_j}{\theta_{n(j)}}\right]}{\displaystyle\sum_{s \in N_{n(j)}} \exp\left[\dfrac{V_s}{\theta_{n(j)}}\right]}, \tag{6.16}$$

denotes the probability of choosing alternative $j \in N_{n(j)}$ given that nest $n(j)$ has been selected and

$$Q_g \equiv \frac{L_g}{\displaystyle\sum_{s=1}^{G} L_s} \tag{6.17}$$

denotes the probability that nest g is chosen, where

$$L_g \equiv \left\{\sum_{k \in N_g} \exp\left[\frac{V_k}{\theta_g}\right]\right\}^{\theta_g} \tag{6.18}$$

is referred to as the inclusive value associated with nest g. Thus the nested logit model implies a structure analogous to two-stage budgeting in the consumer demand literature. In this case, the individual chooses from among the nests (with probabilities Q_g) and, given the nest, chooses from among the available alternatives (N_g) in that nest.

2. The GEV structure in (6.14) implies a block diagonal pattern of correlation among the unobserved components of utility (that is, the ε_js). In particular,

$$\text{corr}(\varepsilon_j, \varepsilon_k) = \begin{cases} \rho_g \geq 0 & n(j) = n(k) = g \\ 0 & n(j) \neq n(k). \end{cases} \tag{6.19}$$

That is, the model assumes the unobserved components of utility are positively correlated for alternatives in the same nest and uncorrelated across nests.[10] The intuition here is straightforward. The nesting structure is chosen so as to group similar alternatives (that is, close substitutes). The correlation pattern in (6.19) is consistent with this notion. For example, consider a nested logit model that nests together the first two alternatives. If the first alternative is preferred to alternative J because $\varepsilon_1 > \varepsilon_J$, then alternative 2 is also more likely to be preferred to alternative J since, given the positive correlation between ε_1 and ε_2, it is more likely that $\varepsilon_1 > \varepsilon_J$.

3. While the nested logit model relaxes some of the structure of the MNL specification, considerable structure remains. In particular, the IIA property still remains for alternatives within the same nest since when $n(j) = n(k) = g$,

$$\frac{P_j}{P_k} = \frac{P_{j|g}}{P_{k|g}} = \exp\left(\frac{V_j - V_k}{\theta_g}\right), \tag{6.20}$$

is independent of all other alternatives. Alternatives in different nests exhibit a property known as the independence of irrelevant nests (IIN), since the relative choice probability P_j/P_k is independent of alternatives outside of the nests $n(j)$ and $n(k)$.[11]

In sum, NL retains many of the advantages of MNL. The choice probabilities, while more complex, still have a convenient closed form. Likewise, assuming a constant marginal utility of income, the welfare implications of changing site availability or characteristics are easily computed since the compensating variation formula has a simple closed form.[12] On the other hand, NL does impose considerable structure on both the choice probabilities and the way in which these probabilities respond to changing individual and alternatives specific characteristics. Furthermore, NL models require that the analyst specify *a priori* the nesting structure. While specification criteria do exist for choosing among competing nesting structures, they are rarely used in practice.[13] A number of studies have attempted to determine the sensitivity of welfare estimates to the choice of nesting structure. Both Kling and Thomson (1996) and Shaw and Ozog (1999) find that welfare estimates can be fairly sensitive to the choice of nesting structure, whereas Hauber and Parsons (2000) find that the nesting structure makes little difference for welfare estimation. A Monte Carlo analysis by Herriges and Kling (1995) suggests that these disparate results are driven in part by the degree of underlying correlation among alternatives and that specification tests should be employed when choosing from among competing nesting structures in practice.

While the RUM models provide an appealing approach to the site selection decision, the discrete framework is less well suited to explaining the decision of how many visits to make to a single or multiple recreation sites. To capture elements of the participation decision, early practitioners estimated separate demand equations to predict the number of trips taken in a season. Various approaches have been used to link this aggregate demand function back to the site selection model. This strand of work began with Bockstael et al. (1987) and has been followed with papers by Creel and Loomis (1992a), Morey et al. (1991), Yen and Adamowicz (1994), Hausman et al. (1995), Feather et al. (1995) and Parsons and Kealy (1995). The basic structure of these so-called 'linked' approaches is to model the total number of trips taken, $y_{iT} = \sum_{j=1}^{j} y_{ij}$ using a relationship of the form

$$y_{iT} = h(L_i, s_i) + \mu_i,$$ (6.21)

where L_i is a variable (or vector of variables) derived from a site selection model. For example, Bockstael et al. (1987) suggest using the expected utility (that is, inclusive value) for L_i computed from the site selection model as an index of the overall utility associated with trip taking. On the other hand, both Parsons and Kealy (1995) and Feather et al. (1995) treat L_i as a vector consisting of expected trip quality and prices. Unfortunately, while these models provide intuitive approaches to tying together the participation and site selection decisions, none is completely utility-theoretic (see, for example, Smith, 1997, 193, fn 18; or Herriges et al., 1999).

HISTORICAL DEVELOPMENT: MODERN VARIATIONS

In the previous section, we outlined the early development of participation and site selection models of recreation demand. In this section, we continue the discussion, focusing on recent innovations. Four classes of models are considered: (1) the Kuhn–Tucker model; (2) systems of count data models; (3) generalized errors structure models of site selection; and (4) the repeated logit model. The first two models naturally trace their roots to the simple trip demand equations used to capture participation (that is, trip quantities), whereas the second two models stem from the site selection literature.

The Kuhn–Tucker Model

The early recreation demand systems (for example, Burt and Brewer, 1971; and Cichetti et al., 1976) represented a significant step towards jointly modeling the site selection and participation decisions. Cichetti et al. (1976), for example, use the system of demand equations

$$
\begin{aligned}
y_{ij} &= \bar{P}_1\beta_1 + v_{ij} \\
y_{ij} &= \bar{P}_2\beta_2 + v_{ij} \\
&\vdots \qquad \vdots \\
y_{ij} &= \bar{P}_J\beta_J + v_{ij},
\end{aligned}
\tag{6.22}
$$

where $y_{ij} = (y_{1j}, ..., y_{Nj})'$ denotes the $N \times 1$ vector of trips to site j by the N individuals in the sample, $\bar{P}_j$ is an $N \times R$ vector of regressors, and v_{ij} is an $N \times 1$ vector of disturbances associated with site j. Including in $\bar{P}_j$ trip costs to sites other than j allows for cross-site substitution effects while still modeling the quantity of trips taken. However, the models themselves were reduced form in nature, both in terms of the demand equations (linear in both cases) and the error specifications (employing additive errors). Welfare calculation in this context is more difficult, lacking a well-defined underlying utility function and making the role of the error terms in welfare calculations uncertain.[14] Furthermore, reduced form systems, such as in equation (6.5), do not naturally incorporate the nonnegativity constraint on trip demands and the frequent occurrences of zeros (or corner solutions).

One strategy for dealing with corner solutions is to apply a statistical fix to the problem along the lines of the Tobit approach for a single equation.[15] In this case, the mass of zeros observed for an alternative is assumed to be the result of censoring what would otherwise be negative latent demand for that alternative. The problem here is that the demand equations, prior to censoring, are assumed to be derived without consideration of the non-negativity constraint and are only after the fact required to lie in the positive orthant. As Phaneuf et al. (1998) note, this approach fails to recognize the different roles of prices in inframarginal versus marginal decisions regarding consumption. Specifically, whereas all prices impact which combination of goods are consumed (or sites visited), only the prices of the consumed commodities affect the marginal consumption decisions.

An alternative approach to tackling this problem is represented by the Kuhn–Tucker (KT) approaches of Wales and Woodland (1983), Hanemann (1984), and Lee and Pitt (1986, 1987). These methods are discussed in Bockstael et al. (1986) for beach recreation (1986) and Morey et al. (1995) and several empirical applications to recreation demand have now appeared in the literature (including Phaneuf et al., 2000; Phaneuf, 1999; Phaneuf and Herriges, 1999; and Morey et al., 1990).

The appeal of the Kuhn–Tucker approach is that it provides a unified and utility theoretic approach to simultaneously modeling both the site selection and participation decisions. In its primal form, the model begins not with the specification of demand equations, but rather with the individual's underlying direct utility function. Specifically, each consumer is assumed to solve

$$\max_{y_j, z} U(y_j, z, \varepsilon_j) \qquad (6.23)$$

subject to the budget constraint

$$p'_j y_j + z \le I \qquad (6.24)$$

and nonnegativity constraints

$$z \ge 0, \ y_j \ge 0 \quad \forall j = 1, ..., J, \qquad (6.25)$$

where $U(\cdot)$ is assumed to be a quasi-concave, increasing, and continuously differentiable function of (y_j, x), $y_j = (y_1, ..., y_J)'$ denotes the vector of goods (that is, trips in recreation demand), z is the numeraire good, $p_j = (p_1, ..., p_J)'$ is a vector of commodity prices (travel costs), I denotes income, and $\varepsilon_j = (\varepsilon_1, ..., \varepsilon_J)'$ is a vector of random disturbances capturing the variation in preferences in the population. Note that, as in the RUM models of site selection, the error terms here have a specific interpretation (that is, preference heterogeneity) and are treated as known by the consumer, but unobserved by the analyst.

Given additional assumptions on the way the error terms enter $U(\cdot)$ (see, for example, Phaneuf et al., 2000, p. 85), the necessary first-order Kuhn–Tucker conditions can then be written in terms of the ε_js; that is,

$$\begin{aligned} &\varepsilon_j \le g_j(y_j, I, p_j) \\ &y_j \ge 0 \\ &y_j[\varepsilon_j - g_j(y_j, I, p_j)] = 0, \end{aligned} \qquad (6.26)$$

where $g_j = g_j(y_j, I, p_j)$ implicitly solves

$$\frac{\partial U(y_j, I - p'_j y_j, g_j)}{\partial y_j} = \frac{\partial U(y_j, I - p'_j y_j, g_j)}{\partial z}. \quad (6.27)$$

Thus, if an individual visits site j, the first of the conditions in (6.26) is binding and the corresponding error term is subject to an equality constraint; that is, $\varepsilon_j = g_j(y_j, I, p_j)$. For those sites that are not visited, the error term is simply bounded from above by $g_j(y_j, I, p_j)$. These restrictions, along with an assumed distribution for the error components, are used to specify each individual's contribution to the likelihood function, which in turn provides the basis for maximum likelihood estimation.[16]

The chief limitation of the KT framework is that, in order to obtain convenient closed-form expressions for the boundary functions, $g_j(y_j, I, p_j)$, relatively simple functional forms for the direct utility function have been used. Most applications have relied upon variants of the linear expenditure system (LES). However, some progress on generalizing the functional form has been made. Von Haefen and Phaneuf (forthcoming) provide a generalization of the basic linear expenditure system (LES) by making parameters a function of individual characteristics as discussed in Willig (1978). Von Haefen et al. (2002) take this a step further by introducing a translated CES specification that includes the LES model as a special case.

In addition to the primal form, a dual version of the KT framework also exists, developed initially by Lee and Pitt (1986, 1987) and recently applied to the recreation demand setting by Phaneuf (1999). The dual model begins with the specification of an indirect utility function, $V(p_j, I, \varepsilon_j)$. This function is in turn used to define virtual prices that rationalize nonconsumption of one or more goods (sites). Like its primal counterpart, the dual approach provides a unified model of both participation and site selection, relying on the error structure to capture preference heterogeneity. However, relatively few applications have emerged to date, due in part to the complexity of the estimation process. Given recent advances in both computing power and simulation estimation procedures, the dual model has the potential for estimating recreation demand under binding nonnegativity constraints using more flexible forms than can feasibly be used for its primal counterpart.

Systems of Counts

A second broad class of models currently receiving considerable attention in the literature is the count demand systems approach exemplified by Englin et al. (1998), Ozuna and Gomez (1994), and Shonkwiler (1999). Like their single-equation counterparts, these models explicitly acknowledge the fact that the numbers of trips taken to each of the available recreation sites are nonnegative integers. Thus, the consumer's problem takes the form[17]

$$\max_{y_j} U(y_j, I - p'_j y_j, \varepsilon_j) \qquad \text{s.t. } y_j \in \{0,1,2, ...\} \, \forall j = 1, ..., J. \qquad (6.28)$$

In practice, analysts do not begin with the general structure in (6.28). Instead, reduced-form expressions for the expected level of demand at each site are specified; for example,

$$E(y_j) = f(p_j, I), \qquad (6.29)$$

where $f(p_j, I)$ is a $J \times 1$ vector value function. For example, a simple exponential version of this model would be $\exp(\beta_0 + \beta_p p_j)$. These average, or representative, demands are then used as the means of a multivariate count distribution. Utility theory is incorporated into the model by requiring that $f(p_j, I)$ satisfy standard integrability conditions.[18]

Most of the recent research in this area has focused on developing count systems that allow for overdispersion (that is, trip variances that exceed trip means), the large number of observed zeros for each site, and demands that are correlated across sites. Ozuna and Gomez (1994), for example, use Holgate's (1964) bivariate Poisson distribution to allow for positive cross-equation correlation in a system of demand equations for two sites. Von Haefen and Phaneuf (forthcoming) account for 'excess zeros' by mixing a spike or mass point at zero with independent negative binomial distributions. This is simply the multivariate counterpart to the double-hurdle models of Haab and McConnell (1996) and Shonkwiler and Shaw (1996). In general, the approach of using mixture models, finite or continuous, to generalize the error structure in count data models appears to be a promising line of future research.

The primary advantage of the count data systems over the KT models of the previous section is that they explicitly account for the discrete nature of trip demands. This may be particularly important when the numbers of trips taken to any given site by an individual are small. However, this comes at the cost of relying on reduced-form demand equations specified for a representative consumer. While integrability restrictions are typically imposed on the average demand equations in (6.29), they need not apply at the individual level. On the other hand, the KT model, while it employs an elegant integrated and utility theoretic framework, ignores the count nature of trip demand for the sake of obtaining the convenience of differentiation. Neither approach is complete and which one is preferred is likely to be an empirical issue depending upon the circumstances of the application (for example, the frequency of trips).

Generalized Error Structures

The RUM models used to characterize the site selection decision have largely been based on either standard logit or the more general nested logit models. As noted above, these specifications, while convenient both for estimation and welfare analysis, impose considerable structure on how choice probabilities change with changing individual and site characteristics. In recent years, there have been a number of generalizations of these models that allow for a richer pattern of correlation (substitution) among alternatives in the individual's choice set.

The first of these generalizations replaces the extreme value and GEV distributions underlying logit and nested logit, respectively, with a multivariate normal distribution. The latter distribution allows for a more flexible pattern of correlation among site utilities.[19] While the multinomial probit model (MNP) has been around for a long time, the computational burden of its estimation has restricted its use in practice. Recent improvements in computing power and in simulation-based estimation procedures have made MNP practical for larger choice set (see, for example, Train, 2002). Nonetheless, it remains a relatively little-used specification and therefore little is known regarding the empirical differences it might generate. Indeed, we are aware of only a single application in the recreation demand literature. Chen et al. (1999) provide a comparison of MNP and logit models in a setting with as many as 42 alternatives in the choice set.[20] In doing so, however, the authors impose considerable structure on the pattern of correlation among alternatives, essentially mimicking a nested logit specification.

A second generalization of the traditional RUM model is the mixed (or random parameters) logit (MXL) specification (McFadden and Train, 2000; Brownstone and Train, 1998; and Revelt and Train, 1998). Applications in the recreation demand literature include Breffle and Morey (2000), Herriges and Phaneuf (2002), and Train (1998, 1999). The mixed logit model begins much like its standard logit counterpart, with the utility that individual i receives from visiting site j given by

$$U_{ij} = V_j(\tilde{x}_{ij}, \tilde{s}_i; \beta_i) + \varepsilon_{ij}, \qquad (6.30)$$

where $\tilde{x}_{ij}$ and $\tilde{s}_i$ denote observed site- and individual-specific characteristics, respectively, and the additive error terms (the ε_{ij}s) are assumed to be i.i.d. (independent and identically distributed) extreme value variates. The distinguishing feature of the mixed logit model is that the parameters (β_i) of the representative utility function (V_j) are no longer assumed to be fixed, but are allowed to vary in the population. For example, the marginal utility of income or fish catch rates can vary across individuals. As with the additive error, ε_{ij}, these random parameters are assumed to be known by the individual, but unobserved by the analyst.[21]

Conditional on observing the random parameter vector β_i, the probability that an individual will choose to visit site j follows the standard logit form, since the remaining errors are i.i.d. extreme value; that is,

$$P_{ij}(\beta_i) = \frac{e^{V_{ij}(\beta_i)}}{\sum\limits_{k=1}^{J} e^{V_k(\beta_i)}}, \qquad (6.31)$$

where $V_{ij}(\beta_i) \equiv V_j(\tilde{x}_{ij}, \tilde{s}_i, \beta_i)$. The unconditional probability that the individual will choose to visit site j, P_{ij}, is then obtained by integrating over the assumed distribution for the $\beta_i s$, $f(\beta \mid \phi)$

$$P_{ij} = \int P_{ij}(\beta) f(\beta \mid \phi) d\beta. \qquad (6.32)$$

Thus, the MXL choice probabilities are a 'mixture' of standard logit probabilities, where $f(\beta \mid \phi)$ is the mixing distributions. Typically, $f(\beta \mid \phi)$ is chosen from among standard distributions, such as the normal, lognormal or uniform. Estimation of the underlying parameters (ϕ) is usually carried out using maximum simulated likelihood (Stern, 1997 and Train, 2002), approximating the integral in the unconditional choice probabilities P_{ij} by simulation.

The appeal of the MXL specification is that it allows one to model greater heterogeneity in consumer preferences than either MNL or NL can accommodate. For example, as Herriges and Phaneuf (2002) illustrate, MXL can mimic the block correlation structure of nested logit by introducing random parameters that are shared by alternatives within a nest. Moreover, it can go further by 'mixing' competing nesting structures, allowing for an explicit test of a given nesting structure, rather than assuming one *a priori*. In a panel setting, as Train (1999) notes, one can introduce correlation in preferences over time, even allowing for an evolution in tastes by specifying the random parameter to exhibit, for example, an autoregressive pattern. A similar approach would seem possible in a spatial setting as well, by allowing correlation across individuals depending on their relative location. The mixed logit specification opens up a myriad of possibilities for capturing rich patterns of heterogeneity and correlation in consumer preferences that are not available in the standard logit or nested logit setting. However, it is not a replacement for careful modeling of preferences based on observed characteristics and, because it opens the door to many alternative specifications, makes sensitivity analysis all the more important.

Repeated Choice Models

Finally, the principal limitation of the standard site selection model is that it ignores the participation decision (that is, how many trips an individual chooses to take). While linked models introduced a trip demand equation to capture changes in overall number of visits taken by an individual or household, they are reduced form in nature, lacking a unifying utility theoretic framework. As an alternative to the linked model, Morey et al. (1993) proposed dealing with the participation decision by introducing one additional alternative to the individual's choice set (the 'stay-at-home' option) and viewing the individual's recreation demand process as a sequence of choice occasions. On each of T choice occasions, the individual chooses whether to stay at home or visit one of the possible recreation sites. The total number of trips in a given season is then simply the number of times they chose not to stay at home.

Formally, the utility from choosing alternative j on choice occasion t is assumed to take the form

$$U_{jt} = V_j(\tilde{x}_{ij}, \tilde{s}) + \varepsilon_{jt}, j = 0,1, ..., J, \qquad (6.33)$$

where $j = 0$ denotes the stay-at-home option. The random component has typically been assumed to be drawn from an extreme value or GEV distribution, independently distributed across choice occasions. Consequently, the choice probabilities on a given choice occasion (P_{jt}) follow the standard logit or nested logit form and, due to the independence assumption, the overall choice probabilities for an individual are then simply the product of the choice occasion probabilities. Estimation is conducted by maximum likelihood and welfare analysis is a simple extension of the welfare analysis for an individual choice occasion. Thus the repeated nested logit (RNL) framework has all of the convenience of the standard NL model, while accounting for both the site selection and participation decision in a unified framework. Not surprisingly, the RNL model has become a popular approach to modeling recreation demand in recent years (for example, Parsons et al. 1999; Herriges and Phaneuf, 2002; Phaneuf et al., 1998; Shaw and Ozog, 1999).

The RNL approach has two principal drawbacks. First, the analyst must fix the number of choice occasions in the given time period. For example, in analyzing annual recreation demand, one might assume that there are 52 choice occasions, one for each week. Second, RNL models have traditionally assumed that the choice occasions are independent of each other (once the observed characteristics are controlled for). There have been a number of recent efforts to relax this assumption. Herriges and Phaneuf (2002) use a repeated mixed logit model to capture unobserved individual effects that persist over time. Provencher et al. (2001) allow for serially correlated errors in an RNL framework.

CROSS-CUTTING CHALLENGES IN IMPLEMENTATION

Regardless of the model structure adopted by a recreation demand analyst, there are a number of difficult empirical issues that must be addressed. In this section, we identify three that we perceive as being key to continued progress in the evolution of recreation demand modeling. For each, we briefly summarize the current state of the art and provide our assessment of future directions for work on the issue. The three cross-cutting issues we identify are: (1) the construction and/or modeling of the 'price' of recreation, particularly as it relates to the opportunity cost of time; (2) the incorporation of dynamic aspects of the choice problem into recreation demand modeling, including the possibilities for intertemporal substitution and habit formation; and (3) the treatment of visits to multiple recreation sites on a single trip. Although we identify these three focus areas for longer discussion here, we hasten to add that there are numerous other empirical and conceptual challenges facing modelers in this field and we very briefly discuss a number of those at the end of the section.

Before proceeding, it is worth noting that, in some cases, these issues have been more identified with one modeling approach over another (for example, site aggregation has been discussed primarily in the context of RUMS). However, we group them together intentionally to point out that these challenges relate to the underlying data, sampling scheme and choice process, and are thus equally relevant for all modeling approaches. Aggregating sites is a good example: regardless of whether a demand system or RUM model approach is selected, the analyst must define the sites and decide the degree to which alternatives can or should be grouped together.

Definition and Measurement of the Opportunity Cost of a Trip

Recreation demand models address the nonmarket nature of the valuation problem by recognizing that the cost of accessing a recreation site is akin to its price. Thus, by collecting and measuring these costs, analysts create a price variable and employ it as if it were a market price in econometric models. The difficulty is of course that the price is constructed with a series of assumptions that are not directly testable. Randall makes this point in his 1994 paper, going so far as to conclude as a consequence of these concerns that recreation demand 'cannot serve as a stand-alone technique for estimating recreation benefits . . .' (p. 88).

In fact, the issue of computing the price of travel, particularly with respect to the time costs, has troubled researchers almost from the beginning of the literature. Cesario (1976) valued time at a fixed ratio of the wage rate, which is a practice researchers continue to commonly employ. McConnell and Strand (1981) provide an approach to directly estimate time costs from the empirical model. They specify a demand for recreation, written here in linear form, as

$$y_i = \alpha + \beta(c_i + sw_i t_i) + \varepsilon_i, \tag{6.34}$$

where c_i is the travel cost, w_i is the wage rate, t_i is travel time, and s is the share of the wage rate at which the individual values time. Although still assuming that the opportunity cost of time is appropriately measured as a fraction of the wage rate, McConnell and Strand cleverly demonstrate that an estimate of s can be recovered directly from (6.34). Although conceptually a significant advance on the assumption of arbitrary shares of the wage rate, multicollinearity often prevents application of this procedure.

In the next significant advance, Bockstael et al. (1987) draw on the labor literature to investigate the more complex situation in which some individuals have fixed work weeks. In that case, the wage rate is not directly linked to the opportunity cost of time. For individuals who cannot trade time for money, these authors demonstrate that the structure of the demand function changes, requiring estimation of a separate model for individuals at corner solutions with respect to the time constraint. Specifically, the following two demand specifications are relevant:

$$y_i = f(c_i + w_i t_i, I_i) + \varepsilon_i \tag{6.35}$$

for individuals who can optimally adjust work hours, and

$$y_i = f(c_i, t_i, I_i) + \varepsilon_i \tag{6.36}$$

for individuals who must work a fixed number of hours. While incorporating the issue of corner solutions in a compelling and tractable way, the model still assumes that those at interior solutions will value their time at the full wage rate. If recreators take pleasure in driving or find driving distasteful, achieve disutility or positive utility from labor, and/or have paid vacation time during which they recreate, the full wage rate will not be appropriate in the short run.

In a useful extension, Feather and Shaw (1999) recognize that information as to whether the individual is over- or under employed can be utilized to improve welfare estimation. Larson (1993a) argues that a long-run view makes the full wage the appropriate opportunity cost of time even when fixed work weeks prevail. Shaw and Feather (1999) consider the appropriate specification for the case of conditional demand systems and two-stage budgeting. Another closely related area is the treatment of on-site time (Kealy and Bishop, 1986; McConnell, 1992; Larson, 1993b; Berman and Kim, 1999).

Despite a flurry of recent activity in this area, the norm in recreation demand modeling continues to be the use of simple, primarily *ad hoc*, specifications for the opportunity cost of time.[22] Even those applications that have developed and estimated a more careful and rigorous treatment of time have fallen short of fully capturing empirically the many sources of influences on the opportunity cost of recreation. This issue should be high on the agenda of recreation demand analysts interested in accurate estimates of surplus values, as recent studies (Azevedo, 2001), as well as some classic works (Bishop and Heberlein, 1979) indicate that alternative treatments of time can have very large influences on resulting welfare estimates. Although questions concerning the treatment of time costs and the overall opportunity cost of recreation have been on the agenda for decades, empirically tractable and fully encompassing solutions continue to elude analysts.

Dynamic Aspects of Recreation Choices

In contrast to the issue of the opportunity cost of time, questions related to the potentially dynamic aspects of recreation choice behavior and the implications for welfare measurement are relatively new. Creel and Loomis's (1992b) work on bag limits recognized that hunters or anglers might wish to take future opportunities into account in their recreation behavior.[23] At first blush, the repeated RUM models discussed above also appear to contain a dynamic element since they explicitly model the decision to visit a site or not on each choice occasion. However, the standard application views each choice occasion as independent, implying that the order of visits could be shuffled with no change in utility. That is, there is not intertemporal interdependence in choices. Current work by Provencher et al. (2001) relaxes the independence assumption, incorporating serially correlated errors in estimation.

The question of the degree to which individuals can substitute intertemporally between visits to a recreation site now and in the future has potentially significant implications for welfare measurement. If substitution is possible not only between sites at a given time period, but also between visits today and later, welfare losses associated with temporary or transient events might be significantly smaller than if the possibilities for intertemporal substitution are not considered.

One of the earliest dynamic effects to be discussed and empirically modeled relates to the issue of habit formation. McConnell et al. (1989), Adamowicz et al. (1990) and Adamowicz (1994) incorporate habit formation through inclusion of the 'stock' of previous visits or lagged site visits into the estimating equations. These models take an important step towards incorporating intertemporal substitution and dynamic behavior into recreation demand models.

The most complete treatment to date of the dynamic aspect of recreation choices appears in Provencher and Bishop (1997). The authors present an explicitly dynamic multinomial logit model of the decision to visit a recreation site. By formally modeling an individual's recreation choices over the course of a season as the solution to a dynamic programming problem, Provencher and Bishop derive the expression for the probability of observing a particular decision on any given choice occasion using a logit formation. The resulting likelihood function incorporates the dynamic aspects of the problem and remains empirically tractable (due to the use of logistic errors). Although not enough work has been done with these models, results suggest that dynamic modeling may be important for welfare assessment (Provencher et al., 2001).

Multiple Site Trips: Choices Among Portfolios

The next challenging issue we address is the treatment of recreation trips for which there are multiple destinations. Most reviews of travel cost and recreation demand models explicitly rule out the application of these methods to recreation trips that are taken with more than a single destination in mind. The difficulty associated with multiple destination trips is akin to multi-product output: the marginal cost of accessing a site cannot be uniquely identified.

Unfortunately, while single destination trips work well in many recreational settings for which values are desired, including single day trips to parks or beaches and multiple day trips to single settings, there are cases where the shoe does not fit as well. Specifically, many families take extended trips on a summer vacation during which they visit numerous large and secondary attractions. If an analyst is interested in valuing price or quality changes at one of these sites, direct application of a traditional recreation demand model will likely be inappropriate.

One promising avenue of approach in modeling multiple destination trips is to analyze such trips as portfolios or trip combinations. Mendelsohn et al. (1992) estimate an inverse demand system for visitors to Bryce

Canyon National Park, treating as separate commodities the single destination trips and various trips combinations (for example to Bryce Canyon
and the Grand Canyon, or Bryce Canyon and Arches). Kridel and Taylor
(1993) take a similar approach, though in a discrete choice setting, to model
consumer demand for telephone calling packages.

Other Issues

Finally, we note a number of other issues of importance in the modeling of
recreation demand.

Functional form
Ziemer et al. (1980), Kling (1989), Adamowicz et al. (1989), and Ozuna et
al. (1993) have examined the implications of alternative functional forms
for demand curves on welfare measures, finding, not surprisingly, that
different forms can yield large differences in consumer surplus. Functional
form is no less a concern in discrete choice models and has been addressed
in part with the inclusion of nonlinear income effects in the indirect utility
function (Herriges and Kling, 1999a; Morey et al., 1993; and Shonkwiler
and Shaw, 1997). Kling and Thomson (1996) investigate the robustness of
welfare measures to changes in variable inclusion and find differences
ranging from almost zero to an order of magnitude.

Aggregation/extent of the market
When there are large numbers of alternatives from which to choose, two
issues arise concerning the extent of the market and aggregation of the
choices into more easily handled numbers for modeling. The issue of extent
of the market or the relevant choice set faced by individuals is often dealt
with on a fairly *ad hoc* basis. Analysts either assume that all individuals have
all sites in their choice set or an arbitrary geographic distance is used to
confine the choice set to all sites within a given distance from the origin of
destination.

   When faced with large numbers of sites, analysts have often aggregated
those alternatives into a smaller number of groupings or zones, implying
that a trip to one site in a particular group is exactly like the trip to another
site within that group. Further, a single aggregated price is used to represent the cost of accessing all sites within the group. Clearly, this practice
adds measurement error to the price variable; the implications of this
practice on welfare measures have been investigated (Parsons and
Needelman, 1992; Kaoru et al., 1995; and Feather, 1994) and have been
found to be significant. Alternative approaches, such as randomly sampling the alternatives in estimation, are promising (Parsons and Kealy,

1992) and deal with both the aggregation and extent of the market issues to some degree.

Much interest remains in this general area: a conference devoted to the topic with specific focus on discrete choice models was organized by NOAA, with several papers published in a special issue of *Marine Resource Economics* (winter, 1999).

Statistical precision and bias

Welfare estimates are random variables since they depend upon estimated coefficients (Bockstael and Strand, 1987; Smith, 1990). At least three approaches have been employed in recreation demand to construct confidence intervals: use of a Taylor's series approximation, a simulation approach due to Krinsky and Robb (1986) (Creel and Loomis, 1991), and a full-blown bootstrapping procedure (Adamowicz et al., 1989; Kling and Sexton, 1990). Comparisons between the three approaches suggest that all are reasonably accurate (Kling, 1991; Krinsky and Robb, 1990 and 1991).

Combining revealed and stated preference data

Recreation demand data have been increasingly combined with stated preference data to estimate a single set of parameter values and/or as validity checks of one another. Cameron (1992) first suggested and implemented this approach in a continuous demand model setting. Adamowicz et al. (1994) extended this idea to the RUM setting and a growing number of applications are making their way into the literature (McConnell et al., 1999; Adamowicz et al., 1994; Niklitschek and Leon, 1996; Huang et al., 1997; Kling, 1997; Azevedo et al., 2002).

One unresolved issue in the combining literature is the degree to which consistency between parameter estimates across methods can be interpreted as a validity test of either method. In a similar vein, the degree to which revealed and stated preference data should be combined is unclear, as stated preference data potentially includes nonuse values. The consequences of employing the weak complementarity assumption inherent in revealed preference applications may need exploration in this regard.

FINAL REFLECTIONS

We hope that the previous sections have provided the reader with a basic understanding of the historical development and current challenges in recreation demand modeling and environmental valuation. While much work remains to be done, there is a substantial body of literature upon which scholars can build. Further, we have little doubt that improved estimation methods for environmental valuation will yield significant social returns. Two trends that show little sign of abating support this notion.

First, benefit–cost analysis is increasingly being called upon to inform public policy by providing estimation of aggregate benefits associated with alternative policies, as well as the disaggregation of benefits so that the net winners and losers can be identified. Second, increased wealth combined with changing preferences in favor of environmental quality imply that the value of environmental goods will be an increasing component of the value of society's 'market basket'. Accurate estimates of these values will continue to be in demand.

While many challenges remain, recreation demand modeling has come a long way since the insightful suggestion of Harold Hotelling. We are optimistic that continued improvements in the methods will provide analysts and policy-makers with more accurate and reliable demand projects and benefit measures.

NOTES

1. A third approach is based on the hedonic method. With notable exceptions (for example, Brown and Mendelsohn, 1984 and Englin and Mendelsohn, 1991), this approach has not been widely developed and is not included in this review.
2. See Haab and McConnell (1996) for discussion in the context of recreation demand and Cameron and Trivedi (1998) in a general setting.
3. In a recent paper, Morey et al. (2001) introduce a generalized version of the trip demand system based on nested CES preferences that does allow for site complementarities.
4. These unobserved characteristics can include a myriad of factors, from the level of an individual's knowledge about the site in question or the type of recreation equipment they own to their mood when they make their decision.
5. Train (2002) provides an excellent discussion of the source of the error term in discrete choice models.
6. While we illustrate the NL model using G nests, as noted above these nests can each be further divided into subnests. Morey (1999), for example, provides an example of a three-level NL model.
7. Note that $\bigcup_{g=1}^{G} N_g = \{1,2, ..., J\}$ and $N_g \cap N_{g'} = \varnothing$ for $g \neq g'$.
8. The dissimilarity coefficient θ_g is typically required to lie in the unit interval in order to insure global consistency with McFadden's (1981) random utility maximization (RUM) hypothesis. It is possible to achieve consistency locally when $\theta_g > 1$, though the resulting restrictions do not appear to allow substantial departures from the unit interval. See Börsch-Supan (1990), Herriges and Kling (1996), and Kling and Herriges (1995).
9. See Morey (1999) for an excellent review of the nested logit model in the context of recreation demand and Train's (2002) ch. 4 for a discussion of GEV models in general. Herriges and Phaneuf (2002) provide a detailed discussion of the correlation and response elasticities implied by the nested logit framework.
10. The degree of correlation, ρ_g, depends upon θ_g. In particular, $\rho_g = 0$ if $\theta_g = 1$ and ρ_g increases as θ_g diminishes towards zero.
11. See Herriges and Phaneuf (2002) for further discussion of the implications of the NL model in terms of implied correlation patterns and response elasticities.

12. When the marginal utility of income is not constant, the compensating variation formula becomes more complex, requiring integration. See McFadden (1999), Herriges and Kling (1999a) and Karlström (2002).
13. One specification criterion is the likelihood dominance ranking, suggested by Pollak and Wales (1991). Alternatively, one can test for consistency with the random utility maximization hypothesis (Herriges and Kling, 1995).
14. As Bockstael and Strand (1987) note, the appropriate role of the error terms in welfare computations depends upon their perceived source; for example, whether they are thought to arise from measurement error or to reflect underlying preference heterogeneity. When the errors are simply added to an *ad hoc* demand specification, the source of the error is often unclear and the appropriate welfare calculations uncertain.
15. Amemiya (1974) generalized the Tobit model for a system of equations. Wales and Woodland (1983) provide a general discussion of the Amemiya–Tobin approach, with an application to meet demand.
16. See the appendix in Phaneuf et al. (2000) for the explicit representation of the log likelihood for the case of a linear expenditure system.
17. See Hellerstein and Mendelsohn (1993) and von Haefen and Phaneuf (forthcoming) for additional discussion of the theory underlying count data demand models. These models are similar in spirit to the earlier trip share equations approach of Morey (1981, 1984, 1985).
18. See LaFrance (1990) and LaFrance and Hanemann (1989) for additional discussion of these conditions.
19. There are, however, limits to the pattern of correlation that can be identified in the discrete choice setting. Train (2002), ch. 5 provides an excellent discussion of these identification issues.
20. Chen and Cosslett (1998) also estimate an MNP model, but restrict the variance–covariance matrix to be diagonal, assuming the errors ε_j to be i.i.d. standard normal variates. They do, however, introduce a more complex correlation structure by allowing some of the parameters of the model to be random.
21. Essentially, the random parameters specification can be interpreted as allowing unobserved characteristics to interact with observed characteristics in the individual function, causing the marginal impact of the observed characteristics to appear random from the analyst's perspective.
22. Other literatures have also investigated the opportunity cost of time including transportation and tourism studies. See Hensher (2001) and Wardman (1998) for recent reviews.
23. Creel and Loomis (1992b) consider the possibility that a deer hunter might pass up the chance to get a deer so as to retain hunting opportunities for a future trip under a regime of bag limits.

REFERENCES

Adamowicz, W. (1994), 'Habit Formation and Variety Seeking in a Discrete Choice Model of Recreation Demand,' *Journal of Agricultural and Resource Economics*, **19**, 9–31.

Adamowicz, W., J. Fletcher and T. Graham-Tomasi (1989), 'Functional Form and the Statistical Properties of Welfare Measures,' *American Journal of Agricultural Economics*, **71**, 414–21.

Adamowicz, W., S. Jennings and A. Coyne (1990), 'A Sequential Choice Model of Recreation Behavior,' *Western Journal of Agricultural Economics*, **15**, 91–9.

Adamowicz, W., J. Louviere and M. Williams (1994), 'Combining Revealed and Stated Preference Methods for Valuing Environmental Amenities,' *Journal of Environmental Economics and Management*, **26**, 271–92.

Amemiya, T. (1974), 'Multivariate Regression and Simultaneous Equation Models when the Dependent Variables are Truncated Normal,' *Econometrica*, **42**, 999–1012.

Azevedo, C. (2001), 'The Effect of Treatments of Time in Recreation Demand Models,' working manuscript, Iowa State University, Ames.

Azevedo, C., J. Herriges and C. Kling (2002), 'Combining Revealed and Stated Preferences: Consistency Tests and Their Interpretations,' draft manuscript, Iowa State University, Ames.

Bateman, I. and K.G. Willis (eds) (1999), *Valuing Environmental Preferences: Theory and Practice of the Contingent Valuation Method in the U.S., E.U., and Developing Countries*, Oxford: Oxford University Press.

Berman, M. and H.J. Kim (1999), 'Endogenous On-Site Time in the Recreation Demand Model,' *Land Economics*, **75**, 603–19.

Bishop, R. and T. Heberlein (1979), 'Travel Cost and Hypothetical Valuation of Outdoor Recreation: Comparisons with an Artificial Market,' Department of Agriculture working paper, University of Wisconsin.

Bockstael, N.E. and I.E. Strand (1987), 'The Effect of Common Sources of Regression Error on Benefit Estimates,' *Land Economics*, **63**, 11–20.

Bockstael, N.E., W.M. Hanemann and C.L. Kling (1987), 'Measuring Recreational Demand in a Multiple Site Framework,' *Water Resources Research*, **23**, 951–60.

Bockstael, N.E., W.M. Hanemann and I.E. Strand (1986), 'Benefit Analysis Using Indirect or Imputed Market Methods,' Volume II, 'Measuring the Benefits of Water Quality Improvements Using Recreation Demand Models,' EPA Cooperative Agreement CR-811043-01-0.

Bockstael, N.E., K.E. McConnell and I.E. Strand (1989), 'A Random Utility Model for Sportfishing: Some Preliminary Results for Florida,' *Marine Resource Economics*, **6**, 245–60.

Bockstael, N.E., K.E. McConnell and I.E. Strand (1991), 'Recreation,' in J. Braden and C. Kolstad (eds), *Measuring the Demand for Environmental Quality*, New York: Elsevier.

Bockstael, N.E., I.E. Strand and W.M. Hanemann (1987), 'Time and the Recreational Demand Model,' *American Journal of Agricultural Economics*, **69**, 293–302.

Bockstael, N.E., I.E. Strand, K.E. McConnell and F. Arsanjani (1990), 'Sample Selection Bias in the Estimation of Recreation Demand Functions: An Application to Sportfishing,' *Land Economics*, **66**, 40–9.

Börsch-Supan, A. (1990), 'On the Compatibility of Nested Logit Models with Utility Maximization,' *Journal of Econometrics*, **43**, 373–88.

Bowes, M.D. and J.B. Loomis (1980), 'A Note on the Use of Travel Cost Models with Unequal Zonal Populations,' *Land Economics*, **56**, 465–70.

Breffle, W. and E.R. Morey (2000), 'Investigating Heterogeneity of Preferences in a Repeated Logit Recreation Demand Model Using RP Data,' *Marine Resource Economics*, **15**, 1–20.

Brown, W.G. and R. Mendelsohn (1984), 'The Hedonic Travel Cost Method,' *Review of Economics and Statistics*, **66**, 427–33.

Brown, W.G. and F. Nawas (1973), 'Impact of Aggregation on the Estimation of Outdoor Recreation Demand Functions,' *American Journal of Agricultural Economics*, **55**, 246–9.

Brown, W.G., C. Sorhus, B. Chou-Yang and J.A. Richards (1983), 'Using Individual

Observations to Estimate Recreation Demand Functions: A Caution,' *American Journal of Agricultural Economics*, **65**, 154–7.

Brownstone, D. and K.E. Train (1998), 'Forecasting New Product Penetration with Flexible Substitution Patterns,' *Journal of Econometrics*, **89**, 109–29.

Burt, O.R. and D. Brewer (1971), 'Estimation of Net Social Benefits from Outdoor Recreation,' *Econometrica*, **39**, 813–27.

Cameron, A.C. and P.K. Trivedi (1998), *Regression Analysis of Count Data*, Cambridge: Cambridge University Press.

Cameron, T. (1992), 'Combining Contingent Valuation and Travel Cost Data for the Valuation of Nonmarket Goods,' *Land Economics*, **68**, 302–17.

Carson, R. (2002), *Contingent Valuation: A Comprehensive Bibliography and History*, Chelenham, UK and Northampton, USA: Edward Elgar.

Caulkins, P., R. Bishop and N. Bouwes (1986), 'The Travel Cost Model for Lake Recreation: A Comparison of Two Methods for Incorporating Site Quality and Substitution Effects,' *American Journal of Agricultural Economics*, **68**, 291–7.

Cesario, F. (1976), 'Value of Time in Recreation Benefit Studies,' *Land Economics*, **52**, 32–41.

Cesario, F. and J. Knetsch (1976), 'A Recreation Site Demand and Benefit Estimation Model,' *Regional Studies*, **10**, 97–104.

Chen, H.Z. and S.R. Cosslett (1998), 'Environmental Quality Preference and Benefit Estimation in Multinomial Probit Models: A Simulation Approach,' *American Journal of Agricultural Economcis*, **80**, 512–20.

Chen, H.Z., F. Lupi and J.P. Hoehn (1999), 'An Empirical Assessment of Multinomial Probit and Logit Models for Recreation Demand,' in J.A. Herriges and C.L. Kling (eds), *Valuing Recreation and the Environment: Revealed Preference Methods in Theory and Practice*, Cheltenham, UK and Northampton, USA: Edward Elgar, 141–61.

Cichetti, C., A. Fisher and V. Smith (1976), 'An Econometric Evaluation of a Generalized Consumer Surplus Measure: The Mineral King Controversy,' *Econometrica*, **44**, 1259–76.

Clawson, M. (1959), *Methods of Measuring the Demand for and Value of Outdoor Recreation*, Washington, DC: Resources for the Future, reprint 10.

Clawson, M. and J. Knetsch (1966), *Economics of Outdoor Recreation*, Washington, DC: Resources for the Future.

Creel, M.D. and J.B. Loomis (1990), 'Theoretical and Empirical Advantages of Truncated Count Data Estimators for Analysis of Deer Hunting in California,' *American Journal of Agricultural Economics*, **72**, 434–41.

Creel, Michael and John Loomis (1991), 'Confidence Intervals for Welfare Measures with Application to a Problem of Truncated Counts,' *Review of Economics and Statistics*, **73**, 370–73.

Creel, M. and J. Loomis (1992a), 'Recreation Value of Water to Wetlands in the San Joaquin Valley: Linked Multinomial Logit and Count Data Trip Frequency Models,' *Water Resources Research*, **28**, 2597–606.

Creel, M. and J. Loomis (1992b), 'Modeling Hunting Demand in the Presence of a Bag Limit with Tests of Alternative Specifications,' *Journal of Environmental Economics and Management*, **22**, 99–113.

Englin, J., P. Boxall and D. Watson (1998), 'Modeling Recreation Demand in a Poisson System of Equations: An Analysis of the Impact of International Exchange Rates,' *American Journal of Agricultural Economics*, **80**, 255–63.

Englin, J. and R. Mendelsohn (1991), 'A Hedonic Travel Cost Analysis for Valuation of Multiple Components of Site Quality: The Recreation Value of Forest Management,' *Journal of Environmental Economics and Management*, **21**, 275–90.

Englin, J. and J. Shonkwiler (1995), 'Estimating Social Welfare Using Count Data Models: An Application to Long-run Recreation Demand Under Conditions of Endogenous Stratification and Truncation,' *Review of Economics and Statistics*, **77**, 104–12.

Feather, P. (1994), 'Sampling and Aggregation Issues in Random Utility Model Estimation,' *American Journal of Agricultural Economics*, **76**, 772–80.

Feather, P. and W.D. Shaw (1999), 'Estimating the Cost of Leisure Time for Recreation Demand Models,' *Journal of Environmental Economics and Management*, **38**, 49–65.

Feather, P., D. Hellerstein and T. Tomasi (1995), 'A Discrete-Count Model of Recreational Demand,' *Journal of Environmental Economics and Management*, **29**, 214–27.

Freeman, M. (1993), *The Measurement of Environmental and Resource Values*, Washington, DC: Resources for the Future.

Haab, T.C. and K.E. McConnell (1996), 'Count Data Models and the Problem of Zeros in Recreation Demand Analysis,' *American Journal of Agricultural Economics*, **78**, 89–102.

Haab, T.C. and K.E. McConnell (2002), *Valuing Environmental and Natural Resources*, Cheltenham, UK and Northampton, USA: Edward Elgar.

Hanemann, W.M. (1978), 'A Methodological and Empirical Study of the Recreation Benefits from Water Quality Improvement,' Ph.D. dissertation, Department of Economics, Harvard University.

Hanemann, W.M. (1984), 'Discrete-Continuous Models of Consumer Demand.' *Econometrica*, **52**, 541–61.

Hanemann, W.M. (1999), 'Welfare Analysis with Discrete Choice Models,' in J.A. Herriges and C.L. Kling (eds), *Valuing Recreation and the Environment: Revealed Preference Methods in Theory and Practice*, Cheltenham, UK and Northampton, USA: Edward Elgar, 33–64.

Hauber, A.B. and G. R. Parsons (2000), 'The Effect of Nesting Structure Specification on Welfare Estimation in a Random Utility Model of Recreation Demand: An Application to the Demand for Recreational Fishing,' *American Journal of Agricultural Economics*, **82**, 501–14.

Hausman, J.A., G.K. Leonard and D. McFadden (1995), 'A Utility-Consistent, Combined Discrete Choice and Count Data Model: Assessing Recreational Use Losses Due to Natural Resource Damage,' *Journal of Public Economics*, **56**, 1–30.

Hellerstein, D. (1991), 'Using Count Data Models in Travel Cost Analysis with Aggregate Data,' *American Journal of Agricultural Economics*, **73**, 860–66.

Hellerstein, D. (1992), 'Estimating Consumer Surplus in the Censored Linear Model,' *Land Economics*, **68**, 83–92.

Hellerstein, D. (1995), 'Welfare Estimation Using Aggregate and Individual-Observation Models: A Comparison Using Monte Carlo Techniques,' *American Journal of Agricultural Economics*, **77**, 620–30.

Hellerstein, D. and R. Mendelsohn (1993), 'A Theoretical Foundation for Count Data Models,' *American Journal of Agricultural Economics*, **75**, 604–11.

Hensher, David (2001), 'Measurement of the Valuation of Travel Time Savings,' *Journal of Transport Economics and Policy*, **35**, 71–98.

Herriges, J.A. and C.L. Kling (1995), 'The Performance of Nested Logit

Models when Welfare Estimation is the Goal,' *American Journal of Agricultural Economics*, **79**, 782–802.

Herriges, J.A. and C.L. Kling (1996), 'Testing the Consistency of Nested Logit Models with Utility Maximization,' *Economics Letters*, **50**, 33–40.

Herriges, J.A. and C.L. Kling (1999a), 'Nonlinear Income Effects in Random Utility Models,' *The Review of Economics and Statistics*, **81**, 62–72.

Herriges, J.A. and C.L. Kling (eds) (1999b), *Valuing Recreation and the Environment: Revealed Preference Methods in Theory and Practice*, Cheltenham, UK and Northampton, USA: Edward Elgar.

Herriges, J.A. and D.J. Phaneuf (2002), 'Inducing Patterns Correlation and Substitution in Repeated Logit Model of Recreation Demand,' *American Journal of Agricultural Economics*, **84**(4), 1076–90.

Herriges, J.A., C.L. Kling and D.J. Phaneuf (1999), 'Corner Solution Models Recreation Demand: A Comparison of Competing Frameworks,' in J.A. Herriges and C.L. Kling (eds), *Valuing Recreation and the Environment: Revealed Preference Methods in Theory and Practice*, Cheltenham, UK and Northampton, USA: Edward Elgar, 163–97.

Holgate, P. (1964), 'Estimation for the Bivariate Poisson Distribution,' *Biometrika*, **51**, 241–5.

Huang, Ju-Chin, Timothy Haab and John Whitehead (1997), 'Willingness to Pay for Quality Improvements: Should Revealed and Stated Preference Data Be Combined?', *Journal of Environmental Economics and Management*, **34**, 240–55.

Huppert, D.D. and C.J. Thomson (1984), 'Demand Analysis of Partyboat Angling in California Using the Travel Cost Method,' Southwest Fisheries Center Administrative Report, NOAA.

Kaoru, Y., V.K. Smith and J.L. Liu (1995), 'Using Random Utility Models to Estimate the Recreational Value of Estuarine Resources,' *American Journal of Agricultural Economics*, **77**, 141–51.

Karlström, A. (2002), 'Hicksian Welfare Measures in a Nonlinear Random Utility Framework,' discussion paper, Systems Analysis and Economics, Royal Institute of Technology, Stockholm, Sweden.

Kealy, M.J. and R.C. Bishop (1986), 'Theoretical and Empirical Specifications Issues in Travel Cost Demand Studies,' *American Journal of Agricultural Economics*, **68**, 660–67.

Kling, C.L. (1988a), 'The Reliability of Estimates of Environmental Benefits from Recreation Demand Models,' *American Journal of Agricultural Economics*, **70**, 892–901.

Kling, C.L. (1988b), 'Comparing Welfare Estimates of Environmental Quality Changes from Recreation Demand Models,' *Journal of Environmental Economics and Management*, **15**, 331–40.

Kling, C.L. (1989), 'The Importance of Functional Form in the Estimation of Welfare,' *Western Journal of Agricultural Economics*, **14**, 168–74.

Kling, C.L. (1991), 'Estimating the Precision of Welfare Measures,' *Journal of Environmental Economics and Management*, **21**, 244–59.

Kling, C.L. (1997), 'The Gains from Combining Travel Cost and Contingent Valuation Data to Value Nonmarket Goods,' *Land Economics*, **73**, 428–39.

Kling, C.L. and J.A. Herriges (1995), 'An Empirical Investigation of the Consistency of Nested Logit Models with Utility Maximization,' *American Journal of Agricultural Economics*, **77**, 875–84.

Kling, C.L. and R.J. Sexton (1990), 'Bootstrapping in Applied Welfare Analysis,' *American Journal of Agricultural Economics*, **69**, 406–18.

Kling, C.L. and C. Thomson (1996), 'The Implications of Model Specification for Welfare Estimation in Nested Logit Models,' *American Journal of Agricultural Economics*, **78**, 103–14.

Kridel, D.J. and L.D. Taylor (1993), 'The Demand for Commodity Packages: The Case of Telephone Custom Calling Features,' *Review of Economics and Statistics*, **75**, 362–8.

Krinsky, I. and A.L. Robb (1986), 'On Approximating the Statistical Properties of Elasticities,' *Review of Economics and Statistics*, **68**, 715–19.

Krinsky, I. and A.L. Robb (1990), 'On Approximating the Statistical Properties of Elasticities: A Correction,' *Review of Economics and Statistics*, **72**, 189–90.

Krinsky, I. and A.L. Robb (1991), 'Three Methods for Calculating the Statistical Properties of Elasticities: A Comparison,' *Empirical Economics*, **16**, 199–209.

LaFrance, J.T. (1990), 'Incomplete Demand Systems and Semi-logarithmic Demand Models,' *Australian Journal of Agricultural Economics*, **34**, 118–131.

LaFrance, J.T. and W.M. Hanemann (1989), 'The Dual Structure of Incomplete Demand Systems,' *American Journal of Agricultural Economics*, **71**, 262–74.

Laitila, T. (1999), 'Estimation of Combined Site-Choice and Trip-Frequency Models of Recreation Demand Using Choice-Base and On-Site Samples,' *Economics Letters*, **64**, 17–23.

Larson, D. (1993a), 'Separability and the Shadow Value of Leisure Time,' *American Journal of Agricultural Economics*, **75**, 572–7.

Larson, D. (1993b), 'Joint Recreation Choices and Implied Values of Time,' *Land Economics*, **69**, 270–86.

Lee, L.F. and M.M. Pitt (1986), 'Microeconometric Demand Systems with Binding Nonnegativity Constraints: The Dual Approach,' *Econometrica*, **54**, 1237–42.

Lee, L.F. and M.M. Pitt (1987), 'Microeconometric Models of Rationing, Imperfect Markets, and Non-Negativity Constraints,' *Journal of Econometrics*, **36**, 89–110.

McConnell, K.E. (1992), 'On-Site Time in the Demand for Recreation,' *American Journal of Agricultural Economics*, **74**, 918–25.

McConnell, K.E. and I.E. Strand (1981), 'Measuring the Cost of Time in Recreation Demand Analysis: An Application to Sport Fishing,' *American Journal of Agricultural Economics*, **63**, 153–6.

McConnell, K.E., I.E. Strand and N.E. Bockstael (1990), 'Habit Formation and the Demand for Recreation: Issues and a Case Study,' in V. Kerry Smith and A. Links (eds), *Advances in Applied Microeconomics*, **5**, 217–35.

McConnell, K.E., Q. Weninger and I.E. Strand (1999), 'Testing the Validity of Contingent Valuation by Combining Referendum Responses with Observed Behavior,' in J.A. Herriges and C.L. Kling (eds), *Valuing Recreation and the Environment: Revealed Preference Methods in Theory and Practice*, Cheltenham, UK and Northampton, USA: Edward Elgar, 65–120.

McFadden, D.L. (1974), 'Conditional Logit Analysis of Qualitative Choice Behavior,' in P. Zarembka (ed.), *Frontiers in Econometrics*, New York: Academic Press, 105–42.

McFadden, D.L. (1978), 'Qualitative Methods for Analyzing Travel Behavior of Individuals,' in David Hensher and Peter Stopher (eds), *Behavioral Travel Modeling*, London: Croom Helm.

McFadden, D.L. (1981), 'Econometric Models of Probabilistic Choice,' in C.F.

Manski and D.L. McFadden (eds), *Structural Analysis of Discrete Data*, Cambridge, MA: MIT Press.

McFadden, D.L. (1999), 'Computing Willingness-to-Pay in Random Utility Models,' in J. Moore, R. Riezman and J. Melvin (eds), *Trade, Theory and Econometrics: Essays in Honor of John S. Chipman*, London: Routledge.

McFadden, D.L. (2001), 'Economic Choice,' *American Economic Review*, **91**, 351–78.

McFadden, D. and K.E. Train (2000), 'Mixed MNL Models for Discrete Response', *Journal of Applied Econometrics*, **15**, 447–70.

Mendelsohn, R., J. Hof, G. Peterson and R. Johnson (1992), 'Measuring Recreation Values with Multiple Destination Trips,' *American Journal of Agricultural Economics*, **74**, 926–33.

Milon, J.W. (1988), 'A Nested Demand Shares Model of Artificial Marine Habitat Choice by Sport Anglers,' *Marine Resource Economics*, **5**, 191–213.

Morey, E. (1981), 'The Demand for Site-Specific Recreational Activities: A Characteristics Approach,' *Journal of Environmental Economics and Management*, **8**, 345–71.

Morey, E. (1984), 'The Choice of Ski Areas: Estimation of a Generalized CES Preference Ordering with Characteristics, Quadratic Expenditure Functions and Non-additivity,' *Review of Economics and Statistics*, **66**, 584–90.

Morey, E. (1985), 'Characteristic, Consumer's Surplus and New Activities: A Proposed Ski Area,' *Journal of Public Economics*, **26**, 221–36.

Morey, E. (1999), 'Two RUMs UnCLOAKED: Nested-Logit Models of Site Choice and Nested-Logit Models of Participation and Site Choice,' in J.A. Herriges and C.L. Kling (eds), *Valuing Recreation and the Environment: Revealed Preference Methods in Theory and Practice*, Cheltenham, UK and Northampton, USA: Edward Elgar, 65–120.

Morey, E.R., W.S. Breffle and P.A. Greene (2001), 'Two Nested Constant-Elasticity-of-Substitution Models of Recreational Participation and Site Choice: An "Alternatives" Model and an "Expenditures' Model,"' *American Journal of Agricultural Economics*, **83**, 414–27.

Morey, E.R., R.D. Rowe and M. Watson (1993), 'A Repeated Nested-Logit Model of Atlantic Salmon Fishing,' *American Journal of Agricultural Economics*, **75**, 578–92.

Morey, E.R., W.D. Shaw and R.D. Rowe (1991), 'A Discrete Choice Model of Recreational Participation, Site Choice, and Activity Valuation When Complete Trip Data Are Not Available,' *Journal of Environmental Economics and Management*, **20**, 181–201.

Morey, E., D. Waldman, D. Assane and D. Shaw (1990), 'Specification and Estimation of a Generalized Corner Solution Model of Consumer Demand: An Amemiya–Tobin Approach,' Department of Economics, University of Colorado, Boulder, manuscript.

Morey, E., D. Waldman, D. Assane and D. Shaw (1995), 'Searching for a Model of Multiple-Site Recreation Demand that Admits Interior and Boundary Solutions,' *American Journal of Agricultural Economics*, **77**, 129–40.

Niklitschek, M. and J. Leon (1996), 'Combining Intended Demand and Yes/No Responses in the Estimation of Contingent Valuation Models,' *Journal of Environmental Economics and Management*, **31**, 387–402.

Ozuna, T. and I.A. Gomez (1994), 'Estimating a System of Recreation Demand Functions Using a Seemingly Unrelated Poisson Regression Approach,' *Review of Economics and Statistics*, **76**, 356–60.

Ozuna, T., L. Jones and O. Capps (1993), 'Functional Form and Welfare Measures in Truncated Recreation Demand Models,' *American Journal of Agricultural Economics*, **75**, 1030–35.

Parsons, G.R. and M.J. Kealy (1992), 'Randomly Drawn Opportunity Sets in a Random Utility Model of Lake Recreation,' *Land Economics*, **68**, 93–106.

Parsons, G.R. and M.J. Kealy (1995), 'A Demand Theory for Number of Trips in a Random Utility Model of Recreation,' *Journal of Environmental Economics and Management*, **29**, 357–67.

Parsons, G.R. and M.S. Needelman (1992), 'Site Aggregation in a Random Utility Model of Recreation,' *Land Economics*, **68**, 418–33.

Parsons, G.R., P. Jakus and T. Tomasi (1999), 'A Comparison of Welfare Estimates from Four Models for Linking Seasonal Recreation Trips to Multinomial Logit Models of Choice,' *Journal of Environmental Economics and Management*, **38**, 143–57.

Phaneuf, D.J. (1999), 'A Dual Approach to Modeling Corner Solutions in Recreation Demand,' *Journal of Environmental Economics and Management*, **37**, 85–105.

Phaneuf, D.J. and J.A. Herriges (1999), 'Choice Set Definition Issues in a Kuhn–Tucker Model of Recreation Demand,' *Marine Resource Economics*, **14**, 343–55.

Phaneuf, D.J. and V.K. Smith (2002), 'Recreation Demand Models,' in K.-G. Mäler and J. Vincent (eds), *Handbook of Environmental Economics*, Amsterdam: Elsevier Science Publishers.

Phaneuf, D.J., C.L. Kling and J.A. Herriges (1998), 'Valuing Water Quality Improvements Using Revealed Preference Methods when Corner Solutions are Prevalent,' *American Journal of Agricultural Economics*, **80**, 1025–31.

Phaneuf, D.J., C.L. Kling and J.A. Herriges (2000), 'Estimation and Welfare Calculations in a Generalized Corner Solution Model with an Application to Recreation Demand,' *The Review of Economics and Statistics*, **82**, 83–92.

Pollak, R. and T. Wales (1991), 'The Likelihood Dominance Criterion: A New Approach to Model Selection,' *Journal of Econometrics*, **47**, 227–42.

Provencher, Bill and Richard C. Bishop (1997), 'An Estimable Dynamic Model of Recreation Behavior with an Application to Great Lakes Angling,' *Journal of Environmental Economics and Management*, **33**, 107–27.

Provencher, Bill, Ken Barenklau and Richard Bishop (2001), 'Using Static Recreation Demand Models to Forecast Angler Responses to Interseasonal Changes in Catch Rates,' draft manuscript, University of Wisconsin.

Randall, A. (1994), 'A Difficulty with the Travel Cost Method,' *Land Economics*, **70**, 88–96.

Revelt, D. and K.E. Train (1998), 'Mixed Logit with Repeated Choices: Households' Choices of Appliance Efficiency Level,' *The Review of Economics and Statistics*, **80**, 647–57.

Shaw, D. (1988), 'On-Site Samples' Regression: Problems of Non-negative Integers, Truncation, and Endogenous Stratification,' *Journal of Econometrics*, **37**, 211–23.

Shaw, W.D. and P. Feather (1999), 'Possibilities for Including the Opportunity Cost of Time in Recreation Demand Systems,' *Land Economics*, **75**, 592–602.

Shaw, W.D. and M.T. Ozog (1999), 'Modeling Overnight Recreation Trip Choice: Application of a Repeated Nested Multinomial Logit Model,' *Environmental and Resource Economics*, **13**, 397–414.

Shonkwiler, J.S. (1999), 'Recreation Demand Systems for Multiple Site Count Data

Travel Cost Models,' in J.A. Herriges and C.L. Kling (eds), *Valuing Recreation and the Environment: Revealed Preference Methods in Theory and Practice*, Cheltenham, UK and Northampton, USA: Edward Elgar, 65–120.

Shonkwiler, J.S. and W.D. Shaw (1996), 'Hurdle Count-Date Models in Recreation Demand Analysis,' *Journal of Agricultural and Resource Economics*, **21**, 210–19.

Shonkwiler, J. Scott and W. Douglas Shaw (1997), 'Shaken, Not Stirred: A Finite Mixture Approach to Analyzing Income Effects in Random Utility Models,' mimeo, Department of Applied Economics and Statistics, University of Nevada, Reno.

Small, K.A. and H.S. Rosen (1981), 'Applied Welfare Economics with Discrete Choice Models,' *Econometrica*, **49**, 105–30.

Smith, V.K. (1988), 'Selection and Recreation Demand,' *American Journal of Agricultural Economics*, **70**, 29–36.

Smith, V.K. (1989), 'Taking Stock of Progress with Recreation Demand Models: Theory and Implementation,' *Marine Resource Economics*, **6**, 279–310.

Smith, V.K. (1990), 'Estimating Recreation Demand Using the Implied Properties of the Consumer Surplus,' *Land Economics*, **66**, 111–20.

Smith, V.K. (1993), 'Nonmarket Valuation of Environmental Resources: An Interpretive Appraisal,' *Land Economics*, **69**, 1–26.

Smith, V.K. (1997), 'Pricing What is Priceless: a Status Report on Non-market Valuation,' ch. 6 in H. Folmer and T. Tietenberg (eds), *The International Yearbook of Environmental and Resource Economics, 1997/1998*, Cheltenham, UK and Lyme, USA: Edward Elgar, 156–204.

Smith, V.K. and W.H. Desvousges (1985), 'The Generalized Travel Cost Model and Water Quality Benefits: A Reconsideration,' *Southern Economic Journal*, **51**, 371–81.

Smith, V.K., W.H. Desvousges and M.P. McGivney (1983a), 'Estimating Water Quality Benefits: An Econometric Analysis,' *Southern Economic Journal*, **50**, 422–37.

Smith, V.K., W.H. Desvousges and M.P. McGivney (1983b), 'The Opportunity Cost of Travel Time in Recreational Demand Models,' *Land Economics*, **59**, 259–77.

Smith, V.K. and R.J. Kopp (1980), 'The Spatial Limits of the Travel Cost Recreational Demand Model,' *Land Economics*, **56**, 64–72.

Stern, S. (1997), 'Simulation-Based Estimation,' *Journal of Economic Literature*, **35**, 2006–39.

Sutherland, R.J. (1982), 'The Sensitivity of Travel Cost Estimates of Recreation Demand to the Functional Form and Definition of Origin Zones,' *Western Journal of Agricultural Economics*, **7**, 87–98.

Train, K.E. (1998), 'Recreation Demand Models with Taste Differences Over People,' *Land Economics*, **74**, 230–39.

Train, K.E. (1999), 'Mixed Logit Models for Recreation Demand.' in J.A. Herriges and C.L. Kling (eds), *Valuing Recreation and the Environment: Revealed Preference Methods in Theory and Practice*, Cheltenham, UK and Northampton, USA: Edward Elgar, 121–40.

Train, K. (2002), *Discrete Choice Methods with Simulation*, Cambridge: Cambridge University Press.

Vaughan, W.J. and C.S. Russell (1982), *Fresh Water Recreational Fishing: The National Benefits of Water Pollution Control*, Washington, DC: Resources for the Future.

Von Haefen, R.H. and D.J. Phaneuf (forthcoming), 'Estimating Preferences for Outdoor Recreation: A Comparison of Continuous and Count Data Demand Systems,' *Journal of Environmental Economics and Management.*

Von Haefen, R.H., D.J. Phaneuf and G. Parsons (2002), 'Modeling the Demand for a Large Set of Quality Differentiated Goods: Estimation and Welfare Results from a Systems Approach,' working paper, presented at the Allied Social Science Association annual meetings, Atlanta, January.

Wales, T.J. and A.D. Woodland (1983), 'Estimation of Consumer Demand Systems with Binding Non-Negativity Constraints,' *Journal of Econometrics*, **21**, 263–85.

Ward, F. and J. Loomis (1986), 'The Travel Cost Demand Model as an Environmental Policy Assessment Tool: A Review of Literature,' *Western Journal of Agricultural Economics*, **11**, 164–78.

Wardman, Mark (1998), 'The Value of Travel Time: A Review of British Evidence,' *Journal of Transport Economics and Policy*, **32**, 285–316.

Wetzstein, M.E. and J.G. McNeely (1980), 'Specification Errors and Inference in Recreation Demand Models,' *American Journal of Agricultural Economics*, **62**, 798–800.

Willig, R. (1978), 'Incremental Consumer's Surplus and Hedonic Price Adjustment,' *Journal of Economic Theory*, **17**, 227–53.

Wood, S. and A. Trice (1958), 'Measurement and Recreation Benefits,' *Land Economics*, **34**, 195–207.

Yen, S.T. and W.L. Adamowicz (1994), 'Participation, Trip Frequency and Site Choice: A Multinomial Poisson Hurdle Model of Recreation Demand,' *Canadian Journal of Agricultural Economics*, **42**, 65–76.

Ziemer, R., W. Musser and R. Hill (1980), 'Recreation Demand Equations: Functional Form and Consumer Surplus,' *American Journal of Agricultural Economics*, **62**, 136–41.

7. Stated preference methods for environmental valuation: a critical look

Bengt Kriström and Thomas Laitila

I. INTRODUCTION

There is now a substantial literature in environmental economics on valuation of non-market goods. Contingent valuation (CV) is the most prominent (and controversial) of the empirical methods in current use. Stripped down to its bare essentials, CV is a carefully structured survey, in which one tries to obtain information about the value subjects place on certain changes of resource usage. In this chapter, we provide a user's guide to a group of similar methods that has risen quickly in popularity within environmental economics. These methods have been used for many years in the transportation and marketing research literature, but seem useful also to environmental economists. There is significant confusion about the nomenclature to be used, and the methods we shall describe are sometimes known as 'conjoint analysis', 'stated preference' or 'stated choice', to name a few popular labels. We might contribute to the terminological inexactitudes by employing our preferred labels for the methods.[1] We describe stated preference (SP) methods and choice experiments (CE). SP methods are used to estimate a utility function defined over attributes (characteristics). CE mimics actual behaviour since respondents make choices within a specified choice set.

We do not provide a survey of the literature, not least because there are many useful and recent accounts to which the interested reader is referred, for example Louviere et al. (2000) and Adamowicz et al. (1998). Bergland (2001) gives a concise technical overview. This account differentiates itself from similar papers, for example Hanley et al. (2001), in that our conclusions tend to be more negative regarding the suitability of these methods for environmental valuation. We include some recent thinking on optimal design, which is a very active field of research on theoretical and applied statistics. Furthermore, we explain why some recent state-of-the-art models (like random coefficient models) should be used with some care in our context. We also present some ideas on welfare measurement that are not standard fare. Because the literature on the subject is relatively new in environmental economics, consensus has not been reached on certain matters, including whether or not CV is to be replaced by a new set of methods that encompasses the CV in all relevant dimensions. We argue that this is not the case and explain in detail why we take this position.

The chapter is structured as follows. We begin in section 2 by describing the SP methods, and focus on ranking and rating experiments. We then turn to choice experiments in section 3. Section 4 includes a brief discussion of relatively advanced topics, such as experimental design and random coefficient models. Section 5 contains a comparison of CE and CV methods from the perspective of applying these methods in environmental economics. Section 6 concludes.

2.   FULL-PROFILE SP EXPERIMENTS

2.1   The Preference Function

The basic problem addressed in applications of SP methods is the estimation of a utility function $U = f(x_1, ..., x_k)$, where U denotes preference for the good considered and $(x_1, ..., x_k)$ denotes k attributes (characteristics) of the good. If $f(x_1, ..., x_k)$ is known, the influence of an attribute on utility is known. In such a case, different combinations of attribute values $(x_1, ..., x_k)$ can be evaluated in terms of their contribution to consumer utility. However, the function $f(x_1, ..., x_k)$ is usually unknown and has to be estimated.[2]

The traditional source of data in economics for estimation of a utility function $f(x_1, ..., x_k)$, is observations of actual consumer behaviour, for example market share data and household expenditure data, or revealed preference (RP) data. A generic problem in environmental economics is that RP data are not always available, but this is of course the case in many other well-known situations. For example, a firm lacks almost by definition data on market performance of a new product. Even if RP data were available they are not without their problems, including those related to measurement errors, multicollinearity and missing observations. Even so, many economists prefer such data, because they are based on actual consumer behaviour.

An alternative source of information for estimation of $f(x_1, ..., x_k)$ is experimental data on consumer preference, which we denote stated preference (SP) data. The basic idea is to let respondents reveal their preferences across hypothetical objects or scenarios. SP data have many advantages, including the fact that the researcher has control over attributes, their values and the context within which data are generated. Measurement errors and correlated attributes can thus be avoided. Attributes which are difficult to analyse using RP data can be handled within an SP experiment. Furthermore, a large number of observations can easily be generated by making repeated measurements from each respondent. Finally, SP data makes it possible to simulate and predict market performance of new products.

Even though the basic principle for SP experiments is simple, a number of different kinds of SP experiments can be used. In this section, we discuss two so-called full-profile designs of SP experiments: rating and ranking experiments.

2.2   Full-profile Experiments

A 'full profile' is a complete description of a hypothetical good; that is, the good is described over all its important attributes. The profile is in practice formulated as a set of levels on a number of attributes. For instance, consider an SP study on anglers' preferences for angling sites. Suppose the attributes licence fee, expected catch and distance to site are studied. An example of a profile is then:

Fee ($):　　　　10
Catch (fish/h):　 5
Distance (km):　 20

Another profile could be:

Fee ($):　　　　8
Catch (fish/h):　 3
Distance (km):　 15

Suppose the researcher is interested in three different levels of the fee (for example $8, $10 and $12), three levels of expected catch (for example 1, 3 and 5 fish/h) and two levels of distance to site (for example 20 and 40 km). The researcher can then construct $3 \times 3 \times 2 = 18$ different profiles. However, if the number of levels of distance is increased to three (for example 20, 40 and 60 km), the number of possible profiles is increased to $3 \times 3 \times 3 = 27$. It is evident that the number of possible profiles increases rapidly with the number of attributes and the number of attribute levels. For instance, six attributes specified at three levels each yields a total of $3^6 = 729$ different profiles. Four attributes specified at four levels each yields a total of $4^4 = 256$ different profiles. Given this kind of combinatorial explosion, a reduced number of profiles is required in practice.

Several methods can be employed for reducing the number of profiles. Some methods are *ad hoc*, for example one either uses some random device or judgemental selection. We do not recommend the use of such approaches, because the resulting design may fail to identify model coefficients, for example. Formal reduction techniques suggested within the statistical literature on experimental design are preferable (for example Montgomery, 1996). Louviere (1988) gives a treatment of such designs within the context of SP experiments. One has to remember, however, that traditional statistical design techniques consider linear models while SP experiments imply estimation of non-linear models. Problems of design for non-linear models are further addressed in section 4.1.

The concept of orthogonal designs is important in the design literature (see also Hensher (1994) regarding design of choice experiments). To illustrate, consider the linear model $Y_j = \beta_0 + \beta_1 X_{j1} + \beta_2 X_{j2} + \beta_3 X_{j3} + \varepsilon_j$, where X_{j1}, X_{j2} and X_{j3} are attributes defined on two levels each, and j denotes the jth profile. Let the levels be represented by -1 (low level) and 1 (high level). Thus, there is a total of $2 \times 2 \times 2 = 8$ different profiles (combinations of attribute levels). These are shown in Table 7.1.

Table 7.1   Possible profiles of three two-level attributes

Profile no.	X_1	X_2	X_3
1	-1	-1	-1
2	-1	-1	1
3	-1	1	-1
4	-1	1	1
5	1	-1	-1
6	1	-1	1
7	1	1	-1
8	1	1	1

Suppose it is desired to reduce the number of profiles to four. Clearly, if the profiles 1–4 are selected, the effect of X_1 cannot be measured since the attribute is constant across those four profiles. Alternatively, assume that an orthogonal main-effects design is desired. A main-effects design assumes that there is no interaction effect among attributes. The design can be obtained in the following way: write down all combinations of the first two attributes and add the levels for the third attribute such that $X_{j1} \cdot X_{j2} \cdot X_{j3} = 1$. The resulting design is shown in Table 7.2.

Table 7.2   Orthogonal subset of profiles in Table 7.1 (Generator $X_1 \cdot X_2 \cdot X_3 = 1$)

Profile no.	X_1	X_2	X_3
1	-1	-1	1
2	-1	1	-1
3	1	-1	-1
4	1	1	1

The orthogonal property of the design in Table 7.2 means that the attributes are 'uncorrelated' over the subset of profiles. That is, consider the vector $X_j = (1 X_{j1} X_{j2} X_{j3})^T$, then

$$\sum_{j=1}^{4} X_j X_j^T = \text{diag} \left\{ \sum_{j=1}^{4} X_{jk}^2 \right\}.$$

Thus the least squares estimators of the coefficients β_0, β_1, β_2 and β_3 are uncorrelated, and the covariance matrix of the least squares estimator equals

$$\text{Cov}(\hat{\beta}_{LS}) = \sigma^2 \text{diag} \left\{ \left(n \sum_{j=1}^{4} X_{jk}^2 \right)^{-1} \right\},$$

where n is the number of respondents (replications) and σ^2 is the variance of the disturbance term in the linear model.

Consequently, orthogonal designs have several interesting properties and provide estimators with good precision in, for example, linear models. Orthogonal designs for linear models have also been frequently used for design of SP experiments. Such designs provide an alternative which can be expected to work better than *ad hoc* methods such as judgemental selection of profiles. However, the design may not be optimal, and if the linear assumption is incorrect, the design may not allow for test or estimation of the correct model.

2.3   Model Formulation and Estimation

Let $X_j = (x_{j1}, \ldots, x_{jk})^T$ denote the jth profile ($j = 1, \ldots, J$) used in an SP experiment. The respondent is assumed to rank the jth profile according to his utility function $U_j = f(X_j)$. In principle, measurements of U_j are required for the estimation of parameters in $f(X_j)$. However, U_j is a latent variable which is not directly observable, but several different methods for indirect measurements have been suggested.

One alternative is to let the respondent rate her preferences on a scale, typically a seven-point scale ranging from 1 (low preference) to 7 (high preference). With this method, the respondent treats each profile separately and does not consider them jointly. Rating experiments have been one of the most popular designs of SP experiments (for example Wittink and Cattin, 1989). The task is not complex and personal interviews can be avoided.

Another popular method for measuring $U_j (j = 1, ..., J)$ is to let the respondent rank the profiles $(j = 1, ..., J)$ from the most preferred to the least preferred. This method is known as 'contingent ranking' in the literature on environmental valuation. If the number of profiles J is large, the ranking procedure can be simplified. For instance, if $J = 10$, the respondent can be instructed to pick the five most preferred and rank them internally. In the second step the respondent can rank the five remaining profiles. The method requires personal interviews, in general. Furthermore, unless very specific distributional assumptions are made, statistical estimation of the utility function becomes very complex. Another serious drawback of the method is that the precision with which respondents do the rankings varies with the rank (Hausman and Ruud, 1987). The top two or three profiles may be easy to identify, while it may be more difficult to rank the remaining profiles.

A third popular measurement method is the pairwise comparison procedure in which the respondent considers two profiles at a time. The task of the respondent is either to pick the most preferred or to make some kind of statement regarding her/his difference in preference for the two profiles. After the first comparison, the respondent is presented with two new profiles, and so on. This alternative is here treated as a special case of the CE method, which is dealt with in section 3. In this section, we focus on modelling and estimation of preference rating and ranking experiments.

For the ith respondent, let U_{ij} denote the preference for the jth profile. Assume preference is measured on an M-point rating scale ranging from 1 (low preference) to M (high preference). Let y_{ij} denote the rating of the jth profile obtained from the ith respondent. Then,

$$Y_{ij} = y \ (1 \leq y \leq M) \quad \text{if} \quad c_{y-1} < U_{ij} \leq c_y,$$

where $c_0 < c_1 < ... < c_M \ (c_0 = -\infty, c_M = +\infty)$ are 'threshold' values.

Under random sampling of respondents, U_{ij} and Y_{ij} can be treated as random variables. Assume a linear utility function,

$$U_{ij} = X_j \beta + \varepsilon_{ij},$$

where X_j denotes the attribute vector of the jth profile, β is an unknown coefficient vector, and ε_{ij} is a random 'error' term defined as $\varepsilon_{ij} = U_{ij} - X_j \beta$.

Let the probability density function (pdf) and the cumulative distribution functions (cdf) for ε_{ij} be $g(\varepsilon)$ and $G(\varepsilon)$, respectively. Then,

$$P(Y_{ij}=y)= P(c_{y-1}< U_{ij}\leq c_y)$$
$$= P(c_{y-1}-X_j\beta<\varepsilon_{ij}\leq c_y-X_j\beta)$$
$$= G(c_y-X_j\beta)-G(c_{y-1}-X_j\beta).$$

If ε_{ij} is assumed to be standard normal distributed, the ordered probit model is obtained. Under an assumption of logistically distributed disturbances, the ordered logit model is obtained.

The contribution to the likelihood from the ith respondent with response vector $y_i^T=(yi1, yi2, ..., yiJ)$ is

$$L_i(b)= \prod_{j=1}^{J} (G(c_{y_{ij}}-X_jb) - G(c_{y_{ij}-1}-X_jb)).$$

The ML estimator of β is defined as the value of b which maximizes

$$L(b)= \prod_{i=1}^{n} L_i(b)$$

or equivalently, the value of b which maximizes the log-likelihood function

$$\log L(b)= \sum_{i=1}^{n} \log L_i(b)$$
$$= \sum_{i=1}^{n} \sum_{j=1}^{J} \log\big(G(c_{y_{ij}}-X_jb)-G(c_{y_{ij}-1}-X_jb)\big).$$

The model considered here is based on the assumption of independent observations. Independence is assumed both over and 'within' individuals. However, since repeated measurements are obtained from respondents, it is likely that 'within'-respondent observations are correlated. One way of modelling such correlation is to introduce an individual specific component, a random effect, into the utility function.

Introducing a random effect component in the model yields

$$U_{ij}=X_j\beta+\alpha_i+\varepsilon_{ij},$$

where α_i denotes the unknown random subject effect. The random effect is assumed distributed with pdf $h(\alpha; \delta)$, where δ is a vector of coefficients. The contribution to the likelihood from a respondent is equal to

$$L_i(b,\,d)=\int_{-\infty}^{\infty}\prod_{j=1}^{J}\Big(G(c_{y_{ij}}-X_jb-\alpha)-G(c_{y_{ij}-1}-X_jb-\alpha)\Big)h(\alpha;\,d)d\alpha.$$

The ML estimator of $(\beta^T,\,\delta^T)^T$ is defined as the values of $(b^T,\,d^T)^T$ which maximizes

$$\log L(b,\,d)=\sum_{i=1}^{n}\log L_i(b,\,d).$$

In a ranking experiment, preference statements from the ith respondent are obtained through her ranks of the profiles. Let j_m denote the profile number of the profile ranked in mth place, that is, the top rank profile is j_1 and the last ranked profile is j_J. Since it is assumed that the respondent ranks the profiles according to her preferences, the ranks obtained give the information

$$U_{ij_1}>U_{ij_2}>\ldots>U_{ij_J}.$$

Under the random effects model $U_{ij}=X_j\beta+\alpha_i+\varepsilon_{ij}$; this is equivalent to

$$X_{j_1}\beta+\varepsilon_{ij_1}>X_{j_2}\beta+\varepsilon_{ij_2}>\ldots>X_{j_J}\beta+\varepsilon_{ij_J}.$$

Note that the individual specific component α_i does not have an effect on the ranks of the profiles. Because it is additive, it only 'adds' to the level of utility and not to the differences in preference between profiles.

For notational convenience, the index for respondents is temporarily surpressed. Now, if the disturbances $\varepsilon_1,\,\varepsilon_2,\,\ldots,\,\varepsilon_J$ are i.i.d. type I extreme-value distributed, then

$$P(j_1,\,\ldots,\,j_J)=P(U_{j_1}>U_{j_2}>\ldots>U_{j_J})$$
$$=\prod_{s=1}^{J}\left[\frac{\exp(X_{j_s}\beta)}{\displaystyle\sum_{t=s}^{J}\exp(X_{j_t}\beta)}\right].$$

This is the model developed by Beggs et al. (1981) for an SP study on consumer preferences for electric cars.

The contribution to the log-likelihood from the ith respondent is

$$\log L_i(b)=\sum_{s=1}^{J}\left[X_{j_s}b-\log\sum_{t=s}^{J}\exp(X_{j_t}b)\right]$$

and the ML estimator of β is defined as the value $\tilde{\beta}_{ML}=b$ which maximizes the log-likelihood

$$logL(b) = \sum_{i=1}^{n} logL_i(b)$$

w.r.t. *b*.

Let θ denote the vector of model coefficients (that is, $\theta = \beta$ in the model for the ranking experiments and $\theta = (\beta^T, \delta^T)^T$ in the model for the rating experiment) and let $\tilde{\theta}_{ML}$ denote the ML estimator of θ. Under appropriate conditions, the ML estimator is consistent and $\sqrt{n}(\theta_{ML} - \theta)$ is asymptotically normal distributed. More specifically,

$$\sqrt{n}(\tilde{\theta}_{ML} - \theta) \xrightarrow{D} N(0, \Omega^{-1}),$$

where

$$\Omega = -\lim_{n \to \infty} n^{-1} \sum_{i=1}^{n} E \frac{\partial^2 \log L_i(\theta)}{\partial\theta\partial\theta^T}$$

2.4 Valuation of Attribute Levels

Suppose one of the attributes in the vector X_j is a cost variable. Then a change of one attribute from one level to another can be valued in terms of Hicksian income variations, like compensating or equivalent variation. For simplicity, let the cost variable be the kth attribute and assume a linear utility function

$$U_{ij} = \alpha_i + \sum_{s=1}^{k-1} X_{js}\beta_s - \gamma c_j + \varepsilon_{ij},$$

where c_j is the cost in the jth profile and γ is the corresponding coefficient (that is, the marginal utility of income, MUI). The marginal value of an attribute is then given by

$$V_s = \beta_s/\gamma.$$

A consistent estimator of V_s is defined by replacing the unknown coefficients with corresponding estimators. This kind of measure is often used within transportation research for measuring the value of travel-time savings (for example Small, 1992).

We have chosen not to denote the marginal value with a willingness-to-pay acronym, since marginal values do not necessarily correspond to measures of willingness to pay. However, Roe et al. (1996) consider the derivation of estimates of compensating variation from conjoint analysis experiments. They conclude that it is possible to derive such estimates if the ratings experiment contains an option describing the *status quo*. The difference in ratings between the *status quo* option and the scenario suggested then contains information on compensating variation. Based on this result, Haefele and Loomis (2001) propose estimated marginal values as measures of willingness to pay.

The measure derived above yields a point estimate when unknown coefficients are replaced by estimates. With an estimate of the standard error for the point estimator, confidence intervals can be constructed. For the general case, let θ denote a vector of unknown coefficients and let $g(\theta)$ be some function of θ. Let $\tilde{\theta}$ denote an estimator of θ such that

$$\sqrt{n}(\tilde{\theta}-\theta) \xrightarrow{D} N(0, \Sigma),$$

Then by Cramér's theorem,

$$\sqrt{n}\big(g(\tilde{\theta})-g(\theta)\big) \xrightarrow{D} N\big(0, \dot{g}(\theta)\Sigma\dot{g}(\theta)^T\big),$$

where $g(\theta) = d\dot{g}(\theta)/d\theta$.

For instance, let $g(\theta) = \beta_s/\gamma \ (\theta = (\beta_1 \ldots \beta_s \ldots \gamma))$, then $g(\theta) = (0 \ldots 1/\gamma \ldots -\beta_s/\gamma^2)$ and

$$\mathrm{Var}(\tilde{V}_s) = (1/\gamma^2)\sigma_{\beta_s}^2 + (\beta_s/\gamma^2)^2\sigma_\gamma^2 - 2(\beta_s/\gamma^3)\sigma_{\beta_s,\gamma},$$

where $\tilde{V}_s = (\tilde{\beta}_s/\tilde{\gamma})$. Replacing unknown coefficients with consistent estimates yields a consistent estimate of the variance. Using Cramér's theorem, an approximate 95 percent confidence interval for V_s is then obtained as

$$\tilde{V}_s \pm 1.96 \cdot \sqrt{\tilde{Var}(\tilde{V}_s)}.$$

It can be noted that the technique of contstructing confidence intervals for functions of coefficients using Cramér's theorem is implemented in the program package LIMDEP (Greene, 1998) in the command Wald.

3. CHOICE EXPERIMENTS

3.1 The Experiment

SP rating and ranking experiments can be used for different research objectives. In the transportation literature the methods are frequently used for valuation of travel time. Estimates of values of travel time are then in turn used for cost–benefit analyses of investments in transportation systems.

Another purpose might be the prediction of travel behaviour for different designs of transportation systems. However, SP methods focus on respondents' preferences for different objects, while many SP results are used for estimation of actual travel behaviour, that is, travel choices made by travellers (choice of mode, choice of destination and so on). That is, SP methods do not directly correspond to choice behaviour, which is often the phenomenon under study.

Choice experiments (CE) were suggested in the 1980s as an alternative to traditional SP experiments (for example Louviere, 1988; Hensher, 1994). One feature of a CE is that it mimics real behaviour since respondents make choices within specified choice sets. Assume the researcher has designed J different profiles of hypothetical objects $(X_1, X_2, ..., X_J)$. A selection of M out of these profiles forms a choice set C, that is, $C = \{j_1, j_2, ..., j_M\}$. The respondent is then presented with the choice set and asked to select one of the profiles in the set. Consider the angling site example in section 2. An example of a choice set containing three profiles is presented in Table 7.3.

Table 7.3   An example of a choice set

Attribute	Site A	Site B	Site C
Fee ($)	10	8	10
Catch (fish/h)	1	3	5
Distance (km)	20	40	40

With this choice set, the respondent would be asked to choose one of the profiles (A, B or C). After the first choice, a new choice set can be presented and the respondent again asked to make a choice. A series of choices can be obtained from the respondent in this manner.

The choice set in a CE adds an extra dimension to the design problem. Not only must it be decided which profiles are to be used, but choice sets must also be created. One alternative is to use a fixed number of profiles in each choice set. Louviere and Hensher (1983) consider a case with eight profiles derived from a reduced design of five attributes defined at two levels each. A cost variable is added to each profile and a reduced design of low/high cost over the eight profiles is employed. The choice set comprises the eight profiles with assigned cost levels for each profile. A more frequently applied size of the choice set is two profiles. One example is given by Adamowicz et al. (1998b), who use choice sets with two constructed profiles in addition to a base case alternative (that is, a no-choice option).

In related literature on analysis of RP choice data, it has been indicated that the design of the choice set is an important factor when analysing choice data (for example, Hensher, 1986). Thus it may be important to allow for different sizes of the choice set, not least for studying the effect of the size of the choice set. Louviere (1988) presents a simple method for designing different sizes of choice set. Suppose J different profiles have been designed. Then we can define J different indicator variables, one for each profile. Each indicator represents the inclusion or exclusion of the associated profile in the choice set. A design of choice sets can then be obtained by reducing the number of combinations of the levels of the indicator variable. As an example, suppose four profiles of a fishing site have been designed, sites A, B, C and D. Let the associated indicators be I_A, I_B, I_C and I_D, each with values -1 (exclude) or $+1$ (include). Using the approach as in section 2.2, write down all combinations of the three first indicators and add the fourth such that $I_A \cdot I_B \cdot I_C \cdot I_D = 1$. This procedure yields the choice sets depicted in Table 7.4. As is seen from Table 7.4, the design yields six choice sets with two profiles and one choice set with all four profiles.

Table 7.4   Choice sets obtained from a $2^{(4-1)}$ fractional design

	I_A	I_B	I_C	I_D	Choice set
1	-1	-1	-1	-1	—
2	-1	-1	$+1$	$+1$	C, D
3	-1	$+1$	-1	$+1$	B, D
4	-1	$+1$	$+1$	-1	B, C
5	$+1$	-1	-1	$+1$	A, D
6	$+1$	-1	$+1$	-1	A, C
7	$+1$	$+1$	-1	-1	A, B
8	$+1$	$+1$	$+1$	$+1$	A, B, C, D

3.2   Modelling and Estimation

Different approaches to the modelling of CE data can be used. The concept of 'random utility maximization' provides a useful microeconomic foundation. In this section, we present the traditional formulation of the RUM theory for the modelling of experimental choice data. This formulation is a direct adaptation of the RUM theory developed for the modelling of discrete choice RP data (McFadden, 1973).

Let Z denote a vector of quantities of goods consumed by an inidividual and let P denote the corresponding price vector. Let there be M different profiles in the choice set and let X_m denote the attribute vector of the mth profile. The utility obtained from a vector Z and a choice of the mth profile can then be written as $U_i^*(Z, X_m)$, where $U_i^*(\cdot)$ is a utility defined as a function of Z and X_m. The task of the respondent in a CE can be formulated as to find the solution to the optimizing problem

$$\max_{Z, m} U_i^* (Z, X_m)$$

$$\text{s.t.} \qquad PZ \leq Y_i - c_m,$$

where Y_i is income and c_m is the cost of the mth profile.

Conditional on the mth profile, utility can be maximized w.r.t. Z, which gives the conditional indirect utility function

$$U_{im}(P, Y_i - c_m, X_m).$$

According to the utility maximization principle, the respondent chooses the profile yielding the highest utility; that is, the respondent chooses profile m iff

$$U_{im} > U_{ij} \ \forall j \in C; j \neq m.$$

Assume a linear utility function,

$$U_{im} = P\lambda + X_m \beta + \gamma (Y_i - c_m) + \alpha_i + \varepsilon_{im},$$

where λ and β are coefficient vectors, γ is the marginal utility of income, α_i is an individual specific component and ε_{im} is an unknown individual/profile specific component. Since $P\lambda$, γY_i and α_i are constant over the alternatives in the choice set C, they do not affect the choice of profile. Thus the decision rule can be restated as: the respondent chooses profile m iff

$$X_m \beta - \gamma c_m + \varepsilon_{im} > X_j \beta - \gamma c_j + \varepsilon_{ij} \qquad \forall j \in C; j \neq m.$$

Suppose respondents are randomly chosen, then the unknown individual/profile specific component can be interpreted as a random disturbance term. Note that the random terms are often given other interpretations, such as lack of information about the 'true' utility function, and so on and so forth.

The probability of obtaining a respondent choosing the mth profile is

$$P(m: C, \beta, \gamma) = P(X_m \beta - \gamma c_m + \varepsilon_{im} > X_j \beta - \gamma c_m + \varepsilon_{ij} \qquad \forall j \in C; j \neq m).$$

If the disturbances $\varepsilon_{i1}, ..., \varepsilon_{iM}$ are i.i.d. with pdf $g(\varepsilon)$ and cdf $G(\varepsilon)$, then

$$P(m: C, \beta, \gamma) = \int_{-\infty}^{\infty} g(u) \prod_{j \neq m}^{M} G\big(u + (X_m - X_j)\beta - \gamma(c_m - c_j)\big) du.$$

In the case of i.i.d. extreme value distributed disturbances, one obtains

$$P(m: C, \beta, \gamma) = \frac{e^{X_m\beta - \gamma c_m}}{\sum_{j \in C} e^{X_j\beta - \gamma c_j}}.$$

Let S denote the number of choice sets presented. Let C_{is}, $(s=1, ..., S)$ denote the sth choice set presented to the ith respondent. Also, let Y_{is} denote the choice of the ith respondent in the sth choice set. If the repeated measurements obtained from a respondent are assumed independent, then the contribution from the ith respondent to the log-likelihood is

$$\log L_i(b, d) = \sum_{s=1}^{S} \log P(y_{is} : C_{is}, b, d).$$

The ML, estimators of β and γ are defined as those values of b and d respectively which maximizes the log-likelihood

$$\log L(b, d) = \sum_{i=1}^{n} \sum_{s=1}^{S} \log L_i (b, d).$$

Again, under appropriate assumptions, the ML estimator is consistent and asymptotically normal distributed (cf. Section 2.3).

3.3 Measuring WTP

Different measures of WTP can be of interest within applications of choice experiments. One measure is given by the marginal value

$$WTP_s = \beta_s/\gamma$$

presented in section 2.4. Using the marginal values of increases in attributes, a change from conditions X_0 to conditions X_1 can be valued as

$$WTP_{\Delta X} = \Delta X\beta/\gamma,$$

where $\Delta X = X_1 - X_0$, for example Garrod and Willis (1999).

Boxall et al. (1996) make use of the expression

$$WTP = (1/\gamma) \left\{ \log \sum_{i \in C} \exp(V_{i1}) - \log \sum_{i \in C} \exp(V_{i0}) \right\},$$

where C is the choice set and V_{i0} and V_{i1} denote the utility before and after the change of the ith choice alternative. Note that in the single alternative case ($\#C=1$) this formula reduces to $WTP=(1/\gamma)\{V_{i1}-V_{i0}\}$, which is equivalent to $WTP_{\Delta X}$ in the linear utility function case.

Care must be taken when using the log-difference formula as a measure of willingness to pay. The reason is that the formula is originally developed within the RP data case and adjusts for selection probabilities. Consider a choice set with only two alternatives and utilities U_1 and U_2. Suppose the second alternative is improved such that utility increases to U_2^*. Then three situations can be identified. First, if $U_1 > U_2^* > U_2$, then the first alternative is selected both before and after the improvement of second alternative. Thus, the improvement of alternative 2 does not yield a subjective utility increase; the consumer is not willing to pay any positive amount for the improvement. Second, if $U_2^* > U_2 > U_1$, then the second alternative is chosen both before and after the improvement of the alternative. The consumer's WTP for the improvement can then be measured in terms of the difference $U_2^* - U_2$ (and then converted into money). The third and final situation, $U_2^* > U_1 > U_2$, yields an intermediate case between the first two. Alternative 1 is chosen before and alternative 2 is chosen after the improvement of alternative 2. In this case, the improvement can be valued in terms of the difference $U_2^* - U_1$ (again we need to convert into money).

For a derivation of the log-difference formula, let there be J alternatives in the choice set and let the indirect conditional utility of the jth alternative be

$$U_j = V_j + \varepsilon_j,$$

where $V_j = X_j\beta$. The index of the individual has been dropped for simplicity. Let $1(j)$ denote an indicator such that $1(j)=1$ if the jth alternative is chosen (that is, $U_j > U_m \; \forall m \neq j$) while $1(j)=0$ otherwise. The utility obtained by the individual can then be expressed as

$$U = \sum_{j=1}^{J} 1(j)U_j = \sum_{j=1}^{J} 1(j)(V_j + \varepsilon_j)$$

and the expected utility for a randomly chosen individual is

$$EU = E \sum_{j=1}^{J} 1(j)(V_j + \varepsilon_j)$$

$$= \sum_{j=1}^{J} E(U_j | U_j > U_m \forall m \neq j)P(j),$$

where $P(j)$ is an abbreviation of $P(j: C, \beta, \gamma)$ defined in section 3.2. If $(\varepsilon_1, \ldots, \varepsilon_J)$ are assumed type I extreme-value distributed, then

$E(U_j|U_j > U_m \; \forall m \neq j) = A + \delta$, where $A = \log \sum_{j=1}^{J} e^{V_j}$ and $\delta \approx 0.5772$ (Euler's constant). Thus, $EU = \delta + \log \sum_{j=1}^{J} e^{V_j}$. The mean WTP for a change of attribute values from X_j to X'_j can then be measured by

$$WTP = \frac{1}{\gamma} \left(\log \sum_{j=1}^{J} e^{V'_j} - \log \sum_{j=1}^{J} e^{V_j} \right),$$

where $V'_j = X'_j \beta$ and γ is the MUI, as before.

Thus, the log-difference formula is appropriate for measuring use values but may be inappropriate for measuring non-use values. Suppose that you are asked to choose between fishing sites 1 and 2, in a scenario when site 2 is to be improved. Include a *status quo* to allow for the fact that you might not be interested in fishing *per se*. You may prefer the *status quo* to an improvement of site, and your choice of the *status quo* signals that this is your utility maximizing choice. However, you might still be willing to pay for the improvement of site 2 (because your best friend is a fisherman, or for whatever reason). From the point of view of the experiment, however, an improvement of site 2 will be interpreted as making you worse off, the problem being that the scenario involves an activity which you are not engaging in. Put simply, you attach passive use values to the site, but the experiment assigns potentially higher utility only to those states of the world where you actually travel.

4.   FURTHER TOPICS

4.1   Experimental Design

To illustrate the problems of designing experiments for non-linear models, suppose the profile X_j ($j = 1, \ldots, J$) is to be used in a dichotomous response experiment with response variable $Y_j \in \{0,1\}$. Assume the logit model, $P(Y_j = 1) = \exp(X_j^T \beta)/(1 + \exp(X_j^T \beta))$, is specified for the analysis. Suppose each respondent is presented with all J profiles. The contribution of the observations from the ith respondent to the log-likelihood is $\log L(\beta)_i = \sum_{j=1}^{J} X_j^T \beta y_{ij} - \log(1 + \exp(X_j^T \beta))$ and the asymptotic covariance matrix[3] of the maximum likelihood (ML) estimator equals

$$\mathrm{Cov}(\tilde{\beta}_{ML}) = \left(\sum_{j=1}^{J} w_j X_j X_j^T \right)^{-1},$$

where $w_j = \exp(X_j \beta)/(1 + \exp(X_j \beta))^2$ (for example Maddala, 1983). Two conclusions regarding the design can be drawn from the structure of the asymptotic covariance matrix:

1. In non-linear models, the ML estimators of the coefficients are, in general, not independent, even if an orthogonal design is used.
2. In non-linear models, the precision with which the coefficients are estimated depends on the unknown coefficient values.

The last observation is generic to optimal design theory in non-linear models and is, to some extent, disheartening.[4] Indeed, we need to know the values of the parameters to derive the optimal design, but with this knowledge there is no need to carry out an experiment! But some ways round this have been suggested, and we discuss some of them below.

It may be useful to see how an orthogonal design may fail to minimize the variance. Consider the design in Table 7.2 and suppose $\beta_1 = 1.0$, $\beta_2 = 0.5$ and $\beta_3 = -0.5$ in the logit model (no constant term). Then the diagonal elements in the asymptotic covariance matrix for the ML, estimator equal 0.54, 0.63 and 0.63, using the design in Table 7.2. Now, if the first profile is replaced with attribute levels $(1, 1, -1)$, the design is not orthogonal. However, the diagonal elements in the corresponding asymptotic covariance matrix equal 0.68, 0.59 and 0.59. Thus both β_2 and β_3 are estimated with greater precision in the non-orthogonal design.[5] A third conclusion to be drawn is therefore:

3. An orthogonal design may give less efficient estimates relative to a non-orthogonal design.

It is perhaps more important to address other topics in profile design than 'optimality' properties. After all, we have to decide upon the optimization criterion first, and there are several reasonable choices. We may want to minimize the variance of the parameters of the model, a function of the parameters, or the variance of prediction. In optimal design theory, each criterion is associated with a letter, such as A-optimality, C-optimality or D-optimality. Thus the optimal design is not independent of what it is we want to measure and, in this sense, there is no generic optimal design in an experiment.

As we have seen, an optimal design requires knowledge of the true model. Certainly, models specified within most fields are usually tentative and exposed to specification testing. The design chosen must therefore allow for more flexible model specifications than the model specified initially. For instance, suppose a linear model as the one above is specified using the orthogonal design in Table 7.2. It follows that the estimable linear effects will be confounded or aliased with interaction effects. The alias pattern of the design in Table 7.2 can be seen from Table 7.5.

The main effect X_1 is aliased with the second-order effect X_2X_3. That is,

Table 7.5   Alias structure of the design in Table 7.2 (generator $X_1 \cdot X_2 \cdot X_3 = 1$)

Profile no.	Main effects			Interaction effects			
	X_1	X_2	X_3	$X_1 X_2$	$X_1 X_3$	$X_2 X_3$	$X_1 X_2 X_3$
1	−1	−1	1	1	−1	−1	1
2	−1	1	−1	−1	1	−1	1
3	1	−1	−1	−1	−1	1	1
4	1	1	1	1	1	1	1

the values of X_1 are perfectly correlated with those of $X_2 X_3$ and the effect of X_1 on preference cannot be separated from the effect of the interaction $X_2 X_3$. Similarly, X_2 is aliased with $X_1 X_3$ and X_3 is aliased with $X_1 X_2$. This alias pattern means that, for example, the effect of $X_2 X_3$ cannot be separated from the effect of X_1, if the design in Table 7.2 is used. The effect estimated, based on the design, is the combined effect of the main effect and its aliased second-order effect. Consequently, if the linear model is inappropriate and the true model contains interaction effects, the interaction effects cannot be tested and the linear model chosen cannot be tested for misspecification.

Without prior knowledge of the true coefficient values it is not possible to obtain reduced designs that are optimal in the traditional sense of giving maximum information about the true model coefficients. However, there are alternative approaches to optimal designs in non-linear model cases (for example Atkinson and Donev, 1992). One alternative is a sequential procedure with optimal design for linearized models. This procedure makes use of a prior point estimate of the unknown coefficients. Such a prior estimate may be obtained from, for example, theory, earlier studies and pilot studies. The use of prior point estimates is also suggested by Kanninen (2001), who specifically considers multinomial choice experiments. She deals with the D-optimality criterion and provides a decomposition of the determinant of the covariance matrix. Based on her findings a sequential approach is suggested.

Another alternative is the use of Bayesian designs. Making a design based on a single point estimate (initial guess) may be a bad procedure if the prior estimate deviates grossly from the true value. In order to include the uncertainty of the prior estimate, a Bayesian design makes use of a 'prior' distribution for the unknown model coefficients. The idea is to incorporate the uncertainty of prior estimates of coefficients by taking expectations of the design criteria over the prior distribution specified for the coeffients. This approach is taken by Zocchi and Atkinson (1999), who propose a Bayesian D-optimal design for multinomial logistic models.

An interesting third alternative is suggested by Häggström and Pettersson (2000). They propose the use of minimax designs for design of an SP experiment on anglers' valuations of angling site characteristics. The idea is to define a parameter space (that is, a uniform prior distribution) and choose the design which minimizes the maximum 'loss' over the parameter space. Here loss means some criteria of the information obtainable from the design. For instance, corresponding to D-optimal designs is a loss function defined as the determinant of the estimator covariance matrix.

4.2 Random Coefficient Models

Random coefficient models have become popular alternatives in econometrics because they provide a direct way of modelling taste variation over the population of consumers. In the standard formulation of the utility function, that is, $U_{ij} = x_{ij}\beta + \varepsilon_{ij}$, individual taste differences, omitted variables, and function approximation errors are collected into the individual specific component ε_{ij}. By specifying individual specific coefficient vectors, β_i, in the utility function, $U_{ij} = x_{ij}\beta_i + \varepsilon_{ij}$, taste variation is explicitly modelled.

Train (1998) considers the modelling of RP choice data and suggests a multinomial logit (MNL) model with random coefficients, the random parameters logit (RPL) model. Conditionally on β_i, let the choice probabilities be defined as

$$P(m:C, \beta_i) = \frac{e^{X_m \beta_i}}{\sum_{j \in C} e^{X_j \beta_i}}$$

(cf. section 3.2). Suppose the coefficient vector β_i is distributed over the population according to a distribution function $G(\beta; \delta)$, where δ is a vector of unknown coefficients determining the specific distribution of the individual coefficients. Then the unconditional choice probabilities are defined as

$$P(m:C, \delta) = \int \cdots \int \frac{e^{X_m b}}{\sum_{j \in C} e^{X_j b}} dG(b; \delta).$$

Suppose each respondent makes a series of choices, for example choice of angling site on S different occasions. Let m_s denote the alternative chosen at the sth occasion. The unconditional probability of observing the choices $\mathbf{m} = (m_1, m_2, ..., m_S)$ is then

$$P(\mathbf{m}:C,\delta)=\int\cdots\int\prod_{S=1}^{S}\frac{e^{X_{mS}b}}{\sum_{j\in C_S}e^{X_j b}}dG(b;\delta).$$

In the random coefficient model framework the vector β_i is not of primary interest in model estimation. Here the main purpose of model estimation is inference on the *distribution* of the coefficients, that is, the coefficient vector δ. The contribution to the log-likelihood from an individual in the random sample is $l_i(\delta)=\log P(\mathbf{m}_i:C,\delta)$, where $\mathbf{m}_i$ includes the choices made by the respondent. The log-likelihood for a whole sample is then specified as the sum of the contributions from each respondent, $l(\delta)=\sum_{i=1}^{n}l_i(\delta)$, and the ML estimator is defined as the value of d which maximizes the log-likelihood function $l(d)$.

The choice probabilities are in general intractable for analytic calculations. In such cases, simulation-based estimators have been proposed (see, for example, Hajivassiliou and Ruud, 1994). The approach taken by Train (1998) is to approximate the probabilities by the averages of probabilities obtained from a random set of coefficients $(b_{i1}, ..., b_{iR})$ drawn from the distribution $G(b;d)$. That is, $P(\mathbf{m}_i:C,d)$ is approximated with

$$SP_i(d)=\frac{1}{R}\sum_{r=1}^{R}\left\{\prod_{s=1}^{S}\frac{e^{X_{ms}b_{ir}}}{\sum_{j=1}^{J}e^{X_j b_{ir}}}\right\}.$$

The simulated ML estimator is then obtained as the value of the coefficient vector d which maximizes the simulated log-likelihood function $SLL(d)=\sum_{i=1}^{n}\log SP_i(d)$. The simulated ML, estimator is consistent and asymptotically normal distributed and, if $R/\sqrt{n}$ converges to infinity as n increases, the simulated ML estimator is asymptotically equivalent to the usual ML estimator (Train, 1998).

Layton (2000) suggests the use of Train's (1998) RPL model for the analysis of SP ranking and CE data. His major consideration is the inability of earlier model suggestions to handle heterogeneity over the rankings in an SP ranking experiment. One major drawback of earlier models is the so-called independence of irrelevant alternatives (IIA) property (see, for example, Maddala, 1983). Layton's results indicate that the RPL model does a better job than earlier ones.

One can argue that the IIA property is not avoided using the RPL model by Train (1998). It is true that on an aggregate level the RPL model does not possess the IIA property. However, conditional on the coefficient vector (that is, β_i) the model is a standard MNL model with probabilities subject to the IIA property. Thus the good performance of the RPL model observed could be ascribed to the explicit modelling of taste variation and not the avoidance of the IIA property.

We find random coefficient models potentially useful for the analysis of choice experiment data. However, our arguments are different from those provided by Layton. As stated earlier, random coefficient models explicitly incorporate taste differences among consumers. Thus the fixed coefficient model is a simplification which may result in lack of model fit. A natural alternative is to include individual specific coefficients in the search for a model with improved ability to describe data.

In standard regression analysis, the error term is usually motivated by referring to taste variation, omitted variables and measurement errors. In the modelling of CE data, utility functions contain a 'systematic' component and a random 'error' component. A major strength of experiments is the control over variables and the levels of the attributes. Thus, in an experiment, the nature and the components of the error term need to be carefully considered.

Suppose there are three alternatives in a choice set in a CE. Let the utility of the first alternative be $U(X_1) = V(X_1) + e(X_1) + r_1$, where $V(X)$ is a systematic component defined by the attributes in the vector X, $e(X)$ is the part of the individual specific component which depends on the vector X, and r is the part of the individual specific component which is independent of X. Now, if the CE is conducted properly, the only difference among the alternatives in the choice set is the differences in attribute levels specified by X_1, X_2 and X_3. Hence, in the expressions for the utilities of the three alternatives, $r_1 = r_2 = r_3$.

This result is of importance since it implies that the error terms r_j ($j = 1$, 2, 3) do not influence the choice of alternative. The error term of interest for modelling is the $e(X)$ part, which depends on the attribute levels. Thus models derived for CE data from assumptions of i.i.d. error terms in the utility function are inappropriate. One such model is the standard MNL model. One possible solution to the modelling problem is to make use of random coefficient models as suggested by Layton (2000). However, his model is based on random coefficients and a random error term while the arguments made here suggest that the model should include random coefficients and exclude a random i.i.d. error term.

5. A COMPARISON OF CV AND CE METHODS

In this section we compare the CV and the CE methods and offer our somewhat off-the-beaten-track arguments on their comparability. Adamowicz et al. (1998b) propose the use of choice experiments for environmental valuation, a proposal largely based on empirical results showing similarities between CE and traditional CV methods. However, the key difference between CE and CV is best understood by contemplating their respective traditions. The CE finds its tradition, as we have noted, in transportation (or marketing). The CV method is a part of applied welfare economics, often used as part of a cost–benefit analysis. A focal point of the literature on CE is the estimation of the marginal utility (converted into money) of certain attributes, while the CV method targets a different quantity, essentially involving a non-marginal utility change (converted into money via the Hicksian measures). This means that comparison is not necessarily straightforward, because one is potentially looking for different quantities.

Furthermore, a key feature of a CE experiment is that the attributes are part of a design; as we have shown, the respondent is asked to choose between goods that are 'constructed' by the researcher. A CV experiment presents a scenario and the individual is asked to state his willingness to pay, or to accept or reject a cost for the change (in the standard set-ups). In a CE, the utility function is defined over a subset of attributes generated by the researcher. Any attribute that is missing, and considered important by the individual, will have an impact on the results generated by a CE. This constraint is not operative in the same way in CV, because the individual can self-select any attribute, presented or not, that he finds important to his decision. Compare the marketing context in which the researcher is interested in a particular set of attributes that can be fixed *ex ante*. This is not possible in the environmental context, because the set of attributes belongs to a set of unknown cardinality.

Thus the question whether CE and CV methods really give the same information must be more carefully addressed. Simple empirical examples showing similarities between methods do not provide sufficient support for the conclusion that CE and CV methods measure the same quantities. Although differences between coefficient estimates are insignificant, they may provide substantially different point estimates of population mean WTP.

It is not within the scope of this chapter to consider fully the differences between the methods. Anyway, suppose that a firm contemplates the appropriate proportion of yellow and green X to produce. It is clearly useful to know the proportion of people that would choose each type of X. Assume now that there is an externality generated by the production of yellow X. A consulting firm obtains willingness to pay by using an open-ended valuation question in a CV experiment. Another consulting firm uses a CE, but does not know that the sole determinant of WTP is the distance between the respondent's house and the X plant and therefore leaves this attribute out of the experiment. Because this distance is constant across the CE, it can reasonably be argued that utility is not affected across alternatives, provided that the utility function is linear (or separable in the right way). This is, however, an assumption that is not needed in the CVM case. Consequently, there is a potential for finding differences in results.

There are two standard assumptions in CE that will affect possibilities of comparison with the CVM:

- The utility function is assumed to have a simple parametric form, often linear.
- The standard assumptions of a multinomial choice model imply that the distribution of WTP follows a logistic distribution, an assumption that finds little support in the CVM literature.

Another aspect that further complicates comparison concerns the construction of choice alternatives (that is, profiles). As we know, orthogonal designs may not be optimal, because the underlying model is non-linear in CE. Future developments are likely to provide more powerful algorithms for *n*-dimensional optimal designs, but as of now, little is known about how the design affects the results in a CE.

The binary response CV method has been suggested as a way of reducing the complexity of the task demanded from the respondent (Bishop and Heberlein, 1979). However, compared with the CV method, CE presents the respondent with a more demanding task. There is a vast literature reporting on problems with CE and conjoint analysis methods related to choice complexity. One problem is the so-called 'numbers-of-levels' effect (for example Wittink et al., 1992). It has been observed that the importance of an attribute is positively correlated with the number of levels the attribute attains in the different profiles. Other problems are learning and fatigue effects, as well as anchoring behaviour by the respondent (for example McFadden, 1986; Lewin et al., 1992; Bradley and Daly, 1994). Since a repeated number of preference judgements are obtained from the respondent, he may change his valuations of the attributes. Another possibility is that the respondent fails to stay interested in the repeated tasks demanded from him. In addition, he may respond to a choice task contingent on earlier responses. Nevertheless, an implicit assumption in CE is that the repeated measurements are uncorrelated. Little is known about the implications of this assumption.

6. SUMMARY

Space has prevented us from doing more than barely scratch the surface of an exciting area of research in environmental economics. The fact that the area is relatively new also means that there may not be complete consensus on a number of issues. But this is as it should be in a lively area of research. We have certainly given a biased account on where important differences of opinion exist, but an important aim of this chapter is to provoke additional discussion about the directions direct valuation methods should take. For example, we firmly believe that there is more to say about welfare measurement in CE, given the fact that the standard formula does not handle choice probabilities correctly, in our view. Furthermore, the use of orthogonal design is standard practice, but such designs are not ideally suited to the non-linear models used in this area. Finally, we believe that direct methods, such as CE and CV, are useful complements that paint different pictures of data and how people make choices. How such methods are to be consistently compared is a subtle issue, and further developments are needed before an 'equal-footing' comparison can be made. Indeed, current comparisons are made within a very limited class of probability models. Extending this class of probability models for the CE, and invoking new insights from optimal design theory, seems to be a useful area for further development. As of now, cost–benefit analysis that needs non-market values should rely more on CV than on CE, although we do not deny that CE methods paint useful pictures of consumer behaviour.

ACKNOWLEDGEMENT

We are most grateful for comments on earlier drafts of the manuscript by Göran Arnoldsson, Mary Evans, Henk Folmer, Ståle Navrud, Kerry Smith and Tom Tietenberg. The usual disclaimer applies.

NOTES

1. Adamowicz et al. (1998) have proposed a thoughtful nomenclature in this area. SP is the generic name for all direct methods of valuation, and contingent valuation, choice experiments and so on are subsets of stated choice methods.
2. Because utility is an ordinal concept, any positive monotone transform of $f(x_1, ..., x_k)$ will describe the same choice behaviour.
3. The expression represents the covariance matrix in the asymptotic distribution of $\sqrt{n}(\beta_{ML}-\beta)$.
4. The general theory of optimal design is developed in Pukelsheim (1993).
5. Furthermore, by creating a different orthogonal design from the one shown in Table 7.2 one may obtain different precision of the estimates.

REFERENCES

Adamowicz, W., J. Louviere and J. Swait (1998a), *Introduction to Attribute-based Stated Choice Methods*, NOAA, US Dept. of Commerce.

Adamowicz, W.L., P.C. Boxall, M. Williams and J. Louviere (1998b), 'Stated Preference Approaches for Measuring Passive Use Values: Choice Experiments and Contingent Valuation', *American Journal of Agricultural Economics*, **80**(1), 64–75.

Atkinson, A.C. and A.N. Donev (1992), *Optimum Experimental Designs*, Oxford: Clarendon Press.

Beggs, S., S. Cardell and J. Hausman (1981), 'Assessing the Potential Demand for Electric Cars', *Journal of Econometrics*, **16**, 1–19.

Bergland, O. (2001), 'Attribute-Based Stated Preference Methods Choice Experiments', paper presented at a conference on Economic Valuation of Environmental Goods, Venice, 11 May, http://arken.nlh.no/~iosob/

Bishop, R.C. and T.A. Heberlein (1979), 'Measuring Values of Extramarket Goods: Are Indirect Measures Biased?', *American Journal of Agricultural Economics*, **61**(5), 926–30.

Boxall, P.C., W.L. Adamowicz, J. Swait, M. Williams and J. Louviere (1996), 'A Comparison of Stated Preference Methods for Environmental Valuation', *Ecological Economics*, **18**, 243–56.

Bradley, M. and A. Daly (1994), 'Use of the Logit Scaling Approach to Test for Rank-order and Fatigue Effects in Stated Preference Data', *Transportation*, **21**, 167–84.

Garrod, G. and K.G. Willis (1999), *Economic Valuation of the Environment*, Cheltenham, UK and Northampton, USA: Edward Elgar.

Greene, W.H. (1998), *LIMDEP Version 7.0: User's Manual*, Econometric Software Inc., New York.

Haefele, M.A. and LB. Loomis (2001), 'Using the Conjoint Analysis Technique for the Estimation of Passive Use Values of Forest Health', *Journal of Forest Economics*, **7**, 9–28.

Häggström, J. and H. Pettersson (2000), 'An Application of Optimum Design to a Binary Choice Experiment', statistical research report 2000–2, University of Umeå.

Hajivassiliou, V.A. and P.A. Ruud (1994), 'Classical Estimation Methods for LDV Models Using Simulation', in R.F. Engle and D.L. McFadden (eds), *Handbook of Econometrics Vol. 4*, Amsterdam: North Holland, pp. 2383–441.

Hanley, N., S. Mourato and R.E. Wright (2001), 'Choice Modelling Approaches: A Superior Alternative for Environmental Valuation?', *Journal of Economic Surveys*, **15**(4), 435–62.

Hausman, J.A. and P.A. Ruud (1987), 'Specifying and Testing Econometric Models for Rank Ordered Data', *Journal of Econometrics*, **34**, 83–104.

Hensher, D.A. (1986), 'Sequential and Full Information Maximum-likelihood-estimation of a Nested Logit Model', *Review of Economics and Statistics*, **68**, 657–67.

Hensher, D.A. (1994), 'Stated Preference Analysis of Travel Choices: The State of Practice', *Transportation*, **21**, 107–33.

Kanninen, B. (2001), 'Optimal Design for Multinomial Choice Experiments', mimeo, Hubert H. Humphrey Institute of Public Affairs, University of Minnesota.

Layton, D.F. (2000), 'Random Coefficient Models for Stated Preference Surveys', *Journal of Environmental Economics and Management*, **40**, 21–36.

Lewin, G., A. Jeuland and S. Struhl (1992), 'An Empirical Investigation of Learning Effects in Conjoint Research', 1992 Sawtooth Software Conference Proceedings.

Louviere, J.J. (1988), *Analyzing Decision Making: Metric Conjoint Analysis*, Newbury Park, CA: Sage Publications.

Louviere, J.J. and D.A. Hensher (1983), 'Using Discrete Choice Models with Experimental Design Data to Forecast Consumer Demand for a Unique Cultural Event', *Journal of Consumer Research*, **10**, 348–61.

Louviere, J., D. Hensher and J. Swait (2000), *Stated Choice Methods: Analysis and Application*, Cambridge: Cambridge University Press.

Maddala, G.S. (1983), *Limited Dependent and Qualitative Variables in Econometrics*, New York: Cambridge University Press.

McFadden (1973), 'Conditional Logit Analysis of Qualitative Choice Behavior', in P. Zarembka (ed.), *Frontiers in Econometrics*, New York: Academic Press, 105–42.

McFadden (1986), 'The Choice Theory Approach to Market Research', *Marketing Science*, **5**, 275–97.

Montgomery, D.C. (1996), *Design and Analysis of Experiments*, 4th ed., New York: Wiley.

Pukelsheim, F. (1993), *Optimal Design of Experiments*, New York: Wiley.

Roe, B., K.J. Boyle and M.F. Teisl (1996), 'Using Conjoint Analysis to Derive Estimates of Compensating Variation', *Journal of Environmental Economics and Management*, **31**, 145–9.

Small, K.A. (1992), *Urban Transportation Economics*, Chur: Harwood Academic Publishers,

Train, K.E. (1998), 'Recreation Demand Models with Taste Differences Over People', *Land Economics*, **74**, 230–39.

Wittink, D.R. and P. Cattin (1989), 'Commercial Use of Conjoint Analysis: An Update', *Journal of Marketing*, **53**, 91–6.

Wittink, D.R., J. Huber, P. Zandan and R.M. Johnson (1992), 'The Number of Levels Effect in Conjoint: Where Does it Come From, and Can it be Eliminated?', Sawtooth Software Conference Proceedings.

Zocchi, S.S. and A.C. Atkinson (1999), 'Optimum Experimental Designs for Multinomial Logistic Models', *Biometrics*, **55**, 437–44.

8. The choice of pollution control policy instruments in developing countries: arguments, evidence and suggestions

Clifford S. Russell and William J. Vaughan

1. BACKGROUND

Concern about the environmental costs of economic development is now both widespread and intense. At one extreme, environmental deterioration, as through air and water pollution and deforestation, is seen as an unavoidable cost of industrialization, urbanization and the growth of consumption (and the change in its composition) that are at the heart of 'development' in the common use of the word. At the other, strongly influenced by the notion of 'sustainability' that has been developed since the Bruntland Report (World Commission on Environment and Development, 1987), is the view that the environmental degradation being accepted by developing countries may well be enough to prevent them from continuing on a development path. Deterioration of natural resources and the health costs of pollution may together overwhelm such growth momentum as has been generated by local and global policies and events. Somewhere in the middle of this polyphonic chorus of projection and advice lies the work on 'environmental Kuznets curves', cross-section phenomena that seem to promise the possibility, at least, that growth and environmental quality may be reconcilable in the long run (for example Stern, 1998).

In the terms of the above perspective, the choice of environmental policy instruments in developing countries has generally, though by no means always, been couched as a matter of 'decoupling' development and the environment (for example Pearce, 1991, p. 51 and World Bank, 1992a, pp. 40 and 43). That is to say, the search has been for ways to attack environmental challenges that promise to have small negative, or perhaps even positive, effects on economic growth as traditionally defined. In the search for such desirable policy approaches, the early literature in environmental economics, when instrument choice was the dominant subject, and enthusiasm for economic incentive approaches was very high, has been notably influential.[1]

Another intellectual thread worth teasing out as part of the background to the current situation is the more general enthusiasm for free markets and undistorted prices that was generated by multilateral development organizations, with the strong backing of developed nations, during the 1980s. This was labeled the 'Washington Consensus' by John Williamson (1990). The particular policy reforms being urged on developing countries under this approach included trade liberalization, unified and competitive exchange rates, fiscal discipline, the institution of secure private property rights, and deregulation (where government intervention was not justified by some clear evidence of market failure). This consensus, which also came to be called the 'Universal Convergence' (Williamson, 1993), was officially extended to environmental matters when the World Bank publicly discovered and endorsed economic (or market-based) instruments (EI/MBI) of environmental policy in the 1992 *World Development Report* (World Bank, 1992a). This extension of the market consensus owed something to the stream of OECD publications in effect advocating the use of economic instruments in both industrial- and developing-country settings (especially OECD, 1989, 1991; Eröcal, 1991).[2] With the World Bank's weight behind it, the idea caught on widely that EI/MBI could be a major part of the resolution of the tension between the developing world's interest in industrialization and economic growth and the fairly obvious environmental damage they were doing themselves. (For an explicit claim that the 'new' policy instruments de-link economic growth and environmental protection, see World Bank, 2000, pp. 40 and 43.) For a sense of the enthusiasm behind this movement, one of the best sources is Panayotou's paper in the Eröcal OECD volume (Panayotou, 1991). Under the prodding of the multilateral lending agencies and the OECD countries, developing countries have adopted a wide variety of EI/MBI, at least on paper. It seems, however, that the extent to which these instruments have been reflected at the level of decision-making for the stack or wastewater outfall is a good deal less clear. On the other hand, some of the economic instruments adopted have been common-sense offshoots of the broader economic policy agenda of the Washington Consensus, for example, getting environmentally relevant prices, such as those for water and energy, 'right' by removing damaging subsidies.

2. DEFINITIONS, DISTINCTIONS, AND THE PLAN OF THE CHAPTER

2.1 Definitions and Distinctions

Before laying out a plan for the rest of the chapter, this section will set out a few definitions and distinctions that will be useful later on:

- Attention will be directed almost exclusively to pollution control policies. Much of the argument will apply with little change to other forms of human-induced environmental stress, but the chapter will not follow up the parallels. It explicitly will not examine environmentally related market pricing, such as that of irrigation water.
- Following the conventions of the literature, the chapter distinguishes between the choice of policy goals or targets and the choice of instruments by which those goals are pursued. In principle, goals and instruments should be chosen together. Or, rather, if the proverbial can opener were available (in this case damage functions for each pollution discharge by source), the instruments as shadow prices (Pigouvian charges) specific to source and pollutant would fall out of the grand minimization of the sum of damages and costs of reducing them. In practice, ambient environmental quality targets are chosen (or in more theoretical work, assumed to be chosen) by a political process, often with quasi-scientific rhetoric surrounding it. The debate about instruments is, then, a debate about how to meet those targets.
- 'Efficiency' (or, more accurately, static efficiency) is, then, the least-cost meeting of the targets in an assumed steady state. It is worth noting two phenomena accompanying this narrow but practical view of efficiency. First, the outcome in physical terms (the pattern of discharges and resulting ambient environmental quality) will not in general bear any resemblance to the Pigouvian ideal in which marginal damages caused by each discharge have been equated to the marginal costs of reducing that discharge. Moreover, damages may be quite a bit higher under a least-cost solution to a regional pollution control problem of ambient quality standard attainment than under some 'inefficient' alternative. For an illustration of this, see the dramatic contrasts in ambient air quality distributions under efficient and inefficient policy instruments in O'Ryan (1996), who examines air pollution control alternatives for Santiago, Chile. Second, it is very difficult to observe efficiency, especially in situations in which location matters, so that marginal costs at the efficient

solution will not in general be equal across sources. Thus, in such a situation, for any policy instrument designed to meet an ambient quality target, there will be a total resource cost of the result. It is possible to say certain things *a priori*, based on economic models of the decision-making of the dischargers in response to the instrument – assuming, importantly, compliance with discharge standards or payment of proper emission charges. But it is a very big job to prove empirically that any one such observed result is or is not, in fact, least cost. To do so would require construction of a complete regional model containing all the dischargers' cost-of-reduction functions and the relevant natural world transfer functions.[3] Notice also that the available *a priori* models of discharger response are quite simple, certainly too simple to predict response to such information-provision instruments as eco-labeling of firms (dischargers) or products.

● The ability to produce static efficiency is only one of the several criteria on which environmental policy instruments may be and have been compared. The additional ones that are emphasized in this chapter are:

– The extent to which the instrument's performance, especially with regard to static efficiency, requires the responsible public agency to have access to information, especially information about polluters' cost of reduction functions.
– The possibility of a 'second dividend' arising from the revenue produced by instruments such as emission charges or auctioned permits, when that revenue is substituted for distorting taxes on labor or products in the government's budget.
– The relative size of the incentive to find and adopt environment-saving technological advances.[4]
– The extent to which the instrument, in a particular application, is consistent with our ability to monitor and enforce continuing compliance.

Notice that the first three of these involve the same sort of application of *a priori* models as does static efficiency; and that compliance with instrument terms is also assumed in those models. The fourth criterion, what might be called 'monitorability', is not symmetric with the efficiency, incentive, and revenue 'theorems'. This one involves empirical assertions about the ability to observe and usually to measure the outcomes relevant to the instrument. Most commonly, it must be possible to verify in a particular application that each pollution source is living within the terms of its permit to discharge, or is paying the correct total emission charge. But other instruments with quite different monitoring requirements exist as well. For example, a prohibition from using a particular input implies that the agency be able to identify when that input is in fact 'slipped in'. The requirement that a particular technology be in place requires that the agency be able to observe the relevant equipment and verify that it is properly installed.[5]

- Finally, it seems desirable to draw attention to a bit of terminology, common in the instrument choice literature, but carrying such a load of misleading meaning as to in fact hinder the debate. This is the label 'command-and-control' (CAC) for every policy instrument not included under the (often very broad) category EI/MBI. There are two problems with this label. The first is that it loads the dice against a very large set of instruments by implying that they have some kinship to or connection with the spectacularly failed command-and-control economies of the former Soviet Union and its Eastern European allies. This connection is made explicitly by Panayotou, 1991 (p. 87):

  > The non-spectacular performance of the regulatory approach and the promising potential of the economic approach have encouraged many countries, including a few in the developing world, to explore more seriously the market-based incentives. The massive collapse of the command economies of Eastern Europe, which incidentally revealed the failure of the command systems not only in economic but also in environmental management, gave added impetus to the search for workable market-based incentives.

  But where is the usefulness of a parallel between an economic system in which production was determined by central planners and technology ordained by those same planners, and the use in pollution control of a permit allowing the owner/operator of a utility boiler, for example, to emit no more than X tons of SO_2 per month or year, with no requirement to use a particular technology to get there?

  This objection should not be taken to imply that CAC methods were never used in pollution control in OECD countries. Indeed, the second objection to the use of CAC as a label for 'everything else' is that it fails to reflect the complexity of the situation. To see this point concretely, consider Figure 8.1, in which four varieties of instrument are distinguished on the bases: does the instrument tell the source what to achieve or not? And, does the instrument tell the source how to go about achieving whatever is achieved or not?

	Tells the polluter what level of pollution to achieve	Does not specify what level of pollution to achieve
Tells the polluter *how* to control pollution	• US auto pollution control: tailpipe emission standards for CO, reactive hydrocarbons, NO$_x$, plus requirement that cars have catalytic conversion exhaust system Command and control	• Landfill design requirements • Secondary treatment requirement for municipal wastewater treatment
Does not specify how to control pollution	• Permit to discharge a certain quantity of air or water pollution per unit time *without* technology specified	• Emission charges • Deposit-refunds • Provision of information about firms or products to investors and consumers Pure economic incentives

Figure 8.1   Varieties of pollution control instruments with examples

The richness of the set of alternatives to 'pure' EI/MBI is illustrated by this pair of distinctions.[6] In particular, the classic alternative of the discharge standard, however derived, is seen to be neither an EI/MBI nor a CAC instrument in any useful sense.[7] Thus, however convenient it may be to have a two-label system for argument's sake, the CAC label carries too much freight to make it useful in that role. It will be useful to substitute Panayotou's 'regulatory alternatives' (RA) when it is necessary to refer to everything other than EI/MBI. More often than not, however, what will actually be at stake is the difference between a non-tradable discharge permit and a charge or marketable permit. (For a more inclusive list of available policy instruments, see Appendix 8.1.)

2.2   The Plan of the Chapter

The next section, 3, will set out the major elements of the case being made by the enthusiasts for application of EI/MBI in the developing-country context. These elements are the same as those found in most discussions of instrument choice in OECD countries, but the relative emphases given them tend to be different because of the differences in the economic situations. In section 4, the case outlined in section 3 will be examined in more detail. In particular, some key places where the assertions of the enthusiasts go too far will be pointed out. More generally, the institutional demands implied by elements of the arguments will be made explicit. Then, in section 5, the institutional theme will be expanded and a different consensus discussed, this one about the relative scarcity of institutional resources, both public and private, in developing countries. In section 4, the chapter turns to the matter of developing-country efforts to employ EI/MBI. It will be seen that many countries have one or more versions of these instruments on their books. The commentary of observers, however, suggests that on the ground, as opposed to on the books, the actual applications are tentative and not hugely successful. The last section, 6, will attempt to tie things together by linking institutional capacity building to 'practice'. In brief, the argument will be that a country is unlikely to be successful in policy result terms if it simply sets out to build 'institutional capacity' through rewriting laws and training a few bureaucrats, and then turns on the EI/MBI policy implementation switch. Rather, it will be argued that institutional capacity is built by attacking policy problems with instruments that are chosen to be appropriate for the existing conditions and then altering and adapting both the institutional forms and rules and the instruments themselves as capacity grows. Bell (1997) has called this process the creation of a 'culture of compliance', a phrase that seems especially apt because the analyses of experience with EI/MBI in developing countries frequently find that failure to achieve compliance with whatever instrument is in use is the single largest implementation problem.[8]

3. THE CASE FOR MARKET-BASED INSTRUMENTS IN THE DEVELOPING-COUNTRY CONTEXT

Many papers in the literature make an *a priori* case for the desirability of EI/MBI in the developing-country context.[9] In the process of distilling their arguments, about a dozen of them will be cited. Because there seems to be broad agreement on the elements of the case, there is broad similarity in the structure and content of the papers, so it is not necessary to be completely inclusive to capture the important elements. Not surprisingly, the arguments depart from two major givens:

- that developing countries are, by definition, poor makes the saving of costs in pollution control especially important;
- that developing countries generally have unsatisfactory tax systems, heavily dependent on distorting import duties and export taxes, makes potential new sources of government revenue especially desirable.

Beyond these fundamentals, other points often, but by no means always, made include:

- that the industrial sectors of developing countries are often made up of many relatively small firms and that knowing much about such details as their pollution control costs would be a daunting task;
- that judicial systems in developing countries may operate with long lags;
- that technology may be a problem, either because industrial process technology tends to be old and 'dirty' or because treatment technology may not be 'appropriate' for local conditions. Both are attributed to the fact that the technologies tend to be imported from the OECD countries.[10]

Building on these foundational observations, the major elements of the case for EI/MBI are: static efficiency; saving of information costs; the 'second dividend' (or more simply, the revenue possibilities); the greater incentives for polluters to seek and put in place environment-saving technology when they face payments or opportunity costs for all units of discharge instead of just a requirement not to exceed a standard; and a 'self-enforcement' aspect to charges in particular. These are presented here and examined in the next major section.

3.1   Static Efficiency

Static efficiency is almost always the first element and cornerstone of the argument, and the motivation for it is almost always based on the observation that a pollution source facing a charge per unit of discharge (or holding a marketable permit with a price per unit discharge, whether buying or selling) will rationally equate his marginal cost of pollution reduction to the charge or price. This is taken, sometimes explicitly, sometimes implicitly, to imply that the aggregate of pollution control costs will be minimized whether the policy goal is stated as a total amount of discharge in a city (or region or nation) or the maintenance of an ambient environmental quality standard. Thus, consider several quotes from papers that span the decade of the 1990s:

> Emission charges are efficient means for achieving the desired level of environmental quality because they minimize the costs of pollution control by leaving the level of individual pollution control and the choice of technology to the polluter. (Panayotou, 1991, p. 100)

> In contrast to a [CAC] regulatory approach, that impose[s] specific mandatory actions on economic agents, economic instruments use market signals for influencing their behavior and are often highly efficient in achieving environmental targets chosen by regulators. Economic instruments leave it to participants to choose their own measures to reduce external environmental effects . . . (UN Commission on Sustainable Development, 1995, p. 17, paragraph 79)

The static efficiency advantages of direct EI instruments stem in part from the fact that they leave firms free to choose abatement technologies that minimize costs in their individual circumstances . . . Perhaps more important, direct EI instruments create incentives for individual firms to choose levels of abatement that minimize the aggregate costs of achieving a given level of environmental quality. (Blackman and Harrington, 2000, p. 11)

Frequently cited original sources for these arguments include Baumol and Oates (1971 and 1988).

3.2 Information Economy

Here the argument is that because the cost minimization cited as the basis for static efficiency is done by each source in a decentralized setting, nothing need be known by the agency about the abatement cost functions of the individual polluters. Again, here are quotes that capture the flavor of the argument against regulatory approaches and for EI/MBI.

This direct regulation . . . suffers from many weaknesses: . . . it requires that the environmental agency masters the technologies of both production and pollution control for hundreds of different types of industries and all their technological alternatives, a monumental task that detracts from the agency's principal monitoring function; [p. 97] [and] 'Enforcement is easier and simpler because charges require no knowledge of the production and abatement technologies of different industries . . . [p. 100] (Both from Panayotou, 1991)

For a CAC policy to achieve the same result [minimization of aggregate costs of achieving a given level of environmental quality], the regulator must know the marginal abatement cost of every polluter . . . (Blackman and Harrington, 2000, p. 11)

Command-and-control approaches could – in theory – achieve this cost-effective solution, but this would require that different standards be set for each pollution source, and, consequently, that policymakers obtain detailed information about the compliance costs each firm faces . . . By contrast, MBI provide for a cost effective allocation of the pollution control burden among sources without requiring the government to have this information (Stavins, 2000, p. 2)

3.3 Government Revenue Possibilities

If the policy instrument chosen for pollution control is either a charge per unit of pollutant emitted or an auctioned permit to emit so many pounds or tons of pollutant per period, the government obtains revenue while, presumably, pushing pollution sources to clean up. In the developing-country setting, new sources of revenue are typically seen as vital, and rather than entering into the complexities of the second dividend debate (for example

Goulder, 1995; Whalley, 1998; Bovenberg and Goulder, 1996; Goulder et al., 1999), the value of supplementing unsatisfactory tax collection systems is taken to be essentially self-evident.[11]

> Taxes and user [discharge] charges can make environmental management self-financing (and possibly even generate a fiscal surplus) rather than posing a continual drain on the government's limited resources. (O'Connor and Turnham, 1992, p. 20)[12]

> Second, market based approaches may have important fiscal consequences for governments . . . by raising revenues through user fees or environmental taxes [which in this source are taken to include emission charges]. These sums may be considerable. (World Bank, 1997a, p. 10)

> While [efficiency] is theoretically interesting, it misses the much more important practical point that . . . pollution taxes generate revenue . . . It is the revenue-raising advantages of MBIs much more than the efficiency gains, which has been most responsible for their application in developing countries. (Steele, 1999, p. 276)

3.4   Incentives for Environment-saving Technological Change

The key observation here is that a charge on emissions applying to all units of emission above zero, or a marketable permit scheme with a fully functioning market, means that every unit of emission has a clear cash or opportunity cost attached to it. This is in contrast, in this line of argument, to the situation with a non-marketable permit. Once the permitted level is achieved by discharge reductions, there is no incentive to reduce further, since only costs and no rewards would result.

> [With an emission charge] . . . the industry will be under constant pressure to develop more cost-efficient ways of reducing or abating pollution in order to reduce its control costs or payment of charges. (Panayotou, 1991, p. 100)

> By acting as continuous charges on pollution . . . MBIs encourage the search for better and better environmentally-friendly technology. While CAC approaches can induce technological change by setting standards slightly ahead of what is the 'best available technology', technology-based standards are typically static in concept. (Pearce, 1991, p. 52)

> [the regulatory approach] provides little incentive to technical improvement once compliance has been achieved. (O'Connor, 1999, p. 92)

> Because firms in direct EI programs can always increase profits by reducing emissions, such programs provide continuing incentives for emission reducing innovation. (Blackman and Harrington, 2000, p. 12)

> In contrast to command-and-control regulations, market based instruments have the potential to provide powerful incentives for companies to adopt cheaper and better pollution-control technologies. (Stavins, 2000, p. 2)

3.5 Self-enforcing Character

The phrase 'self-enforcing' is something of a show-stopper for economists generally, for the profession has a tendency to assume that parties subject to any policy instrument wielded by an environmental management agency, be these regulations or charges or whatever, will be motivated to try to find ways around the situation, that is, to cheat, in very direct common language. It appears, however, that the meaning of the phrase is that the use of charges on emissions, assuming accurate measurement of those emissions, implies that there is no need to enforce anything, as there would be if the instrument were a permit. Thus, if the measurements revealed a violation of the terms of a permit, the discharger would have to be penalized (perhaps after warnings and a chance to 'voluntarily' come into compliance). The penalty is the enforcement mechanism and its imposition might well require passage through a hugely inefficient judicial system. With the charge, the measurement leads to a bill – at least in a simple schematic version of the full process. So long as the bill is paid, there is no need to pursue 'enforcement' as a separate and resource-using activity.[13] Thus:

> . . . the incentive structure facing the polluter is such that it promotes self-enforcement. (Panayotou, 1991, p. 100)

> In a broad sense the term 'Market-based instruments of environmental policy' is used to cover all price-related and/or regulatory instruments that harness the commercial self-interest of actors (i.e. industry, farmers, transport users, or the population at large) for environmental goals. (GTZ, 1995, p. 1)

Taken together, the arguments presented above, in our words and those of the enthusiasts, seem to make a powerful case for the adoption of EI/MBI in developing countries. They are examined more closely in the following section in order to make clear just how powerful the case really is, for that in effect is what will be given up if other instruments are chosen for reasons such as the fragility of developing-country institutions.

4. THE CASE FOR EI/MBI EXAMINED AND RELATED TO INSTITUTIONAL DEMANDS

In this section, the case as just presented is examined in some detail, its strengths and weaknesses assessed, and its elements related to the demands they imply on institutional capacity, both public and private.

4.1 Static Efficiency

This is the weakest part of the case. The result that the enthusiasts take as writ (the result from the 1971 Baumol and Oates paper) is a special case. It assumes that only the sum of discharges matters, not the discharge locations. In the more general situation, as for regional air and water pollution, location does matter. This implies that a single charge level applied to all sources (or a single market price for discharge permits) cannot, in general, produce the lowest-cost meeting of given ambient quality standards. (This is demonstrated in Bohm and Russell, 1985.) Further, it has been shown (Russell, 1986) that the single charge or permit price solution cannot be asserted to be second best – more costly than that produced by individually tailored (to the sources) charges or the ambient permit system of Montgomery (1972), but cheaper than an arbitrary set of standards. (In the paper cited, the RA was a set of discharge standards determined by the 'rollback' method.) Evidence from a set of the regional models referred to above that demonstrates the result in particular settings may be found in Tietenberg (1985, table 9, pp. 68–9). There, cost results for 11 runs from eight models are summarized, with one column showing the ratio of costs of meeting the ambient requirements for the particular model using some version of a regulatory alternative to the cost using an emission permit trading system. In five of the 11 cases, the regulatory approach produces a cheaper solution. The lowest ratio is less than 0.5. That is, the regulatory approach is less than half as expensive as emission trading in that run.

As hinted at in the quotations reproduced above, part of the argument for efficiency in the proponent literature is the notion that, because each source minimizes its costs, the aggregate of costs is minimized. This amounts to a version of the fallacy of composition. Each source is minimizing the *sum* of its abatement costs and its charge payments. But if the marginal charge payment – the charge itself – is incorrect for the attainment of the least-cost solution to the regional ambient quality problem, then the sum of the individual costs will not be a minimum. (It *is* true that whatever total of discharges is attained will be attained at lowest total cost.)

As noted in section 2, there is a good reason why little is said about static efficiency in connection with newer EI/MBI, in particular the provision of information on polluters or their products. That reason is the lack of persuasive economic models by which the effect of information provision can be predicted. Proponents are thus limited to noting that it appears information can make a desirable difference (for example, on the environmental performance of firms: Afsah et al., 1996; Konar and Cohen, 1997; on consumer response to environmental product labels: Bjørner et al., 2002) and that it is comparatively cheap, especially if the agency relies on data supplied by the companies.

Finally, because it will be relevant in the next subsection, notice that a trial-and-error approach to finding a single charge resulting in the meeting of a given ambient standard is conceivable (if not necessarily desirable).[14] But if individualized charges are required, trial and error will be impossible in any even remotely practical sense.

4.2 Information Economy

If static efficiency is to be attained (lowest-cost meeting of given ambient quality standards) with either an EI/MBI or an RA, information on the marginal abatement costs of the sources involved will be required. This is true even in the simple case where location does not matter. The only way around this requirement is trial and error, and, as just noted, that only seems even conceptually feasible when a single charge for all sources can be optimal.[15] If a marketable discharge permit approach is chosen, in the context of ambient standards, the problem is more complex. Even though a single permit price cannot produce static efficiency in general, the total of permits available has to be chosen with an eye to the ambient standard. In particular, some attention has to be paid to the possibility of 'hot spots' – violations of the standards resulting from a particular pattern of trades. With information on marginal costs, this process would be a good deal more satisfactory than without, for patterns of likely trades could be predicted in a regional trading model, and the total of permits to be created could be tailored so that predicted trades did not lead to hot spots. Without that cost information, to be completely confident of avoiding hot spots, the total of permitted discharge would have to be reduced until no set of trades (tending to aggregate discharges at one or a few points) could produce hot spots. This would probably lead to serious over control. (See Kruitwagen et al., 2000 for a suggestion for 'guided' trading to attain the cost-effective solution while avoiding hot spots.)

In summary, attaining static efficiency requires cost information and, in the general case, a modeling exercise to find the optimal price or permit set. Alternatively it requires an ambient permit system, which demands sophisticated trading from private business people.

4.3 Government Revenue Possibilities

This may be the strongest part of the case for at least the revenue-raising versions of EI/MBI. At one level, if a developing country is chronically short of revenue, and probably under pressure from international agencies to fix a tax system heavily dependent on import and export levies, any new source of revenue, but especially one with the side benefit of pollution abatement, will be attractive. At a more sophisticated level, recent work (for example Goulder et al., 1999) has shown that, in the second-best world of pre-existing factor taxes, the tax interaction effect, which raises the costs to society of policy interventions aimed at pollution control, non-auctioned, even if tradable, permits are much less attractive relative to pollution taxes or auctioned permits because the revenue recycling of those instruments partially offsets the tax interaction effect.

But it does seem desirable not to oversell this, and some of the enthusiasts have responsibly pointed out the tension between the abatement and revenue goals (for example Serôa da Motta et al., 1999; UN Commission on Sustainable Development, 1995, p. 25, paragraphs 138 and 139). This tension can be expressed in different ways. One is to observe that only by the greatest good fortune will a charge (or permit auction price) that results in meeting the desired ambient quality standard be the one that maximizes government revenue. Another is to notice that the technology-encouraging characteristic of these instruments amounts to a constant pressure on the tax 'base'. An additional complication, as noted below, is that earmarking of the funds raised is often suggested, or even assumed, as part of the price of political feasibility. Earmarked funds, whether for environmental or other programs, are not, of course, equivalent to general revenues.

In addition, it is reasonable to ask just how important pollution-related EI/MBI revenues can be in the total revenue picture of a developing country. The answer would appear to be not very, though this is not to deny that every little bit can help. For example, the Swedish tax on carbon is said by Blackman and Harrington (2000) to have generated revenue in 1995 amounting to about 1 percent of the country's GDP, or perhaps 2–2.5 percent of government revenue needs. This is the result from a tax on a production (and consumption) input for which demand is almost certainly quite inelastic, at a level that doubled natural gas prices and almost doubled coal prices (though oil prices were only raised by 20 percent) and in a country with a highly efficient and reputedly honest tax service.[16] It would seem unlikely that more could be accomplished taxing discharges for which reduction technology is available, at rates consistent with political acceptability, and where tax collection is liable to corruption. As support for this speculation, note the figures quoted by Blackman and Harrington (2000) for Sweden's sulfur tax. This tax is said to generate only about 0.005 percent of the revenue of the carbon tax. It is set at a level equivalent to about $1 per pound of SO_2 generation, said to have been chosen to approximate the 'average marginal cost of abating sulfur emissions' (Blackman and Harrington, 2000, p. 19). Finally, a back-of-the-envelope calculation can be done based on some pollution control models of industrial processes created at Resources for the Future back in the 1970s (Russell, 1973; Russell and Vaughan, 1976). In these models, at levels of discharge reduction in the range roughly 60–80 percent (from the uncontrolled levels) charge payments were roughly equal to the resource costs of abatement.[17] Estimates of the national costs of abatement are of course subject to manifold caveats and no two seem to agree exactly, but figures well under 5 percent of GDP are common. While less pessimistic than the Swedish carbon tax results as a predictor of total charge revenue, this calculation does not suggest that a developing-country government should pin high hopes for fiscal betterment on pollution-related charges or permit auctions. In any case, these (effective) taxes are by no means trivial to collect. Monitoring is required, as discussed in the next subsection. Bills must be prepared, and payments made checked against emission reality.

4.4 Incentives for Technical Change

The relevant literature by now leaves no doubt that the incentives for environment-saving technical change produced by emission charges and regularly auctioned marketable permits are greater than those produced by unmarketable permits (the most likely regulatory alternative). And, certainly, technology specification tends to freeze in place the technology specified, thus in effect anchoring the scale of possible effects at zero. Some of the enthusiasts, including several quoted above, however, imply that the non-marketable permit offers no incentive to improve technology. This overstates the contrast between instrument types, but is perhaps understandable because it is clear that, with a non-marketable permit (a fixed discharge standard), there is no incentive to reduce discharges below the standard. It is still possible, however, to save costs by finding and adopting technology offering lower costs of getting to the permitted level. A problem for policy in the RA case, therefore, is how to gain an environmental quality improvement from the new technology. This would occur automatically with a charge or auctioned permit; as marginal abatement costs fell, so would discharges. To achieve this effect with a regulatory approach implies some version of 'ratcheting down'. For example, if the permit terms are 'technology based', as they are in US water pollution control law, the definition of 'best available technology' could be changed to take advantage of the technical advance. But, if it were known in advance that this were going to be done, the prospective gain from seeking the advance would be reduced – possibly even eliminated. Even if it were not known in advance the first time, it would be assumed for the future once the ratchet had been applied. Finally, however, it is worth pointing out that this line of argument goes beyond the social desirability of cost savings in pursuit of a given level of environmental quality and assumes the social desirability of better quality. This may have intuitive appeal, but it is clearly not logically supportable as a general proposition.[18] See, however, note 4.

4.5 Self-enforcing Character

It has already been suggested that the interpretation of this asserted characteristic rests on an assumption of meaningful monitoring. And monitoring is by far the tougher half of the monitoring and enforcement problem. In the context of this chapter, the point is that the 'self-enforcement' claim amounts to very little. Any policy instrument that sets limits or prices for discharges of pollutants requires the same sort of monitoring enterprise – one sophisticated enough to have a significant probability of detecting a violation of a limit or an incorrect charge payment. Setting up and operating of such a credible system is institutionally demanding, arguably at least as demanding as the collection of fines for the violation established by it. In addition, charge payments will in general be substantially larger than non-compliance fees and will therefore generate larger incentives for corruption of responsible officials, a problem mentioned frequently in the literature on the actual efforts at implementation of environmental controls generally in developing countries.

4.6 Summary

The lessons that emerge from the above examination of the case for using EI/MBI in developing country contexts are:

1. That case has frequently been exaggerated by its proponents. In particular:
   (a) Static efficiency (cost-effectiveness in the attainment of ambient quality standards) does not follow as the night the day from the adoption of an emission charge or marketable permit. Rather it would require a great deal of technical knowledge, including knowledge of abatement cost functions, unless an ambient marketable permit system were put in place – an experiment that no nation, in or out of the OECD club, has tried.
   (b) The asserted 'self-enforcing' character of EI/MBI has little practical meaning. Monitoring is necessary, whether to ensure that marketable permits are lived up to (and not used two or three times over after trades) or that the proper quantity of emissions

is being paid for under a charge. And successful monitoring takes organization, technical skill, and freedom from corruption.

(c)   The revenue aspect of charges or auctioned permits and the extra spur, which being the source of this revenue gives to polluters to search for better technology, are both real and potentially valuable. The revenue is probably quite limited, however, relative to government needs even in the short run. In the longer run, the two characteristics are clearly at odds, since the second erodes the tax base on which the first depends. Further, collecting this public revenue is by no means obviously easier than improving other parts of the tax system. It requires a well-organized, efficient and honest civil service.

2.   As emphasized above, capturing the advantages of EI/MBI is institutionally demanding – at least as much so as the RA routes. There is, fortunately for the world-view of the economics profession, no free lunch.

5.   INSTITUTIONAL CAPACITY AS A SCARCE RESOURCE IN DEVELOPING COUNTRIES

Section 4 stressed the institutional demands of environmental quality management, and the proposition that EI/MBI are at least as demanding on this dimension as the regulatory alternatives. This is important because there appears to be widespread agreement on the scarcity of such resources in developing countries. This is true both at what might called the synoptic level – data on many components of institutional design and functioning for many countries – and at the level of country- (or region-)specific commentary aimed specifically at analyzing environmental performance.

At the synoptic level, consider Table 8.1, which shows the characterization of public institutions by region modified from table 5 of Straub (2000, pp. 25–6). These characterizations are based on factor analysis of 17 variables covering 57 countries.

A very similar, though considerably more detailed picture, is painted by Payne and Losada (2000). These authors constructed their own data set for what they call 'institutional output categories' covering seven dimensions of what in this context may be called institutional capacity:

1.   (a)   Respect for the rule of law, enforcement
      (b)   Respect for the rule of law, corruption
2.   Predictability of policies and the legal framework
3.   Strength of system of checks and balances
4.   Extent of democratic political freedoms and civil liberties

Table 8.1   Characterization of public institutions by region

Region	Characteristics
Europe, North America and Oceania (High level of development)	Democratic and equilibrated political system Good institutions
Latin America and Caribbean (Relatively high level of development)	Democratic and equilibrated political system Bad institutions
Middle East and North Africa (Low level of development)	Undemocratic political system with few checks and balances Rather bad-quality institutions
Asia (Relatively low level of development)	Rather undemocratic political system with few checks and balances Intermediate institutional quality
Sub-Saharan Africa (Very low level of development)	Undemocratic political system with few checks and balances Relatively bad institutions

5. Effectiveness of market regulations and sectoral economic policies
6. Effectiveness in ensuring the efficient and equitable delivery of public goods and services.

The number of countries for which they have observations for all the underlying variables within each dimension is different across the dimensions, and, perhaps to skirt this limitation, they present the results relevant to our discussion as averages of dimension scores across groupings of countries. For every dimension, the 'high-income' countries score substantially higher on average than the next-best country grouping. That next grouping is Central and Eastern Europe for four dimensions, East Asia for two, and Latin America and the Caribbean for one. At the other end of this scale, the worst average scores are those for Sub-Saharan Africa, three times (tied twice); Former Soviet Republics, three times; Middle East and North Africa, twice (tied once); and South Asia (tied once).

Another example of quantitative comparison of institutional strength is shown in Table 8.2: aggregated data from Global Leaders of Tomorrow Environmental Task Force (2001), Annex 4, table of scores on the indicator labeled 'Regulation and Management', an environment-specific effort

*Table 8.2   Average regional scores on the regulation and management
indicator*

Region or group	Score
High-income countries (23)	0.74
South Asian countries (8)	0.24
Latin American/Caribbean countries (22)	−0.15
East Asian countries (8)	−0.22
Sub-Saharan African countries (25)	−0.26
Central and Eastern European countries (14)	−0.28
Former Soviet Union countries (10)	−0.59
Middle Eastern and North African countries (12)	−0.64

Source: Global Leaders of Tomorrow Environment Task Force (2001), Annex 4.

to capture regulatory capacity. The component indices of this summary indicator are: stringency and consistency of environmental regulation; degree to which environmental regulations promote innovation; percentage of land area under protected status; and number of sectoral environmental impact assessment guidelines. The scoring has been 'normalized' so that the mean of the country scores is zero. One suspects that the inclusion of the (nominally at least) protected land sub-indicator is responsible for a good deal of the difference in orderings observed between this and the previously reported rankings. In particular, the eastern and southern African countries show up well here and tend to pull up the Sub-Saharan country average. But the message is not fundamentally different: attempts to objectively compare institutional capacity across countries consistently show the poorest having the weakest public institutions.

Finally, not to flog the proverbial dead horse, qualitative comments about institutional weaknesses in developing countries are common in assessments of their experience with environmental policy alternatives and of their readiness to innovate in the direction (usually) of EI/MBI. Examples include: Gray (1991); Bernstein (1993); Oxford Analytica (1994); Lovei (1995); BCFSD (1995); IADB (1996); BNA (1997); Hirschmann (1999); Nolet (2000); Romero-Lankao (2000); and UNEP (2000).

At a finer level of detail, consider the specific weaknesses identified by commentators on developing-country institutions. Four problem areas are noted quite consistently.

1. A lack of well-trained people in the civil service bureaucracy – whether the training be technical, as in running and maintaining complex equipment; implementing regulations in the field; translating laws into

regulations; preparing cases against violators of regulations; or maintaining large databases. (For example, see Gray, 1991; Tribe, 1996;
UNEP, 2000; Huber et al. 1996; Kozeltsev and Markandya, 1997;
Romero-Lankao, 2000; Bell, 2001; and perhaps most comprehensively,
Hirschmann, 1999, who provides a history of changing fashions in
development, of failed efforts to fix the civil service in line with the
fashions of the decade, and of the negative impact all this has had on
public institutional capabilities.)

2. Lack of information available to responsible agencies, including such
    fundamental information as inventories of polluters and pollutants in
    the baseline situation. (For example Tribe, 1996; BNA, 1997; UNEP,
    2000.)
3. Quite specifically, a lack of point-source pollution monitoring equip-
    ment and of people trained to use it and analyze and interpret the
    results. (For example IADB, 1996; BNA, 1997; Kozeltsev and
    Markandya, 1997; Lakhan et al., 2000; and Nolet, 2000.)
4. A ubiquitous problem of corruption, usually traceable to underpayment
    of the civil service and a sort of tacit acceptance of the result – the use
    of the regulatory system for private gain rather than the achievement of
    intended public benefit. (For example Oxford Analytica, 1994, especially
    ch. 7; Buscaglia et al., 1995; BNA, 1997; Ardila, 2000; Nolet, 2000.)

The result, regularly noted in surveys of country experience, tends to be a
gulf between the laws and regulation on the books and what polluters are
actually responding to in the field. Probably most important is the widespread failure to monitor discharges effectively. The frequency of measurement tends to be too low to imply a significant probability of finding a
violation of permit terms or a mispayment of a charge. There may also be
a failure to measure with 'surprise', so that what is observed is not a sample
of what is actually happening; rather it is a sample of what the polluter is
capable of achieving given sufficient advance warning. When courts are
relied on for enforcement (punishment) the process can be hugely drawn
out so that, even if a penalty is eventually extracted, its present value at the
time non-compliance is chosen as a strategy is very low. This reflects inadequate resources devoted to the judicial system, the availability of delay-
ing tactics, and quite possibly better lawyering available to the private sector
(for example Buscaglia et al., 1995).

Short of even going to court, the search by civil servants for 'rents' to
supplement low salaries means that discovered violators are likely to be able
to make side-payments, amounting to less than possible penalties, directly
to the local enforcement group.

When charges for pollution emissions are in place, their values seem regularly to be set and more or less forgotten, so that their real values are eroded by inflation. And, since high levels of inflation have been endemic in the developing world (including here the states of the former Soviet Union and its Eastern European allies), the erosion can be quite rapid and dramatic (for example Golub and Gurvich, 1997 on the Russian experience from 1990 to 1996 with pollution charges).

While it is fairly easy to identify the symptoms of institutional weakness, it has proved to be far from easy to fix the problem. Indeed, Hirschmann (1999) is pessimistic about even the possibility of repair, finding that the enthusiasm for privatization and the shrinking of governments, coupled with the budget crises that have reduced salaries of civil servants to very low levels, may together have pushed 'morale and ethics of the bureaucracy' so low as to preclude turning things around (p. 303). Further, studies such as that by Straub (2000), attempting to 'explain' differential institutional quality across countries, are not encouraging. Straub concludes: 'the results prove not robust . . . yielding no clear insights. We conclude regarding the fragility of existing data, in particular with respect to the incentive structure, and the need for a better theoretical understanding of the underlying mechanisms.' This has not stopped national and multilateral development agencies from generating recommendations for 'institutional capacity building'. Prominent examples include OECD reports stressing the development of legal structure, including property rights (OECD, 1993 and Opschoor, 1994); work by and for the Inter-American Development Bank (for example, Dourojeanni, 1994; Oxford Analytica, 1994; Tlaiye and Biller, 1994; and IADB, 1996); the UN Environment Program (UNEP, 2000); and USAID (for example, the work of the Harvard Institute for International Development, as in C4EP/NIS 1996). The ideas and recommendations to be found in these published and unpublished works are neither surprising nor outrageous. They attempt to identify solutions for exactly the weaknesses noted above:

- Designing better organizations and legislation
- Training civil servants and judges in necessary technical matters for implementation, monitoring and enforcement of policies
- Encouraging greater and better-informed public participation
- Identifying sources of 'sustainable' funding for environmental institutions.

Nonetheless, the institutional problems persist. Though particular observers argue that real improvements can be identified in particular places, seen broadly it would appear that progress is slow. Consider this statement from UNEP (2000), referring to Latin America (p. 92):

Environmental policy implementation is often difficult given the lack of appropriate control, monitoring and start-up mechanisms. In some cases the legal framework for environmental management is diluted in numerous legal texts and throughout diverse institutions, and environmental matters are often delegated to several public institutions at different political levels. The creation of new policies and institutions does not always include a revision of previous legislation.

It is not necessary, nor is it particularly helpful, to posit incompetence on the one side or perversity on the other as an explanation for slow progress. Changing institutions is inevitably slow work, if for no other reason than that institutions reflect and are part of culture more broadly. But there may be one or two more specific observations that imply actions other than just exercising patience. One is from Turnham, a long-time student of the environmental management process in developing countries (Turnham, 1991). He worried, back in the early days of the 'new thrust on environmental management', that relatively too much effort was going into the design of new programs and relatively too little into the analysis of their subsequent success or failure. Arguing from what he, at least, saw as the failure of the World Bank's assault on poverty under Robert McNamara, he claims there was then too little learning from experience, a result that seemed likely to be repeated in the environmental policy area (pp. 377–8). A second sort of observation comes from Bell, who has participated in institution building in several countries in Central and Eastern Europe. Her analyses of successes and failures suggest that obstacles to progress are created by the combination of the inevitable awkwardness of outside-in efforts ('We're from Washington [or London or Paris] and we're here to help you'); the fundamental difficulties of communication across language and cultural barriers; and the asymmetry of motivations of the parties (for example Bell, 2001).

6.   EXPERIMENT AND EXPERIENCE WITH EI/MBI IN DEVELOPING COUNTRIES

To say that more than a few observers share our concern about institutional capacity, and that fixing the problems identified is proving to be far from easy is, of course, not to say that EI/MBI are absent from the pollution control policy tool kits actually employed by developing countries. Quite the contrary, a large number of countries have adopted specific versions of these instruments, and the adoptions have involved a variety of pollution settings.[19] Inventories and at least qualitative assessments of performance are available. Several of these have already been referred to in the institutional sections, because the performance remarks made in them tend to identify institutional weakness as the key to poor instrument performance when that is observed. In any case, Table 8.3 summarizes information on the prevalence of the instruments, and Table 8.4 contains a list of country-specific studies of applications of EI/MBI. (Most of the country studies include many instruments that are outside the terms of reference chosen here. These include changing subsidies on energy and water, and introducing new fishery and forestry management tools.)

Table 8.3 contains some interesting patterns. Most obviously there appear to be regional 'fashions' in adoptions of EI/MBI. The countries of Central and Eastern Europe (plus Russia) are committed to emission charges on specific air and water pollutants. A couple of Asian countries have air or water charges, and five use sewage treatment charges, as do four Latin American nations. But the latter regional group is far more committed to using lump sum and marginal subsidies (the latter as deposit–refund systems), albeit in fairly limited contexts. Both Asian and Latin American nations have information provision programs in place, the most widely publicized of which is the PROPER program in Indonesia (with a spin-off to the Philippines). It is not clear from our sources why these patterns exist, though some reflection suggests that one causal factor may well be the nature of the environmental challenges faced. Thus, in Central and Eastern Europe, there exists a substantial amount of heavy industry, much of it with an aging and energy-inefficient capital stock, and often with a history of using 'dirty' fuels such as 'brown' coal. It is easy to see that air pollution could seem the most urgent problem in such circumstances. Latin America, on the other hand, faces challenges created by rapid and essentially uncontrolled urbanization. Prominent among these are lack of piped water supplies with intake treatment, and 'neighborhood' water pollution from lack of household sanitation facilities. Water supply, sewering and sewage treatment are high-priority efforts (for example Russell et al., 2001).

Beyond those observations, however, it is difficult to see reasons for some parts of the pattern. For example, why should the Latin American and Caribbean countries so enthusiastically have embraced subsidies, both lump sum and marginal (in particular, deposit–refund systems for beverage containers)? Granted that the latter instrument changes the burden of proof in situations of difficult monitoring, but why confine the application to beverage containers (with the one Mexican car-battery exception)? Along similar lines, the information-provision programs aimed at the performance of firms (as opposed to the characteristics of products) have explicitly been sold as substitutes for highly imperfect systems of monitoring and enforcement. The descriptions of the results in Indonesia (for example, Asfah et al., 1996; Wheeler, 1997) tend to be enthusiastic, and the World Bank's clout lies behind the effort. So perhaps a similar survey in 2005 will see a significant expansion of their application. For now, the

Table 8.3 Use of economic instruments in transition and less developed countries

Instrument	Asia	Central/Eastern Europe	Former Soviet Union	Latin America & Caribbean	Other
1. Emission charges, air[c] (a) Carbon monoxide		Czech Rep. (e)[a] Estonia (e) Lithuania (e 70) Poland (e) Slovakia (e)	Russia (e)		
(b) Sulfur dioxide	China	Bulgaria (e 70) Czech Rep. (e) Estonia (e 50) Hungary (e 70) Lithuania (e 70) Poland (e) Slovakia (e)	Russia (e)		
(c) Nitrogen oxides		Bulgaria (e 70) Czech Rep. (e) Estonia (e 50) Hungary (e 70) Lithuania (e 70) Poland (e) Slovakia (e)	Russia (e)		
(d) Combined or unspecified	China [Korea][b]		Kazakhstan		Egypt

2. Emission charges (water)

(a) BOD

Malaysia	Bulgaria (e 70)	Brazil
Philippines	Czech Rep.	Colombia (e)
[Korea]	Estonia (e)	
	Lithuania (e 70)	
	Poland	
	Romania	
	Slovakia	
	Slovenia	

(b) Total suspended solids

[Korea]	Bulgaria (e 70)	Colombia (e)
	Estonia (e)	
	Lithuania (e 70)	
	Poland (e)	

(c) Nitrogen and phosphorus

	Estonia (e)	
	Lithuania (e 70)	

(d) Combined or unspecified

China	Latvia	Brazil
India	Slovakia (e)	Mexico
[Korea]		
Malaysia		
Philippines		
Thailand		

(e) Sewage treatment charges

China		Brazil
Indonesia		Chile
Malaysia		Colombia
Singapore		Mexico
Thailand		

Table 8.3 (continued)

Instrument	Asia	Central/Eastern Europe	Former Soviet Union	Latin America & Caribbean	Other
3. Solid waste disposal fees	[Korea] Thailand	Czech Rep. Estonia (e) Hungary Latvia Poland (e) Slovakia	Russia	Ecuador Venezuela	
4. Hazardous waste disposal fees	China Thailand				
5. Other taxes/fees					
(a) Leaded gas price differential	Philippines Turkey			Mexico	Egypt
6. Tradable permits or quotas					
(a) Air pollution		Czech Rep. Poland (e)	Kazakhstan	Chile	
(b) Ozone-depleting substances	Singapore				
(c) Vehicles	Singapore	Latvia		Mexico	
7. Subsidies					
(a) Capital or lump sum	Sri Lanka	Bulgaria Czech Rep. Estonia Hungary	Russia	Barbados Brazil Chile Colombia	

		Lithuania Poland Slovakia	Ecuador Jamaica Mexico Venezuela
(b) Marginal/deposit–refund			
(i) Beverage containers	[Korea] Taiwan	Czech Rep. Hungary Poland	Barbados Bolivia Brazil Chile Colombia Ecuador Jamaica Mexico Peru Trinidad and Tobago Venezuela
(ii) Auto batteries			Mexico
(iii) Other or unspecified	Bangladesh [Korea] Philippines		
8. Information – firm or product 'labels'	Bangladesh China Indonesia [Korea] Philippines Taiwan Thailand	Hungary	Bolivia Brazil Chile Ecuador Mexico

Table 8.3 (continued)

Instrument	Asia	Central/Eastern Europe	Former Soviet Union	Latin America & Caribbean	Other
9. Liability				Bolivia Colombia Trinidad and Tobago	

Notes:
[a] Stavins's table 1 indicates where it is known that revenue from charges is earmarked and the percentage split between environmentally earmarked and general fund uses. Here (e) means that 100 percent of revenues are earmarked for environmental funds at one or more jurisdictional levels; (e 50) or (e 70) indicate 50 percent or 70 percent of revenue is earmarked.
[b] Korea, that is the Republic of South Korea, is put in brackets because it recently joined the OECD, but is still in some ways institutionally 'developing'.
[c] Anderson and Lohot (1997) list Romania as having air pollution charges but describe them as penalties for failing to meet a standard.

Sources: Serôa da Motta et al. (1999); Stavins (2000); World Bank (1997a); Anderson and Lohof (1997).

Table 8.4 Citations to sources of case studies of particular countries

Argentina	IADB (1996); Margulis (n.d.)
Barbados	Huber et al. (1996)
Bolivia	IADB (1996); Huber et al. (1996)
Brazil	Tlaiye and Biller (1994); Huber et al. (1996); IADB (1996); Benjamin and Weiss (1997)
Chile	Huber et al. (1996)
China	Blackman and Harrington (2000)
Colombia	Tlaiye and Biller (1994); Huber et al. (1996); Ardila (2000)
Czech Republic	Opschoor (1994)
Ecuador	Huber et al. (1996)
Estonia	Opschoor (1994)
Guyana	Lakhan et al. (2000)
Hungary	Opschoor (1994)
India	Bradley (1998)
Indonesia	O'Connor (1993)
Jamaica	Huber et al. (1996)
Kenya	Ayoo and Jama (1999)
Korea	O'Connor (1993)
Mexico	Huber et al. (1996); Margulis (n.d.); Bradley (1998)
Paraguay	IADB (1996)
Peru	Huber et al. (1996)
Poland	Opschoor (1994); Żylicz (1995); Anderson and Fiedor (1997); Bradley (1998); Blackman and Harrington (2000)
Russia	Opschoor (1994); Kozeltsev and Markandya (1997)
Slovak Republic	Opschoor (1994)
South Pacific Island States	Hunt (1997)
Sri Lanka	Steele (1999)
Taiwan	O'Connor (1993)
Thailand	O'Connor (1993)
Uruguay	IADB (1996)
Venezuela	Huber et al. (1996); Ardila (2000)

information-provision instrument seems to be spreading in Asia with outposts – less well documented – in Latin America.

So much for cataloging efforts to use EI/MBI. Eventually, it will be useful to have a reasonably comprehensive assessment of these efforts. For now, much of what is in the law books appears to be only imperfectly implemented in the field, and even for systems that are in operation, the periods involved have been quite short. (Alternatively, as in Russia and Central and Eastern Europe, charging schemes dating back to Communist days, but admittedly ineffective then, are being 'repaired' by new governments and responded to by newly privatized industry.) Relying on the research reported in the Table 8.4 sources, however, one can at least get an impression of the experience so far. Some of this has already been referred to; in particular, if there is an over-arching theme it is that monitoring (and thus enforcement) has been almost everywhere weak, for all the reasons noted in the section on institutional weakness.

In addition, there is a widespread problem of the levels of charges being too low, either because they were set that way for political reasons or because inflation has eroded their real value. On a more positive note, there has been reasonably good experience, so far, with the use of 'environmental funds' at every level of jurisdiction, from local to national. These have most often been funded from the proceeds of emission taxes (see Table 8.3 for evidence on the extensive use of earmarking) and used to pay for pollution control equipment, both public and private. The effect seems to be that charges do little to affect discharges, but subsidized investment in control equipment is seen as more successful, at least in the short run.[20]

7.   A CONCLUDING SUGGESTION

The environmental economics literature on policy instruments rests on a carefully developed base of *a priori* arguments (including regional modeling studies under this label) exploring the advantages of EI/MBI in relation to regulatory alternatives. Two aspects of this literature seem to have been underplayed – even ignored – by the most enthusiastic proponents of the application of EI/MBI in developing countries. The first of these is that there are links among the dimensions of advantage that imply the impossibility of the proberbial free lunch. Two important examples are: (1) achieving static efficiency in the general case in which source location matters requires either that the responsible agency have an enormous amount of polluter-specific knowledge and the technical ability to use it in a regional optimizing model, or that tradable ambient permit systems be put in place, which would place heavy demands on the skills of the sources themselves; and (2) revenues gained from charges are in tension with desired incentive effects, are politically expensive, and over time tend to erode the tax base by encouraging technological innovation that cuts discharges. The second major aspect of the literature that requires emphasizing is that it is all based on assumed compliance, whether this means emitting no more than is consistent with owned (tradable or non-tradable) permits or paying a charge on actual emissions.

The first observation serves as a reminder that the cost of not adopting EI/MBI is a good deal lower than many of the proponents implicitly or explicitly claim. The second, when taken with the near-universal observation that compliance monitoring is the weakest link in the developing-country institutional chain, suggests that it may be worth considering alternative paths into the future. Such paths would be designed to avoid overtaxing weak institutions in the early days, and to be adjustable as institutional capability grew. Indeed, it is possible to view the process of policy evolution as part of the institutional development exercise – as cause as well as result. The goal may be seen as creating Bell's 'culture of compliance', in which social norms make compliance the first rather than the last choice (Bell, 1997). Two examples will give a bit more life to this rather abstract notion:

1. One possible path would begin with a technology requirement – all sources in a certain industry would be required to install a particular technology. This is easy to monitor. Almost as easy would be the requirement that it be kept operational. (For some technologies, the remaining variable costs of actual operation would be small, raising the probability that this would occur.)

    As discharge monitoring capability and general civil service morale increased, the technology requirement could be translated into a technology-based discharge standard, as in the US water pollution control system permits. These would not require the technology *per se*, but only the results it was judged by experts as capable of achieving.

    Finally, the permits could be made marketable when the information and record-keeping infrastructure was judged ready to support the move. For some small water pollution sources, or any source appropriately located, the path might be short-circuited with a requirement that they be connected to sewers (possibly with pre-treatment) and that all sewage be treated in certain ways before discharge. Sewer charges could be presumptive, based on industry, capital vintage and size.

Lest this proposal be seen as merely the nattering of eccentric 'instrument Luddites', compare it with the analysis by Cole and Grossman (1999) of pollution control policy in the USA. Their view is essentially that, whether by conscious design or happy political accident, policy evolved here along similar lines – from instruments that economists found less than desirable, toward applications of EI/MBI – as institutional capabilities grew.

A second possible example could build on the notion of the self-financed marginal subsidy found most often in deposit–refund systems.

2. The idea would be to begin with a tax on inputs based on their presumed implications for pollution discharges in the absence of control

efforts. The source could claim a *pro rata* refund by proving to the satisfaction of the responsible agency that it was engaged in predischarge control that was accounting for some claimed percentage reduction. This owes something to the presumptive charge of Eskeland, to which it is a close cousin (Eskeland and Devarajan, 1996). The system could be started at the simplest end, where input characteristics translate very directly into pollution loads (as in sulfur in coal and fuel oil used in utility boilers) and gradually extended to more complex settings, such as sulfur in crude oil charged to refineries, where intervening technologies leads to multiple fates and release pathways.

The point, to make it a final time, is not to deny that EI/MBI are useful tools, or to oppose their use in appropriate settings. It is rather that they are being oversold to developing countries, many of which will find it difficult to meet the implied institutional demands. And it seems there are other ways to skin the cat of sustainable development – ways that both take current institutional weakness seriously and provide practice fields on which new strengths can be developed. The above suggestions only scratch the surface of the set of such possibilities. The application of imagination and technical skill, with which the environmental policy world has been blessed, will doubtless produce new and more promising ideas, if it can free itself from infatuation with EI/MBI.[21]

NOTES

1. For example, almost ubiquitously cited is the 1971 paper by Baumol and Oates that sets out some efficiency results to be discussed further below. Also Baumol and Oates (1988).
2. As Taylor (1993) points out, however, it is not easy to trace the lineage of the World Bank's enthusiasm, since the Bank tended to cite primarily its own publications and working papers. In particular, it did not cite any of the OECD papers noted in the text.
3. A section of the literature (for example Johnson, 1967; Atkinson and Lewis, 1974; Roach et al., 1981; Eheart et al., 1983; Krupnick, 1986; Seskin et al., 1983; Spofford, 1984; and O'Ryan, 1996; summarized by Tietenberg, 1996) 'demonstrates' the efficiency results for EI/MBI using such regional cost minimization models containing empirically based control cost models and mathematical representations of the regional environment. These are, however, just numerical extensions of the assumptions behind the more abstract results, not demonstrations that those assumptions are accurate representations of reality. For example, one cannot prove with a model that real tradable permit markets will proceed in a purely competitive and rational fashion.
4. This criterion may be seen as the practical fallback position when the 'gold standard' would be dynamic efficiency with endogenous technological change. It is important to remember that there is no guarantee that a larger incentive is better in the full dynamic efficiency sense. It is emphasized in the literature because that is the problem economists can currently solve.
5. Monitoring is logically prior to 'enforcement', which is generally taken to mean the steps taken to punish noncompliance, most often application of fines. The existence of money

penalties at the enforcement stage has led to a certain amount of terminological confusion in the literature on instrument choice (for example, Panayotou, 1991, p. 94; Opschoor, 1994, p. 21; UN Commission on Sustainable Development, 1995; Serôa da Motta et al., 1999; Steele, 1999).

6. Marketable permits might arguably go in either of the bottom two boxes. At any one time, the source does face an upper limit on pollution discharge (what to achieve). That upper limit can be modified by market transactions; but this is not possible for all the sources collectively. The total upper limit is fixed. The provision of information as a regulatory tool certainly belongs in the lower right-hand box (not what/not how), but because information operates on polluters via perceptions and decisions of investors or consumers, it is clearly not entirely symmetric with emission charges.

7. Discharge permits can be derived from optimizing regional models, from the *notional* application of 'best' technologies (as in US water pollution permits) or via something as simple as equal percentage 'rollbacks'.

8. 'Compliance' when the instrument is a permit clearly means living within it. 'Compliance' in the context of a charge system has to mean paying for the correct amount of discharge per unit time.

9. Here is a sample that covers the decade of the 1990s, including 2000. No claim for completeness should be inferred: Lyon (1989); Anderson (1990); Eröcal (1991, including Panayotou, 1991 and Pearce, 1991); Halter (1991); Eskeland and Jimenez (1992); O'Connor and Turnham (1992); Bernstein (1993); Bruce and Ellis (1993); Panayotou (1994); GTZ (1995); Hansen (1995); UN Commission on Sustainable Development (1995); World Bank (1997a); O'Connor (1999); Steele (1999); Blackman and Harrington (2000); Stavins (2000); World Bank (2000); and Seckler (n.d.).

10. This point about technology may suggest to the reader the 'clean development mechanism' (CDM), created by the Kyoto Protocol. This is an internationally created policy instrument that, in effect, legitimizes greenhouse gas emission trades between developed and developing countries (for example Fichtner et al., 2001). Developing countries are free to participate or not in such trades, but the adoption (or not) of the instrument itself is not within their purview. Should a country choose to trade under the CDM by selling emission 'rights', it would face a separate decision on how to live up to its end of the bargain – what purely domestic policy instruments to choose. The CDM is not included in the rest of this chapter, but the interested reader may want to consult Painuly (2001); Philibert (2000); and Forsyth (1999); in addition to the paper noted above.

11. The second dividend was originally proposed as an additional advantage of revenue-raising EI/MBI, for the revenue came without a deadweight loss – or so it seemed in the partial equilibrium setting – but substituted for taxes on labor or product sales that produced such losses. Things are much more complicated in the general equilibrium setting. See, for example, the papers cited above in the text.

12. This quote raises the question of earmarking of the funds raised – by assuming it will be done. While earmarking is generally frowned on in the public finance literature it is often taken to be politically necessary to getting EI/MBI adopted in developing countries (for example O'Connor, 1999, pp. 99 and 106; Steele, 1999, p. 275).

13. A certain amount of confusion is introduced into the discussion when some commentators classify the enforcement fines themselves (non-compliance penalties) as EI/MBI. For example, Bernstein (1993); Steele (1999); Serôa da Motta et al. (1999).

14. Trial and error seems unlikely to be desirable because of the costs of the errors – stranded capital from overinvestment and cost penalties for building up capacity in too-small increments – and because of the long lag each trial would imply.

15. If the agency knew the marginal damage attributable to each source, and if that were constant, there would be no need for any cost information. This, in essence, is the earliest case for charges provided by Kneese (1964). If the marginal damages were not constant (damages were non-linear functions of discharge), the form of the charge would have to be more complicated, but if it were properly structured, cost information would not be necessary.

16. The tax is quite complicated in detail, and discriminates against CO_2 emitters who do

not compete in world markets. But it does cover 'almost all CO_2 emissions' (personal communication from Peter Bohm, July 2002). Bohm also confirms the above rough estimate of government revenue produced.

17. Had the marginal cost of abatement been linear, it is easy to show that equality of charge payments and resource costs would occur at an emission charge that inspired a reduction to one-third of the uncontrolled level.

18. Not usually mentioned in the case for EI/MBI in developing countries is the advantage of flexibility in the face of change that is a property of marketable permits. In the developing, which is of course to say, changing, context, a charge would require constant updating just to maintain the originally desired ambient quality level, forgetting efficiency. This would not be necessary with a marketable permit system, though the caveat about hot spots would apply.

19. The number of countries involved is not noticeably affected by adopting modest limits on what constitutes an EI/MBI. In particular, non-compliance fines are not taken to be EI/MBI, but part of the enforcement structure required with any regulatory or economic approach. Nor is the abandonment of environmentally harmful subsidies counted, though this is a useful policy action and undoubtedly 'economic'.

20. It is worth pointing out that earmarking and 'recycling' into environmental investments is not what the double-dividend argument is about, unless those subsidies would have been paid out of other revenue sources. The country assessments lead the reader to conclude that the charge revenues are treated as extra, not as a substitute for labor or sales taxes.

21. It is worth reminding readers here that the first operational version of something very like a tradable discharge permit system was created by imaginative perople within US EPA as a way around the political train wreck looming because new businesses would not have been allowed to start up within air quality non-attainment areas.

REFERENCES

Afsah, S., B. Laplante and D. Wheeler (1996), 'Controlling Industrial Pollution: A New Paradigm,' policy research working paper 1672, Washington, DC: World Bank (October).

Anderson, Dennis (1990), 'Environmental Policy and the Public Revenue in Developing Countries,' environment working paper No. 36, Environment Dept, Washington, DC: World Bank (July).

Anderson, Glen D. and Boguslaw Fiedor (1997), 'Environmental Change in Poland,' environmental discussion paper No. 16, C4EP Project, Harvard Institute for International Development (January).

Anderson, Robert and Andrew Lohof (1997), *The United States Experience with Economic Instruments in Environmental Pollution Control Policy*, Washington, DC: Environmental Law Institute, http://yosemite.epa.gov/ee/epalib/incent.nsf/.

Ardila, Sergio (2000), 'Lessons From Water Pollution Control Efforts in Colombia and Venezuela,' in R. López and J.C. Jordán (eds), *Sustainable Development in Latin America: Financing and Policy Working in Synergy*, Washington, DC: Organization of American States.

Atkinson, Scott and D. Lewis (1974), 'A Cost-Effective Analysis of Alternative Air Quality Control Strategies,' *Journal of Environmental Economics and Management*, **1**(3) November, 237–50.

Ayoo, C. and M.A. Jama (1999), 'Environmental Taxation in Kenya,' in T. Sterner (ed.), *The Market and the Environment: The Effectiveness of Market-Based Policy Instruments for Environmental Reform*, Cheltenham, UK and Northampton, USA: Edward Elgar, 301–18.

Baumol, William and Wallace Oates (1971), 'The Use of Standards and Prices for Protection of the Environment,' *Swedish Journal of Economics*, **73**(1), 42–54.

Baumol, William and Wallace Oates (1988), *The Theory of Environmental Policy*, 2nd edn, Cambridge: Cambridge University Press, ch. 11.

BCFSD (Business Council for Sustainable Development) (1995), *Environmental Policies in Latin America*, Policy Series No. 1, Business Council for Sustainable Development, Monterrey, Mexico (January).

Bell, Ruth Greenspan (1997), 'Developing a Culture of Compliance in the International Environmental Regime,' *Environmental Law Reporter*, **XXVII**(8), 10402–12.

Bell, Ruth Greenspan (1999), 'Environmental Policy, Legislation and Regulation in Central and Eastern Europe,' *The Environdialogue Website: Mapping Environmental Change* [www.environdialogue.net/legpol.shtml].

Bell, Ruth Greenspan (2001), 'Reaching Across the Communication Gulf: Reflections on the Challenges of Environmental Assistance Programs,' discussion paper 01–05; Washington, DC: Resources for the Future (January).

Benjamin, A.H. and Charles Weiss Jr (1997), 'Economic and Market Incentives as Instruments of Environmental Policy in Brazil and the United States,' *Texas International Law Journal*, **32**, 67–95.

Bernstein, J.D. (1993), *Alternative Approaches to Pollution Control and Waste Management: Regulatory and Economic Instruments*, Urban Management and the Environment, Washington, DC: World Bank.

Bjørner, Thomas Bue, Lars Gårn Hansen and Clifford S. Russell (2002), 'Environmental Labelling and Consumer Choice: An Empirical Analysis of the Effect of the Nordic Swan,' AKF working paper, Copenhagen, DK (April).

Blackman, Allen and W. Harrington (2000), 'The Use of Economic Incentives in Developing Countries: Lessons From International Experience With Industrial Air Pollution,' *Journal of Environment and Development*, **9**(1), 5–44.

BNA (1997), *Environmental Laws on the Books in Latin America. But Enforcement, Environmental Infrastructure Lacking*, special report, Washington, DC: Bureau of National Affairs (19 February), 176–81.

Bohm, Peter and Clifford S. Russell (1985), 'Comparative Analysis of Alternative Policy Instruments,' in A.V. Kneese and J. Sweeney (eds), *Handbook of Natural Resource and Energy Economics*, New York: North-Holland, 395–460.

Borregaard, Nicola, Claudia Sepúlveda and Patrico Bernal Edmundo Claro (1997), 'Instrumento económicos al servicio de la politica ambiental en Chile,' *Ambiente y Desarrolo*, **13**(1), 6–19.

Bovenberg, A.L. and L.H. Goulder (1996), 'Optimal Environmental Taxation in the Presence of Other Taxes: General Equilibrium Analysis,' *American Economic Review*, **86**(4), 985–1000.

Bradley, Theresa (ed.) (1998), *Public Finance Restructuring for Sustainable Development in Emerging Market Economies*, Washington, DC: World Resources Institute (September).

Bruce, N. and Gregory M. Ellis (1993), 'Environmental Taxes and Policies for Developing Countries,' working paper, Policy Research/Public Economics, Policy Research Department, Washington, DC: World Bank (September).

Buscaglia, Edgardo, Jr, Maria Dakolias and William Ratliff (1995), 'Judicial Reform in Latin America: A Framework for National Development,' Stanford, CA: Hoover Institution, Stanford University.

Cole, D.H. and P.Z. Grossman (1999), 'When is Command-and-control Efficient?'

Institutions, Technology, and the Comparative Efficiency of Alternative Regulatory Regimes for Environmental Protection,' *Wisconsin Law Review*, **5**, 887–938.

Dourojeanni, Marc J. (1994), 'Environmental Performance of IDB Member Countries,' Washington, DC: Inter-American Development Bank memo (7 March).

Eheart, J., E. Brill and R. Lyon (1983). 'Transferable Discharge Permits for Control of BOD: An Overview,' in E. Joeres and M. David (eds), *Buying a Better Environment: Cost-Effective Regulation Through Permit Trading*, Madison, WI: University of Wisconsin Press, 163–95.

Eröcal, D. (ed.) (1991), *Environmental Management in Developing Countries*, papers from an OECD Development Centre Conference, Paris: OECD.

Eskeland, Gunnar S. and E. Jimenez (1992), 'Policy Instruments for Pollution Control in Developing Countries,' *The World Bank Observer*, **7**(2), July, 145–69.

Eskeland, Gunnar S. and Shantayanan Devarajan (1996), *Taxing Bads by Taxing Goods: Pollution Control with Presumptive Charges*, Directions in Development Series, Washington, DC: The World Bank.

Fichtner, W., M. Goebelt and O. Rentz (2001), 'The Efficiency of International Cooperation in Mitigating Climate Change: Analysis of Joint Implementation, the Clean Development Mechanism and Emission Tracking for the Federal Republic of Germany, The Russian Federation, and Indonesia,' *Energy Policy*, **29**(10), 817–30.

Forsyth, Timothy (1999), 'Flexible Mechanisms of Climate Change Technology Transfer,' *Journal of Environment and Development*, **8**(3), 238–57.

Global Leaders of Tomorrow Environmental Task Force (2001), *2001 Environmental Sustainability Index*, World Economic Forum, New Haven: Yale Center for Environmental Law and Policy.

Golub, Alexander and Evgeny Gurvich (1997), *Options for Revising the System of Pollution Charges in Russia: Results of an Aggregate Modeling Analysis*, environment discussion paper No. 21, July, Harvard Institute for International Development, International Environment Program, Cambridge, MA: Harvard Institute for International Development.

Goulder, L.H. (1995), 'Environmental Taxation and the "Double Dividend": A Reader's Guide,' *International Tax and Public Finance*, **2**(2), 157–83.

Goulder, L.H., Ian W.H. Parry, Robertson C. Williams, III and Dallas Burtraw (1999), 'The Cost-effectiveness of Alternative Instruments for Environmental Protection in a Second-best Setting,' *Journal of Public Economics*, **27**(3), 329–60.

Gray, C.W. (1991), 'Legal Process and Economic Development: A Case Study,' *World Development*, **19**(7), 763–77.

GTZ (Deutsche Gesellschaft für Technische Zusammenarbeit) (1995), *Market-based Instruments in Developing Countries*, Eschborn, Germany.

Halter, F. (1991), 'Toward More Effective Environmental Regulation in Developing Countries,' in D. Eröcal (ed.), *Environmental Management in Developing Countries*, Paris: OECD, 223–54.

Hansen, J.K. (1995), 'Policy Instruments for Pollution Control in Developing Countries,' consulting report to the Inter-American Development Bank, Washington, DC (March).

Hirschmann, D. (1999), 'Development Management Versus Third World Bureaucracies: A Brief History of Conflicting Interests,' *Development and Change*, **30**, 287–305.

Huber, Richard, Jack Ruitenbeek and Ronaldo Seroa da Motta (1996), 'Market

Based Instruments for Environmental Policymaking in Latin America and the Carribbean: Lessons from Eleven Countries,' Washington, DC: World Bank.

Hunt, Colin (1997), *Economic Instruments for Environmental and Natural Resource Conservation and Management in the South Pacific*, working paper in Ecological Economics No. 9706, CRES, Canberra, Australian National University.

IADB (Inter-American Development Bank) (1996), *Environmental Management in the Southern Cone: A Study on the Legal and Institutional Framework* (ATN/IT-5109–96) final report, Washington, DC: Inter-American Development Bank (December).

Johnson, Edward (1967), 'A Study in the Economics of Water Quality Management,' *Water Resources Research*, **3**(2), 291–305.

Kneese, Allen V. (1964), *The Economics of Regional Water Quality Management*, Baltimore, MD: Johns Hopkins University Press (for Resources for the Future).

Konar, S. and M.A. Cohen (1997). 'Information as Regulation: The Effect of Community Right to Know Laws on Toxic Emissions,' *Journal of Environmental Economics and Management*, **32**(1), 109–24.

Kozeltsev, Michael and Anil Markandya (1997), 'Pollution Charges in Russia: The Experience of 1990–1995,' environment discussion paper No. 15, NISEEP Project, Harvard Institute for International Development (January).

Kruitwagen, S., H. Folmer, E. Hendrix, L. Hordijk and E. Van Ierland (2000), 'Trading Sulphur Emissions in Europe: Guided Bilateral Trade,' *Environmental and Resource Economics*, **16**(4), 423–41.

Krupnick, Alan (1986), 'Costs of Alternative Policies for the Control of NO_2 in Baltimore,' *Journal of Environmental Economics and Management*, **13**(2), 189–97.

Lakhan, V. Chris, A.S. Trenhaile and P.D. LaValle (2000), 'Environmental Protection Efforts in a Developing Country: The Case of Guyana,' *Electronic Green Journal*, **13**, December, 2000 [http://egj.lib.uidaho.edu/].

Lovei, Magda (1995), 'Financing Pollution Abatement: Theory and Practice,' Washington, DC: The World Bank.

Lyon, R.M. (1989), 'Transferable Discharge Permit Systems and Environmental Management in Developing Countries,' *World Development*, **17**(8), 1299–312.

Margulis, Sergio (n.d.), 'The Experiences of Brazil, Mexico, Chile and Argentina in the Use of Economic Instruments in Environmental Policy,' Washington, DC: World Bank.

Montgomery, David (1972), 'Markets in Licenses and Efficient Pollution Control Programs,' *Journal of Economic Theory*, **5**, 395–418.

Nolet, Gil (2000), 'Environmental Enforcement in Latin America and the Caribbean,' in R. López and J.C. Jordán (eds), *Sustainable Development in Latin America: Financing and Policies Working in Synergy*, Washington, DC: Organization of American States.

O'Connor, David (1993), *The Use of Economic Instruments for Environmental Management in Developing Countries*, Paris: OECD.

O'Connor, David (1999), 'Applying Economic Instruments in Developing Countries: From Theory to Implementation,' *Environment and Development Economics*, (4), 91–110.

O'Connor, David and David Turnham (1992), *Managing the Environment in Developing Countries*, policy brief No. 2, OECD Development Centre, Paris: OECD.

OECD (1989), *Economic Instruments for Environmental Protection*, Paris: OECD.
OECD (1991), *Environmental Policy: How to Apply Economic Instruments*, Paris: OECD.
OECD (1993), *Economic Instruments for Environmental Management in Developing Countries*, Paris: OECD.
Opschoor, J.B. (1994), *Managing the Environment: The Role of Economic Instruments*, Paris: OECD.
O'Ryan, Raul E. (1996), 'Cost-effective Policies to Improve Urban Air Quality in Santiago, Chile,' *Journal of Environmental Economics and Management*, **31**, 302–13.
Oxford Analytica (1994), *The Role of the Public Sector in Latin America in the 1990s and Beyond* (a report to the Inter-American Development Bank), Oxford: Oxford Analytica.
Painuly, Jyoti (2001), 'The Kyoto Protocol, Emissions Trading, and the CDM: An Analysis from Developing Countries' Perspectives,' *The Energy Journal*, **22**(3), 147–60.
Panayotou, Theodore (1991), 'Economic Incentives in Environmental Management and Their Relevance to Developing Countries,' in D. Eröcal (ed.), *Environmental Management in Developing Countries*, papers from an OECD Development Centre Conference, Paris: OECD, 83–132.
Panayotou, T. (1994), *Economic Instruments for Environmental Management and Sustainable Development*, environmental economics series, paper No. 16, Nairobi: United Nations Environment Programme.
Payne, Mark and Carlos Losada (2000), *Institutions and Development in Latin America: An Approach Toward Quantitatively Describing Institutional Capacity in the Region*, technical study, Washington, DC: Inter-American Development Bank.
Pearce, D. (1991), 'New Environmental Policies: The Recent Experience of OECD Countries and its Relevance to the Developing World,' in D. Eröcal (ed.), *Environmental Management in Developing Countries*, papers from an OECD Development Centre Conference, Paris: OECD, 47–82.
Philibert, Cedric (2000), 'How Could Emissions Trading Benefit Developing Countries,' *Energy Policy*, **28**, 947–56.
Roach, F., C. Kolstad, A. Kneese, R. Tokin and M. Williams (1981), 'Alternative Air Quality Policy Options in the Four Corners Region,' *Southwest Review*, **1**(2), 29–58.
Romero-Lankao, Patricia (2000), 'Sustainability and Public Management Forum: Two Challenges for Mexican Environmental Policy,' *American Review of Public Administration*, **30**(4), 389–99.
Russell, C.S. (1973), *Residuals Management in Industry: A Case Study of Petroleum Refining*, Baltimore, MD: Johns Hopkins University Press for Resources for the Future.
Russell, C.S. (1986), 'Note on the Efficiency Ranking of Two Second-Best Policy Instruments for Pollution Control,' *Journal of Environmental Economics and Management*, **13**(1), 13–17.
Russell, C.S. and P.T. Powell (1999), 'Practical Considerations and Comparison of Instruments of Environmental Policy,' in Jeroen C.J.M. van den Bergh (ed.), *Handbook of Environmental and Resource Economics*, Cheltenham, UK and Northampton, USA: Edward Elgar, 307–28.
Russell, C.S. and W.J. Vaughan (1976), *Steel Production: Processes, Products and*

Residuals, Baltimore, MD: Johns Hopkins University Press for Resources for the Future.

Russell, C.S., P.T. Powell and W.J. Vaughan (1998), 'Rethinking Advice on Environmental Policy Instrument Choice in Developing Countries,' paper prepared for the World Congress of Environmental Economics, Venice, Italy, (June).

Russell, C.S., William J. Vaughan, Christopher D. Clark, Diego J. Rodriguez and Arthur H. Darling (2001), *Investing in Water Quality: Measuring Benefits, Costs and Risks*, Washington, DC: Inter-American Development Bank.

Seckler, D. (n.d.) 'Environmental and Natural Resource Policy Issues in Developing Countries,' discussion paper No.1, Arlington, VA, Environmental Policy and Training Project, Winrock International.

Serôa da Motta, Ronaldo, Richard M. Huber and H. Jack Ruitenbeek (1999), 'Market Based Instruments for Environmental Policymaking in Latin America and the Caribbean: Lessons from Eleven Countries,' *Environment and Development Economics*, **4**(2), 177–201.

Seskin, E., R. Anderson and R. Reid (1983), 'An Empirical Analysis of Economic Strategies for Controlling Air Pollution,' *Journal of Environmental Economics and Management*, **10**(2) 112–24.

Spofford, Walter O. Jr (1984), 'Efficiency Properties of Alternative Source Control Policies for Meeting Ambient Air Quality Standards: An Empirical Application to the Lower Delaware Valley,' Washington, DC: Resources for the Future, discussion paper D-118 (February).

Stavins, Robert N. (2000), 'Experience with Market-based Environmental Policy Instruments,' discussion paper 00-09, Washington, DC: Resources for the Future.

Steele, P. (1999), 'Market-Based Instruments for Environmental Policy in Developing Countries – from Theory to Practice with a Case Study of Sri Lanka's Recent Experience,' in T. Sterner (ed.), *The Market and the Environment: The Effectiveness of Market-Based Policy Instruments for Environmental Reform*, Cheltenham, UK and Northampton, USA: Edward Elgar, 274–300.

Stern, David I. (1998), 'Progress on the Environmental Kuznets Curve?', *Environment and Development Economics*, **3**(2), 173–96.

Straub, Stéphane (2000), 'Empirical Determinants of Good Institutions: Do We Know Anything?', working paper No. 423, Research Department, Washington, DC: Inter-American Development Bank (June).

Taylor, Lance (1993), 'The World Bank and the Environment: The World Development Report, 1992,' *World Development*, **21**, 869–81.

Tietenberg, T.H. (1985), *Emissions Trading, An Exercise in Reforming Pollution Policy*, Washington, DC: Resources for the Future.

Tietenberg, T.H. (1996), *Environmental and Natural Resource Economics*, 4th edn, New York: HarperCollins.

Tlaiye, Laura and Dan Biller (1994), 'Successful Environmental Institutions: Lessons From Colombia and Curitiba, Brazil,' Washington, DC: World Bank.

Tribe, Michael (1996), 'Environmental Control and Industrial Projects in Less Developed Countries,' *Project Appraisal*, **11**(1), 13–26.

Turnham, David (1991), 'Multilateral Development Banks and Environmental Management,' *Public Administration and Development*, **11**, 363–79.

United Nations Commission on Sustainable Development (1995), *Finance Resources and Mechanisms for Sustainable Development: Overview of Current Issues and Developments*, Report of the Secretary-General, New York: United Nations (February).

United Nations Environment Program (2000), *Latin America and the Caribbean: Environment Outlook*, Mexico City (DF): UNEP Regional Office.

Whalley, John (1998), 'Environmental Considerations in Tax Policy Design,' *Environment and Development Economics*, **4**(1), 111–24.

Wheeler, David (1997), 'Information in Pollution Management: The New Model,' in *Brazil: Managing Pollution Problems, The Brown Environmental Agenda*, report 16513–BR, Washington, DC: World Bank (June), 165–95.

Williamson, John (1990), 'Latin American Adjustment: How Much Has Happened?' Washington, DC: Institute for Economics.

Williamson, John (1993), 'Democracy and the "Washington Consensus",' *World Development*, **21**(8), 1329–36.

World Bank (1992), *World Development Report*, New York: Oxford University Press for the World Bank.

World Bank (1997), 'Five Years after Rio: Innovation in Environmental Policy,' Environmentally Sustainable Development Studies and Monographs Series No. 18, Washington, DC: World Bank.

World Bank (2000), *Greening Industry: New Roles for Communities, Markets and Governments*, New York: Oxford University Press for the World Bank.

World Commission on Environment and Development (1987), *Our Common Future*, New York: Oxford University Press.

Żylicz, Tomasz (1995), 'Cost-Effectiveness of Air Pollution Abatement in Poland,' *Environmental and Resource Economics*, **5**(2), 131–49.

APPENDIX 8.1   INSTRUMENTS OF ENVIRONMENTAL POLICY

1. Prohibition (of inputs, processes or products)
2. Technology specification (for production, recycling or waste treatment)
3. Technological basis for discharge standard[a]
4. Performance specification (discharge permits)[b]
5. Tradable performance specification (tradable permits)
6. Pollution charges
7. Subsidies
   (i)   Lump sum for capital cost
   (ii) Marginal for desired results[c]
8. Liability law provisions
9. Provision of information
   (i)   To polluters (technical assistants)
   (ii) To investors, consumers, activists (for example US Toxics Release Inventory)
   (iii) To consumers (green product or process)
10. Challenge regulation and voluntary agreements

Notes:
[a] In a technology-based standard setting, the amount of allowed pollution is determined via an engineering study in which a legally designated technology is applied on paper to a particular polluting operation with known uncontrolled pollution load (raw load). The result of this exercise is an achievable discharge amount.
[b] Performance specification can be based on any of a number of rules or methods from uniform percentage reduction by all sources to modeling that determines the cheapest way to attain a given ambient quality standard.
[c] The deposit–refund system, for example for drinks containers, is a self-financed marginal study for container return.

Source: Russell and Powell (1999).

Index